PEARLS OF FUNCTIONAL ALGORITHM DESIGN

In *Pearls of Functional Algorithm Design* Richard Bird takes a radically new approach to algorithm design, namely design by calculation. The body of the text is divided into 30 short chapters, called pearls, each of which deals with a particular programming problem. These problems, some of which are completely new, are drawn from sources as diverse as games and puzzles, intriguing combinatorial tasks and more familiar algorithms in areas such as data compression and string matching.

Each pearl starts with the statement of the problem expressed using the functional programming language Haskell, a powerful yet succinct language for capturing algorithmic ideas clearly and simply. The novel aspect of the book is that each solution is calculated from the problem statement by appealing to the laws of functional programming.

Pearls of Functional Algorithm Design will appeal to the aspiring functional programmer, students and teachers interested in the principles of algorithm design, and anyone seeking to master the techniques of reasoning about programs in an equational style.

RICHARD BIRD is Professor of Computer Science at Oxford University and Fellow of Lincoln College, Oxford.

PEARLS OF FUNCTIONAL ALGORITHM DESIGN

RICHARD BIRD

University of Oxford

CAMBRIDGE
UNIVERSITY PRESS

CAMBRIDGE
UNIVERSITY PRESS

University Printing House, Cambridge CB2 8BS, United Kingdom

Cambridge University Press is part of the University of Cambridge.

It furthers the University's mission by disseminating knowledge in the pursuit of education, learning and research at the highest international levels of excellence.

www.cambridge.org
Information on this title: www.cambridge.org/9780521513388

© Cambridge University Press 2010

First published 2010
7th printing 2014

A catalogue record for this publication is available from the British Library

Library of Congress Cataloguing in Publication data

Bird, Richard, 1943–
Pearls of functional algorithm design / Richard Bird.
p.   cm.
ISBN 978-0-521-51338-8 (Hardback)
1. Functional programming (Computer science)   2. Computer algorithms.   I. Title.
QA76.62.B57 2010
006.3′1–dc22
2010022871

ISBN 978-0-521-51338-8 Hardback

Dedicated to my wife, Norma.

Contents

Preface

In 1990, when the *Journal of Functional Programming* (JFP) was in the stages of being planned, I was asked by the then editors, Simon Peyton Jones and Philip Wadler, to contribute a regular column to be called *Functional Pearls*. The idea they had in mind was to emulate the very successful series of essays that Jon Bentley had written in the 1980s under the title "Programming Pearls" in the *Communications of the ACM*. Bentley wrote about his pearls:

Just as natural pearls grow from grains of sand that have irritated oysters, these programming pearls have grown from real problems that have irritated programmers. The programs are fun, and they teach important programming techniques and fundamental design principles.

I think the editors had asked me because I was interested in the specific task of taking a clear but inefficient functional program, a program that acted as a specification of the problem in hand, and using equational reasoning to calculate a more efficient one. One factor that stimulated growing interest in functional languages in the 1990s was that such languages were good for equational reasoning. Indeed, the functional language GOFER, invented by Mark Jones, captured this thought as an acronym. GOFER was one of the languages that contributed to the development of Haskell, the language on which this book is based. Equational reasoning dominates everything in this book.

In the past 20 years, some 80 pearls have appeared in the JFP, together with a sprinkling of pearls at conferences such as the *International Conference of Functional Programming* (ICFP) and the *Mathematics of Program Construction Conference* (MPC). I have written about a quarter of them, but most have been written by others. The topics of these pearls include interesting program calculations, novel data structures and small but elegant domain-specific languages embedded in Haskell and ML for particular applications.

My interest has always been in algorithms and their design. Hence the title of this book is *Pearls of Functional Algorithm Design* rather than the more general *Functional Pearls*. Many, though by no means all, of the pearls start with a specification in Haskell and then go on to calculate a more efficient version. My aim in writing these particular pearls is to see to what extent algorithm design can be cast in a familiar mathematical tradition of calculating a result by using well-established mathematical principles, theorems and laws. While it is generally true in mathematics that calculations are designed to simplify complicated things, in algorithm design it is usually the other way around: simple but inefficient programs are transformed into more efficient versions that can be completely opaque. It is not the final program that is the pearl; rather it is the calculation that yields it. Other pearls, some of which contain very few calculations, are devoted to trying to give simple explanations of some interesting and subtle algorithms. Explaining the ideas behind an algorithm is so much easier in a functional style than in a procedural one: the constituent functions can be more easily separated, they are brief and they capture powerful patterns of computation.

The pearls in this book that have appeared before in the JFP and other places have been polished and repolished. In fact, many do not bear much resemblance to the original. Even so, they could easily be polished more. The gold standard for beauty in mathematics is *Proofs from The Book* by Aigner and Ziegler (third edition, Springer, 2003), which contains some perfect proofs for mathematical theorems. I have always had this book in mind as an ideal towards which to strive.

About a third of the pearls are new. With some exceptions, clearly indicated, the pearls can be read in any order, though the chapters have been arranged to some extent in themes, such as divide and conquer, greedy algorithms, exhaustive search and so on. There is some repetition of material in the pearls, mostly concerning the properties of the library functions that we use, as well as more general laws, such as the fusion laws of various folds. A brief index has been included to guide the reader when necessary.

Finally, many people have contributed to the material. Indeed, several pearls were originally composed in collaboration with other authors. I would like to thank Sharon Curtis, Jeremy Gibbons, Ralf Hinze, Geraint Jones and Shin-Cheng Mu, my co-authors on these pearls, for their kind generosity in allowing me to rework the material. Jeremy Gibbons read the final draft and made numerous useful suggestions for improving the presentation. Some pearls have also been subject to close scrutiny at meetings of the Algebra of Programming research group at Oxford. While a number of flaws and errors have been removed, no doubt additional ones have been introduced. Apart from those mentioned above, I would like to thank Stephen Drape, Tom Harper, Daniel James, Jeffrey Lake, Meng Wang and Nicholas Wu for many positive suggestions for improving presentation. I would also like to thank Lambert Meertens and Oege de Moor for much fruitful collaboration over the years. Finally, I am indebted to David Tranah, my editor at Cambridge University Press, for encouragement and support, including much needed technical advice in the preparation of the final copy.

Richard Bird

1

The smallest free number

Introduction

Consider the problem of computing the smallest natural number not in a given finite set X of natural numbers. The problem is a simplification of a common programming task in which the numbers name objects and X is the set of objects currently in use. The task is to find some object not in use, say the one with the smallest name.

The solution to the problem depends, of course, on how X is represented. If X is given as a list without duplicates and in increasing order, then the solution is straightforward: simply look for the first gap. But suppose X is given as a list of distinct numbers in no particular order. For example,

$$[08, 23, 09, 00, 12, 11, 01, 10, 13, 07, 41, 04, 14, 21, 05, 17, 03, 19, 02, 06]$$

How would you find the smallest number not in this list?

It is not immediately clear that there is a linear-time solution to the problem; after all, sorting an arbitrary list of numbers cannot be done in linear time. Nevertheless, linear-time solutions do exist and the aim of this pearl is to describe two of them: one is based on Haskell arrays and the other on divide and conquer.

An array-based solution

The problem can be specified as a function *minfree*, defined by

$$minfree \quad :: \quad [Nat] \to Nat$$
$$minfree\ xs \quad = \quad head\ ([0\ ..\ ]\ \backslash\backslash\ xs)$$

The expression $us \backslash\backslash vs$ denotes the list of those elements of us that remain after removing any elements in vs:

$$(\backslash\backslash) \quad :: \quad Eq\ a \Rightarrow [a] \to [a] \to [a]$$
$$us \backslash\backslash vs \quad = \quad filter\ (\notin vs)\ us$$

1

The function *minfree* is executable but requires $\Theta(n^2)$ steps on a list of length n in the worst case. For example, evaluating *minfree* $[n-1, n-2 .. 0]$ requires evaluating $i \notin [n-1, n-2 .. 0]$ for $0 \leq i \leq n$, and thus $n(n+1)/2$ equality tests.

The key fact for both the array-based and divide and conquer solutions is that not every number in the range $[0 .. length \; xs]$ can be in *xs*. Thus the smallest number not in *xs* is the smallest number not in *filter* $(\leq n) \; xs$, where $n = length \; xs$. The array-based program uses this fact to build a checklist of those numbers present in *filter* $(\leq n) \; xs$. The checklist is a Boolean array with $n+1$ slots, numbered from 0 to n, whose initial entries are everywhere *False*. For each element x in *xs* and provided $x \leq n$ we set the array element at position x to *True*. The smallest free number is then found as the position of the first *False* entry. Thus, *minfree* = *search* · *checklist*, where

$$search \quad :: \quad Array \; Int \; Bool \rightarrow Int$$
$$search \quad = \quad length \cdot takeWhile \; id \cdot elems$$

The function *search* takes an array of Booleans, converts the array into a list of Booleans and returns the length of the longest initial segment consisting of *True* entries. This number will be the position of the first *False* entry.

One way to implement *checklist* in linear time is to use the function *accumArray* in the Haskell library *Data.Array*. This function has the rather daunting type

$$Ix \; i \Rightarrow (e \rightarrow v \rightarrow e) \rightarrow e \rightarrow (i, i) \rightarrow [(i, v)] \rightarrow Array \; i \; e$$

The type constraint $Ix \; i$ restricts i to be an *Index* type, such as *Int* or *Char*, for naming the indices or positions of the array. The first argument is an "accumulating" function for transforming array entries and values into new entries, the second argument is an initial entry for each index, the third argument is a pair naming the lower and upper indices and the fourth is an association list of index–value pairs. The function *accumArray* builds an array by processing the association list from left to right, combining entries and values into new entries using the accumulating function. This process takes linear time in the length of the association list, assuming the accumulating function takes constant time.

The function *checklist* is defined as an instance of *accumArray*:

$$checklist \quad :: \quad [Int] \rightarrow Array \; Int \; Bool$$
$$checklist \; xs \quad = \quad accumArray \; (\vee) \; False \; (0, n)$$
$$(zip \; (filter \; (\leq n) \; xs) \; (repeat \; True))$$
$$\textbf{where} \; n = length \; xs$$

This implementation does not require the elements of xs to be distinct, but does require them to be natural numbers.

It is worth mentioning that *accumArray* can be used to sort a list of numbers in linear time, provided the elements of the list all lie in some known range $(0, n)$. We replace *checklist* by *countlist*, where

$$
\begin{array}{lcl}
countlist & :: & [Int] \rightarrow Array\ Int\ Int \\
countlist\ xs & = & accumArray\ (+)\ 0\ (0, n)\ (zip\ xs\ (repeat\ 1))
\end{array}
$$

Then $sort\ xs = concat\ [replicate\ k\ x \mid (x, k) \leftarrow countlist\ xs]$. In fact, if we use *countlist* instead of *checklist*, then we can implement *minfree* as the position of the first 0 entry.

The above implementation builds the array in one go using a clever library function. A more prosaic way to implement *checklist* is to tick off entries step by step using a constant-time update operation. This is possible in Haskell only if the necessary array operations are executed in a suitable monad, such as the state monad. The following program for *checklist* makes use of the library *Data.Array.ST*:

$$
\begin{array}{lcl}
checklist\ xs & = & runSTArray\ (\mathbf{do} \\
& & \quad \{a \leftarrow newArray\ (0, n)\ False; \\
& & \quad\ sequence\ [writeArray\ a\ x\ True \mid x \leftarrow xs,\ x \leq n]; \\
& & \quad\ return\ a\}) \\
& & \mathbf{where}\ n = length\ xs
\end{array}
$$

This solution would not satisfy the pure functional programmer because it is essentially a procedural program in functional clothing.

A divide and conquer solution

Now we turn to a divide and conquer solution to the problem. The idea is to express $minfree\ (xs +\!\!+ ys)$ in terms of $minfree\ xs$ and $minfree\ ys$. We begin by recording the following properties of $\backslash\backslash$:

$$
\begin{array}{lcl}
(as +\!\!+ bs) \backslash\backslash\ cs & = & (as \backslash\backslash\ cs) +\!\!+ (bs \backslash\backslash\ cs) \\
as \backslash\backslash\ (bs +\!\!+ cs) & = & (as \backslash\backslash\ bs) \backslash\backslash\ cs \\
(as \backslash\backslash\ bs) \backslash\backslash\ cs & = & (as \backslash\backslash\ cs) \backslash\backslash\ bs
\end{array}
$$

These properties reflect similar laws about sets in which set union $\cup$ replaces $+\!\!+$ and set difference $\backslash$ replaces $\backslash\backslash$. Suppose now that as and vs are disjoint, meaning $as \backslash\backslash\ vs = as$, and that bs and us are also disjoint, so $bs \backslash\backslash\ us = bs$. It follows from these properties of $+\!\!+$ and $\backslash\backslash$ that

$$
(as +\!\!+ bs) \backslash\backslash\ (us +\!\!+ vs) = (as \backslash\backslash\ us) +\!\!+ (bs \backslash\backslash\ vs)
$$

Now, choose any natural number b and let $as = [0 .. b-1]$ and $bs = [b..]$. Furthermore, let $us = filter\ (< b)\ xs$ and $vs = filter\ (\geq b)\ xs$. Then as and vs are disjoint, and so are bs and us. Hence

$$[0 ..\,] \setminus\!\setminus xs \quad = \quad ([0 .. b-1] \setminus\!\setminus us) +\!\!+ ([b ..\,] \setminus\!\setminus vs)$$
$$\textbf{where}\ (us, vs) = partition\ (< b)\ xs$$

Haskell provides an efficient implementation of a function *partition p* that partitions a list into those elements that satisfy p and those that do not. Since

$$head\ (xs +\!\!+ ys) \quad = \quad \textbf{if}\ null\ xs\ \textbf{then}\ head\ ys\ \textbf{else}\ head\ xs$$

we obtain, still for any natural number b, that

$$minfree\ xs \quad = \quad \textbf{if}\ null\ ([0 .. b-1] \setminus\!\setminus us)$$
$$\textbf{then}\ head\ ([b ..\,] \setminus\!\setminus vs)$$
$$\textbf{else}\ head\ ([0 ..\,] \setminus\!\setminus us)$$
$$\textbf{where}\ (us, vs) = partition\ (< b)\ xs$$

The next question is: can we implement the test $null\ ([0 .. b-1] \setminus\!\setminus us)$ more efficiently than by direct computation, which takes quadratic time in the length of us? Yes, the input is a list of distinct natural numbers, so is us. And every element of us is less than b. Hence

$$null\ ([0 .. b-1] \setminus\!\setminus us) \quad \equiv \quad length\ us == b$$

Note that the array-based solution did not depend on the assumption that the given list did not contain duplicates, but it is a crucial one for an efficient divide and conquer solution.

Further inspection of the above code for *minfree* suggests that we should generalise *minfree* to a function, *minfrom* say, defined by

$$minfrom \qquad :: \quad Nat \to [Nat] \to Nat$$
$$minfrom\ a\ xs \quad = \quad head\ ([a ..\,] \setminus\!\setminus xs)$$

where every element of xs is assumed to be greater than or equal to a. Then, provided b is chosen so that both *length us* and *length vs* are less than *length xs*, the following recursive definition of *minfree* is well-founded:

$$minfree\ xs \qquad = \quad minfrom\ 0\ xs$$
$$minfrom\ a\ xs \quad | \quad null\ xs \qquad\qquad = \quad a$$
$$| \quad length\ us == b - a \quad = \quad minfrom\ b\ vs$$
$$| \quad \textbf{otherwise} \qquad\quad = \quad minfrom\ a\ us$$
$$\textbf{where}\ (us, vs) = partition\ (< b)\ xs$$

It remains to choose b. Clearly, we want $b > a$. And we would also like to choose b so that the maximum of the lengths of us and vs is as small as possible. The right choice of b to satisfy these requirements is

$$b \;=\; a + 1 + n \operatorname{div} 2$$

where $n = length \; xs$. If $n \neq 0$ and $length \; us < b - a$, then

$$length \; us \leq n \operatorname{div} 2 < n$$

And, if $length \; us = b - a$, then

$$length \; vs = n - n \operatorname{div} 2 - 1 \leq n \operatorname{div} 2$$

With this choice the number of steps $T(n)$ for evaluating $minfrom \; 0 \; xs$ when $n = length \; xs$ satisfies $T(n) = T(n \operatorname{div} 2) + \Theta(n)$, with the solution $T(n) = \Theta(n)$.

As a final optimisation we can avoid repeatedly computing $length$ with a simple data refinement, representing xs by a pair $(length \; xs, xs)$. That leads to the final program

$$
\begin{aligned}
minfree \; xs \quad\quad &= \quad minfrom \; 0 \; (length \; xs, xs) \\
minfrom \; a \; (n, xs) \quad | \quad & n == 0 \quad\quad = \quad a \\
| \quad & m == b - a \quad = \quad minfrom \; b \; (n - m, vs) \\
| \quad & \textbf{otherwise} \quad = \quad minfrom \; a \; (m, us) \\
& \textbf{where} \; (us, vs) \quad = \quad partition \; (< b) \; xs \\
& \qquad\quad\; b \quad\quad\;\; = \quad a + 1 + n \operatorname{div} 2 \\
& \qquad\quad\; m \quad\quad\;\; = \quad length \; us
\end{aligned}
$$

It turns out that the above program is about twice as fast as the incremental array-based program, and about 20% faster than the one using $accumArray$.

Final remarks

This was a simple problem with at least two simple solutions. The second solution was based on a common technique of algorithm design, namely divide and conquer. The idea of partitioning a list into those elements less than a given value, and the rest, arises in a number of algorithms, most notably Quicksort. When seeking a $\Theta(n)$ algorithm involving a list of n elements, it is tempting to head at once for a method that processes each element of the list in constant time, or at least in amortized constant time. But a recursive process that performs $\Theta(n)$ processing steps in order to reduce the problem to another instance of at most half the size is also good enough.

One of the differences between a pure functional algorithm designer and a procedural one is that the former does not assume the existence of arrays with a constant-time update operation, at least not without a certain amount of plumbing. For a pure functional programmer, an update operation takes logarithmic time in the size of the array.[1] That explains why there sometimes seems to be a logarithmic gap between the best functional and procedural solutions to a problem. But sometimes, as here, the gap vanishes on a closer inspection.

---

[1] To be fair, procedural programmers also appreciate that constant-time indexing and updating are only possible when the arrays are small.

2

A surpassing problem

Introduction

In this pearl we solve a small programming exercise of Martin Rem (1988a). While Rem's solution uses binary search, our solution is another application of divide and conquer. By definition, a *surpasser* of an element of an array is a greater element to the right, so $x[j]$ is a surpasser of $x[i]$ if $i < j$ and $x[i] < x[j]$. The *surpasser count* of an element is the number of its surpassers. For example, the surpasser counts of the letters of the string GENERATING are given by

G	E	N	E	R	A	T	I	N	G
5	6	2	5	1	4	0	1	0	0

The maximum surpasser count is six. The first occurrence of letter E has six surpassers, namely N, R, T, I, N and G. Rem's problem is to compute the maximum surpasser count of an array of length $n > 1$ and to do so with an $O(n \log n)$ algorithm.

Specification

We will suppose that the input is given as a list rather than an array. The function *msc* (short for maximum surpasser count) is specified by

$$msc \qquad :: \quad Ord\ a \Rightarrow [a] \rightarrow Int$$
$$msc\ xs \quad = \quad maximum\ [scount\ z\ zs \mid z : zs \leftarrow tails\ xs]$$
$$scount\ x\ xs \quad = \quad length\ (filter\ (x <)\ xs)$$

The value of *scount x xs* is the surpasser count of x in the list xs and *tails* returns the *nonempty* tails of a nonempty list in decreasing order of length:[1]

$$tails\ [\ ] \qquad = \quad [\ ]$$
$$tails\ (x : xs) \quad = \quad (x : xs) : tails\ xs$$

The definition of *msc* is executable but takes quadratic time.

---

[1] Unlike the standard Haskell function of the same name, which returns the possibly empty tails of a possibly empty list.

Divide and conquer

Given the target complexity of $O(n \log n)$ steps, it seems reasonable to head for a divide and conquer algorithm. If we can find a function *join* so that

$$msc \; (xs \; +\!\!+ \; ys) \;\; = \;\; join \; (msc \; xs) \; (msc \; ys)$$

and *join* can be computed in linear time, then the time complexity $T(n)$ of the divide and conquer algorithm for computing *msc* on a list of length n satisfies $T(n) = 2\,T(n/2) + O(n)$, with solution $T(n) = O(n \log n)$. But it is fairly obvious that no such *join* can exist: too little information is provided by the single number *msc xs* for any such decomposition.

The minimal generalisation is to start out with the table of *all* surpasser counts:

$$table \; xs \;\; = \;\; [(z, scount \; z \; zs) \mid z : zs \leftarrow tails \; xs]$$

Then $msc = maximum \cdot map \; snd \cdot table$. Can we find a linear-time *join* to satisfy

$$table \; (xs \; +\!\!+ \; ys) \;\; = \;\; join \; (table \; xs) \; (table \; ys)$$

Well, let us see. We will need the following divide and conquer property of *tails*:

$$tails \; (xs \; +\!\!+ \; ys) \;\; = \;\; map \; (+\!\!+ys) \; (tails \; xs) \; +\!\!+ \; tails \; ys$$

The calculation goes as follows:

$$table \; (xs \; +\!\!+ \; ys)$$
$= \quad$ {definition}
$$[(z, scount \; z \; zs) \mid z : zs \leftarrow tails \; (xs \; +\!\!+ \; ys)]$$
$= \quad$ {divide and conquer property of *tails*}
$$[(z, scount \; z \; zs) \mid z : zs \leftarrow map \; (+\!\!+ys) \; (tails \; xs) \; +\!\!+ \; tails \; ys]$$
$= \quad$ {distributing $\leftarrow$ over $+\!\!+$}
$$[(z, scount \; z \; (zs \; +\!\!+ \; ys)) \mid z : zs \leftarrow tails \; xs] \; +\!\!+$$
$$[(z, scount \; z \; zs) \mid z : zs \leftarrow tails \; ys])$$
$= \quad$ {since $scount \; z \; (zs \; +\!\!+ \; ys) = scount \; z \; zs + scount \; z \; ys$}
$$[(z, scount \; z \; zs + scount \; z \; ys) \mid z : zs \leftarrow tails \; xs] \; +\!\!+$$
$$[(z, scount \; z \; zs) \mid z : zs \leftarrow tails \; ys])$$
$= \quad$ {definition of *table* and $ys = map \; fst \; (table \; ys)$}
$$[(z, c + scount \; z \; (map \; fst \; (table \; ys))) \mid (z, c) \leftarrow table \; xs] \; +\!\!+ \; table \; ys$$

Hence *join* can be defined by

$$join\ txs\ tys\ =\ [(z, c + tcount\ z\ tys)\ |\ (z, c) \leftarrow txs]\ \text{+\!+}\ tys$$
$$tcount\ z\ tys\ =\ scount\ z\ (map\ fst\ tys)$$

The problem with this definition, however, is that *join txs tys* does not take linear time in the length of *txs* and *tys*.

We could improve the computation of *tcount* if *tys* were sorted in ascending order of first component. Then we can reason:

$$\qquad tcount\ z\ tys$$
$$=\qquad \{\text{definition of } tcount \text{ and } scount\}$$
$$length\ (filter\ (z\ <)\ (map\ fst\ tys))$$
$$=\qquad \{\text{since } filter\ p \cdot map\ f = map\ f \cdot filter\ (p \cdot f)\}$$
$$length\ (map\ fst\ (filter\ ((z\ <) \cdot fst)\ tys))$$
$$=\qquad \{\text{since } length \cdot map\ f = length\}$$
$$length\ (filter\ ((z\ <) \cdot fst)\ tys)$$
$$=\qquad \{\text{since } tys \text{ is sorted on first argument}\}$$
$$length\ (dropWhile\ ((z \geq) \cdot fst)\ tys)$$

Hence

$$tcount\ z\ tys\ =\ length\ (dropWhile((z \geq) \cdot fst)\ tys) \qquad (2.1)$$

This calculation suggests it would be sensible to maintain *table* in ascending order of first component:

$$table\ xs\ =\ sort\ [(z, scount\ z\ zs)\ |\ z : zs \leftarrow tails\ xs]$$

Repeating the calculation above, but for the sorted version of *table*, we find that

$$join\ txs\ tys\ =\ [(x, c + tcount\ x\ tys)\ |\ (x, c) \leftarrow txs]\ \text{⋀}\ tys \qquad (2.2)$$

where ⋀ merges two sorted lists. Using this identity we can now calculate a more efficient recursive definition of *join*. One of the base cases, namely *join* [ ] *tys* = *tys*, is immediate. The other base case, *join txs* [ ] = *txs*, follows because *tcount x* [ ] = 0. For the recursive case we simplify

$$join\ txs@((x, c) : txs')\ tys@((y, d) : tys') \qquad (2.3)$$

by comparing *x* and *y*. (In Haskell, the @ sign introduces a synonym, so *txs* is a synonym for $(x, c) : txs'$; similarly for *tys*.) Using (2.2), (2.3) reduces to

$$((x, c + tcount\ x\ tys) : [(x, c + tcount\ x\ tys)\ |\ (x, c) \leftarrow txs'])\ \text{⋀}\ tys$$

To see which element is produced first by $\wedge$ we need to compare x and y. If $x < y$, then it is the element on the left and, since $tcount\ x\ tys = length\ tys$ by (2.1), expression (2.3) reduces to

$(x, c + length\ tys) : join\ txs'\ tys$

If $x = y$, we need to compare $c + tcount\ x\ tys$ and d. But $d = tcount\ x\ tys'$ by the definition of *table* and $tcount\ x\ tys = tcount\ x\ tys'$ by (2.1), so (2.3) reduces to $(y, d) : join\ txs\ tys'$. This is also the result in the final case $x > y$.

Putting these results together, and introducing *length tys* as an additional argument to *join* in order to avoid repeating length calculations, we arrive at the following divide and conquer algorithm for *table*:

$$
\begin{aligned}
table\ [x] \quad &= \quad [(x, 0)] \\
table\ xs \quad &= \quad join\ (m - n)\ (table\ ys)\ (table\ zs) \\
&\qquad \textbf{where}\ m \quad = \quad length\ xs \\
&\qquad\qquad\quad\ n \quad = \quad m\ \text{div}\ 2 \\
&\qquad\qquad\ (ys, zs) \quad = \quad splitAt\ n\ xs
\end{aligned}
$$

$$
\begin{aligned}
join\ 0\ txs\ [\,] \quad &= \quad txs \\
join\ n\ [\,]\ tys \quad &= \quad tys \\
join\ n\ txs@((x, c) : txs')\ &tys@((y, d) : tys') \\
&\mid\ x < y \quad = \quad (x, c + n) : join\ n\ txs'\ tys \\
&\mid\ x \geq y \quad = \quad (y, d) : join\ (n{-}1)\ txs\ tys'
\end{aligned}
$$

Since *join* takes linear time, *table* is computed in $O(n \log n)$ steps, and so is *msc*.

Final remarks

It is not possible to do better than an $O(n \log n)$ algorithm for computing *table*. The reason is that if xs is a list of distinct elements, then *table xs* provides enough information to determine the permutation of xs that sorts xs. Moreover, no further comparisons between list elements are required. In fact, *table xs* is related to the *inversion table* of a permutation of n elements; see Knuth (1998): *table xs* is just the inversion table of *reverse xs*. Since comparison-based sorting of n elements requires $\Omega(n \log n)$ steps, so does the computation of *table*.

As we said in the Introduction for this pearl, the solution in Rem (1998b) is different, in that it is based on an iterative algorithm and uses binary search. A procedural programmer could also head for a divide and conquer algorithm, but would probably prefer an in-place array-based algorithm simply because it consumes less space.

References

Knuth, D. E. (1998). *The Art of Computer Programming, Volume 3: Sorting and Searching*, second edition. Reading, MA: Addison-Wesley.

Rem, M. (1988a). Small programming exercises 20. *Science of Computer Programming* **10** (1), 99–105.

Rem, M. (1998b). Small programming exercises 21. *Science of Computer Programming* **10** (3), 319–25.

3

Improving on saddleback search

The setting is a tutorial on functional algorithm design. There are four students: Anne, Jack, Mary and Theo.

Teacher: Good morning class. Today I would like you design a function *invert* that takes two arguments: a function f from pairs of natural numbers to natural numbers, and a natural number z. The value *invert* f z is a list of all pairs (x, y) satisfying $f(x, y) = z$. You can assume that f is strictly increasing in each argument, but nothing else.

Jack: That seems an easy problem. Since f is a function on naturals and is increasing in each argument, we know that $f(x, y) = z$ implies $x \leq z$ and $y \leq z$. Hence we can define *invert* by a simple search of all possible pairs of values:

$$invert\ f\ z\ =\ [(x, y)\ |\ x \leftarrow [0 \mathinner{..} z],\ y \leftarrow [0 \mathinner{..} z],\ f(x, y) == z]$$

Doesn't this solve the problem?

Teacher: Yes it does, but your solution involves $(z + 1)^2$ evaluations of f. Since f may be very expensive to compute, I would like a solution with as few evaluations of f as possible.

Theo: Well, it is easy to halve the evaluations. Since $f(x, y) \geq x + y$ if f is increasing, the search can be confined to values on or below the diagonal of the square:

$$invert\ f\ z\ =\ [(x, y)\ |\ x \leftarrow [0 \mathinner{..} z],\ y \leftarrow [0 \mathinner{..} z - x],\ f(x, y) == z]$$

Come to think of it, you can replace the two upper bounds by $z - f(0, 0)$ and $z - x - f(0, 0)$. Then if $z < f(0, 0)$ the search terminates at once.

Anne: Assuming it doesn't matter in which order the solutions are found, I think you can do better still. Jack's method searches a square of size $z + 1$

from the origin at the bottom left, and proceeds upwards column by column.
We can do better if we start at the top-left corner $(0, z)$ of the square. At any
stage the search space is constrained to be a rectangle with top-left corner
(u, v) and bottom-right corner $(z, 0)$. Here is the picture:

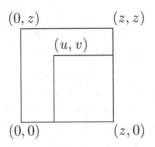

Let me define

$$find\ (u, v)\ f\ z\ =\ [(x, y)\ |\ x \leftarrow [u\ ..\ z],\ y \leftarrow [v, v - 1\ ..\ 0],\ f(x, y) == z]$$

so that *invert* $f\ z = find\ (0, z)\ f\ z$. It is now easy enough to calculate a more
efficient implementation of *find*.

First of all, if $u > z$ or $v < 0$, then, clearly, $find\ (u, v)\ f\ z = [\ ]$. Otherwise,
we carry out a case analysis on the value $f(u, v)$. If $f(u, v) < z$, then
the rest of column u can be eliminated, since $f(u, v') < f(u, v) < z$ for
$v' < v$. If $f(u, v) > z$, we can similarly eliminate, the rest of row v. Finally,
if $f(u, v) = z$, then we can record (u, v) and eliminate the rest of both
column u and row v.

Here is my improved version of *invert*:

$$invert\ f\ z\ =\ find\ (0, z)\ f\ z$$
$$find\ (u, v)\ f\ z$$
$$|\quad u > z \lor v < 0\quad =\quad [\ ]$$
$$|\quad z' < z\quad\quad\quad =\quad find\ (u{+}1, v)\ f\ z$$
$$|\quad z' == z\quad\quad\quad =\quad (u, v) : find\ (u{+}1, v{-}1)\ f\ z$$
$$|\quad z' > z\quad\quad\quad =\quad find\ (u, v{-}1)\ f\ z$$
$$\textbf{where}\ z' = f(u, v)$$

In the worst case, when *find* traverses the perimeter of the square from the
top-left corner to the bottom-right corner, it performs $2z + 1$ evaluations
of f. In the best case, when *find* proceeds directly to either the bottom or
rightmost boundary, it requires only $z + 1$ evaluations.

Theo: You can reduce the search space still further because the initial
square with top-left corner $(0, z)$ and bottom-right corner $(z, 0)$ is an overly

generous estimate of where the required values lie. Suppose we first compute m and n, where

$$
\begin{aligned}
m &= maximum\ (filter\ (\lambda y \to f(0, y) \le z)\ [0 .. z]) \\
n &= maximum\ (filter\ (\lambda x \to f(x, 0) \le z)\ [0 .. z])
\end{aligned}
$$

Then we can define *invert* $f\ z = find\ (0, m)\ f\ z$, where *find* has exactly the same form that Anne gave, except that the first guard becomes $u > n \lor v < 0$. In other words, rather than search a $(z+1) \times (z+1)$ square we can get away with searching an $(m+1) \times (n+1)$ rectangle.

The crucial point is that we can compute m and n by binary search. Let g be an increasing function on the natural numbers and suppose x, y and z satisfy $g\ x \le z < g\ y$. To determine the unique value m, where $m = bsearch\ g\ (x, y)\ z$, in the range $x \le m < y$ such that $g\ m \le z < g\ (m+1)$ we can maintain the invariants $g\ a \le z < g\ b$ and $x \le a < b \le y$. This leads to the program

$$
\begin{aligned}
&bsearch\ g\ (a, b)\ z \\
&\quad |\quad a+1 == b \quad = \quad a \\
&\quad |\quad g\ m \le z \quad = \quad bsearch\ g\ (m, b)\ z \\
&\quad |\quad \textbf{otherwise} \quad = \quad bsearch\ g\ (a, m)\ z \\
&\quad\quad \textbf{where}\ m = (a + b)\ \text{div}\ 2
\end{aligned}
$$

Since $a+1 < b \Rightarrow a < m < y$ it follows that neither $g\ x$ nor $g\ y$ are evaluated by the algorithm, so they can be fictitious values. In particular, we have

$$
\begin{aligned}
m &= bsearch\ (\lambda y \to f(0, y))\ (-1, z+1)\ z \\
n &= bsearch\ (\lambda x \to f(x, 0))\ (-1, z+1)\ z
\end{aligned}
$$

where we extend f with fictitious values $f(0, -1) = 0$ and $f(-1, 0) = 0$.

This version of *invert* takes about $2 \log z + m + n$ evaluations of f in the worst case and $2 \log z + m \min n$ in the best case. Since m or n may be substantially less than z, for example when $f(x, y) = 2^x + 3^y$, we can end up with an algorithm that takes only $O(\log z)$ steps in the worst case.

Teacher: Congratulations, Anne and Theo, you have rediscovered an important search strategy, dubbed *saddleback search* by David Gries; see Backhouse (1986), Dijkstra (1985) and Gries (1981). I imagine Gries called it that because the shape of the three-dimensional plot of f, with the smallest element at the bottom left, the largest at the top right and two wings, is a bit like a saddle. The crucial idea, as Anne has spotted, is to start the search at the tip of one of the wings rather than at the smallest or highest value. In his treatment of the problem, Dijkstra (1985) also mentioned the advantage of using a logarithmic search to find the appropriate starting rectangle.

Mary: What happens if we go for a divide and conquer solution? I mean, why not look at the middle element of the rectangle first? Surely it is reasonable to investigate the two-dimensional analogue of binary search.

Suppose we have confined the search to a rectangle with top-left corner (u, v) and bottom-right corner (r, s). Instead of looking at $f(u, v)$, why not inspect $f(p, q)$, where $p = (u + r)$ div 2 and $q = (v + s)$ div 2? Here is the picture:

If $f(p, q) < z$, then we can throw away all elements of the lower-left rectangle A. Similarly, if $f(p, q) > z$, then we can throw away the upper-right rectangle B. And if $f(p, q) = z$, then we can throw away both.

I know that this strategy does not maintain Anne's property that the search space is always a rectangle; instead, we have two rectangles or an L-shape. But we are functional programmers and don't have to confine ourselves to simple loops: a divide and conquer algorithm is as easy for us to implement as an iterative one because both have to be expressed recursively.

Jack: You have to deal with the L-shape though. You can split an L-shape into two rectangles of course. In fact you can do it in two ways, either with a horizontal cut or a vertical one. Let me do a rough calculation. Consider an $m \times n$ rectangle and let $T(m, n)$ denote the number of evaluations of f required to search it. If $m = 0$ or $n = 0$ then there is nothing to search. If $m = 1$ or $n = 1$ we have

$$
\begin{aligned}
T(1, n) &= 1 + T(1, \lceil n/2 \rceil) \\
T(m, 1) &= 1 + T(\lceil m/2 \rceil, 1)
\end{aligned}
$$

Otherwise, when $m \geq 2$ and $n \geq 2$, we can throw away a rectangle of size at least $\lfloor m/2 \rfloor \times \lfloor n/2 \rfloor$. If we make a horizontal cut, then we are left with two rectangles, one of size $\lfloor m/2 \rfloor \times \lceil n/2 \rceil$ and the other of size $\lceil m/2 \rceil \times n$. Hence

$$
T(m, n) = 1 + T(\lfloor m/2 \rfloor, \lceil n/2 \rceil) + T(\lceil m/2 \rceil, n)
$$

If we make a vertical cut, then we have

$$
T(m, n) = 1 + T(\lceil m/2 \rceil, \lfloor n/2 \rfloor) + T(m, \lceil n/2 \rceil)
$$

I don't immediately see the solutions to these recurrence relations.

Theo: If you make both a horizontal and a vertical cut, you are left with three rectangles, so when $m \geq 2$ and $n \geq 2$ we have

$$T(m, n) \;=\; 1 + T(\lceil m/2 \rceil, \lfloor n/2 \rfloor) + T(\lceil m/2 \rceil, \lceil n/2 \rceil) + T(\lfloor m/2 \rfloor, \lceil n/2 \rceil)$$

I can solve this recurrence. Set $U(i, j) = T(2^i, 2^j)$, so

$$
\begin{aligned}
U(i, 0) &= i \\
U(0, j) &= j \\
U(i+1, j+1) &= 1 + 3U(i, j)
\end{aligned}
$$

The solution is $U(i, j) = 3^k(|j - i| + 1/2) - 1/2$, where $k = i \min j$, as one can check by induction. Hence, if $m \leq n$ we have

$$T(m, n) \leq 3^{\log m} \log(2n/m) = m^{1.59} \log(2n/m)$$

That's better than $m + n$ when m is much smaller than n.

Jack: I don't think the three-rectangle solution is as good as the two-rectangle one. Following your approach, Theo, let me set $U(i, j) = T(2^i, 2^j)$. Supposing $i \leq j$ and making a horizontal cut, we have

$$
\begin{aligned}
U(0, j) &= j \\
U(i+1, j+1) &= 1 + U(i, j) + U(i, j+1)
\end{aligned}
$$

The solution is $U(i, j) = 2^i(j - i/2 + 1) - 1$, as one can check by induction. Hence

$$T(m, n) \leq m \log(2n/\sqrt{m})$$

If $i \geq j$ we should make a vertical cut rather than a horizontal one; then we get an algorithm with at most $n \log(2m/\sqrt{n})$ evaluations of f. In either case, if one of m or n is much smaller than the other we get a better algorithm than saddleback search.

Anne: While you two have been solving recurrences I have been thinking of a lower bound on the complexity of *invert*. Consider the different possible outputs when we have an $m \times n$ rectangle to search. Suppose there are $A(m, n)$ different possible answers. Each test of $f(x, y)$ against z has three possible outcomes, so the height h of the ternary tree of tests has to satisfy $h \geq \log_3 A(m, n)$. Provided we can estimate $A(m, n)$ this gives us a lower bound on the number of tests that have to be performed. The situation is the same with sorting n items by binary comparisons; there are $n!$ possible outcomes, so any sorting algorithm has to make at least $\log_2 n!$ comparisons in the worst case.

It is easy to estimate $A(m, n)$: each list of pairs (x, y) in the range $0 \leq x < n$ and $0 \leq y < m$ with $f(x, y) = z$ is in a one-to-one correspondence with a step shape from the top-left corner of the $m \times n$ rectangle to the bottom-right corner, in which the value z appears at the inner corners of the steps. Of course, this step shape is not necessarily the one traced by the function *find*. The number of such paths is $\binom{m+n}{n}$, so that is the value of $A(m, n)$.

Another way to see this result is to suppose there are k solutions. The value z can appear in k rows in exactly $\binom{m}{k}$ ways, and for each way there are $\binom{n}{k}$ possible choices for the columns. Hence

$$A(m, n) = \sum_{k=0}^{m} \binom{m}{k} \binom{n}{k} = \binom{m + n}{n}$$

since the summation is an instance of Vandermonde's convolution; see Graham *et al.* (1989). Taking logarithms, we obtain the lower bound

$$\log A(m, n) \quad = \quad \Omega(m \log(1 + n/m) + n \log(1 + m/n))$$

This estimate shows that when $m = n$ we cannot do better than $\Omega(m + n)$ steps. But if $m \leq n$ then $m \leq n \log(1 + m/n)$, since $x \leq \log(1 + x)$ if $0 \leq x \leq 1$. Thus $A(m, n) = \Omega(m \log(n/m))$. Jack's solution does not quite achieve this bound because he obtains only an $O(m \log(n/\sqrt{m}))$ algorithm in the case $m \leq n$.

Mary: I don't think that Jack's divide and conquer solution is really necessary; there are other ways of using binary search to solve the problem. One is simply to carry out m binary searches, one on each row. That gives an $O(m \log n)$ solution. But I think we can do better and achieve the optimal asymptotic $O(m \log(n/m))$ bound, assuming $m \leq n$.

Suppose, as before, we have confined the search to a rectangle with top-left corner (u, v) and bottom-right corner (r, s). Thus, there are $r - u$ columns and $s - v$ rows. Furthermore, assume $v - s \leq r - u$, so there at least as many columns as rows. Suppose we carry out a binary search along the middle row, $q = (v+s)$ div 2, in order to determine a p such that $f(p, q) \leq z < f(p+1, q)$. If $f(p, q) < z$, then we need continue the search only on the two rectangles $((u, v), (p, q+1))$ and $((p+1, q-1), (r, s))$. If $f(p, q) = z$ then we can cut out column p and can continue the search only on the rectangles $((u, v), (p-1, q+1))$ and $((p+1, q-1), (r, s))$. The reasoning is dual if there are more rows than columns. As a result, we can eliminate about half the elements of the array with a logarithmic number of probes.

$$find\ (u, v)\ (r, s)\ f\ z$$

$$
\begin{array}{lll}
\quad |\quad u > r \vee v < s & = & [\,] \\
\quad |\quad v - s \le r - u & = & rfind\ (bsearch\ (\lambda x \to f(x, q))\ (u-1, r+1)\ z) \\
\quad |\quad \textbf{otherwise} & = & cfind\ (bsearch\ (\lambda y \to f(p, y))\ (s-1, v+1)\ z)
\end{array}
$$

$\quad\textbf{where}$

$$
\begin{array}{lll}
p & = & (u+r)\ \text{div}\ 2 \\
q & = & (v+s)\ \text{div}\ 2 \\
rfind\ p & = & (\textbf{if}\ f(p, q) = z\ \textbf{then}\ (p, q) : find\ (u, v)\ (p-1, q+1)\ f\ z \\
& & \textbf{else}\ find\ (u, v)\ (p, q+1)\ f\ z)\ +\!\!+ \\
& & find\ (p+1, q-1)\ (r, s)\ f\ z \\
cfind\ q & = & find\ (u, v)\ (p-1, q+1)\ f\ z\ +\!\!+ \\
& & (\textbf{if}\ f(p, q) = z\ \textbf{then}(p, q) : find\ (p+1, q-1)\ (r, s)\ f\ z \\
& & \textbf{else}\ find\ (p+1, q)\ (r, s)\ f\ z)
\end{array}
$$

Fig. 3.1 The revised definition of *find*

Here is the algorithm I have in mind: we implement *invert* by

$$
\begin{array}{lll}
invert\ f\ z & = & find\ (0, m)\ (n, 0)\ f\ z \\
\textbf{where}\ m & = & bsearch\ (\lambda y \to f(0, y))\ (-1, z+1)\ z \\
n & = & bsearch\ (\lambda x \to f(x, 0))\ (-1, z+1)\ z
\end{array}
$$

where $find\ (u, v)\ (r, s)\ f\ z$, given in Figure 3.1, searches a rectangle with top-left corner (u, v) and bottom-right corner (r, s).

As to the analysis, again let $T(m, n)$ denote the number of evaluations required to search an $m \times n$ rectangle. Suppose $m \le n$. In the best case, when for example each binary search on a row returns the leftmost or rightmost element, we have $T(m, n) = \log n + T(m/2, n)$ with solution $T(m, n) = O(\log m \times \log n)$. In the worst case, when each binary search returns the middle element, we have

$$T(m, n) = \log n + 2T(m/2, n/2)$$

To solve this, set $U(i, j) = T(2^i, 2^j)$. Then we have

$$U(i, j) = \sum_{k=0}^{i-1} 2^k(j - k) = O(2^i(j - i))$$

Hence $T(m, n) = O(m \log(n/m))$. This is asymptotically optimal by Anne's lower bound.

Teacher: Well done the four of you! It is surprising that in the 25 years or so that saddleback search has been presented as a paradigm of formal program construction nobody has seemed to notice that it is not asymptotically the best algorithm for searching.

Algorithm	f_0	f_1	f_2	f_3	f_4
Anne	7501	5011	6668	5068	9989
Theo	2537	38	1749	157	5025
Mary	121	42	445	181	134

Fig. 3.2 Number of evaluations

Algorithm	f_0	f_1	f_2	f_3	f_4
Anne	0.42	0.40	0.17	0.15	0.54
Theo	0.06	0.01	0.05	0.01	0.15
Mary	0.01	0.01	0.02	0.02	0.01

Fig. 3.3 Absolute running times

Afterword

The real story behind this pearl was that I decided to use saddleback search as an exercise when interviewing candidates for entry to Oxford. They were given a two-dimensional array of numbers, increasing along each row and up each column and asked for a systematic way to spot all occurrences of a given number. My aim was to get them to realise that searching from the top-left or bottom-right was a good strategy. But those candidates who had done some computing at school kept wanting to use binary search, either by going for the middle of each row or for the middle element of the rectangle. Thinking that saddleback search was the gold standard for this problem, I steered them away from pursuing the thought. Only afterwards did I wonder whether they might have had a point.

Apart from describing a new algorithm for an old problem, I think that two other methodological aspects are worthy of note. First, formal program calculation is heavily influenced by the available computational methods of the target language. While nobody would say it was elegant, Mary's final program is simple enough, given recursion and list concatenation as basic constructs, but would be more difficult to express with just arrays and loops. Second, as algorithm designers fully appreciate, formal program calculation has to be supplemented by insight into possible directions for improving efficiency. Such insight is provided, in part, by solving recurrence relations and determining lower bounds.

This pearl originally appeared in Bird (2006). One of the referees of the original paper wrote:

Complexity brings with it its own efficiency overheads, which are so often neglected in the sort of analyses included in the paper. If the author really wants to convince us that his algorithms are better than Gries's, then he should show some concrete evidence. Run the algorithm for specific functions on specific data, and compare the results.

Figures 3.2 and 3.3 provide such evidence. Five functions were chosen almost at random:

$$
\begin{array}{rcl}
f_0\,(x,y) & = & 2^y(2x+1)-1 \\
f_1\,(x,y) & = & x2^x + y2^y + 2x + y \\
f_2\,(x,y) & = & 3x + 27y + y^2 \\
f_3\,(x,y) & = & x^2 + y^2 + x + y \\
f_4\,(x,y) & = & x + 2^y + y - 1
\end{array}
$$

Figure 3.2 lists the exact number of evaluations of f_i required in the computation of *invert* f_i 5000 using Anne's initial version of saddleback search, Theo's version (with binary search to compute the boundaries) and Mary's final version. Figure 3.3 lists absolute running times in seconds under GHCi. The close correspondence with the first table shows that the number of evaluations is a reasonable guide to absolute running time.

References

Backhouse, R. (1986). *Program Construction and Verification*. International Series in Computer Science. Prentice Hall.

Bird, R. (2006). Improving saddleback search: a lesson in algorithm design. *Mathematics of Program Construction*, LNCS 4014, pp. 82–9.

Dijkstra, E. W. (1985). The saddleback search. EWD-934.
http://www.cs.utexas.edu/users/EWD/index09xx.html.

Gries, D. (1981). *The Science of Programming*. Springer-Verlag.

Graham, R. L., Knuth, D. E. and Patashnik, O. (1989). *Concrete Mathematics*. Reading, MA: Addison-Wesley.

4

A selection problem

Introduction

Let X and Y be two finite disjoint sets of elements over some ordered type and of combined size greater than k. Consider the problem of computing the kth smallest element of $X \cup Y$. By definition, the kth smallest element of a set is one for which there are exactly k elements smaller than it, so the zeroth smallest is the smallest. How long does such a computation take?

The answer depends, of course, on how the sets X and Y are represented. If they are both given as sorted lists, then $O(|X| + |Y|)$ steps are sufficient. The two lists can be merged in linear time and the kth smallest can be found at position k in the merged list in a further $O(k)$ steps. In fact, the total time is $O(k)$ steps, since only the first $k + 1$ elements of the merged list need be computed. But if the two sets are given as sorted arrays, then – as we show below – the time can further be reduced to $O(\log |X| + \log |Y|)$ steps. This bound depends on arrays having a constant-time access function. The same bound is attainable if both X and Y are represented by balanced binary search trees, despite the fact that two such trees cannot be merged in less than linear time.

The fast algorithm is another example of divide and conquer, and the proof that it works hinges on a particular relationship between merging and selection. Our aim in this pearl is to spell out the relationship, calculate the list-based divide and conquer algorithm and then implement it for the array representation of lists.

Formalisation and first steps

In terms of two sorted disjoint lists xs and ys, the problem is to compute

$$
\begin{array}{lll}
smallest & :: & Ord\ a \Rightarrow Int \rightarrow ([a], [a]) \rightarrow a \\
smallest\ k\ (xs, ys) & = & union\ (xs, ys) \mathbin{!!} k
\end{array}
$$

The value of $xs \mathbin{!!} k$ is the element of xs at position k, counting from zero. The function $union :: Ord\ a \Rightarrow ([a], [a]) \to [a]$ for merging two disjoint lists, each in increasing order, is defined by

$$
\begin{aligned}
union\ (xs, [\,]) &&= && xs \\
union\ ([\,], ys) &&= && ys \\
union\ (x : xs, y : ys) &\mid\ x < y &= && x : union\ (xs, y : ys) \\
&\mid\ x > y &= && y : union\ (x : xs, ys)
\end{aligned}
$$

Our aim is to derive a divide and conquer algorithm for *smallest*, so we need some decomposition rules for $\mathbin{!!}$ and *union*. For the former, abbreviating *length xs* to $|xs|$, we have

$$
(xs \mathbin{+\!\!+} ys) \mathbin{!!} k \;=\; \textbf{if } k < |xs| \textbf{ then } xs \mathbin{!!} k \textbf{ else } ys \mathbin{!!} (k - |xs|) \tag{4.1}
$$

The straightforward proof is omitted. For *union* we have the following property. Suppose $xs \mathbin{+\!\!+} ys$ and $us \mathbin{+\!\!+} vs$ are two sorted disjoint lists such that

$$
union\ (xs, vs) = xs \mathbin{+\!\!+} vs \quad \text{and} \quad union\ (us, ys) = us \mathbin{+\!\!+} ys
$$

In other words, no element of xs is greater than or equal to any element of vs; similarly for us and ys. Then

$$
union\ (xs \mathbin{+\!\!+} ys,\ us \mathbin{+\!\!+} vs) \;=\; union\ (xs, us) \mathbin{+\!\!+} union\ (ys, vs) \tag{4.2}
$$

It is instructive to rewrite (4.2) using an infix symbol $\cup$ for *union*:

$$
(xs \mathbin{+\!\!+} ys) \cup (us \mathbin{+\!\!+} vs) \;=\; (xs \cup us) \mathbin{+\!\!+} (ys \cup vs)
$$

Compare this with the similar identity[1] involving list difference $\setminus\!\setminus$:

$$
(xs \mathbin{+\!\!+} ys) \setminus\!\setminus (us \mathbin{+\!\!+} vs) \;=\; (xs \setminus\!\setminus us) \mathbin{+\!\!+} (ys \setminus\!\setminus vs)
$$

which holds when $xs \setminus\!\setminus vs = xs$ and $ys \setminus\!\setminus us = ys$. When two operators, $\mathbin{+\!\!+}$ and $\cup$, or $\mathbin{+\!\!+}$ and $\setminus\!\setminus$, interact in this way, they are said to *abide*[2] with one another. The abides property (4.2) of $\mathbin{+\!\!+}$ and $\cup$ is, we hope, sufficiently clear that we can omit a formal proof.

In what follows, the condition $union\ (xs, ys) = xs \mathbin{+\!\!+} ys$ is abbreviated to $xs \mathbin{\lhd} ys$. Thus, $xs \mathbin{\lhd} ys$ if $x < y$ for all elements x of xs and y of ys. Note that, restricted to nonempty lists, $\lhd$ is a transitive relation.

---

[1] Used in Pearl 1: "The smallest free number".

[2] "Abide" is a contraction of above-beside, in analogy with two operations on picture objects, one placing two equal-height pictures beside one another, and the other placing two equal-width pictures one above the other.

Divide and conquer

The aim of this section is to decompose the expression

$$smallest\ k\ (xs +\!\!+ [a] +\!\!+ ys, us +\!\!+ [b] +\!\!+ vs)$$

We deal only with the case $a < b$, since the case $a > b$, is entirely dual. The key point is that $(xs +\!\!+ [a]) \lhd ([b] +\!\!+ vs)$ if $a < b$ because all lists are in increasing order.

Assume first that $k < |xs +\!\!+ [a] +\!\!+ us|$, which is equivalent to $k \leq |xs +\!\!+ us|$. We calculate:

$$smallest\ k\ (xs +\!\!+ [a] +\!\!+ ys, us +\!\!+ [b] +\!\!+ vs)$$

$=$ {definition}

    $union\ (xs +\!\!+ [a] +\!\!+ ys, us +\!\!+ [b] +\!\!+ vs)\ !!\ k$

$=$ {choose ys_1 and ys_2 so that $ys = ys_1 +\!\!+ ys_2$ and
$(xs +\!\!+ [a] +\!\!+ ys_1) \lhd ([b] +\!\!+ vs)$ and $us \lhd ys_2$}

    $union\ (xs +\!\!+ [a] +\!\!+ ys_1 +\!\!+ ys_2, us +\!\!+ [b] +\!\!+ vs)\ !!\ k$

$=$ {abides property of $+\!\!+$ and $\cup$ and choice of ys_1 and ys_2}

    $(union\ (xs +\!\!+ [a] +\!\!+ ys_1, us) +\!\!+ union\ (ys_2, [b] +\!\!+ vs))\ !!\ k$

$=$ {using (4.1) and assumption that $k < |xs +\!\!+ [a] +\!\!+ us|$}

    $union\ (xs +\!\!+ [a] +\!\!+ ys_1, us)\ !!\ k$

$=$ {using (4.1) again}

    $(union\ (xs +\!\!+ [a] +\!\!+ ys_1, us) +\!\!+ union\ (ys_2, [\,]))\ !!\ k$

$=$ {abides property again, since $xs +\!\!+ [a] +\!\!+ ys_1 \lhd [\,]$}

    $union\ (xs +\!\!+ [a] +\!\!+ ys_1 +\!\!+ ys_2, us +\!\!+ [\,])\ !!\ k$

$=$ {definition of ys and $smallest$}

    $smallest\ k\ (xs +\!\!+ [a] +\!\!+ ys, us)$

Next, assume that $k \geq |xs +\!\!+ [a] +\!\!+ us|$. A symmetric argument gives

$$smallest\ k\ (xs +\!\!+ [a] +\!\!+ ys, us +\!\!+ [b] +\!\!+ vs)$$

$=$ {definition}

    $union\ (xs +\!\!+ [a] +\!\!+ ys, us +\!\!+ [b] +\!\!+ vs)\ !!\ k$

$=$ {choose us_1 and us_2 so that $us = us_1 +\!\!+ us_2$ and
$us_1 \lhd ys$ and $(xs +\!\!+ [a]) \lhd (us_2 +\!\!+ [b] +\!\!+ vs)$}

    $union\ (xs +\!\!+ [a] +\!\!+ ys, us_1 +\!\!+ us_2 +\!\!+ [b] +\!\!+ vs)\ !!\ k$

$=$ {abides property of $+\!\!+$ and $\cup$ and choice of us_1 and us_2}

    $(union\ (xs +\!\!+ [a], us_1) +\!\!+ union\ (ys, us_2 +\!\!+ [b] +\!\!+ vs))\ !!\ k$

$$= \quad \{\text{using (4.1) and assumption that } k \geq |xs + [a] + us|\}$$
$$union\ (ys, us_2 + [b] + vs) \mathbin{!!} (k - |xs + [a] + us_1|)$$
$$= \quad \{\text{using (4.1) again}\}$$
$$(union\ ([\,], us_1) + union\ (ys, us_2 + [b] + vs)) \mathbin{!!} (k - |xs + [a]|)$$
$$= \quad \{\text{as before}\}$$
$$smallest\ (k - |xs + [a]|)\ (ys, us + [b] + vs)$$

Summarising, we have that if $a < b$, then

$$smallest\ k\ (xs + [a] + ys,\ us + [b] + vs)$$
$$\mid \quad k \leq p+q \quad = \quad smallest\ k\ (xs + [a] + ys,\ us)$$
$$\mid \quad k > p+q \quad = \quad smallest\ (k-p-1)\ (ys,\ us + [b] + vs)$$
$$\textbf{where }(p, q) = (length\ xs,\ length\ us)$$

Entirely dual reasoning in the case $a > b$ yields

$$smallest\ k\ (xs + [a] + ys,\ us + [b] + vs)$$
$$\mid \quad k \leq p+q \quad = \quad smallest\ k\ (xs,\ us + [b] + vs)$$
$$\mid \quad k > p+q \quad = \quad smallest\ (k-q-1)\ (xs + [a] + ys,\ vs)$$
$$\textbf{where }(p, q) = (length\ xs,\ length\ us)$$

To complete the divide and conquer algorithm for *smallest* we have to consider the base cases when one or other of the argument lists is empty. This is easy, and we arrive at the following program:

$$smallest\ k\ ([\,], ws) = ws \mathbin{!!} k$$
$$smallest\ k\ (zs, [\,]) = zs \mathbin{!!} k$$
$$smallest\ k\ (zs, ws) =$$
$$\quad \textbf{case }(a < b,\ k \leq p+q)\ \textbf{of}$$

$(True, True)$	$\rightarrow$	$smallest\ k\ (zs, us)$
$(True, False)$	$\rightarrow$	$smallest\ (k-p-1)\ (ys, ws)$
$(False, True)$	$\rightarrow$	$smallest\ k\ (xs, ws)$
$(False, False)$	$\rightarrow$	$smallest\ (k-q-1)\ (zs, vs)$

$$\textbf{where } p \qquad\quad = \quad (length\ zs)\ \text{div}\ 2$$
$$q \qquad\qquad = \quad (length\ ws)\ \text{div}\ 2$$
$$(xs, a : ys) \quad = \quad splitAt\ p\ zs$$
$$(us, b : vs) \quad = \quad splitAt\ q\ ws$$

The running time of *smallest* $k\ (xs, ys)$ is linear in the lengths of the lists xs and ys, so the divide and conquer algorithm is no faster than the specification. The payoff comes when xs and ys are given as sorted arrays rather than lists. Then the program can be modified to run in logarithmic time in the sizes of

search k (lx, rx) $(ly\ ry)$
   | $lx == rx$ = $ya\ !\ k$
   | $ly == ry$ = $xa\ !\ k$
   | **otherwise**   =   **case** $(xa\ !\ mx < ya\ !\ my, k \leq mx+my)$ **of**
                        $(True, True) \rightarrow$ *search k* (lx, rx) (ly, my)
                        $(True, False) \rightarrow$ *search* $(k-mx-1)$ (mx, rx) (ly, ry)
                        $(False, True) \rightarrow$ *search k* (lx, mx) (ly, ry)
                        $(False, False) \rightarrow$ *search* $(k-my-1)$ (lx, rx) (my, ry)
                 where $mx = (lx+rx)$ div 2; $my = (ly+ry)$ div 2

Fig. 4.1 Definition of *search*

---

the arrays. Instead of repeatedly splitting the two lists, everything can be done with array indices. More precisely, a list xs is represented by an array xa and two indices (lx, rx) under the abstraction $xs = map\ (xa!)\ [lx\ ..\ rx-1]$, where (!) is the array indexing operator in the Haskell library *Data.Array*. This library provides efficient operations on *immutable* arrays, arrays that are constructed in one go. In particular, (!) takes constant time. A list xs can be converted into an array xa indexed from zero by

$$xa = listArray\ (0, length\ xs - 1)\ xs$$

We can now define

> *smallest*   :: $Int \rightarrow (Array\ Int\ a, Array\ Int\ a) \rightarrow a$
> *smallest k* (xa, ya) =   *search k* $(0, m+1)$ $(0, n+1)$
>   **where** $(0, m)$ =   *bounds xa*
> $(0, n)$ =   *bounds ya*

The function *bounds* returns the lower and upper bounds on an array, here indexed from zero. Finally, the function *search*, which is local to *smallest* because it refers to the arrays xa and ya, is given in Figure 4.1.

There is a constant amount of work at each recursive call, and each call halves one or other of the two intervals, so the running time of *search* is logarithmic.

Final remarks

Although we have phrased the problem in terms of disjoint sets represented by lists in increasing order, there is a variation on the problem in which the lists are not necessarily disjoint and are only in weakly increasing order. Such lists represents multisets or bags. Consider the computation of *merge* (xs, ys) !! k, where *merge* merges two lists in ascending order, so *merge* = *uncurry* ($\curlywedge$):

$$
\begin{aligned}
merge\ ([\,], ys) &= ys \\
merge\ (xs, [\,]) &= xs \\
merge\ (x : xs, y : ys) &\mid x \le y = x : merge\ (xs, y : ys) \\
&\mid x \ge y = y : merge\ (x : xs,\ ys)
\end{aligned}
$$

Thus, *merge* has the same definition as *union* except that $<$ and $>$ are replaced by $\le$ and $\ge$. Of course, the result is no longer necessarily the kth smallest element of the combined lists. Furthermore, provided we replace $\lhd$ by $\unlhd$, where $xs \unlhd ys$ if *merge* $(xs, ys) = xs \mathbin{+\!\!+} ys$, and equivalently if $x \le y$ for all x in xs and y in ys, then the calculation recorded above remains valid provided the cases $a < b$ and $a > b$ are weakened to $a \le b$ and $a \ge b$.

As a final remark, this pearl originally appeared, under a different title, in Bird (1997). But do not look at it, because it made heavy weather of the crucial relationship between merging and selection. Subsequently, Jeremy Gibbons (1997) spotted a much simpler way to proceed, and it is really his calculation that has been recorded above.

References

Bird, R. S. (1997). On merging and selection. *Journal of Functional Programming* **7** (3), 349–54.

Gibbons, J. (1997). More on merging and selection. Technical Report CMS-TR-97-08, Oxford Brookes University, UK.

5

Sorting pairwise sums

Introduction

Let A be some linearly ordered set and $(\oplus) :: A \to A \to A$ some monotonic binary operation on A, so $x \leq x' \wedge y \leq y' \Rightarrow x \oplus y \leq x' \oplus y'$. Consider the problem of computing

$$
\begin{aligned}
sortsums & \quad :: \quad [A] \to [A] \to [A] \\
sortsums\ xs\ ys & \quad = \quad sort\ [x \oplus y \mid x \leftarrow xs,\ y \leftarrow ys]
\end{aligned}
$$

Counting just comparisons, and supposing xs and ys have the same length n, how long does $sortsums\ xs\ ys$ take?

Certainly $O(n^2 \log n)$ comparisons are sufficient. There are n^2 sums and sorting a list of length n^2 can be done with $O(n^2 \log n)$ comparisons. This upper bound does not depend on $\oplus$ being monotonic. In fact, without further information about $\oplus$ and A this bound is also a lower bound. The assumption that $\oplus$ is monotonic does not reduce the asymptotic complexity, only the constant factor.

But now suppose we know more about $\oplus$ and A: specifically that $(\oplus, A)$ is an *Abelian group*. Thus, $\oplus$ is associative and commutative, with identity element e and an operation $negate :: A \to A$ such that $x \oplus negate\ x = e$. Given this extra information, Jean-Luc Lambert (1992) proved that $sortsums$ can be computed with $O(n^2)$ comparisons. However, his algorithm also requires $Cn^2 \log n$ additional operations, where C is quite large. It remains an open problem, some 35 years after it was first posed by Harper *et al.* (1975), as to whether the total cost of computing $sortsums$ can be reduced to $O(n^2)$ comparisons and $O(n^2)$ other steps.

Lambert's algorithm is another nifty example of divide and conquer. Our aim in this pearl is just to present the essential ideas and give an implementation in Haskell.

Lambert's algorithm

Let's first prove the $\Omega(n^2 \log n)$ lower bound on *sortsums* when the only assumption is that $(\oplus)$ is monotonic. Suppose xs and ys are both sorted into increasing order and consider the $n \times n$ matrix

$$[[x \oplus y \mid y \leftarrow ys] \mid x \leftarrow xs]$$

Each row and column of the matrix is therefore in increasing order. The matrix is an example of a standard Young tableau, and it follows from Theorem H of Section 5.1.4 of Knuth (1998) that there are precisely

$$E(n) = (n^2)! \left/ \left(\frac{(2n-1)!}{(n-1)!} \frac{(2n-2)!}{(n-2)!} \cdots \frac{n!}{0!} \right) \right.$$

ways of assigning the values 1 to n^2 to the elements of the matrix, and so exactly $E(n)$ potential permutations that sort the input. Using the fact that $\log E(n) = \Omega(n^2 \log n)$, we conclude that at least this number of comparisons is required.

Now for the meat of the exercise. Lambert's algorithm depends on two simple facts. Define the subtraction operation $(\ominus) :: A \to A \to A$ by $x \ominus y = x \oplus \text{negate } y$. Then:

$$x \oplus y \ = \ x \ominus \text{negate } y \tag{5.1}$$
$$x \ominus y \leq x' \ominus y' \ \equiv \ x \ominus x' \leq y \ominus y' \tag{5.2}$$

Verification of (5.1) is easy, but (5.2), which we leave as an exercise, requires all the properties of an Abelian group. In effect, (5.1) says that the problem of sorting sums can be reduced to the problem of sorting subtractions and (5.2) says that the latter problem is, in turn, reducible to the problem of sorting subtractions over a single list.

Here is how (5.1) and (5.2) are used. Consider the list *subs xs ys* of *labelled* subtractions defined by

$$
\begin{array}{lll}
subs & :: & [A] \to [A] \to [Label\ A] \\
subs\ xs\ ys & = & [(x \ominus y, (i,j)) \mid (x,i) \leftarrow zip\ xs\ [1..],\ (y,j) \leftarrow zip\ ys\ [1..]]
\end{array}
$$

where *Label a* is a synonym for $(a, (Int, Int))$. Thus, each term $x \ominus y$ is labelled with the position of x in xs and y in ys. Labelling information will be needed later on. The first fact (5.1) gives

$$
\begin{array}{lll}
sortsums\ xs\ ys & = & map\ fst\ (sortsubs\ xs\ (map\ negate\ ys)) \\
sortsubs\ xs\ ys & = & sort\ (subs\ xs\ ys)
\end{array}
$$

The sums are sorted by sorting the associated labelled subtractions and throwing away the labels.

The next step is to exploit (5.2) to show how to compute *sortsubs xs ys* with a quadratic number of comparisons. Construct the list *table* by

$$
\begin{array}{lcl}
table & :: & [A] \to [A] \to [(Int, Int, Int)] \\
table\ xs\ ys & = & map\ snd\ (map\ (tag\ 1)\ xxs \curlywedge map\ (tag\ 2)\ yys) \\
& \textbf{where}\ xxs & = & sortsubs\ xs\ xs \\
& yys & = & sortsubs\ ys\ ys \\
tag\ i\ (x, (j, k)) & = & (x, (i, j, k))
\end{array}
$$

Here, $\curlywedge$ merges two sorted lists. In words, *table* is constructed by merging the two sorted lists *xxs* and *yys* after first tagging each list in order to be able to determine the origin of each element in the merged list. According to (5.2), *table* contains sufficient information to enable *sortsubs xs ys* to be computed with *no* comparisons over A. For suppose that $x \ominus y$ has label (i, j) and $x' \ominus y'$ has label (k, ℓ). Then $x \ominus y \leq x' \ominus y'$ if and only if $(1, i, k)$ precedes $(2, j, \ell)$ in *table*. No comparisons of elements of A are needed beyond those required to construct *table*.

To implement the idea we need to be able to compute precedence information quickly. This is most simply achieved by converting *table* into a Haskell array:

$$
\begin{array}{lcl}
mkArray\ xs\ ys & = & array\ b\ (zip\ (table\ xs\ ys)\ [1..]) \\
& \textbf{where}\ b & = & ((1, 1, 1), (2, p, p)) \\
& p & = & max\ (length\ xs)\ (length\ ys)
\end{array}
$$

The definition of *mkArray* makes use of the library *Data.Array* of Haskell arrays. The first argument b of *array* is a pair of bounds, the lowest and highest indices in the array. The second argument of *array* is an association list of index–value pairs. With this representation, $(1, i, k)$ precedes $(2, j, \ell)$ in *table* if $a!(1, i, k) < a!(2, j, \ell)$, where $a = mkArray\ xs\ ys$. The array indexing operation (!) takes constant time, so a precedence test takes constant time. We can now compute *sortsubs xs ys* using the Haskell utility function *sortBy*:

$$
\begin{array}{lcl}
sortsubs\ xs\ ys & = & sortBy\ (cmp\ (mkArray\ xs\ ys))\ (subs\ xs\ ys) \\
cmp\ a\ (x, (i, j))\ (y, (k, \ell)) \\
& = & compare\ (a\ !\ (1, i, k))\ (a\ !\ (2, j, \ell))
\end{array}
$$

The function *compare* is a method in the type class *Ord*. In particular, *sort* = *sortBy compare* and ($\curlywedge$) = *mergeBy compare*. We omit the divide and conquer definition of *sortBy* in terms of *mergeBy*.

The program so far is summarised in Figure 5.1. It is complete apart from the definition of *sortsubs'*, where *sortsubs' xs* = *sortsubs xs xs*. However, this definition cannot be used in *sortsums* because the recursion would not be

$$
\begin{aligned}
sortsums\ xs\ ys\ &=\ map\ fst\ (sortsubs\ xs\ (map\ negate\ ys))\\
sortsubs\ xs\ ys\ &=\ sortBy\ (cmp\ (mkArray\ xs\ ys))\ (subs\ xs\ ys)
\end{aligned}
$$

$$
subs\ xs\ ys\ =\ [(x \ominus y, (i,j)) \mid (x,i) \leftarrow zip\ xs\ [1..], (y,j) \leftarrow zip\ ys\ [1..]]
$$

$$
cmp\ a\ (x,(i,j))\ (y,(k,\ell))\ =\ compare\ (a\ !\ (1,i,k))\ (a\ !\ (2,j,\ell))
$$

$$
\begin{aligned}
mkArray\ xs\ ys\ &=\ array\ b\ (zip\ (table\ xs\ ys)\ [1..])\\
&\mathbf{where}\ b\ =\ ((1,1,1),(2,p,p))\\
&\qquad\quad\ p\ =\ max\ (length\ xs)\ (length\ ys)\\
table\ xs\ ys\ &=\ map\ snd\ (map\ (tag\ 1)\ xxs \wedge\!\!\wedge map\ (tag\ 2)\ yys)\\
&\mathbf{where}\ xxs\ =\ sortsubs'\ xs\\
&\qquad\quad\ yys\ =\ sortsubs'\ ys\\
tag\ i\ (x,(j,k))\ &=\ (x,(i,j,k))
\end{aligned}
$$

Fig. 5.1 The complete code for *sortsums*, except for *sortsubs'*

---

well founded. Although computing *sortsubs xs ys* takes $O(mn \log mn)$ steps, it uses no comparisons on A beyond those needed to construct *table*. And *table* needs only $O(m^2 + n^2)$ comparisons plus those comparisons needed to construct *sortsubs' xs* and *sortsubs' ys*. What remains is to show how to compute *sortsubs'* with a quadratic number of comparisons.

Divide and conquer

Ignoring labels for the moment and writing $xs \ominus ys$ for $[x \ominus y \mid x \leftarrow xs, y \leftarrow ys]$, the key to a divide and conquer algorithm is the identity

$$
\begin{aligned}
&(xs \mathbin{+\!\!+} ys) \ominus (xs \mathbin{+\!\!+} ys)\\
&=\ (xs \ominus xs) \mathbin{+\!\!+} (xs \ominus ys) \mathbin{+\!\!+} (ys \ominus xs) \mathbin{+\!\!+} (ys \ominus ys)
\end{aligned}
$$

Hence, to sort the list on the left, we can sort the four lists on the right and merge them together. The presence of labels complicates the divide and conquer algorithm slightly because the labels have to be adjusted correctly. The labelled version reads

$$
\begin{aligned}
&subs\ (xs \mathbin{+\!\!+} ys)\ (xs \mathbin{+\!\!+} ys)\\
&=\ subs\ xs\ xs \mathbin{+\!\!+} map\ (incr\ m)\ (subs\ xs\ ys) \mathbin{+\!\!+}\\
&\qquad map\ (incl\ m)\ (subs\ ys\ xs) \mathbin{+\!\!+} map\ (incb\ m)\ (subs\ ys\ ys)
\end{aligned}
$$

where $m = length\ xs$ and

$$
\begin{aligned}
incl\ m\ (x,(i,j))\ &=\ (x,(m{+}i,j))\\
incr\ m\ (x,(i,j))\ &=\ (x,(i,m{+}j))\\
incb\ m\ (x,(i,j))\ &=\ (x,(m{+}i,m{+}j))
\end{aligned}
$$

$$
\begin{aligned}
sortsubs'\,[\,] \;\; &= \;\; [\,] \\
sortsubs'\,[w] \;\; &= \;\; [(w \ominus w, (1,1))] \\
sortsubs'\,ws \;\; &= \;\; foldr1\,(\wedge)\,[xxs,\,map\,(incr\,m)\,xys, \\
&\qquad\qquad\qquad map\,(incl\,m)\,yxs,\,map\,(incb\,m)\,yys]
\end{aligned}
$$

$$
\begin{aligned}
\textbf{where } xxs \;\; &= \;\; sortsubs'\,xs \\
xys \;\; &= \;\; sortBy\,(cmp\,(mkArray\,xs\,ys))\,(subs\,xs\,ys) \\
yxs \;\; &= \;\; map\,switch\,(reverse\,xys) \\
yys \;\; &= \;\; sortsubs'\,ys \\
(xs, ys) \;\; &= \;\; splitAt\,m\,ws \\
m \;\; &= \;\; length\,ws \text{ div } 2
\end{aligned}
$$

$$
\begin{aligned}
incl\,m\,(x, (i, j)) \;\; &= \;\; (x, (m + i, j)) \\
incr\,m\,(x, (i, j)) \;\; &= \;\; (x, (i, m + j)) \\
incb\,m\,(x, (i, j)) \;\; &= \;\; (x, (m + i, m + j)) \\
\\
switch\,(x, (i, j)) \;\; &= \;\; (negate\,x, (j, i))
\end{aligned}
$$

Fig. 5.2 The code for *sortsubs'*

To compute *sortsubs' ws* we split *ws* into two equal halves *xs* and *ys*. The lists *sortsubs' xs* and *sortsubs' ys* are computed recursively. The list *sortsubs xs ys* is computed by applying the algorithm of the previous section. We can also compute *sortsubs ys xs* in the same way, but an alternative is simply to reverse *sortsubs xs ys* and negate its elements:

$$
\begin{aligned}
sortsubs\,ys\,xs \;\; &= \;\; map\,switch\,(reverse\,(sortsubs\,xs\,ys)) \\
switch\,(x, (i, j)) \;\; &= \;\; (negate\,x, (j, i))
\end{aligned}
$$

The program for *sortsubs'* is given in Figure 5.2. The number $C(n)$ of comparisons required to compute *sortsubs'* on a list of length n satisfies the recurrence $C(n) = 2C(n/2) + O(n^2)$ with solution $C(n) = O(n^2)$. That means *sortsums* can be computed with $O(n^2)$ comparisons. However, the total time $T(n)$ satisfies $T(n) = 2T(n/2) + O(n^2 \log n)$ with solution $T(n) = O(n^2 \log n)$. The logarithmic factor can be removed from $T(n)$ if *sortBy cmp* can be computed in quadratic time, but this result remains elusive. In any case, the additional complexity arising from replacing comparisons by other operations makes the algorithm very inefficient in practice.

Final remarks

The problem of sorting pairwise sums is given as Problem 41 in the Open Problems Project (Demaine *et al.*, 2009), a web resource devoted to recording open problems of interest to researchers in computational geometry and related fields. The earliest known reference to the problem is Fedman (1976), who attributes the problem to Elwyn Berlekamp. All these references consider the problem in terms of numbers rather than Abelian groups, but the idea is the same.

References

Demaine, E. D., Mitchell, J. S. B. and O'Rourke, J. (2009). The Open Problems Project. http://mave,smith.edu/~orourke/TOPP/.

Fedman, M. L. (1976). How good is the information theory lower bound in sorting? *Theoretical Computer Science* **1**, 355–61.

Harper, L. H., Payne, T. H., Savage, J. E. and Straus, E. (1975). Sorting $X + Y$. *Communications of the ACM* **18** (6), 347–9.

Knuth, D. E. (1998). *The Art of Computer Programming: Volume 3, Sorting and Searching*, second edition. Reading, MA: Addison-Wesley.

Lambert, J.-L. (1992). Sorting the sums $(x_i + y_j)$ in $O(n^2)$ comparisons. *Theoretical Computer Science* **103**, 137–41.

6

Making a century

Introduction

The problem of making a century is to list all the ways the operations $+$ and $\times$ can be inserted into the list of digits $[1 .. 9]$ so as to make a total of 100. Two such ways are:

$$100 = 12 + 34 + 5{\times}6 + 7 + 8 + 9$$
$$100 = 1 + 2{\times}3 + 4 + 5 + 67 + 8 + 9$$

Note that no parentheses are allowed in expressions and $\times$ binds more tightly than $+$. The only way to solve the problem seems to be by searching through all possible expressions, in other words to carry out an *exhaustive search*. The primary aim of this pearl is to examine a little of the theory of exhaustive search in order to identify any features that can improve its performance. The theory is then applied to the problem of making a century.

A little theory

We begin with the three types *Data*, *Candidate* and *Value* and three functions:

$$
\begin{array}{lll}
candidates & :: & Data \rightarrow [Candidate] \\
value & :: & Candidate \rightarrow Value \\
good & :: & Value \rightarrow Bool
\end{array}
$$

These three functions are be used to construct a function *solutions*:

$$
\begin{array}{lll}
solutions & :: & Data \rightarrow [Candidate] \\
solutions & = & filter\,(good \cdot value) \cdot candidates
\end{array}
$$

The function *solutions* carries out an exhaustive search through the list of candidates to find all those having good value. No special steps have to be taken if only one answer is required because lazy evaluation will ensure that only the work needed to evaluate the first solution will be performed. Apart from this general remark about the benefits of lazy evaluation, nothing much more can be said about *solutions* unless we make some assumptions about the ingredients.

The first assumption is that *Data* is a list of values, say [*Datum*], and that *candidates* :: [*Datum*] → [*Candidate*] takes the form

$$candidates \quad = \quad foldr\ extend\ [\ ] \tag{6.1}$$

where *extend* :: *Datum* → [*Candidate*] → [*Candidate*] is some function that builds a list of extended candidates from a given datum and a list of candidates.

The second assumption is in two parts. First, there is a predicate *ok* such that every *good* value is necessarily an *ok* value, so *good v* ⇒ *ok v* for all *v*. Hence

$$filter\ (good \cdot value) \quad = \quad filter\ (good \cdot value) \cdot filter\ (ok \cdot value) \tag{6.2}$$

The second part is that candidates with *ok* values are the extensions of candidates with *ok* values:

$$filter\ (ok \cdot value) \cdot extend\ x$$
$$= \quad filter\ (ok \cdot value) \cdot extend\ x \cdot filter\ (ok \cdot value) \tag{6.3}$$

Using these assumptions, we calculate:

$$solutions$$
$$= \quad \{\text{definition of } solutions\}$$
$$filter\ (good \cdot value) \cdot candidates$$
$$= \quad \{\text{equation (6.1)}\}$$
$$filter\ (good \cdot value) \cdot foldr\ extend\ [\ ]$$
$$= \quad \{\text{equation (6.2)}\}$$
$$filter\ (good \cdot value) \cdot filter\ (ok \cdot value) \cdot foldr\ extend\ [\ ]$$
$$= \quad \{\text{with } extend'\ x = filter\ (ok \cdot value) \cdot extend\ x; \text{ see below}\}$$
$$filter\ (good \cdot value) \cdot foldr\ extend'\ [\ ]$$

The last step in this calculation is an appeal to the *fusion law* of *foldr*. Recall that this laws states that *f* · *foldr g a* = *foldr h b* provided three conditions are satisfied: (i) *f* is a strict function; (ii) *f a* = *b*; (iii) *f* (*g x y*) = *h x* (*f y*) for all *x* and *y*. In particular, taking *f* = *filter* (*ok* · *value*) and *g* = *extend*, we have that (i) is satisfied, (ii) holds for *a* = *b* = [ ] and (iii) is just (6.3) with *h* = *extend'*.

We have shown that

$$solutions \; = \; filter \, (good \cdot value) \cdot foldr \; extend' \,[\,]$$

The new version of *solutions* is better than the previous one, as a potentially much smaller list of candidates is constructed at each stage, namely only those with an *ok* value. On the other hand, the function *value* is recomputed at each evaluation of *extend'*.

We can avoid recomputing *value* with the help of yet a third assumption:

$$map \; value \cdot extend \; x \; = \; modify \; x \cdot map \; value \tag{6.4}$$

Assumption (6.4) states that the values of an extended set of candidates can be obtained by modifying the values of the candidates out of which the extensions are built.

Suppose we redefine *candidates* to read

$$candidates \; = \; map \, (fork \, (id, value)) \cdot foldr \; extend' \,[\,]$$

where $fork \, (f, g) \, x = (f \, x, g \, x)$. The new version of *candidates* returns a list of pairs of candidates and their values. The form of the new definition suggests another appeal to the fusion law of *foldr*. For the main fusion condition we have to find a function, *expand* say, satisfying

$$map \, (fork \, (id, value)) \cdot extend' \; x \; = \; expand \; x \cdot map \, (fork \, (id, value))$$

Then we obtain *candidates* = *foldr expand* [ ].

We are going to use simple equational reasoning to discover *expand*. In order to do so, we need a number of combinatorial laws about *fork*, laws that are used in many program calculations. The first law is that

$$fst \cdot fork \, (f, g) = f \quad and \quad snd \cdot fork \, (f, g) = g \tag{6.5}$$

The second law is a simple fusion law:

$$fork \, (f, g) \cdot h \; = \; fork \, (f \cdot h, g \cdot h) \tag{6.6}$$

For the third law, define *cross* by $cross \, (f, g) \, (x, y) = (f \, x, g \, y)$. Then we have

$$fork \, (f \cdot h, g \cdot k) \; = \; cross \, (f, g) \cdot fork \, (h, k) \tag{6.7}$$

The next two laws relate *fork* to two functions, *zip* and *unzip*. The function *unzip* is defined by

$$unzip \quad :: \quad [(a, b)] \to ([a], [b])$$
$$unzip \quad = \quad fork \, (map \; fst, map \; snd)$$

and $zip :: ([a], [b]) \rightarrow [(a, b)]$ is specified by the condition $zip \cdot unzip = id.$[1]
In particular, we can reason:

$$unzip \cdot map \ (fork \ (f, g))$$
$$= \quad \{\text{definition of } unzip\}$$
$$fork \ (map \ fst, map \ snd) \cdot map \ (fork \ (f, g))$$
$$= \quad \{(6.6) \text{ and } map \ (f \cdot g) = map \ f \cdot map \ g\}$$
$$fork \ (map \ (fst \cdot fork \ (f, g)), map \ (snd \cdot fork \ (f, g)))$$
$$= \quad \{(6.5)\}$$
$$fork \ (map \ f, map \ g)$$

Hence

$$fork \ (map \ f, map \ g) \quad = \quad unzip \cdot map \ (fork \ (f, g)) \tag{6.8}$$

Using $zip \cdot unzip = id$ we have from (6.8) that

$$map \ (fork \ (f, g)) \quad = \quad zip \cdot fork \ (map \ f, map \ g) \tag{6.9}$$

The final law relates *fork* to *filter*:

$$map \ (fork \ (f, g)) \cdot filter \ (p \cdot g)$$
$$= \quad filter \ (p \cdot snd) \cdot map \ (fork \ (f, g)) \tag{6.10}$$

Evaluating the expression on the right is more efficient than evaluating the expression on the left because g is evaluated just once for each element of the argument list.

Having identified the various plumbing combinators and the rules that relate them, we are ready for the final calculation:

$$map \ (fork \ (id, value)) \cdot extend' \ x$$
$$= \quad \{\text{definition of } extend'\}$$
$$map \ (fork \ (id, value)) \cdot filter \ (ok \cdot value) \cdot extend \ x$$
$$= \quad \{(6.10)\}$$
$$filter \ (ok \cdot snd) \cdot map \ (fork \ (id, value)) \cdot extend \ x$$

We now focus on the second two terms, and continue:

$$map \ (fork \ (id, value)) \cdot extend \ x$$
$$= \quad \{(6.9) \text{ and } map \ id = id\}$$
$$zip \cdot fork \ (id, map \ value) \cdot extend \ x$$

---

[1] The Haskell function $zip :: [a] \rightarrow [b] \rightarrow [(a, b)]$ is defined as a curried function.

$$= \quad \{(6.6)\}$$
$$zip \cdot fork \ (extend \ x, map \ value \cdot extend \ x)$$
$$= \quad \{(6.4)\}$$
$$zip \cdot fork \ (extend \ x, modify \ x \cdot map \ value)$$
$$= \quad \{(6.7)\}$$
$$zip \cdot cross \ (extend \ x, modify \ x) \cdot fork \ (id, map \ value)$$
$$= \quad \{(6.8)\}$$
$$zip \cdot cross \ (extend \ x, modify \ x) \cdot unzip \cdot map \ (fork \ (id, value))$$

Putting the two calculations together, we arrive at

$$
\begin{aligned}
solutions &= map \ fst \cdot filter \ (good \cdot snd) \cdot foldr \ expand \ [\,] \\
expand \ x &= filter \ (ok \cdot snd) \cdot zip \cdot cross \ (extend \ x, modify \ x) \cdot unzip
\end{aligned}
$$

This is our final version of *solutions*. It depends only on the definitions of *good*, *ok*, *extend* and *modify*. The term *foldr expand* [ ] builds a list of candidates along with their values, and *solutions* picks those candidates whose values satisfy *good*. The function *expand x* builds an extended list of candidates, maintaining the property that all extended candidates have values that satisfy *ok*.

Making a century

Let us now return to the problem in hand, which was to list all the ways the operations + and × can be inserted into the list of digits $[1 \mathbin{..} 9]$ so as to make a total of 100.

Candidate solutions are expressions built from + and ×. Each expression is the sum of a list of terms, each term is the product of a list of factors and each factor is a list of digits. That means we can define expressions, terms and factors just with the help of suitable type synonyms:

$$
\begin{aligned}
\textbf{type } Expression &= [Term] \\
\textbf{type } Term &= [Factor] \\
\textbf{type } Factor &= [Digit] \\
\textbf{type } Digit &= Int
\end{aligned}
$$

Thus, *Expression* is synonymous with $[[[Int]]]$.

The value of an expression is given by a function *valExpr*, defined by

$$
\begin{aligned}
valExpr \ &:: \ Expression \to Int \\
valExpr \ &= \ sum \cdot map \ valTerm
\end{aligned}
$$

$$valTerm \quad :: \quad Term \to Int$$
$$valTerm \quad = \quad product \cdot map \; valFact$$

$$valFact \quad :: \quad Factor \to Int$$
$$valFact \quad = \quad foldl1 \; (\lambda n \; d \to 10 * n + d)$$

A good expression is one whose value is 100:

$$good \quad :: \quad Int \to Bool$$
$$good \; v \quad = \quad (v \mathbin{==} 100)$$

To complete the formulation we need to define a function *expressions* that generates a list of all possible expressions that can be built out of a given list of digits. We can do this in two ways. One is to invoke the standard function *partitions* of type $[a] \to [[[a]]]$ that partitions a list into one or more sublists in all possible ways. If we apply *partitions* to a list of digits xs we get a list of all possible ways of splitting xs into a list of factors. Then, by applying *partitions* again to each list of factors, we obtain a list of all possible ways a list of factors can be split into lists of terms. Hence

$$expressions \quad :: \quad [Digit] \to [Expression]$$
$$expressions \quad = \quad concatMap \; partitions \cdot partitions$$

Alternatively, we can define *expressions* by $expressions = foldr \; extend \; [\,]$, where

$$extend \qquad\qquad :: \quad Digit \to [Expression] \to [Expression]$$
$$extend \; x \; [\,] \qquad\quad = \quad [[[[x]]]]$$
$$extend \; x \; es \qquad\quad = \quad concatMap \; (glue \; x) \; es$$

$$glue \qquad\qquad\qquad :: \quad Digit \to Expression \to [Expression]$$
$$glue \; x \; ((xs : xss) : xsss) \; = \; [((x : xs) : xss) : xsss,$$
$$([x] : xs : xss) : xsss,$$
$$[[x]] : (xs : xss) : xsss]$$

To explain these definitions, observe that only one expression can be built from a single digit x, namely $[[[x]]]$. This justifies the first clause of *extend*. An expression built from more than one digit can be decomposed into a leading factor (a list of digits, xs say), a leading term (a list of factors, xss say) and a remaining expression (a list of terms, $xsss$ say). A new digit x can be inserted into an expression in exactly three different ways: by extending the current factor on the left with the new digit, by starting a new factor or by starting a new term. This justifies the second clause of *extend* and the definition of *glue*. One advantage of the second definition is that it is immediate that there are $6561 = 3^8$ expressions one can build using the digits $[1 .. 9]$; indeed, 3^{n-1} expressions for a list of n digits.

Evaluating *filter (good · valExpr) · expressions* and displaying the results in a suitable fashion, yields the seven possible answers:

$$100 = 1 \times 2 \times 3 + 4 + 5 + 6 + 7 + 8 \times 9$$
$$100 = 1 + 2 + 3 + 4 + 5 + 6 + 7 + 8 \times 9$$
$$100 = 1 \times 2 \times 3 \times 4 + 5 + 6 + 7 \times 8 + 9$$
$$100 = 12 + 3 \times 4 + 5 + 6 + 7 \times 8 + 9$$
$$100 = 1 + 2 \times 3 + 4 + 5 + 67 + 8 + 9$$
$$100 = 1 \times 2 + 34 + 5 + 6 \times 7 + 8 + 9$$
$$100 = 12 + 34 + 5 \times 6 + 7 + 8 + 9$$

The computation does not take too long because there are only 6561 possibilities to check. But on another day the input might consist of a different target value and many more digits, so it is worth spending a little time seeing whether the search can be improved.

According to the little theory of exhaustive search given above, we have to find some definition of *ok* such that all *good* expressions are *ok* expressions, and such that *ok* expressions are necessarily constructed out of *ok* subexpressions. Given that *good* $v = (v == c)$, where c is the target value, the only sensible definition of *ok* is *ok* $v = (v \leq c)$. Since the only operations are $+$ and $\times$, every expression with a target value c has to be built out of subexpressions with target values at most c.

We also have to find a definition of *modify* so that

$$map\ valExpr \cdot extend\ x = modify\ x \cdot map\ valExpr$$

Here we run into a small difficulty, because not all the values of expressions in *glue x e* can be determined simply from the value of e: we need the values of the leading factor and leading term as well. So we define *value* not to be *valExpr* but

$$value\ ((xs : xss) : xsss) = (10^n, valFact\ xs, valTerm\ xss, valExpr\ xsss)$$
$$\textbf{where } n = length\ xs$$

The extra first component 10^n is included simply to make the evaluation of *valFact* $(x : xs)$ more efficient. Now we obtain

$$modify\ x\ (k, f, t, e)$$
$$= [(10 * k, k * x + f, t, e), (10, x, f * t, e), (10, x, 1, f * t + e)]$$

Accordingly, the definitions of *good* and *ok* are revised to read:

$$good\ c\ (k, f, t, e) = (f * t + e == c)$$
$$ok\ c\ (k, f, t, e) = (f * t + e \leq c)$$

Installing these definitions in the definition of *expand* gives a faster exhaustive search:

$$solutions\ c = map\ fst \cdot filter\ (good\ c \cdot snd) \cdot foldr\ (expand\ c)\ [\ ]$$
$$expand\ c\ x = filter\ (ok\ c \cdot snd) \cdot zip \cdot cross\ (extend\ x, modify\ x) \cdot unzip$$

The definition of *expand* can be simplified to read:

$$expand\ c\ x\ [\ ] \quad = \quad [(([[[x]]], (10, x, 1, 0))]$$
$$expand\ c\ x\ evs \quad = \quad concat\ (map\ (filter\ (ok\ c \cdot snd) \cdot glue\ x)\ evs)$$

$$glue\ x\ ((xs : xss) : xsss, (k, f, t, e)) =$$
$$[(((x : xs) : xss) : xsss, (10*k, k*x + f, t, e)),$$
$$(([x] : xs : xss) : xsss, (10, x, f*t, e)),$$
$$([[x]] : (xs : xss) : xsss, (10, x, 1, f*t + e))]$$

The result is a program for *solutions c* that is many times faster than the first version. As just one experimental test, taking $c = 1000$ and the first 14 digits of π as input, the second version was over 200 times faster.

Final remarks

The problem of making a century is discussed in Exercise 122 of Knuth (2006), which also considers other variants of the problem, such as allowing parentheses and other arithmetical operators; see also the Countdown pearl later in the book (Pearl 20). One moral of the exercise is that, when seeking candidates whose value satisfies some criterion, it is a good idea to combine the generation of the candidates with the generation of their values. That way, we can avoid recomputing values. Usually, it is clear enough how to do this directly without formally instantiating the recipe described above, but it is nice to know that a recipe does exist. The other moral is that it is useful to see whether or not a good value can be weakened to some kind of *ok* value that can be maintained for all candidates. That way, the set of candidates that have to be considered is reduced in size.

References

Knuth, D. E. (2006). *The Art of Computer Programming, Volume 4, Fascicle 4: Generating All Trees*. Reading, MA: Addison-Wesley.

7

Building a tree with minimum height

Introduction

Consider the problem of building a leaf-labelled tree of minimum height with a given list of integers as fringe. Leaf-labelled trees are defined by

data *Tree* = *Leaf Int* | *Fork Tree Tree*

and the fringe of a tree is the list of labels at the leaves in left-to-right order. There are two well-known algorithms for this problem, both of which can be implemented in linear time. One is recursive, or top-down, and works by splitting the list into two equal halves, recursively building a tree for each half, and then combining the two results with a *Fork*. The other method is iterative, or bottom-up, and works by first turning the fringe into a list of leaves and then repeatedly combining all adjacent pairs until just one tree remains. The two methods will lead to different trees, but in each case the result is a tree with minimum height.

The form of the bottom-up algorithm suggests an intriguing generalisation: given an arbitrary list of trees together with their heights, is there a linear-time algorithm to combine them into a single tree of minimum height? The restriction, of course, is that the trees should appear as subtrees of the final tree in the same order as they appear in the list. In the special case that the input is a list of leaves, the problem reduces to the one above, but there is no immediate reason why the more general problem should be solvable in linear time. Nevertheless, our aim in this pearl is to derive precisely such an algorithm.

First steps

An alternative, but equivalent, version of the problem is to ask: given a sequence $xs = [x_1, x_2, \ldots, x_n]$ of natural numbers (representing the heights of the given trees), can one find a linear-time algorithm to build a tree with fringe xs that minimises *cost*, where

41

$$cost\,(Leaf\;x) \quad = \quad x$$
$$cost\,(Fork\;u\;v) \quad = \quad 1 + (cost\;u \;\mathrm{max}\; cost\;v)$$

Thus, *cost* has the same definition as *height* except that the "height" of *Leaf x* is *x* rather than zero.

Formulated in this way, the problem is to compute

$$mincost\,Tree \quad = \quad minBy\;cost \cdot trees$$

where *trees* builds all possible trees with a given fringe and *minBy cost* selects one with minimum cost. A constructive definition of *trees* can be formulated in a number of ways, following either a top-down or bottom-up scheme. However, we are going for a third option, namely an inductive algorithm:

$$trees \qquad\qquad :: \quad [Int] \rightarrow [Tree]$$
$$trees\,[x] \qquad\; = \quad [Leaf\;x]$$
$$trees\,(x:xs) \quad = \quad concatMap\,(prefixes\;x)\,(trees\;xs)$$

The Haskell function *concatMap f* abbreviates *concat · map f*. The value *prefixes x t* is a list of all the ways *x* can be inserted as a leftmost leaf in the tree *t*:

$$prefixes \qquad\qquad\qquad :: \quad Int \rightarrow Tree \rightarrow [Tree]$$
$$prefixes\;x\;t@(Leaf\;y) \quad = \quad [Fork\,(Leaf\;x)\;t]$$
$$prefixes\;x\;t@(Fork\;u\;v) \quad = \quad [Fork\,(Leaf\;x)\;t] \;+\!\!+$$
$$\qquad\qquad\qquad\qquad\qquad\quad [Fork\;u'\;v \mid u' \leftarrow prefixes\;x\;u]$$

We could have taken *trees* [ ] = [ ], and so defined *trees* as an instance of *foldr*. But *minBy cost* is not defined on an empty set of trees and it is best to restrict the input to nonempty lists. Haskell does not provide a general fold function on nonempty lists (the function *foldr1* is not quite general enough), but if we define *foldrn* by

$$foldrn \qquad\qquad :: \quad (a \rightarrow b \rightarrow b) \rightarrow (a \rightarrow b) \rightarrow [a] \rightarrow b$$
$$foldrn\;f\;g\,[x] \qquad = \quad g\;x$$
$$foldrn\;f\;g\,(x:xs) \quad = \quad f\;x\,(foldrn\;f\;g\;xs)$$

then *trees* can be expressed as an instance of *foldrn*:

$$trees \quad = \quad foldrn\,(concatMap \cdot prefixes)\,(wrap \cdot Leaf)$$
$$wrap\;x \quad = \quad [x]$$

Wherever there are trees there are also forests, and many definitions involving the former can be phrased, often more cleanly, in terms of the latter. So it is with *trees*. A cleaner definition is obtained by first building a list of forests (where a forest is itself a list of trees) and then rolling up each forest into a tree:

$$
\begin{aligned}
\mathit{trees} \quad\quad &= \quad \mathit{map\ rollup} \cdot \mathit{forests} \\[4pt]
\mathit{forests} \quad\quad &= \quad [\mathit{Int}] \rightarrow [\mathit{Forest}] \\
\mathit{forests} \quad\quad &= \quad \mathit{foldrn}\ (\mathit{concatMap} \cdot \mathit{prefixes})\ (\mathit{wrap} \cdot \mathit{wrap} \cdot \mathit{Leaf}) \\[4pt]
\mathit{prefixes} \quad\quad &:: \quad \mathit{Int} \rightarrow \mathit{Forest} \rightarrow [\mathit{Forest}] \\
\mathit{prefixes}\ x\ \mathit{ts} \quad &= \quad [\mathit{Leaf}\ x : \mathit{rollup}\ (\mathit{take}\ k\ \mathit{ts}) : \mathit{drop}\ k\ \mathit{ts} \\
&\quad\quad\ |\ k \leftarrow [1 .. \mathit{length}\ \mathit{ts}]] \\[4pt]
\mathit{rollup} \quad\quad &:: \quad \mathit{Forest} \rightarrow \mathit{Tree} \\
\mathit{rollup} \quad\quad &= \quad \mathit{foldl1}\ \mathit{Fork}
\end{aligned}
$$

In this version of *trees* each forest represents the *left spine* of a tree; that is, the sequence of right subtrees along the path from leftmost leaf to the root. The first element in the spine is the leftmost leaf itself. Rolling up the spine gives the tree. We prefer the second definition of *prefixes* to the first because it reveals more clearly what is going on in building the final trees. We will come back to this definition of *trees* later on.

It remains to define *minBy cost* :: $[\mathit{Tree}] \rightarrow \mathit{Tree}$. The requirement is that it should return some tree with minimum cost:

$$
\mathit{minBy}\ \mathit{cost}\ \mathit{ts} \in \mathit{ts} \quad \wedge \quad (\forall t \in \mathit{ts} : \mathit{cost}\ (\mathit{minBy}\ \mathit{cost}\ \mathit{ts}) \leq \mathit{cost}\ t)
$$

The output is not determined uniquely by this specification, so *minBy cost* is a *nondeterministic* function. One can implement it by defining

$$
\begin{aligned}
\mathit{minBy}\ f \quad &= \quad \mathit{foldl1}\ (\mathit{cmp}\ f) \\
\mathit{cmp}\ f\ u\ v \quad &= \quad \textbf{if}\ f\ u \leq f\ v\ \textbf{then}\ u\ \textbf{else}\ v
\end{aligned}
$$

But this implementation selects the first tree in *ts* with minimum cost, and so depends on the order in which the trees appear in *ts*. An unbiased but deterministic implementation can be obtained by inventing a total linear ordering $\preceq$ that respects *cost*, so $u \preceq v \Rightarrow \mathit{cost}\ u \leq \mathit{cost}\ v$, and replacing *cmp f* by *cmp*, where

$$
\mathit{cmp}\ u\ v \quad = \quad \textbf{if}\ u \preceq v\ \textbf{then}\ u\ \textbf{else}\ v
$$

But this definition depends on the invention of $\preceq$ and is again too specific. So we will leave *minBy cost* as a nondeterministic function.

Fusion

Implemented directly, *minBy cost* · *trees* takes exponential time, and the obvious way to make it faster is to appeal to the fusion law of *foldrn*. In its simplest form the fusion law states

$$
h\ (\mathit{foldrn}\ f\ g\ \mathit{xs}) \quad = \quad \mathit{foldrn}\ f'\ g'\ \mathit{xs}
$$

for all finite nonempty lists xs provided $h\,(g\,x) = g'\,x$ and $h\,(f\,x\,y) = f'\,x\,(h\,y)$ for all x and y. However, asking for equality of both terms when h is a nondeterministic function is unreasonable: we need only that the right-hand term is a *refinement* of the left-hand one. Suppose we define $f\,x \rightsquigarrow g\,x$ to mean that the set of possible outputs of $f\,x$ includes the (nonempty) set of possible outputs of $g\,x$. In particular, if g is a normal deterministic function, then $f\,x \rightsquigarrow g\,x$ means that $g\,x$ is a possible output of $f\,x$. A weaker statement of fusion is that

$$h\,(foldrn\ f\ g\ xs) \quad \rightsquigarrow \quad foldrn\ f'\ g'\ xs$$

for all finite nonempty lists xs provided $h\,(g\,x) \rightsquigarrow g'\,x$ for all x, and $h\,y \rightsquigarrow y'$ implies $h\,(f\,x\,y) \rightsquigarrow f'\,x\,y'$ for all x, y and y'.

   Since $minBy\ cost \cdot wrap = id$, we obtain on appeal to fusion that

$$
\begin{aligned}
&minBy\ cost\ (foldrn\ (concatMap \cdot prefixes)\ (wrap \cdot Leaf)\ xs)\\
&\quad \rightsquigarrow \quad foldrn\ insert\ Leaf\ xs
\end{aligned}
$$

provided a function *insert* can be defined to satisfy the fusion condition

$$
\begin{aligned}
&minBy\ cost\ ts \rightsquigarrow t\\
&\quad \Rightarrow \quad minBy\ cost\ (concatMap\ (prefixes\ x)\ ts) \rightsquigarrow insert\ x\ t
\end{aligned}
\qquad (7.1)
$$

Suppose we specify *insert* by the condition

$$minBy\ cost \cdot prefixes\ x \quad \rightsquigarrow \quad insert\ x$$

In words, $insert\ x\ t$ returns some minimum cost tree in $prefixes\ x\ t$. Then we claim that (7.1) holds if the following does:

$$
\begin{aligned}
&minBy\ cost\ ts \rightsquigarrow t\\
&\quad \Rightarrow \quad minBy\ cost\ (map\ (insert\ x)\ ts) \rightsquigarrow insert\ x\ t
\end{aligned}
\qquad (7.2)
$$

For the proof we need the fact that

$$minBy\ cost \cdot concat \quad = \quad minBy\ cost \cdot map\ minBy\ cost$$

over nonempty lists of nonempty lists. In words, every possible result of the left-hand side is a possible result of the right-hand side and vice versa. Now we argue

$$
\begin{aligned}
&minBy\ cost\ (concatMap\ (prefixes\ x)\ ts)\\
&= \quad \{\text{expanding } concatMap\}\\
&\qquad minBy\ cost\ (concat\ (map\ (prefixes\ x)\ ts))
\end{aligned}
$$

$$= \quad \{\text{above fact}\}$$

$$minBy\ cost\ (map\ (minBy\ cost \cdot prefixes\ x)\ ts)$$

$$\rightsquigarrow \quad \{\text{since } f \rightsquigarrow f' \text{ implies } map\ f \rightsquigarrow map\ f' \text{ and } g \cdot f \rightsquigarrow g \cdot f'\}$$

$$minBy\ cost\ (map\ (insert\ x)\ ts)$$

The fusion condition (7.2) holds provided that

$$cost\ u \leq cost\ v \quad \Rightarrow \quad cost\ (insert\ x\ u) \leq cost\ (insert\ x\ v) \tag{7.3}$$

for all trees u and v with the same fringe. However (7.3) does not hold. Consider the trees u and v given by

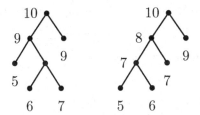

In each tree the left spines have been labelled with cost information, so the cost of both trees is 10. Inserting 8 into the left tree u gives a tree with minimum cost 11, but inserting 8 into the right tree v gives a tree with cost 10. So (7.3) fails.

But notice that the costs $[10, 8, 7, 5]$ reading downwards along the left spine of v are lexicographically less than the costs $[10, 9, 5]$ along the left spine of u. What we *can* establish is the monotonicity condition

$$cost'\ u \leq cost'\ v \quad \Rightarrow \quad cost'\ (insert\ x\ u) \leq cost'\ (insert\ x\ v) \tag{7.4}$$

where

$$cost' \quad = \quad map\ cost \cdot reverse \cdot spine$$

The function *spine* is the inverse of *rollup*, so $spine \cdot rollup = id$. Minimising $cost'$ also minimises $cost$, since $xs \leq ys \Rightarrow head\ xs \leq head\ ys$. As we will show in a moment, (7.4) implies that

$$minBy\ cost' \cdot map(insert\ x) \quad \rightsquigarrow \quad insert\ x \cdot minBy\ cost'$$

Since spines have appeared on the scene it is sensible to make use of the definition of *trees* in terms of spines and summarise the calculation so far in the following way:

$$minBy\ cost \cdot trees$$

$$\rightsquigarrow \quad \{\text{refinement}\}$$

$\quad\quad minBy\ cost' \cdot trees$

$\quad=\quad$ {definition of *trees* in terms of forests}

$\quad\quad minBy\ cost' \cdot map\ rollup\ \cdot$
$\quad\quad foldrn\ (concatMap \cdot prefixes)\ (wrap \cdot wrap \cdot Leaf)$

$\quad=\quad$ {defining *costs* = *map cost · reverse*}

$\quad\quad minBy\ (costs \cdot spine) \cdot map\ rollup\ \cdot$
$\quad\quad foldrn\ (concatMap \cdot prefixes)\ (wrap \cdot wrap \cdot Leaf)$

$\quad=\quad$ {claim: see below}

$\quad\quad rollup \cdot minBy\ costs\ \cdot$
$\quad\quad foldrn\ (concatMap \cdot prefixes)\ (wrap \cdot wrap \cdot Leaf)$

$\quad\rightsquigarrow\quad$ {fusion, with $minBy\ costs \cdot prefixes\ x \rightsquigarrow insert\ x$}

$\quad\quad rollup \cdot foldrn\ insert\ (wrap \cdot Leaf)$

The claim is that

$$minBy\ (costs \cdot spine) \cdot map\ rollup\quad =\quad rollup \cdot minBy\ costs$$

This follows from the definition of *minBy* and the fact that *spine* and *rollup* are each other's inverse.

It remains to implement *insert*, to show that (7.4) holds and to prove that it leads to a linear-time program.

Optimal insertion

Consider the two trees of Figure 7.1. The tree on the left has spine *ts*, where $ts = [t_1, t_2, \ldots, t_n]$. The one on the right has spine *Leaf x* : *rollup* (*take j ts*) : *drop j ts*. Each spine is also labelled with cost information: c_k is defined for $2 \leq k \leq n$ by

$$c_k\quad =\quad 1 + (c_{k-1}\ max\ cost\ t_k)$$

and c_1 is the value at the leaf t_1. A similar equation defines c'_k for k in the range $j+1 \leq k \leq n$. Note that $c'_j > c_j$ and $c'_k \geq c_k$ for $j+1 \leq k \leq n$. Bearing (7.4) in mind, we want to choose some j in the range $1 \leq j \leq n$ that minimises

$$[c'_n, c'_{n-1}, \ldots, c'_{j+1}, c'_j, x]$$

We claim that the minimum is obtained by choosing j to be the smallest value in the range $1 \leq j < n$, if it exists, such that

$$1 + (x\ max\ c_j) < c_{j+1} \tag{7.5}$$

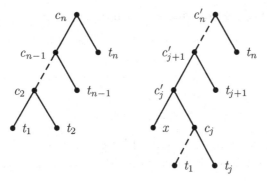

Fig. 7.1 Inserting x into a tree

Otherwise, choose $j = n$. To prove the claim, observe that if (7.5) holds, then

$$c'_j = 1 + (x \max c_j) < c_{j+1}$$

and so $c'_k = c_k$ for $j+1 \leq k \leq n$. Moreover, if (7.5) also holds for $i < j$, then

$$[c'_n, c'_{n-1}, \ldots, c'_{i+1}, c'_i, x]$$
$$= \quad \{\text{because } c'_k = c_k \text{ for } i+1 \leq k \leq n \text{ and } i < j\}$$
$$[c_n, c_{n-1}, \ldots, c_{j+1}, c_j, \ldots c_{i+1}, c'_i, x]$$
$$< \quad \{\text{because } c_j < c'_j\}$$
$$[c_n, c_{n-1}, \ldots, c_{j+1}, c'_j, x]$$
$$= \quad \{\text{because } c'_k = c_k \text{ for } j+1 \leq k \leq n\}$$
$$[c'_n, c'_{n-1}, \ldots, c'_{j+1}, c'_j, x]$$

So, the smaller the j to satisfy (7.5) the better. If (7.5) does not hold for j, then $c'_{j+1} > c_{j+1}$ and $c'_k \geq c_k$ for $j+2 \leq k \leq n$, so the cost is worse.

Next we prove the monotonicity condition (7.4). Let u and v be two trees with costs $cost'\, u$ and $cost'\, v$. Clearly, if these costs are equal, then so are the costs of inserting an arbitrary x in either of them. Otherwise, suppose

$$cost'\, u = [c_n, c_{n-1}, \ldots] < [d_m, d_{m-1}, \ldots, d_1] = cost'\, v$$

Removing the common prefix of these costs, say one of length k, we are left with $[c_{n-k}, \ldots, c_1]$ and $[d_{m-k}, \ldots, d_1]$, where $c_{n-k} < d_{m-k}$. But inserting x into the corresponding subtree of u gives a tree with no larger costs than inserting x into the corresponding subtree of v.

Finally, since (7.5) is equivalent to $x \max c_j < cost\, t_{j+1}$, we can implement *insert* by

$$
\begin{array}{lcl}
insert\ x\ ts & = & Leaf\ x : split\ x\ ts \\
split\ x\ [u] & = & [u] \\
split\ x\ (u : v : ts) & = & \textbf{if}\ \ x \max cost\ u < cost\ v\ \textbf{then}\ \ u : v : ts \\
& & \textbf{else}\ \ split\ x\ (Fork\ u\ v : ts)
\end{array}
$$

Cost computations can be eliminated by a simple data refinement in which each tree t is represented by a pair $(cost\ t, t)$, leading to the final algorithm

$$
\begin{array}{lcl}
mincostTree & = & foldl1\ Fork \cdot map\ snd \cdot foldrn\ insert\ (wrap \cdot leaf) \\
insert\ x\ ts & = & leaf\ x : split\ x\ ts \\
split\ x\ [u] & = & [u] \\
split\ x\ (u : v : ts) & = & \textbf{if}\ \ x \max fst\ u < fst\ v\ \textbf{then}\ \ u : v : ts \\
& & \textbf{else}\ \ split\ x\ (fork\ u\ v : ts) \\
leaf\ x & = & (x, Leaf\ x) \\
fork\ (a, u)\ (b, v) & = & (1 + a \max b, Fork\ u\ v)
\end{array}
$$

The smart constructors *leaf* and *fork* each construct a pair consisting of a cost and a tree.

It remains to time the program, which we can do by counting the calls to *split*. By induction we prove that *foldrn insert* $(wrap \cdot leaf)$ applied to a list of length n and returning a forest of length m involves at most $2n - m$ calls to *split*. The base case, $n = 1$ and $m = 1$, is obvious. For the induction step, note that *split* applied to a list of length m' and returning a list of length m is called $m' - m$ times. And since $2(n - 1) - m' + m' - m + 1 \le 2n - m$, the induction is established. Hence the algorithm takes linear time.

Final remarks

The minimum-cost tree problem and its derivation is an exercise in constructing a *greedy* algorithm. Greedy algorithms are tricky, not so much because the final algorithm is opaque, but because of the delicate reasoning required to prove that they work. First, one usually has to invent a strengthening of the cost function and to minimise that at each step. Here, the monotonicity condition (7.4) is crucial to the success of the enterprise. Second, in dealing with most optimisation problems there is a need to bring relations, or nondeterministic functions, into the derivation. The outcome of the derivation is not equivalent to the initial specification, but a refinement of it. Our treatment of relations has been "light touch", and relied on Haskell-like notation for carrying the derivation forward. In Bird and de Moor (1997), the treatment of relations and their use in program derivation is made much more systematic.

Finally, it is worth mentioning that another way to solve the minimum-cost tree problem is by using, the Hu–Tucker (or the more modern version, the Garsia–Wachs) algorithm; see Hu (1982) or Knuth (1998). The Hu–Tucker algorithm applies because *cost* is a *regular* cost function in the sense of Hu (1982). But the best implementation of that algorithm has a running time of $\Theta(n \log n)$.

References

Bird, R. S. and de Moor, O. (1997). *Algebra of Programming.* Hemel Hempstead: Prentice Hall.

Hu, T. C. (1982). *Combinatorial Algorithms.* Reading, MA: Addison-Wesley.

Knuth, D. E. (1998). *The Art of Computer Programming, Volume 3: Searching and Sorting*, second edition. Reading, MA: Addison-Wesley.

8

Unravelling greedy algorithms

Make you to ravel all this matter out.

Hamlet, Act 3, Scene 4

Introduction

As we said in the previous pearl, greedy algorithms are tricky things. So the subject deserves a second example. Here is another problem that can be solved by a greedy algorithm, and the path to the solution has much in common with the previous one.

An *unravel*[1] of a sequence xs is a bag of nonempty subsequences of xs that when shuffled together can give back xs. For example, the letters of "accompany" can be unravelled into three lists: "acm", "an" and "copy". The order of these lists is not important, but duplications do matter; for example, "peptet" can be unravelled into two copies of "pet". Thus, an unravel is essentially a bag of sequences, not a set or a list.

An unravel is called an *upravel* if all its component sequences are weakly increasing. Since each of "acm", "an" and "copy" is increasing, they give an upravel of "accompany", and so do "aany", "ccmp" and "o". Each nonempty sequence has at least one upravel, namely the upravel consisting of just singleton sequences. However, of all possible upravels, we want to determine one with shortest size.

Specification

Here is the specification of the function *supravel* (short for shortest upravel):

$$supravel \quad :: \quad Ord\ a \Rightarrow [a] \rightarrow [[a]]$$
$$supravel \quad = \quad minBy\ length \cdot filter\ (all\ up) \cdot unravels$$

---

[1] By the way, "to unravel" and "to ravel" mean the same thing, just as "to unloose" and "to loose". The prefix "un-" serves both to negate an action and to emphasize it.

We represent the bag of sequences in a shortest upravel by a list. The function $minBy\ f$ is the non-deterministic function introduced in the previous pearl and specified by

$$minBy\ f\ xs \in xs \quad \wedge \quad (\forall x \in xs : f\ (minBy\ f\ xs) \leq f\ x)$$

The predicate up, whose definition is omitted, determines whether its argument is in ascending order. The function $unravels$ returns all unravels of a sequence and can be defined inductively by

$$
\begin{array}{lcl}
unravels & :: & [a] \rightarrow [[[a]]] \\
unravels & = & foldr\ (concatMap \cdot prefixes)\ [[\,]] \\
prefixes\ x\ [\,] & = & [[[x]]] \\
prefixes\ x\ (xs : xss) & = & [(x : xs) : xss] \mathbin{+\!\!+} map\ (xs\ :)\ (prefixes\ x\ xss)
\end{array}
$$

The function $prefixes\ x$ adds x as a new first element to an unravel by prefixing it in all possible ways to each sequence in the unravel.

Derivation

The first step is to employ the fusion law of $foldr$ to fuse $filter\ (all\ up)$ and $unravels$. Define $upravels$ by

$$upravels \;=\; filter\ (all\ up) \cdot unravels$$

An easy application of the fusion law of $foldr$ gives the following definition of $upravels$:

$$
\begin{array}{lcl}
upravels & :: & Ord\ a \Rightarrow [a] \rightarrow [[[a]]] \\
upravels & = & foldr\ (concatMap \cdot uprefixes)\ [[\,]] \\
uprefixes\ x\ [\,] & = & [[[x]]] \\
uprefixes\ x\ (xs : xss) & = & \textbf{if}\ x \leq head\ xs\ \textbf{then} \\
 & & \quad [(x : xs) : xss] \mathbin{+\!\!+} map\ (xs\ :)\ (uprefixes\ x\ xss) \\
 & & \textbf{else}\ map\ (xs\ :)\ (uprefixes\ x\ xss)
\end{array}
$$

Here, $uprefixes\ x$ adds x as a new first element to an unravel by prefixing it in all possible ways to each sequence in the unravel whose first element is at least x.

Now we have arrived at the nub of the problem, which is how to fuse $minBy\ length$ with $upravels$. Recall from the previous pearl the meaning of the refinement relation $\leadsto$: for non-deterministic function f and normal deterministic function g we have that $f \leadsto g$ if for all x the result of $g\ x$ is a possible result of $f\ x$. Suppose the function $insert$ is specified by

$$minBy\ length \cdot uprefixes\ x \quad \leadsto \quad insert\ x$$

Thus, *insert x ur* returns some shortest possible way of inserting *x* into the upravel *ur*. By appealing to the weaker fusion law of *foldr* in terms of refinement rather than equality, we then obtain

$$minBy\ length\ (upravels\ xs)\ \ \rightsquigarrow\ \ foldr\ insert\ [\ ]\ xs$$

for all finite lists *xs*, provided the fusion condition

$$minBy\ length\ urs \rightsquigarrow ur$$
$$\Rightarrow\ minBy\ length\ (map\ (insert\ x)\ urs) \rightsquigarrow insert\ x\ ur$$

holds for all upravels *urs* of a list. And, in turn, the fusion condition holds if

$$length\ ur \le length\ vr$$
$$\Rightarrow\ length\ (insert\ x\ ur) \le length\ (insert\ x\ vr) \tag{8.1}$$

for any two upravels *ur* and *vr* of the same list.

Unfortunately, (8.1) does not hold. Take the two equal-length upravels ["ad", "a"] and ["aa", "d"] of "ada". Inserting "c" in the first upravel gives the best possible upravel ["ad", "a", "c"], but ["aa", "cd"] is a better upravel of the second.

The conclusion is that, just as in the problem of finding a minimum cost tree, we have to strengthen the cost function being minimised. It is fairly clear that the length of *insert x ur* depends only on *x* and the first element of each sequence in *ur*. Suppose we define *heads* by

$$heads\ \ ::\ \ Ord\ a \Rightarrow [[a]] \to [a]$$
$$heads\ \ =\ \ sort \cdot map\ head$$

Informally, the larger (lexicographically speaking) that *heads ur* is, the more likely it is that *x* can be prefixed to some sequence in *ur*, thereby ensuring *insert x ur* is no longer than *ur*. The problem with replacing *minBy length* by *maxBy heads* is that

$$heads\ ur \ge heads\ vr\ \ \not\Rightarrow\ \ length\ ur \le length\ vr$$

even for upravels *ur* and *vr* of the same sequence. So, we need something else.

One way out is to abandon the lexicographic ordering and consider instead the *partial preorder* $\preceq$, defined by

$$ur \preceq vr\ \ =\ \ heads\ ur \unlhd heads\ yr$$

where $[x_1, x_2, \ldots, x_m] \unlhd [y_1, y_2, \ldots, y_n]$ if $m \le n$ and $x_j \ge y_j$ for all *j* in the range $1 \le j \le n$. Thus, $ur \preceq vr$ if *length ur* $\le$ *length vr* and the elements of *heads ur* are pointwise no smaller than those of *heads vr*. Since $\preceq$ clearly respects *length*, we can replace *minBy length* by *minWith* ($\preceq$), where

$$minWith\ (\preceq)\ urs \in urs \quad \text{and} \quad (\forall ur \in urs : minWith\ (\preceq)\ urs \preceq ur)$$

and establish the monotonicity condition

$$ur \preceq vr \quad \Rightarrow \quad insert\ x\ ur \preceq insert\ x\ vr \tag{8.2}$$

where *insert x* is some refinement of *minWith* ($\preceq$) $\cdot$ *uprefixes x*. Condition (8.2) then gives

$$minWith\ (\preceq) \cdot upravels \quad \leadsto \quad foldr\ insert\ [\,]$$

However, there is a slight technical difficulty with partial orderings: in general there is no guarantee that minimum, as distinct from *minimal*, elements exist. An element is minimum if it is smaller than all other candidates, but minimal only if there is no candidate smaller than it. For example, the set $\{\{a, b\}, \{a, c\}, \{a, b, c\}\}$ has no minimum elements under $\subseteq$, but two minimal elements, namely $\{a, b\}$ and $\{a, c\}$. So we have to check that $minWith\,(\preceq)\,(upravels\,xs)$ is inhabited. But this is easily proved by induction on *xs*, given that $minWith\,(\preceq) \cdot uprefixes\ x \leadsto insert\ x$ and (8.2).

Let us next show how to construct *insert x*. Suppose

$$heads\ ur \quad = \quad [x_1, x_2, \ldots, x_m]$$

so $x_i \leq x_j$ for $1 \leq i \leq j \leq m$. Define k by the condition $x_k < x \leq x_{k+1}$, where we can set $x_{m+1} = \infty$. Then

$$heads\ (uprefixes\ x\ ur) \quad = \quad map\ ([x_1, x_2, \ldots, x_k, x]\!+\!\!+)\ xss$$

where *xss* are the lists

$$[x_{k+2}, x_{k+3}, \ldots, x_m]$$
$$[x_{k+1}, x_{k+3}, \ldots, x_m]$$
$$\cdots$$
$$[x_{k+1}, x_{k+2}, \ldots, x_{m-1}]$$
$$[x_{k+1}, x_{k+2}, \ldots, x_{m-1}, x_m]$$

Of these, the first list is pointwise largest (though not necessarily the only one that is) and hence a minimum under $\unlhd$. In words, we can minimise $\preceq$ by prefixing x to a sequence whose first element is the shortest one greater than or equal to x. In fact we can define *insert* by

$$\begin{aligned}
insert\ x\ [\,] \quad &= \quad [[x]] \\
insert\ x\ (xs : xss) \quad &= \quad \textbf{if}\ x \leq head\ xs\ \textbf{then}\ (x : xs) : xss \\
&\qquad \textbf{else}\ xs : insert\ x\ xss
\end{aligned}$$

It is an invariant on *insert x ur* that *map head ur* is in strictly increasing order. Hence the best way to insert x is by prefixing x to the first sequence in ur whose head is at least x. The definition of *insert x ur* takes linear time in the length of ur, but the complexity can be reduced to logarithmic time either by representing upravels as arrays of lists and employing binary search, or by making use of balanced trees. We omit further details and just claim that *foldr insert* [ ] can be implemented to run in $O(n \log n)$ steps.

Let us now turn to the proof of (8.2). Let *heads ur* $= [x_1, x_2, \ldots, x_m]$ and *heads vr* $= [y_1, y_2, \ldots, y_n]$, so $m \leq n$ and $y_i \leq x_i$ for $1 \leq i \leq m$. As we saw above:

$$
\begin{aligned}
heads\,(insert\ x\ ur) &= [x_1, x_2, \ldots, x_k, x, x_{k+2}, x_{k+3}, \ldots, x_m] \\
heads\,(insert\ x\ vr) &= [y_1, y_2, \ldots, y_\ell, x, x_{\ell+2}, x_{\ell+3}, \ldots, y_n]
\end{aligned}
$$

where $x_k < x \leq x_{k+1}$ and $y_\ell < x \leq y_{\ell+1}$. But $y_k \leq x_k$, so $k \leq \ell$. Lining up the two lists, as in

$$
\begin{aligned}
&[x_1, x_2, \ldots, x_k, x, \quad x_{k+2}, \ldots, x_\ell, x_{\ell+1}, x_{\ell+2}, \ldots, x_m] \\
&[y_1, y_2, \ldots, y_k, y_{k+1}, y_{k+2}, \ldots, y_\ell, x, \quad y_{\ell+2}, \ldots, y_m]
\end{aligned}
$$

we see that the first is pointwise larger than the second because $y_{k+1} \leq x$ and $x \leq x_{l+1}$.

In summary, the problem of computing the shortest upravel of a given list can be solved by a greedy algorithm that takes $O(n \log n)$ steps in the length of the list.

Final remarks

The problem of the shortest upravel was first posed and solved by Lambert Meertens in September 1984, at a meeting of IFIP Working Group 2.1 in Pont-à-Mousson, France (Meertens, 1984). Subsequently, Kaldewaij (1985) published a quite different solution. Kaldewaij's (one-page!) solution was based on a constructive proof of a specialisation of Dilworth's theorem: the size of a shortest upravel of xs is equal to the length of the longest decreasing subsequence of xs. This fact can be combined with a well-known algorithm for finding the length of a longest decreasing subsequence in $O(n \log n)$ steps to produce an algorithm for the shortest upravel with the same time complexity. The present pearl is based on Bird (1992), which also considers another greedy algorithm that starts off with the following definition of *unravels*:

$$
\begin{aligned}
unravels\ [\,] &= [[\,]] \\
unravels\ xs &= [ys : yss \mid ys \leftarrow subseqs\ xs,\ not\ (null\ ys), \\
&\qquad\qquad yss \leftarrow unravels\ (xs \setminus\!\setminus ys)]
\end{aligned}
$$

A shortest upravel can then obtained by extracting the *rightmost maximal upsequence* at each stage, computed by $rmu = foldr\ op\ [\ ]$, where

$$
\begin{aligned}
op\ x\ [\ ] \quad &= \quad [x] \\
op\ x\ (y : ys) \quad &= \quad \textbf{if}\ x \le y\ \textbf{then}\ x : y : ys\ \textbf{else}\ y : ys
\end{aligned}
$$

The derivation of the alternative algorithm is left as an exercise.

References

Bird, R. S. (1992). The smallest upravel. *Science of Computer Programming* **18**, 281–92.

Kaldewaij, A. (1985). On the decomposition of sequences into ascending subsequences. *Information Processing Letters* **21**, 69.

Meertens, L. G. L. T. (1984). Some more examples of algorithmic developments. *IFIP WG2.1 Working Paper*, Pont-à-Mousson, France. See also *An Abstracto Reader prepared for IFIP WG 2.1*. Technical Report CWI Note CS-N8702, Centrum voor Wiskunde en Informatica, April 1987.

9

Finding celebrities

The setting is a tutorial on functional algorithm design. There are four students: Anne, Jack, Mary and Theo.

Teacher: Good morning class. Today I would like you to solve the following problem. Imagine a set P of people at a party. Say a subset C of P forms a *celebrity clique* if C is nonempty, everybody at the party knows every member of C, but members of C know only each other. Assuming there is such a clique at the party, your problem is to write a functional program for finding it. As data for the problem you are given a binary predicate *knows* and the set P as a list *ps* not containing duplicates.

Jack: Just to be clear, does every member of a celebrity clique actually know everyone else in the clique? And does everyone know themselves?

Teacher: As to the first question, yes, it follows from the definition: everyone in the clique is known by everyone at the party. As to the second question, the answer is not really relevant to the problem, so ask a philosopher. If it simplifies things to assume that x knows x for all x, then go ahead and do so.

Theo: This is going to be a hard problem, isn't it? I mean, the problem of determining whether there is a clique of size k in a party of n people will take $\Omega(n^k)$ steps, so we are looking at an exponential time algorithm.

Anne: That doesn't follow, since being a celebrity clique is a much stronger property than being a clique. In a directed graph, a clique is a set of nodes in which each pair of nodes has an arc in both directions between them, but a celebrity clique also requires an arc from every node in the graph to every node in the clique, and no arcs from the clique to nodes outside the clique.

Mary: Yes, while there can be many cliques in a graph, there is at most one celebrity clique. Suppose that C_1 and C_2 are two celebrity cliques. Pick any c_1 in C_1 and c_2 in C_2. We have that c_1 knows c_2 from the fact that everybody in the clique C_2 is known by everybody at the party. But since clique members know only other members of the clique, it follows that $c_2 \in C_1$. Since c_2 was arbitrary, we have $C_2 \subseteq C_1$ and, by symmetry, $C_1 \subseteq C_2$.

Theo: Agreed, they are different problems. Let me formalise the problem. To simplify matters I am going to suppose that x knows x is true for all x. By definition C is a celebrity clique of P if $\emptyset \subset C \subseteq P$ and

$$(\forall x \in P, \ y \in C :: x \text{ knows } y \wedge (y \text{ knows } x \Rightarrow x \in C))$$

Let me abbreviate this last condition to $C \vartriangleleft P$. Given lists ps and cs representing P and C respectively, we can translate the condition into a list comprehension:

$$cs \vartriangleleft ps \ = \ and \ [x \text{ knows } y \wedge (y \text{ knows } x \Rightarrow x \in cs) \mid x \leftarrow ps, y \leftarrow cs]$$

Now define $cclique\ ps = head\ (filter\ (\vartriangleleft ps)\ (subseqs\ ps))$, where $subseqs\ ps$ is a list of all subsequences of ps:

$$\begin{aligned} subseqs\ [\,] \quad &= \quad [[\,]] \\ subseqs\ (x:xs) \quad &= \quad map\ (x:)\ (subseqs\ xs) \mathbin{+\!\!+} subseqs\ xs \end{aligned}$$

Since $subseqs\ ps$ generates subsequences in descending order of length, the value of $cclique\ ps$ is either the empty list if there is no celebrity clique, or the unique celebrity clique.

Jack: Theo's exhaustive search program seems a reasonable place to start I would say. Clearly, the way to achieve greater efficiency is to fuse the filtering with the generation of subsequences. For the base case when there are no people at the party we have $filter\ (\vartriangleleft [\,])\ (subseqs\ [\,]) = [[\,]]$ since $cs \vartriangleleft [\,] = True$. For the inductive case we can reason

$$\begin{aligned} &\quad filter\ (\vartriangleleft(p:ps))\ (subseqs\ (p:ps)) \\ =& \quad \{\text{definition of } subseqs\} \\ &\quad filter\ (\vartriangleleft (p:ps))\ (map\ (p:)\ (subseqs\ ps) \mathbin{+\!\!+} subseqs\ ps) \\ =& \quad \{\text{since } filter \text{ distributes over } +\!\!+\} \\ &\quad filter\ (\vartriangleleft (p:ps))\ (map\ (p:)\ (subseqs\ ps)) \mathbin{+\!\!+} \\ &\quad filter\ (\vartriangleleft (p:ps))\ (subseqs\ ps) \end{aligned}$$

What next?

Anne: We have to simplify $(p : cs) \lhd (p : ps)$ and $cs \lhd (p : ps)$ when cs is a subsequence of ps and p is not in cs. Let us deal with the second case first. The definition of $\lhd$ gives that $cs \lhd (p{:}ps)$ just in the case that $cs \lhd ps$, that no celebrity in cs knows p and that p knows every celebrity in cs. In symbols:

$$cs \lhd (p : ps) \quad = \quad cs \lhd ps \wedge nonmember\ p\ cs$$

where

$$nonmember\ p\ cs \quad = \quad and\ [p \text{ knows } c \wedge not\ (c \text{ knows } p) \mid c \leftarrow cs]\ .$$

Now we can reason

$$\begin{aligned}
&filter\ (\lhd (p : ps))\ (subseqs\ ps) \\
=\quad &\{\text{above simplification of } cs \lhd (p : ps)\} \\
&filter\ (\lambda cs \to cs \lhd ps \wedge nonmember\ p\ cs)\ (subseqs\ ps) \\
=\quad &\{\text{since } filter\ (\lambda x \to p\ x \wedge q\ x) = filter\ q \cdot filter\ p\} \\
&filter\ (nonmember\ p)\ (filter\ (\lhd ps)\ (subseqs\ ps))
\end{aligned}$$

Now for the other case. We have that $(p : cs) \lhd (p : ps)$ holds just in the case that $cs \lhd ps$, and p is a new celebrity, meaning that everyone knows p and p knows all and only members of cs. In symbols:

$$(p : cs) \lhd (p : ps) \quad = \quad cs \lhd ps \wedge member\ p\ ps\ cs$$

where

$$member\ p\ ps\ cs \quad = \quad and\ [x \text{ knows } p \wedge (p \text{ knows } x \Leftrightarrow x \in cs) \mid x \leftarrow ps]$$

A similar calculation to the one above now gives

$$\begin{aligned}
&filter\ (\lhd (p : ps))\ (map\ (p{:})\ (subseqs\ ps)) \\
=\quad &map\ (p{:})\ (filter\ (member\ p\ ps)\ (filter\ (\lhd ps)\ (subseqs\ ps)))
\end{aligned}$$

Putting the two pieces together, we have $cclique = head \cdot ccliques$, where

$$\begin{aligned}
ccliques\ [\,]\quad &=\quad [[\,]] \\
ccliques\ (p : ps)\quad &=\quad map\ (p{:})\ (filter\ (member\ p\ ps)\ css) \mathbin{+\!\!+} \\
&\qquad filter\ (nonmember\ p)\ css \\
&\quad \textbf{where } css = ccliques\ ps
\end{aligned}$$

The predicates *member* and *nonmember* can be evaluated in linear time and, as *ccliques* returns at most two lists, a proper celebrity clique and an empty list, we have reduced an exponential algorithm to a quadratic one.

Theo: Well, you can't do better than a quadratic algorithm, at least in the worst case. Suppose there was a sub-quadratic one, so at least one entry in the *knows* matrix is not inspected. Suppose, furthermore, that all entries are true, so everyone knows everyone else and the celebrity clique is the whole party. Now change the non-inspected entry, *knows x y* say, to false. Then *y* is no longer a celebrity. But everyone apart from *x* still knows *y*, so they cannot be celebrities. That leaves *x* as the only possible celebrity; but unless *x* and *y* are the only people at the party, there is some non-celebrity that *x* knows, so *x* is not a celebrity either. That means there is no celebrity clique at the modified party, and the sub-quadratic algorithm returns the wrong answer. So, in the worst case, every element of the *knows* matrix has to be inspected to arrive at the correct answer.

Teacher: Very good, Theo, and quite correct, but the problem was not to determine whether or not there was a celebrity clique. All I asked for was to identify a celebrity clique assuming one exists. In your scenario the answer *ps* will suffice for both cases: in the first case it is the correct answer and in the second case there is no celebrity clique, so any answer will do.

There is a pause while the class digests this information.

Mary: I have an idea. Anne's reasoning shows that for all *xs*

$$xs \lhd (p : ps) \quad \Rightarrow \quad (xs \setminus\setminus [p]) \lhd ps$$

where $\setminus\setminus$ denotes list difference. In other words, if $cs \lhd ps$ and p is someone new who joins the party *ps*, then the only possible values of *xs* satisfying $xs \lhd (p : ps)$ are $[\,]$, $[p]$, cs, or $p : cs$. I think this gives us another way of solving the problem. Suppose first that *cs* is empty, so the only possible celebrity clique of $p : ps$ is $[p]$. In symbols:

$$null\ (cclique\ ps) \quad \Rightarrow \quad cclique\ (p : ps) \in \{[\,], [p]\}$$

On the other hand, suppose *cs* is not empty and contains some celebrity *c*. What are the possible outcomes when a new person *p* joins the party? Well, assume first that *p* does not know *c*. Then *c* is no longer a celebrity in the extended party, and neither is any other member of *cs* because they all know *c*. Hence

$$c \in cclique\ ps \wedge not\ (p\ knows\ c) \quad \Rightarrow \quad cclique\ (p : ps)) \in \{[\,], [p]\}$$

Assume next that p does know c but c does not know p. In this case cs is also the celebrity clique of the extended party:

$$c \in cclique\ ps \wedge p \text{ knows } c \wedge not\ (c \text{ knows } p)$$
$$\Rightarrow\quad cclique\ (p : ps) = cclique\ ps$$

Finally, if p and c know each other, then the only celebrity clique of $p : ps$ is $p : cs$; in symbols:

$$c \in cclique\ ps \wedge p \text{ knows } c \wedge c \text{ knows } p$$
$$\Rightarrow\quad cclique\ (p : ps) \in \{[\,], p : cs\}$$

Theo: While I agree that your reasoning is correct, Mary, I do not see how it leads to a solution. All you have shown is that if we know the value of *cclique ps* and if the party $p : ps$ contains a celebrity clique, then we can quickly determine it. But how do we know the value of *cclique ps* in the first place? You seem to be suggesting that if we define *cclique′* by

$$
\begin{array}{lll}
cclique' & = & foldr\ op\ [\,] \\
op\ p\ cs & |\quad null\ cs & =\quad [p] \\
& |\quad not\ (p \text{ knows } c) & =\quad [p] \\
& |\quad not\ (c \text{ knows } p) & =\quad cs \\
& |\quad \textbf{otherwise} & =\quad p : cs \\
& \textbf{where } c = head\ cs
\end{array}
$$

then

$$not\ (null\ (cclique\ ps)) \quad \Rightarrow \quad cclique\ ps = cclique'\ ps \qquad (9.1)$$

But I don't see how your reasoning proves (9.1).

Mary: Let me try again then. I will prove (9.1) by induction on ps. There are two cases:

Case $[\,]$. We have $cclique\ [\,] = [\,]$, so (9.1) is true by default.

Case $p : ps$. Assume $cclique\ (p : ps)$ is not empty. There are two subcases, depending on whether $cclique\ ps$ is empty or not. If not, then $cclique\ ps = cclique'\ ps$ by induction. We then have

$$
\begin{array}{ll}
& cclique\ (p : ps) \\
= & \{\text{my previous reasoning and definition of } op\} \\
& op\ p\ (cclique\ ps) \\
= & \{\text{since } cclique\ ps = cclique'\ ps\} \\
& op\ p\ (cclique'\ ps) \\
= & \{\text{definition of } cclique'\} \\
& cclique'\ (p : ps)
\end{array}
$$

If, on the other hand, *cclique ps* is empty, then

$\quad$ *cclique* $(p : ps)$

$=\quad$ {assumption that *cclique* $(p : ps)$ is not empty,
$\qquad$ and first case of my previous reasoning}

$\quad [p]$

$=\quad$ {p is the unique celebrity,
$\qquad$ so *not* $(p$ knows $c)$ for any $c \in cclique'\ ps$}

$\quad$ *op p* $(cclique'\ ps)$

$=\quad$ {as before}

$\quad$ *cclique'* $(p : ps)$

This establishes the case and the induction.

Anne: That's amazing, a simple linear-time algorithm! But we have only arrived at the solution because of Mary's cleverness. I still want a formal derivation of *cclique'* from some suitable fusion law.

Teacher: Thank you, Anne, it's good to have you in the class.

Anne: We can write *subseqs* using *foldr*:

$$subseqs \quad = \quad foldr\ add\ [[\,]]$$
$$add\ x\ xss \quad = \quad map\ (x:)\ xss \mathbin{+\!\!+} xss$$

So it appears that we are appealing to some fusion law of *foldr*. The textbook statement of the fusion law for *foldr* states that $f \cdot foldr\ g\ a = foldr\ h\ b$ provided f is strict, $f\ a = b$, and $f\ (g\ x\ y) = h\ x\ (f\ y)$ for all x and y. The strictness condition is not needed if we want only to assert that $f\ (foldr\ g\ a\ xs) = foldr\ h\ b\ xs$ for all finite lists xs. This fusion rule does not apply directly to the celebrity clique problem, namely *filter* $(\lhd ps)$ $(subseqs\ ps)$, first because *filter* $(\lhd ps)$ has ps as a parameter and second because we want something more general than the equality of both sides.

Theo: The first restriction is not really a problem. We can always define a version of *subseqs* that returns both the subsequences of a list and the list itself. Suppose we define

$$subseqs' \quad = \quad foldr\ step\ ([\,], [[\,]])$$
$$step\ x\ (xs, xss) \quad = \quad (x : xs, map\ (x:)\ xss \mathbin{+\!\!+} xss)$$

Then *cclique* $= f \cdot subseqs'$, where $f\ (ps, css) = head\ (filter\ (\lhd ps)\ css)$. In this way the additional parameter is eliminated.

Mary: The textbook statement of the fusion rule is not general enough for the problem. Let $\leadsto$ be some relation on values; I don't care what. Then it is easy to show by induction that

$$f\ (foldr\ g\ a\ xs)\quad \leadsto\quad foldr\ h\ b\ xs$$

for all finite lists xs provided $f\ a \leadsto b$ and $f\ y \leadsto z \Rightarrow f\ (g\ x\ y) \leadsto h\ x\ z$ for all x, y and z.

Jack: Yes, that's it. We want to define $xs \leadsto ys$ by

$$xs \leadsto ys\quad =\quad not\ (null\ xs) \Rightarrow xs = ys$$

Then the conditions we have to establish are first that

$$head\ (filter\ (\triangleleft\ [\,])\ [[\,]]) \leadsto [\,]$$

and second that

$$head\ (filter\ (\triangleleft\ ps)\ css) \leadsto cs$$
$$\Rightarrow\quad head\ (filter\ (\triangleleft(p:ps))(map\ (p:)\ css + css)) \leadsto op\ p\ cs$$

Mary's reasoning establishes exactly these conditions.

Teacher: Yes. The more general statement of fusion is the one provided by parametricity in Wadler's (1989) "Theorems for free!" paper. It is nice to see an example where the more general statement is needed. What is interesting about the problem is that it is the first example I have seen in which it is asymptotically more efficient to find a solution assuming one exists than to check that it actually is a solution. A similar problem is the *majority voting* problem – see, for example, Morgan (1994), Chapter 18 – in which one is given a list xs and it is required to determine whether there is a value in xs that occurs strictly greater than $\lfloor length\ xs/2 \rfloor$ times. It is easier to first compute a putative majority and then check whether it is actually a majority afterwards. But checking for a majority takes linear time rather than quadratic time, so there is no asymptotic gap.

Afterword

The true story of the celebrity clique problem was as follows. I was giving a course of lectures on Formal Program Design, in an imperative rather than functional framework, and thought of the problem as a generalisation of the one in Kaldewaij's (1990) book. But despite a day of struggling with loop invariants, I could not produce a sufficiently simple solution to present to the class, so I set it as a challenge. I also talked about it at a research meeting the following Friday. Over the weekend, Sharon Curtis produced a simple linear-time algorithm and Julian Tibble, a second-year undergraduate, provided a good way to reason about the problem.

In the belief that whatever can be done with loops and invariants can also be done at least as easily using the laws of functional program derivation, the problem was translated into a functional setting and the dialogue above was composed. Afterwards, the problem was tried out at a WG2.1 meeting in Nottingham in September, 2004. Gratifyingly, the actual discussion followed the early part of the dialogue quite closely. On repeatedly being urged to try harder, Andres Löh and Johan Jeuring came up a day later with the linear-time solution.

References

Kaldewaij, A. (1990). *Programming the Derivation of Algorithms*. Hemel Hempstead: Prentice Hall.

Morgan, C. (1994). *Programming from Specifications*, 2nd edition. Hemel Hempstead: Prentice Hall.

Wadler, P. (1989). Theorems for free! *Fourth International Symposium on Functional Programming Languages and Computer Architecture*. ACM Press, pp. 347–59.

10

Removing duplicates

Introduction

The Haskell library function *nub* removes duplicates from a list:

$$nub \qquad :: \quad Eq\ a \Rightarrow [a] \rightarrow [a]$$
$$nub\ [\,] \qquad = \quad [\,]$$
$$nub\ (x : xs) \quad = \quad x : nub\ (xs \setminus\!\setminus [x])$$

The value $xs \setminus\!\setminus ys$ is what remains of xs after all the elements in ys have been deleted. For example, *nub* "calculus" = "calus". Evaluation of *nub* on a list of length n takes $\Theta(n^2)$ steps. This is the best one can hope for, since any algorithm for the problem requires $\Omega(n^2)$ equality tests in the worst case. With the definition above, *nub xs* returns a list of the distinct elements in xs in the order in which they first appear in xs. In other words, the position of *nub xs* as a subsequence of xs is lexicographically the least among the positions of all possible solutions.

Let us now change the problem and ask that $nub :: Ord\ a \Rightarrow [a] \rightarrow [a]$ simply returns the lexicographically least solution. Note the subtle difference: before it was the position of the subsequence that was lexicographically the least; now it is the subsequence itself. For example, *nub* "calculus" = "aclus" under the second definition. The change of type of *nub* is necessary to make the new problem meaningful. Changing the type of *nub* changes the lower bound complexity: only $\Omega(n \log n)$ comparison tests are needed in the worst case. A pretty proof of this claim is given by Bloom and Wright (2003). Can we find an $\Theta(n \log n)$ program for the new version of *nub*? The answer turns out to be yes, but the algorithm is not obvious and calculating it requires some work. So, be prepared.

A first version

We begin with the specification

$$nub \quad = \quad minimum \cdot longest \cdot filter\ nodups \cdot subseqs$$

In words, compute all possible subsequences of the given list (*subseqs*), filter this list of subsequences for just those that do not contain duplicates (*filter nodups*), compute all the longest ones (*longest*) and finally select the smallest one (*minimum*).

It is not too difficult to calculate the following recursive definition of *nub* from the specification:

$$
\begin{aligned}
nub\,[\,] \quad &= \quad [\,] \\
nub\,(x:xs) \quad &= \quad \textbf{if } x \notin xs \textbf{ then } x:nub\,xs \textbf{ else} \\
&\qquad (x:nub\,(xs \setminus\!\setminus [x]))\ \min\ (nub\,xs)
\end{aligned}
$$

We omit the details, leaving them as an exercise for the interested reader. Anyway, the recursive version is reasonably intuitive: in the case $x:xs$, either x does not appear in xs, so there is no choice, or it does, in which case the result is the smaller of two alternatives, choosing x now or later on.

The problem with the recursive definition of *nub* is that it can take exponential time because the number of recursive calls can double at each step. We therefore have some work to do in reaching an $\Theta(n \log n)$ algorithm.

A generalisation

The first thought, given the target time complexity, is a divide and conquer algorithm, seeking a function *join* for which

$$
nub\,(xs \mathbin{+\!\!+} ys) \quad = \quad join\,(nub\,xs)\,(nub\,ys) \tag{10.1}
$$

But no such function can exist. For instance, (10.1) requires

$$
join\,\text{``bca''}\,\text{``c''} = join\,(nub\,\text{``bca''})\,(nub\,\text{``c''}) = nub\,\text{``bcac''} = \text{``bac''}
$$

But also (10.1) requires

$$
join\,\text{``bca''}\,\text{``c''} = join\,(nub\,\text{``bcab''})\,(nub\,\text{``c''}) = nub\,\text{``bcabc''} = \text{``abc''}
$$

This example also shows that *nub* cannot be expressed as an instance of *foldl*. It is also easy to construct an example to show that *nub* cannot be expressed as an instance of *foldr*.

We therefore need some generalisation of *nub*. To see what it might be, consider a list of the form $x:y:xs$ with $x \in xs$ and $y \in xs$ and $x \neq y$. Unfolding the definition of $nub(x:y:xs)$, and exploiting both the associativity of min and the fact that $(x:)$ distributes through min, we find

$$nub\ (x : y : xs) \quad = \quad x : y : nub\ (xs \setminus\!\setminus [x, y])\ \ min$$
$$x : nub\ (xs \setminus\!\setminus [x]))\ \ min$$
$$y : nub\ (xs \setminus\!\setminus [y])\ \ min$$
$$nub\ xs$$

Now suppose that $x < y$, so the second term is lexicographically smaller than the third. That means the third term can be dropped:

$$nub\ (x : y : xs) \quad = \quad x : y : nub\ (xs \setminus\!\setminus [x, y])\ \ min$$
$$x : nub\ (xs \setminus\!\setminus [x]))\ \ min$$
$$nub\ xs$$

If, on the other hand, $x > y$, then the first two terms can be dropped:

$$nub\ (x : y : xs) \quad = \quad y : nub\ (xs \setminus\!\setminus [y])\ \ min$$
$$nub\ xs$$

The forms of these two expressions suggest our generalisation, which we will call *hub*. To help keep expressions reasonably short, abbreviate *minimum* to *min* in all that follows. The definition of *hub* is

$$hub\ ws\ xs \quad = \quad min\ [is \mathbin{+\!\!+} nub\ (xs \setminus\!\setminus is) \mid is \leftarrow inits\ ws] \tag{10.2}$$

where *ws* is a list in *strictly increasing* order. The standard function *inits* returns a list of all the initial segments, or prefixes, of a list. The example above now reads

$$nub\ (x : y : xs) \quad = \quad \textbf{if}\ x < y\ \textbf{then}\ hub\ [x, y]\ xs\ \textbf{else}\ hub\ [y]\ xs$$

The function *hub* generalises *nub*, for *inits* $[\,] = [[\,]]$ and $xs \setminus\!\setminus [\,] = xs$, so $nub\ xs = hub\ [\,]\ xs$. Two other immediate facts about *hub* are that *hub ws xs* begins with a prefix of *ws*, and that $hub\ ws\ xs \leq nub\ xs$ since the empty list is a prefix of every list.

The aim now is to derive an inductive definition of *hub*. For the base case we reason

$$hub\ ws\ [\,]$$
$$=\quad \{\text{definition}\}$$
$$min\ [is \mathbin{+\!\!+} nub\ ([\,] \setminus\!\setminus is) \mid is \leftarrow inits\ ws]$$
$$=\quad \{\text{since } [\,] \setminus\!\setminus is = [\,]\ \text{and}\ nub\ [\,] = [\,]\}$$
$$min\ [is \mid is \leftarrow inits\ ws]$$
$$=\quad \{\text{since } [\,]\ \text{is the lexicographically least list in } inits\ ws\}$$
$$[\,]$$

Hence *hub ws* [ ] = [ ]. For the inductive case, (10.2) gives

$$hub\ ws\ (x : xs) \quad = \quad min\ [is \mathbin{+\mkern-10mu+} nub\ ((x : xs) \setminus\setminus is) \mid is \leftarrow inits\ ws] \quad (10.3)$$

To simplify the right-hand side we need to know whether or not $x \in ws$, so we start by splitting *ws* into two lists, *us* and *vs*, defined by

$$(us, vs) \quad = \quad (takeWhile\ (< x)\ ws, dropWhile\ (< x)\ ws)$$

More briefly, $(us, vs) = span\ (< x)\ ws$, where *span* is a standard Haskell library function. Since $ws = us \mathbin{+\mkern-10mu+} vs$ and *ws* is in increasing order, both *us* and *vs* are also in increasing order. Moreover, if $x \in ws$, then $x = head\ vs$; if not, then either *vs* is empty or $x < head\ vs$.

The following property of *inits* is key to the simplification of (10.3):

$$inits\ (us \mathbin{+\mkern-10mu+} vs) \quad = \quad inits\ us \mathbin{+\mkern-10mu+} map\ (us\mathbin{+\mkern-10mu+})\ (inits^+\ vs) \quad (10.4)$$

where $inits^+\ vs$ returns the list of *nonempty* prefixes of *vs*. Using this expression for *inits* in (10.3) and splitting the comprehension into two parts, we obtain that $hub\ ws\ (x : xs) = A\ min\ B$, where

$$A \quad = \quad min\ [is\mathbin{+\mkern-10mu+}nub\ ((x : xs) \setminus\setminus is) \mid is \leftarrow inits\ us] \quad (10.5)$$

$$B \quad = \quad min\ [us\mathbin{+\mkern-10mu+}is\mathbin{+\mkern-10mu+}nub\ ((x : xs) \setminus\setminus (us\mathbin{+\mkern-10mu+}is)) \mid is \leftarrow inits^+\ vs] \quad (10.6)$$

To discover $A\ min\ B$ we deal with A first, distinguishing the two cases $x \notin xs$ and $x \in xs$. In the first case, $x \notin xs$, we argue:

A

$=$ {definition (10.5)}

$min\ [is \mathbin{+\mkern-10mu+} nub\ ((x : xs) \setminus\setminus is) \mid is \leftarrow inits\ us]$

$=$ {recursive definition of *nub* since $x \notin xs$ and $x \notin us$}

$min\ [is \mathbin{+\mkern-10mu+} [x] \mathbin{+\mkern-10mu+} nub\ (xs \setminus\setminus is) \mid is \leftarrow inits\ us]$

$=$ {since $us < is \mathbin{+\mkern-10mu+} [x]$ for $is \in inits\ us$}

$us \mathbin{+\mkern-10mu+} [x] \mathbin{+\mkern-10mu+} nub\ (xs \setminus\setminus us)$

$=$ {since $nub\ xs = hub\ [\,]\ xs$}

$us \mathbin{+\mkern-10mu+} [x] \mathbin{+\mkern-10mu+} hub\ [\,]\ (xs \setminus\setminus us)$

In the second case, $x \in xs$, we argue:

A

$=$ {recursive definition of *nub* since $x \in xs$ and $x \notin us$}

$min\ [is \mathbin{+\mkern-10mu+} ([x] \mathbin{+\mkern-10mu+} nub\ (xs \setminus\setminus (is \mathbin{+\mkern-10mu+} [x])))\ min\ nub\ (xs \setminus\setminus is))$
$\qquad \mid is \leftarrow inits\ us]$

=   {taking min outside the comprehension}

$min\ [is + [x] + nub\ (xs \setminus\setminus (is + [x])) \mid is \leftarrow inits\ us]$ min
$min\ [is + nub\ (xs \setminus\setminus is) \mid is \leftarrow inits\ us]$

=   {since $us < is + [x]$ for $is \in inits\ us$}

$(us + [x] + nub\ (xs \setminus\setminus (us + [x])))$ min
$min\ [is + nub\ (xs \setminus\setminus is) \mid is \leftarrow inits\ us]$

=   {since $inits\ (us + [x]) = inits\ us + [us + [x]]$}

$min\ [is + nub\ (xs \setminus\setminus is) \mid is \leftarrow inits\ (us + [x])]$

=   {definition (10.2)}

$hub\ (us + [x])\ xs$

Summarising, A equals

if $x \in xs$ **then** $hub\ (us + [x])\ xs$ **else** $us + [x] + hub\ [\,]\ (xs \setminus\setminus us)$

Now we turn to B. According to (10.6), if vs is empty (so $inits^+ vs$ is empty), then B is the fictitious value $min\ [\,]$. Otherwise, we reason:

B

=   {definition (10.6)}

$min\ [us + is + nub\ ((x : xs) \setminus\setminus (us + is)) \mid is \leftarrow inits^+ (v : vs')]$

=   {since $inits^+ (v : vs') = map\ (v :)\ (inits\ vs')$}

$min\ [us + [v] + is + nub\ ((x : xs) \setminus\setminus (us + [v] + is)) \mid is \leftarrow inits\ vs']$

=   {since $min \cdot map\ (ys+) = (ys+) \cdot min$}

$us + [v] + min\ [is + nub\ ((x : xs) \setminus\setminus (us + [v] + is)) \mid is \leftarrow inits\ vs']$

In particular, B begins with $us + [v]$. Without going further we now have enough information to determine $hub\ ws\ (x : xs)$ in the case $x \notin ws$. In this case, either vs is empty, so $A < B$, or vs is not empty and begins with v where $x < v$. In the latter situation we again have $A < B$ because A begins with a prefix of $us + [x]$ and $us + [x] < us + [v]$. Hence

$x \notin ws \quad \Rightarrow \quad hub\ ws\ (x : xs) = A$

It remains to deal with the case $x \in ws$, so $x = v$. In this case B simplifies to

$us + [x] + min\ [is + nub\ (xs \setminus\setminus (us + [x] + is)) \mid is \leftarrow inits\ vs']$

Now we need a final case analysis. Assume first that $x \notin xs$. We calculate:

B

=   {above}

$us + [x] + min\ [is + nub\ (xs \setminus\setminus (us + [x] + is)) \mid is \leftarrow inits\ vs']$

$$
\begin{aligned}
nub &= hub\,[\,] \\
hub\ ws\,[\,] &= [\,] \\
hub\ ws\,(x:xs) &= \textbf{case}\ (x \in xs, x \in ws)\ \textbf{of}
\end{aligned}
$$

$$
\begin{array}{lll}
(\textit{False}, \textit{False}) & \rightarrow & us \mathbin{+\!\!+} [x] \mathbin{+\!\!+} hub\,[\,]\,(xs \setminus\!\setminus us) \\
(\textit{False}, \textit{True}) & \rightarrow & us \mathbin{+\!\!+} [x] \mathbin{+\!\!+} hub\,(\textit{tail}\ vs)\,(xs \setminus\!\setminus us) \\
(\textit{True}, \textit{False}) & \rightarrow & hub\,(us \mathbin{+\!\!+} [x])\ xs \\
(\textit{True}, \textit{True}) & \rightarrow & hub\ ws\ xs
\end{array}
$$

$$\textbf{where}\ (us, vs) = span\,(< x)\ ws$$

Fig. 10.1 Second definition of *nub*

$$
\begin{aligned}
= &\quad \{\text{since } xs \setminus\!\setminus (us \mathbin{+\!\!+} [x] \mathbin{+\!\!+} is) = xs \setminus\!\setminus (us \mathbin{+\!\!+} is) = (xs \setminus\!\setminus us) \setminus\!\setminus is\} \\
&\quad us \mathbin{+\!\!+} [x] \mathbin{+\!\!+} min\,[is \mathbin{+\!\!+} nub\,((xs \setminus\!\setminus us) \setminus\!\setminus is) \mid is \leftarrow inits\ vs'] \\
= &\quad \{\text{definition (10.2)}\} \\
&\quad us \mathbin{+\!\!+} [x] \mathbin{+\!\!+} hub\ vs'\,(xs \setminus\!\setminus us)
\end{aligned}
$$

Hence:

$$
\begin{aligned}
&\quad hub\ ws\,(x:xs) \\
= &\quad \{\text{expressions for } A \text{ and } B, \text{ assuming } x \notin xs\} \\
&\quad (us \mathbin{+\!\!+} [x] \mathbin{+\!\!+} nub\,(xs \setminus\!\setminus us))\ min\ (us \mathbin{+\!\!+} [x] \mathbin{+\!\!+} hub\ vs'\,(xs \setminus\!\setminus us)) \\
= &\quad \{\text{since } hub\ vs'\,(xs \setminus\!\setminus us) \leq nub\,(xs \setminus\!\setminus us)\} \\
&\quad us \mathbin{+\!\!+} [x] \mathbin{+\!\!+} hub\ vs'\,(xs \setminus\!\setminus us)
\end{aligned}
$$

In the final case $x \in xs$ we can reason:

$$
\begin{aligned}
&\quad hub\ ws\,(x:xs) \\
= &\quad \{\text{expressions for } A \text{ and } B, \text{ assuming } x \in xs\} \\
&\quad hub\,(us \mathbin{+\!\!+} [x])\ xs\ min \\
&\quad us \mathbin{+\!\!+} [x] \mathbin{+\!\!+} min\,[is \mathbin{+\!\!+} nub\,(xs \setminus\!\setminus (us \mathbin{+\!\!+} [x] \mathbin{+\!\!+} is)) \mid is \leftarrow inits\ vs'] \\
= &\quad \{\text{since } ws = us \mathbin{+\!\!+} [x] \mathbin{+\!\!+} vs' \text{ and (10.4)}\} \\
&\quad min\,[is \mathbin{+\!\!+} nub\,(xs \setminus\!\setminus is) \mid is \leftarrow inits\ ws] \\
= &\quad \{\text{definition of } hub\} \\
&\quad hub\ ws\ xs
\end{aligned}
$$

The result of these calculations is summarised in Figure 10.1. Each membership test, list difference operation and evaluation of *span* takes linear time, so evaluation of *hub* takes linear time at each recursive call and quadratic time in total.

Introducing sets

The final step is to introduce an efficient representation of sets to reduce the complexity of the subsidiary operations from linear to logarithmic. Rather than program the set operations ourselves, we can invoke the Haskell library *Data.Set*. This library provides a data type *Set a* and the following operations (among others):

$$
\begin{array}{lll}
empty & :: & Set\ a \\
member & :: & Ord\ a \Rightarrow a \rightarrow Set\ a \rightarrow Bool \\
insert & :: & Ord\ a \Rightarrow a \rightarrow Set\ a \rightarrow Set\ a \\
split & :: & Ord\ a \Rightarrow a \rightarrow Set\ a \rightarrow (Set\ a, Set\ a) \\
elems & :: & Ord\ a \Rightarrow Set\ a \rightarrow [a]
\end{array}
$$

The value *empty* denotes the empty set, *member* is the membership test, *insert x xs* inserts a new element x into the set xs, while *split x* splits a set into those elements less than x and those greater than x, and *elems* returns the elements of a set in increasing order. As to the costs, *empty* takes constant time, *member*, *insert* and *split* take $O(\log n)$ steps on a set of size n, while *elems* takes $O(n)$ steps.

   In order to introduce sets into the definition of *nub* we need a preprocessing phase that associates with each element x of xs the set of elements that come after it. That is, we need to compute

$$(x_1, \{x_2, x_3, \ldots x_n\}), (x_2, \{x_3, \ldots, x_n\}), \ldots (x_n, \{\})$$

This list can be computed using the Haskell function *scanr*:

$$
\begin{array}{lll}
preprocess & :: & Ord\ a \Rightarrow [a] \rightarrow [(a, Set\ a)] \\
preprocess\ xs & = & zip\ xs\ (tail\ (scanr\ insert\ empty\ xs))
\end{array}
$$

The expression *scanr insert empty* $[x_1, x_2, \ldots x_n]$ returns the list

$$[\{x_1, x_2, \ldots, x_n\}, \{x_2, \ldots, x_n\}, \ldots, \{x_n\}, \{\}]$$

and takes $O(n \log n)$ steps to do so.

   The result of installing sets in Figure 10.1 is given in Figure 10.2. Unfortunately, its running time is not $O(n \log n)$. To see why, let us estimate the costs of the various operations. Each membership test contributes $O(\log n)$ steps to the cost at each recursive call. So does *split*. Let m be the size of us. Since *elems* takes $O(m)$ steps, as does concatenating the result with the rest of the list, and there are at most n elements in the final list, the total contribution of *elems* and $+\!\!+$ to the final cost is $O(n)$ steps. However, the

$$
\begin{array}{lll}
nub & = & hub\ empty \cdot preprocess \\
preprocess\ xs & = & zip\ xs\ (tail\ (scanr\ insert\ empty\ xs)) \\
hub\ ws\ [\,] & = & [\,] \\
hub\ ws\ ((x, xs) : xss) & = &
\end{array}
$$

> **case** $(member\ x\ xs, member\ x\ ws)$ **of**
>
> $$
> \begin{array}{lll}
> (False, False) & \rightarrow & eus + \hspace{-0.3em}+ [x] + \hspace{-0.3em}+ hub\ empty\ yss \\
> (False, True) & \rightarrow & eus + \hspace{-0.3em}+ [x] + \hspace{-0.3em}+ hub\ vs\ yss \\
> (True, False) & \rightarrow & hub\ (insert\ x\ us)\ xss \\
> (True, True) & \rightarrow & hub\ ws\ xss
> \end{array}
> $$
>
> **where** $\begin{array}[t]{lll}
> (us, vs) & = & split\ x\ ws \\
> eus & = & elems\ us \\
> yss & = & [(x, xs) \mid (x, xs) \leftarrow xss, not\ (member\ x\ us)]
> \end{array}$

Fig. 10.2 Introducing sets

---

cost of computing yss is $\Omega(n \log m)$ steps at each call, and summing this cost gives $\Omega(n^2)$ steps. As a specific example, consider the input

$$
[1 .. n] + \hspace{-0.3em}+ [j \mid j \leftarrow [1 .. n],\ j \bmod 3 \neq 0]
$$

The output is $[1 .. n]$. Each multiple of 3 causes the program to flush two elements from the set ws, namely $[1, 2]$, $[4, 5]$, $[7, 8]$ and so on, and the total cost of computing yss is quadratic in n.

One way to solve this problem is to introduce an additional argument ps into hub, defining hub' by

$$
\begin{array}{lll}
hub' & :: & Set\ a \rightarrow Set\ a \rightarrow [(a, Set\ a)] \rightarrow [a] \\
hub'\ ps\ ws\ xss & = & hub\ ws\ [(x, xs) \mid (x, xs) \leftarrow xss,\ x \notin ps]
\end{array}
$$

Then we obtain the program of Figure 10.3. The cost of computing qs is $O(m \log n)$, where m is the size of us, rather than the $O(n \log m)$ cost of computing yss in the previous version. Since the combined size of the sets us for which this operation is performed is at most n, the total running time is $O(n \log n)$ steps.

Final remarks

It was quite a lot of work to achieve the result, and the final algorithm is neither pretty nor intuitive. A nagging doubt remains that there might be a much simpler solution to such a simply stated problem. But so far I have not been able to find one. The main calculation turned out to be quite intricate and bedevilled by case analysis. Nevertheless, the battle plan is common enough: obtain a recursive formulation of the problem and then

$$
\begin{aligned}
nub &= hub' \; empty \; empty \cdot preprocess \\
preprocess \; xs &= zip \; xs \; (tail \; (scanr \; insert \; empty \; xs)) \\
hub' \; ps \; ws \; [\,] &= [\,] \\
\end{aligned}
$$

$hub' \; ps \; ws \; ((x, xs) : xss) =$

    if *member x ps* **then** *hub' ps ws xss* **else**

    case (*member x xs, member x ws*) **of**

$$
\begin{aligned}
(False, False) &\rightarrow \quad eus \mathbin{+\!\!+} [x] \mathbin{+\!\!+} hub' \; qs \; empty \; xss \\
(False, True) &\rightarrow \quad eus \mathbin{+\!\!+} [x] \mathbin{+\!\!+} hub' \; qs \; vs \; xss \\
(True, False) &\rightarrow \quad hub' \; ps \; (insert \; x \; us) \; xss \\
(True, True) &\rightarrow \quad hub' \; ps \; ws \; xss
\end{aligned}
$$

    where
$$
\begin{aligned}
(us, vs) &= split \; x \; ws \\
eus &= elems \; us \\
qs &= foldr \; insert \; ps \; eus
\end{aligned}
$$

Fig. 10.3 The final version

---

seek a generalised version that can be implemented efficiently. The same plan arises in the derivation of many efficient algorithms.

References

Bloom, S. L. and Wright, R. S. (2003). Some lower bounds on comparison-based algorithms. Unpublished research paper. Department of Computer Science, Steven's Institute of Technology, Hoboken, NJ, USA.

11

Not the maximum segment sum

Introduction

The maximum segment sum problem enjoyed a burst of popularity at the end of the 1980s, mostly as a showcase for programmers to illustrate their favourite style of program development or their particular theorem prover. The problem is to compute the maximum of the sums of all possible segments of a list of integers, positive or negative. But this pearl is not about the maximum segment sum. Instead, it is about the maximum *non-segment* sum. A segment of a list is a contiguous subsequence, while a non-segment is a subsequence that is not a segment. For example,

$$[-4, -3, -7, +2, +1, -2, -1, -4]$$

has maximum segment sum 3 (from the segment $[+2, +1]$) and maximum non-segment sum 2 (from the non-segment $[+2, +1, -1]$). There are no non-segments of a list with two or fewer elements. While there are $\Theta(n^2)$ segments of a list of length n, there are $\Theta(2^n)$ subsequences, and so many more non-segments than segments. Can one compute the maximum non-segment sum in linear time? Yes. There is a simple linear-time algorithm, and the aim of this pearl is to calculate it.

Specification

Here is the specification of *mnss*, the maximum non-segment sum:

$$mnss \quad :: \quad [Int] \to Int$$
$$mnss \quad = \quad maximum \cdot map\ sum \cdot nonsegs$$

The function *nonsegs* returns a list of all non-segments of a list. To define this function we can mark each element of the list with a Boolean value: *True* to signify it is to be included in the non-segment and *False* to indicate it is not. We mark in all possible ways, filter the markings for those that correspond to non-segments and then extract those non-segments whose elements are marked *True*. The function *markings* returns all possible markings:

$$markings \qquad :: \quad [a] \to [[(a, Bool)]]$$
$$markings \; xs \qquad = \quad [zip \; xs \; bs \mid bs \leftarrow booleans \; (length \; xs)]$$

$$booleans \; 0 \qquad = \quad [[\,]]$$
$$booleans \; (n{+}1) \quad = \quad [b : bs \mid b \leftarrow [True, False], \; bs \leftarrow booleans \; n]$$

Markings are in one-to-one correspondence with subsequences. We can now define

$$nonsegs \quad :: \quad [a] \to [[a]]$$
$$nonsegs \quad = \quad extract \cdot filter \; nonseg \cdot markings$$

$$extract \quad :: \quad [[(a, Bool)]] \to [[a]]$$
$$extract \quad = \quad map \; (map \; fst \cdot filter \; snd)$$

The function $nonseg :: [(a, Bool)] \to Bool$ returns *True* on a list xms if and only if $map \; snd \; xms$ describes a non-segment marking. The Boolean list ms is a non-segment marking if and only if it is an element of the set represented by the regular expression

$$F^* T^+ F^+ T (T + F)^*$$

in which *True* is abbreviated to T and *False* to F. The regular expression identifies the leftmost gap $T^+ F^+ T$ that makes the sequence a non-segment.

The finite automaton for recognising members of the corresponding regular set needs four states:

data *State* $= \quad E \mid S \mid M \mid N$

State E (for Empty) is the starting state; when the automaton is in state E, markings only in the set F^* have been recognised. State S (for Suffix) is when the automaton has processed one or more Ts, so indicates markings in the set $F^* T^+$, a non-empty suffix of Ts. State M (for Middle) is to indicate markings in the set $F^* T^+ F^+$, a middle segment, and state N (for Non-segment) for non-segment markings. We can now define

$$nonseg \quad = \quad (== N) \cdot foldl \; step \; E \cdot map \; snd$$

where the middle term $foldl \; step \; E$ executes the steps of the finite automaton:

step E False = E	step M False = M
step E True = S	step M True = N
step S False = M	step N False = N
step S True = S	step N True = N

Finite automata process their input from left to right, which explains the use of *foldl*. We could equally as well have processed lists from right to left, and looked for the rightmost gap, but why break with convention unnecessarily? Notice also that there is nothing special here about the *nonseg* property: any property of markings that can be recognised by a finite-state automaton yields to exactly the same treatment.

Derivation

Here is the definition of *mnss* again:

$$
\begin{aligned}
mnss &= maximum \cdot map\ sum \cdot extract \cdot filter\ nonseg \cdot markings \\
extract &= map\ (map\ fst \cdot filter\ snd) \\
nonseg &= (== N) \cdot foldl\ step\ E \cdot map\ snd
\end{aligned}
$$

Our plan of attack is to express *extract · filter nonseg · markings* as an instance of *foldl* and then to apply the fusion law of *foldl* to complete the passage to a better algorithm. To this end, define *pick* by

$$
\begin{aligned}
pick &\ ::\ State \rightarrow [a] \rightarrow [[a]] \\
pick\ q &= extract \cdot filter\ ((== q) \cdot foldl\ step\ E \cdot map\ snd) \cdot markings
\end{aligned}
$$

In particular, *nonsegs = pick N*. We claim that the following seven equations hold:

$$
\begin{aligned}
pick\ E\ xs &= [[\,]] \\
pick\ S\ [\,] &= [\,] \\
pick\ S\ (xs + [x]) &= map\ (+[x])\ (pick\ S\ xs + pick\ E\ xs) \\
pick\ M\ [\,] &= [\,] \\
pick\ M\ (xs + [x]) &= pick\ M\ xs + pick\ S\ xs \\
pick\ N\ [\,] &= [\,] \\
pick\ N\ (xs + [x]) &= pick\ N\ xs + \\
&\quad\ map\ (+[x])\ (pick\ N\ xs + pick\ M\ xs)
\end{aligned}
$$

The pukka way to derive these equations is through due process of calculation from the definition of *pick q*, but the steps are tedious and we will not bother. Instead, each equation can be justified by appeal to *step*. For example, the equation for *pick E* is justified because *step* returns *E* only on empty subsequences. Similarly for *pick S*, because *step* returns *S* only when x is marked *True* and preceded either by an element of *pick E* or *pick S*. The other definitions can be justified in a similar way. Again, there is nothing specific to non-segments: any finite automaton with k states that recognises correct markings can be systematically transformed into essentially k functions that operate directly on the given input.

The next step is to recast the definition of *pick* as an instance of *foldl*. Consider the function *pickall*, specified by

$$pickall\ xs\ =\ (pick\ E\ xs, pick\ S\ xs, pick\ M\ xs, pick\ N\ xs)$$

The following definition of *pickall* as an instance of *foldl* follows from the definitions above:

$$
\begin{aligned}
pickall\qquad\qquad\quad &=\ foldl\ step\ ([[\,]], [\,], [\,], [\,])\\
step\ (ess, nss, mss, sss)\ x\ &=\ (ess,\\
&\qquad map\ (+\!\!\!+[x])\ (sss +\!\!\!+ ess),\\
&\qquad mss +\!\!\!+ sss,\\
&\qquad nss +\!\!\!+ map\ (+\!\!\!+[x])\ (nss +\!\!\!+ mss))
\end{aligned}
$$

Our problem now takes the form

$$mnss\ =\ maximum \cdot map\ sum \cdot fourth \cdot pickall$$

where *fourth* returns the fourth element of a quadruple. We can move the *fourth* to the front of the expression on the right by introducing

$$tuple\ f\ (w, x, y, z) = (f\ w, f\ x, f\ y, f\ z)$$

Then we have

$$maximum \cdot map\ sum \cdot fourth\ =\ fourth \cdot tuple\ (maximum \cdot map\ sum)$$

so $mnss = fourth \cdot tuple\ (maximum \cdot map\ sum) \cdot pickall$.

As hoped for, we are now in a position to apply the fusion law of *foldl*. This law states that $f\ (foldl\ g\ a\ xs) = foldl\ h\ b\ xs$ for all finite lists xs provided that $f\ a = b$ and $f\ (g\ x\ y) = h\ (f\ x)\ y$ for all x and y. In our problem we have the instantiations

$$
\begin{aligned}
f\ &=\ tuple\ (maximum \cdot map\ sum)\\
g\ &=\ step\\
a\ &=\ ([[\,]], [\,], [\,], [\,])
\end{aligned}
$$

It remains to find h and b to satisfy the fusion conditions. First:

$$tuple\ (maximum \cdot map\ sum)\ ([[\,]], [\,], [\,], [\,])\ =\ (0, -\infty, -\infty, -\infty)$$

because the maximum of an empty set of numbers is $-\infty$. This gives the definition of b. For h we need to satisfy the equation

$$
\begin{aligned}
&tuple\ (maximum \cdot map\ sum)\ (step\ (ess, sss, mss, nss)\ x)\\
&=\ h\ (tuple\ (maximum \cdot map\ sum)\ (ess, sss, mss, nss))\ x
\end{aligned}
$$

To derive h we look at each component in turn. To keep expressions short, abbreviate *maximum* to *max*. For the fourth component we reason:

$$max \ (map \ sum \ (nss \hspace{0.7mm}+\hspace{-2mm}+ \ map \ (+\hspace{-1mm}+[x]) \ (nss \hspace{0.7mm}+\hspace{-2mm}+ \ mss)))$$

$=$ {definition of *map*}

$$max \ (map \ sum \ nss \hspace{0.7mm}+\hspace{-2mm}+ \ map \ (sum \cdot (+\hspace{-1mm}+[x])) \ (nss \hspace{0.7mm}+\hspace{-2mm}+ \ mss))$$

$=$ {since $sum \cdot (+\hspace{-1mm}+[x]) = (+x) \cdot sum$}

$$max \ (map \ sum \ nss \hspace{0.7mm}+\hspace{-2mm}+ \ map \ ((+x) \cdot sum) \ (nss \hspace{0.7mm}+\hspace{-2mm}+ \ mss))$$

$=$ {since $max \ (xs \hspace{0.7mm}+\hspace{-2mm}+ \ ys) = (max \ xs) \ max \ (max \ ys)$}

$$max \ (map \ sum \ nss) \ max \ max \ (map \ ((+x) \cdot sum) \ (nss \hspace{0.7mm}+\hspace{-2mm}+ \ mss))$$

$=$ {since $max \cdot map \ (+x) = (+x) \cdot max$}

$$max \ (map \ sum \ nss) \ max \ (max \ (map \ sum \ (nss \hspace{0.7mm}+\hspace{-2mm}+ \ mss)) + x)$$

$=$ {introducing $n = max \ (map \ sum \ nss)$ and
$m = max \ (map \ sum \ mss)$}

$$n \ max \ ((n \ max \ m) + x)$$

The other three components are treated similarly, and we arrive at

$$h \ (e, s, m, n) \ x$$
$$= \ (e, (s \ max \ e) + x, m \ max \ s, n \ max \ ((n \ max \ m) + x))$$

and $mnss = fourth \cdot foldl \ h \ (0, -\infty, -\infty, -\infty)$.

That, basically, is it. Well, we still have to deal with the fictitious $-\infty$ values. Perhaps the best method is to eliminate them entirely by considering the first three elements of the list separately:

$$mnss \ xs \quad = \quad fourth \ (foldl \ h \ (start \ (take \ 3 \ xs)) \ (drop \ 3 \ xs))$$
$$start \ [x, y, z] \quad = \quad (0, max \ [x{+}y{+}z, y{+}z, z], max \ [x, x{+}y, y], x{+}z)$$

Not quite as pretty, but more effective.

Final remarks

The origins of the maximum segment sum problem go back to about 1975, and its history is described in one of Bentley's (1987) programming pearls. For a derivation using invariant assertions, see Gries (1990); for an algebraic approach, see Bird (1989). The problem refuses to go away, and variations are still an active topic for algorithm designers because of potential applications in data-mining and bioinformatics; see Mu (2008) for recent results.

The interest in the non-segment problem is what it tells us about any maximum marking problem in which the marking criterion can be formulated as a regular expression. For instance, it is immediate that there is an $O(nk)$ algorithm for computing the maximum at-least-length-k segment problem because $F^* T^n F^*$ ($n \geq k$) can be recognised by a k-state automaton. And even non-regular conditions such as $F^* T^n F^* T^n F^*$ ($n \geq 0$), whose recogniser requires an unbounded number of states, is susceptible to the same method. What is more, the restriction to lists is not necessary either; one can solve maximum marking problems about a whole variety of data types in a similar way.

References

Bentley, J. R. (1987). *Programming Pearls*. Reading, MA: Addison-Wesley.

Bird, R. S. (1989). Algebraic identities for program calculation. *Computer Journal* **32** (2), 122–6.

Gries, D. (1990). The maximum segment sum problem. In *Formal Development of Programs and Proofs*, ed. E. W. Dijkstra *et al.* University of Texas at Austin Year of Programming Series. Menlo Park. Addison-Wesley, pp. 43–5.

Mu, S.-C. (2008). The maximum segment sum is back. *Partial Evaluation and Program Manipulation (PEPM '08)*, pp. 31–9.

12

Ranking suffixes

Introduction

The idea of ranking the elements of a list crops up frequently. An element x is assigned rank r if there are exactly r elements of the list less than x. For example, $rank\ [51, 38, 29, 51, 63, 38] = [3, 1, 0, 3, 5, 1]$. This scheme ranks from 0 and from lowest to highest, but one can also rank from 1 and from highest to lowest, as when ranking candidates by their marks in an examination. Rankings are distinct if and only if the list does not contain duplicates, in which case $rank\ xs$ is a permutation of $[0 .. length\ xs - 1]$.

In this pearl we consider the problem of ranking the *suffixes* of a list rather than the list itself. It takes $\Theta(n \log n)$ steps to rank a list of length n, assuming a test $x < y$ takes constant time. Since in the worst case it takes $\Theta(n)$ such tests to make one lexicographic comparison between two suffixes of a list of length n, it seems that ranking the suffixes of a list should require $\Theta(n^2 \log n)$ basic comparisons. The point of this pearl is to show that only $\Theta(n \log n)$ steps are necessary. Asymptotically speaking, it takes no more time to rank the suffixes of a list than it does to rank the list itself. Surprising but true.

Specification

In Haskell the suffixes of a list are called its *tails*, and henceforth we will refer to tails rather than suffixes. The function *tails* returns the *nonempty* tails of a list in decreasing order of length:

$$
\begin{array}{lll}
tails & :: & [a] \to [[a]] \\
tails\ [\,] & = & [\,] \\
tails\ xs & = & xs : tails\ (tail\ xs)
\end{array}
$$

This definition of *tails* differs from the standard Haskell function of the same name, which returns all the tails, including the empty tail. The function *rank* can be specified by

$$rank \quad :: \quad Ord\ a \Rightarrow [a] \to [Int]$$
$$rank\ xs \quad = \quad map\ (\lambda x \to length\ (filter\ (< x)\ xs))\ xs$$

This definition takes $\Theta(n^2)$ steps on a list of length n, but *rank* can be improved to take $\Theta(n \log n)$ steps, something we will take up later on.

The required function, *ranktails* say, can now be defined by

$$ranktails \quad :: \quad Ord\ a \Rightarrow [a] \to [Int]$$
$$ranktails \quad = \quad rank \cdot tails$$

Our task is to implement *ranktails* to take $\Theta(n \log n)$ steps.

Properties of rank

We will need various properties of *rank*, the most important of which is that *rank* maintains order: if we know only *rank xs*, then we know everything about the relative order of the elements of *xs*, though nothing about the nature of the elements themselves. Suppose we define $xs \approx ys$ to mean *rank xs = rank ys*. Then $xs \approx ys$ if the elements in *xs* have the same relative order as the elements in *ys*. As two examples among many:

$$xs \approx zip\ xs\ xs \quad \text{and} \quad zip\ (zip\ xs\ ys)\ zs \approx zip\ xs\ (zip\ ys\ zs)$$

We will also need the following property of *rank*. Let *select* $:: [a] \to [a]$ be any function such that:

(i) every element in *select xs* is in *xs*;
(ii) *select* $\cdot$ *map f* = *map f* $\cdot$ *select* for any *f*.

Then

$$rank \cdot select \cdot rank \quad = \quad rank \cdot select \tag{12.1}$$

In particular, taking *select* = *id* we have *rank* $\cdot$ *rank* = *rank*, and taking *select* = *tail*, we have *rank* $\cdot$ *tail* $\cdot$ *rank* = *rank* $\cdot$ *tail*. The proof of (12.1) is left as an instructive exercise to the interested reader.

Finally, a useful idea associated with ranking is that of *refining* one ranking by another one. Suppose we define the operation $\ll$, pronounced "refined by", by

$$xs \ll ys \quad = \quad rank\ (zip\ xs\ ys) \tag{12.2}$$

For example, $[3, 1, 3, 0, 1] \ll [2, 0, 3, 4, 0] = [2, 1, 3, 0, 1]$. Thus, equal ranks in *xs* may be refined to distinct ranks in $xs \ll ys$. The operation $\ll$ is associative. Here is the proof:

$$(xs \ll ys) \ll zs$$

$$= \quad \{(12.2)\}$$

$$rank\ (zip\ (rank\ (zip\ xs\ ys))\ zs)$$

$$= \quad \{\text{since } zip\ us\ vs \approx zip\ (rank\ us)\ vs\}$$

$$rank\ (zip\ (zip\ xs\ ys)\ zs)$$

$$= \quad \{\text{since } zip\ (zip\ xs\ ys)\ zs \approx zip\ xs\ (zip\ ys\ zs)\}$$

$$rank\ (zip\ xs\ (zip\ ys\ zs))$$

$$= \quad \{\text{as before}\}$$

$$xs \ll (ys \ll zs)$$

Observe also that if a ranking xs consists of distinct elements, and therefore is a permutation of $[0 .. n-1]$, where $n = length\ xs$, then $xs \ll ys = xs$ for any ys of the same length as xs. In words, once a ranking is a permutation it cannot be further refined.

A better algorithm

One obvious approach to improving the performance of *ranktails*, given its target complexity, is to look for a divide and conquer solution based on the decomposition

$$tails\ (xs \mathbin{+\!\!+} ys) \quad = \quad map\ (\mathbin{+\!\!+} ys)\ (tails\ xs) \mathbin{+\!\!+} tails\ ys$$

But this does not seem to lead anywhere. Instead, we take another approach and first generalise *ranktails* to a function *rats* by replacing the lexicographic comparison test ($<$) with ($<_k$), where $xs <_k ys = take\ k\ xs < take\ k\ ys$. In other words, we rank the tails of a list by looking only at the first k elements of each tail. Define *rats* by

$$rats\ k \quad = \quad rank \cdot map\ (take\ k) \cdot tails \tag{12.3}$$

We have *ranktails* $xs = rats\ (length\ xs)\ xs$, so *rats* is a generalisation of *ranktails*. The main reason for the name *rats*, apart from being a compression of both rank and tails, is that it is pronounceable and short enough to avoid lengthy expressions in calculations.

The key to the derivation of a faster algorithm for *ranktails* is the following property of *rats*:

$$rats\ (2{*}k)\ xs \quad = \quad rats\ k\ xs \ll shiftBy\ k\ (rats\ k\ xs) \tag{12.4}$$

We will prove this, and also give the definition of *shiftBy*, later on. Since $xs \approx map\,(take\,1)\,(tails\,xs)$ we have $rats\,1 = rank$. The idea is to use (12.4) to successively rank $map\,(take\,2)\,(tails\,xs)$, $map\,(take\,4)\,(tails\,xs)$ and so on until we reach a permutation. Thus, we propose the following algorithm for *ranktails*:

$$
\begin{array}{lcl}
ranktails & = & apply\,Until\ isperm\ rerankings \cdot rank \\
rerankings & = & map\ rerank\ (iterate\ (*2)\ 1) \\
rerank\ k\ rs & = & rs \ll shiftBy\ k\ rs
\end{array}
$$

The function *applyUntil* is a variant of the standard function *until* and is defined by

$$
\begin{array}{lcl}
apply\,Until & :: & (a \rightarrow Bool) \rightarrow [a \rightarrow a] \rightarrow a \rightarrow a \\
apply\,Until\ p\ (f:fs)\ x & = & \textbf{if}\ \ p\ x\ \ \textbf{then}\ \ x\ \ \textbf{else}\ \ apply\,Until\ p\ fs\ (f\ x)
\end{array}
$$

The function *isperm* tests whether a ranking is a permutation and can be defined using a Haskell array:[1]

$$
\begin{array}{lcl}
isperm & :: & [Int] \rightarrow Bool \\
isperm\ is & = & and\,(elems \\
& & \quad (accumArray\,(\vee)\ False\ (0, n{-}1)\,(zip\ is\,(repeat\ True)))) \\
& & \textbf{where}\ n = length\ is
\end{array}
$$

This definition of *isperm* takes linear time.

In words, *ranktails* first ranks the elements of the input and then successively applies *rerank* 1, *rerank* 2, *rerank* 4 and so on until the result is a permutation. Note that it is only the very first ranking that inspects the input; the remaining rerankings deal exclusively with ranks; that is, lists of integers. At worst, *ranktails* xs requires $\log n$ rerankings where $n = length\,xs$. Assuming *rank* takes $\Theta(n \log n)$ steps and *shiftBy* takes $\Theta(n)$ steps, the new version of *ranktails* takes $\Theta(n \log^2 n)$ steps. Better than $\Theta(n^2 \log n)$, but not yet at our target complexity of $\Theta(n \log n)$.

Proof

Now we prove (12.4), and at the same time discover a definition of *shiftBy*. We are going to need a number of additional properties involving lists, tails and rankings, the first of which is that

$$
all\,(not \cdot null)\ xss\ \Rightarrow\ xss = zip\,With\,(:)\,(map\ head\ xss)\,(map\ tail\ xss)
$$

---

[1] An almost identical program was used in the pearl "The smallest free number"; see pearl 1.

To reduce the parenthesis count in expressions we rewrite the consequent in the form

$$id \;\; = \;\; zipWith \, (:) \cdot fork \, (map \; head, map \; tail) \qquad\qquad (12.5)$$

where $fork \, (f, g) \, x = (f \, x, g \, x)$ and $zipWith \, (:)$ is quietly assumed to be non-curried. Proofs of this and other properties are omitted.

We start by calculating

$$rats \, (k{+}1)$$
$$= \quad \{(12.3)\}$$
$$rank \cdot map \, (take \, (k{+}1)) \cdot tails$$
$$= \quad \{(12.5) \text{ since } all \, (not \cdot null) \cdot map \, (take \, (k{+}1)) \cdot tails\}$$
$$rank \cdot zipWith \, (:) \cdot fork \, (map \; head, map \; tail) \cdot$$
$$map \, (take \, (k{+}1)) \cdot tails$$

Now, $fork \, (f, g) \cdot h = fork \, (f \cdot h, g \cdot h)$ and

$$map \; head \cdot map \, (take \, (k{+}1)) \cdot tails = id$$
$$map \; tail \cdot map \, (take \, (k{+}1)) \cdot tails \; = snoc \, [\,] \cdot tail \cdot map \, (take \, k) \cdot tails$$

where $snoc \; x \; xs = xs \, \text{++} \, [x]$. Hence we can continue:

$$rank \cdot zipWith \, (:) \cdot fork \, (map \; head, map \; tail) \cdot$$
$$map \, (take \, (k{+}1)) \cdot tails$$
$$= \quad \{\text{above}\}$$
$$rank \cdot zipWith \, (:) \cdot fork \, (id, snoc \, [\,] \cdot tail \cdot map \, (take \, k) \cdot tails)$$

The next step is to see that $zipWith \, (:) \; xs \; xss \approx zip \; xs \; xss$, or, more briefly, $zipWith \, (:) \approx zip$, where zip is also quietly assumed to be non-curried. Hence we obtain

$$rats \, (k{+}1) \;\; = \;\; rank \cdot zip \cdot fork \, (id, snoc \, [\,] \cdot tail \cdot map \, (take \, k) \cdot tails)$$

Now $rank \cdot zip = (\ll)$ by (12.2). And since $xs \ll ys = xs \ll rank \; ys$, that gets us to

$$rats \, (k{+}1) \;\; = \;\; (\ll) \cdot fork \, (id, rank \cdot snoc \, [\,] \cdot tail \cdot map \, (take \, k) \cdot tails)$$

Now $rank \cdot snoc \, [\,] = lift \cdot rank$, where $lift = snoc \; 0 \cdot map \, (+1)$, so

$$rats \, (k{+}1) \;\; = \;\; (\ll) \cdot fork \, (id, lift \cdot rank \cdot tail \cdot map \, (take \, k) \cdot tails)$$

Next we claim that $lift \cdot rank \cdot tail \approx lift \cdot tail \cdot rank$. Here is the proof:

$$lift \, (rank \, (tail \; xs)) \approx lift \, (tail \, (rank \; xs))$$

$\Leftarrow$ {since $xs \approx ys$ implies $lift\ xs \approx lift\ ys$}

   $rank\ (tail\ xs) \approx tail\ (rank\ xs)$

$\equiv$ {definition of $\approx$}

   $rank\ (rank\ (tail\ xs)) = rank\ (tail\ (rank\ xs))$

$\Leftarrow$ {using (12.1) twice, once for $subseq = id$

      and once for $subseq = tail$}

   $true$

Hence $rats\ (k{+}1) = (\ll) \cdot fork\ (id, lift \cdot tail \cdot rats\ k)$. Equivalently:

$$rats\ (k{+}1)\ xs \quad = \quad rank\ xs \ll shift\ (rats\ k\ xs) \tag{12.6}$$

where $shift = lift \cdot tail$ and $lift\ is = map\ (+1)\ is \mathbin{+\!\!+} [0]$.

   The next step is to exploit the fact that

$$shift\ (is \ll js) \quad = \quad shift\ is \ll shift\ js$$

and the associativity of $\ll$. Then we obtain from (12.6) that

$$rats\ k\ xs \quad = \quad rs \ll shift\ rs \ll shift^2\ rs \ll \cdots \ll shift^{k-1}\ rs$$

where $rs = rank\ xs$ and $shift^k$ is the k-fold composition of $shift$ with itself. It is now easy to group terms in this series expansion for $rats$ to obtain

$$rats\ (2{*}k)\ xs \quad = \quad rats\ k\ xs \ll shift^k\ (rats\ k\ xs)$$

Finally, we can set $shiftBy\ k = shift^k$ to establish (12.4). In fact, we have

$$shiftBy\ k\ rs \quad = \quad map\ (+k)\ (drop\ k\ rs) \mathbin{+\!\!+} [k{-}1, k{-}2\ ..\ 0]$$

Evaluation of $shiftBy\ k\ rs$ takes $\Theta(n)$ steps where $n = length\ rs$.

A better rank

We turn next to a better method for computing $rank$. As every examiner knows, the way to rank a list of candidate–mark pairs, given in candidate order, is first to partition the candidates by sorting them according to their marks, and placing candidates with equal marks into groups. Then each candidate in the first group receives rank 0, each candidate in the second group receives rank g_0, where g_0 is the size of the first group, each candidate in the third group receives rank $g_0 + g_1$, where g_1 is the size of the second group, and so on. The result is then resorted in the original candidate order. This method is formalised by

$$rank \quad = \quad resort \cdot concat \cdot label \cdot psort \cdot zip\ [0..]$$

$$
\begin{array}{lll}
\textit{psort} & :: & \textit{Ord } b \Rightarrow [(a, b)] \to [[a]] \\
\textit{psort xys} & = & \textit{pass xys } [\,] \\[4pt]
\textit{pass } [\,] \textit{ xss} & = & \textit{xss} \\
\textit{pass } (e@(x, y) : xys) \textit{ xss} & = & \textit{step xys } [\,] [x] [\,] \textit{ xss} \\
\quad \textbf{where} \\
\quad \textit{step } [\,] \textit{ as bs cs xss} & = & \textit{pass as } (bs : \textit{pass cs xss}) \\
\quad \textit{step } (e@(x, y') : xys) \textit{ as bs cs xss} & \mid & y' < y = \textit{step xs } (e : as) \textit{ bs cs xss} \\
& \mid & y' = y = \textit{step xs as } (x : bs) \textit{ cs xss} \\
& \mid & y' > y = \textit{step xs as bs } (e : cs) \textit{ xss}
\end{array}
$$

Fig. 12.1 Partition sorting

The function *psort*, short for partition sort, partitions a list of candidate–mark pairs by sorting by mark and grouping candidates with equal marks into runs. The marks, having served their purpose, are discarded. One way of implementing *psort* is presented in Figure 12.1. The method used is a version of *ternary quicksort* in which the head of a list is chosen as the pivot in the partitioning step. As a consequence, *psort* takes $\Theta(n^2)$ steps in the worst case. Choosing the pivot to be the median element brings the cost down to $\Theta(n \log n)$ steps.

The function *label* is defined by

$$
\begin{array}{lll}
\textit{label} & :: & [[a]] \to [[(a, Int)]] \\
\textit{label xss} & = & \textit{zipWith tag xss } (\textit{scanl } (+) \, 0 \, (\textit{map length xss})) \\
\textit{tag xs k} & = & [(x, k) \mid x \gets xs]
\end{array}
$$

Finally, *resort* can be implemented by using a Haskell array:

$$
\begin{array}{lll}
\textit{resort} & :: & [(Int, Int)] \to [Int] \\
\textit{resort ijs} & = & \textit{elems } (\textit{array } (0, \textit{length ijs} - 1) \, ijs)
\end{array}
$$

The value *array* $(0, n{-}1)$ *ijs* builds an array indexed from 0 to $n{-}1$ whose index–value pairs are given by the association list *ijs*. The first components of *ijs* have to be a permutation of $[0 .. n{-}1]$ for the result to be well defined. Both *array* and *elems* take linear time, so *resort* takes linear time.

The final algorithm

The revised implementation of *rank* leads to an alternative implementation of *ranktails* in which ranking is subordinated to partitioning. Suppose we introduce

$$
\begin{array}{lll}
\textit{partition} & :: & \textit{Ord } a \Rightarrow [a] \to [[Int]] \\
\textit{partition} & = & \textit{psort} \cdot \textit{zip } [0..]
\end{array}
$$

Then $rank = resort \cdot concat \cdot label \cdot partition$. Furthermore, $\ll$ can be expressed in terms of *partition* because it is expressed in terms of *rank*. That means we can regroup terms and express *ranktails* in terms of *partition* rather than *rank*. One advantage of doing so is that *rank* returns a permutation if and only if *partition* returns a list all of whose elements are singletons, so *isperm* can be replaced by *all single*, where *single* determines whether its argument is a singleton list. Installing these changes leads to

$$
\begin{aligned}
ranktails \quad &= \quad resort \cdot concat \cdot label \cdot \\
&\quad\quad applyUntil\,(all\ single)\ repartitions \cdot partition \\
repartitions \quad &= \quad map\ repartition\,(iterate\,(*2)\,1) \\
repartition\ k\ iss \quad &= \quad partition(zip\ rs\,(shiftBy\ k\ rs)) \\
&\quad \mathbf{where}\ rs = resort\,(concat\,(label\ iss))
\end{aligned}
$$

This version has the same time complexity as the previous one, but it opens up the route for further optimisation. In fact, we are now just two steps away from our goal of a $\Theta(n \log n)$ algorithm for *ranktails*.

The first of these is to make use of the identity

$$
\begin{aligned}
&partition\,(zip\ xs\ ys) \\
&= \quad concatMap\,(psort \cdot map\,(install\ ys))\,(partition\ xs) \quad\quad (12.7)
\end{aligned}
$$

where

$$
install\ ys\ i \quad = \quad (i, ys\ !!\ i) \quad\quad\quad\quad\quad (12.8)
$$

In words, one can partition a list of pairs by first partitioning with respect to first components and refining the result using the second components. The correct second components can be installed in each run because each run is a list of positions. After installation, each run is partition sorted and the results concatenated.

To be accurate, (12.7) holds only if *psort* is a *stable* sorting algorithm and the implementation in Figure 12.1 is not stable. If *psort* is not stable then the elements in each run will appear in a different order in the left- and right-hand sides. But (12.7) does hold if we interpret equality of two partitions to mean equal up to some permutation of the elements in each run. Since the computation of *ranktails* does not depend on the precise order of the elements in a run, that is all that is required.

We are now ready to rewrite *repartition*:

$$
\begin{aligned}
&repartition\ k\ iss \\
&= \quad \{\text{definition, setting } rs = resort\,(concat\,(label\ iss))\} \\
&\quad\quad partition(zip\ rs\,(shiftBy\ k\ rs))
\end{aligned}
$$

$=$ $\{(12.7)\}$

$concatMap\ (psort \cdot map\ (install\ (shiftBy\ k\ rs)))\ (partition\ rs)$

$=$ $\{$since $iss = partition\ xs$ implies $rs = rank\ xs$
        and $partition \cdot rank = partition\}$

$concatMap\ (psort \cdot map\ (install\ (shiftBy\ k\ rs)))\ iss$

Hence

$$repartition\ k\ iss\ =\ concatMap\ (psort \cdot map\ (install\ rs))\ iss$$
$$\mathbf{where}\ rs = shiftBy\ k\ (resort\ (concat\ (label\ iss)))$$

We are nearly there, but (12.8) gives an inefficient way of computing *install* because it uses list-indexing (!!) which is not constant time. Better is to use array-indexing (!) which does take constant time. The final step is to rewrite *install*:

$(shiftBy\ k\ (resort\ (concat\ (label\ iss))))\ !!\ i$

$=$ $\{$definition of $shiftBy\}$

$(map\ (+k)\ (drop\ k\ (resort\ (concat\ (label\ iss))))\ +\!\!+$
$[k\!-\!1, k\!-\!2 .. 0])\ !!\ i$

$=$ $\{$arithmetic, with $n = length(concat\ (label\ iss))$ and $j = i+k\}$

$\mathbf{if}\ j < n\ \mathbf{then}\ k + (resort\ (concat\ (label\ iss)))\ !!\ j\ \mathbf{else}\ n\!-\!i\!-\!1$

$=$ $\{$definition of *resort* and $elems\ a\ !!\ i = a\ !\ i\}$

$\mathbf{if}\ j < n\ \mathbf{then}\ k + array\ (0, n\!-\!1)\ (concat\ (label\ iss))))\ !\ j$
$\mathbf{else}\ n\!-\!i\!-\!1$

The final program for *ranktails* is recorded in Figure 12.2. The length of the input is computed once and passed to the various subsidiary functions that need it.

Analysis

It remains to time *ranktails*. We will do this by estimating the total number of comparisons $T(n, k)$ required to carry out k repartitions on a list of length n. The key to the analysis is to appreciate that the computation of *ranktails* is essentially the same as partition sorting a list of n vectors, each of dimension k, by sorting on each dimension in turn. The first components of these vectors consist of the elements of the input, but each subsequent component is an integer which is determined dynamically from the result of sorting with respect to previous components. Unlike the implementation of *psort* given in Figure 12.1 we will suppose that each partition step chooses

$$
\begin{array}{rcl}
\textit{ranktails} & :: & \textit{Ord } a \Rightarrow [a] \rightarrow [\textit{Int}] \\
\textit{ranktails xs} & = & (\textit{resort } n \cdot \textit{concat} \cdot \textit{label} \cdot \\
& & \quad \textit{applyUntil } (\textit{all single}) \, (\textit{repartitions } n) \cdot \\
& & \quad \textit{psort} \cdot \textit{zip } [0..]) \; \textit{xs} \\
& & \textbf{where } n = \textit{length xs} \\
\textit{resort } n & = & \textit{elems} \cdot \textit{array } (0, n-1) \\
\textit{label iss} & = & \textit{zipWith tag iss } (\textit{scanl } (+) \, 0 \, (\textit{map length iss})) \\
\textit{tag is j} & = & [(i, j) \mid i \leftarrow \textit{is}] \\
\textit{repartitions } n & = & \textit{map } (\textit{repartition } n) \, (\textit{iterate } (*2) \, 1) \\
\textit{repartition } n \, k \, \textit{iss} & = & \textit{concatMap } (\textit{psort} \cdot \textit{map install}) \, \textit{iss} \\
\quad \textbf{where } \textit{install } i & = & (i, \textbf{if } j < n \textbf{ then } k + a \, ! \, j \textbf{ else } n-i-1) \\
\quad\quad a & = & \textit{array } (0, n-1) \, (\textit{concat } (\textit{label iss}))
\end{array}
$$

Fig. 12.2 The final algorithm for *ranktails*

---

a pivot that is the median of the possible pivots. For example, in sorting on the first component, a pivot p is chosen so that some positive number, say x, of elements of the list have first components equal to p and an equal number, namely $(n-x)/2$, of elements whose first components are less than p, and elements whose second components are greater than p. The run of x elements are sorted on first component, so it remains to sort them on the remaining components. But the other two lists have still to be sorted on all components. Since partitioning n elements requires $n-1$ comparisons, we can define $T(n, k)$ by the recurrence relation

$$
\begin{array}{rcl}
T(0, k) & = & 0 \\
T(n, 0) & = & 0 \\
T(n, k) & = & (\max x : 1 \leq x \leq n : n-1 + T(x, k-1) + 2\, T((n-x)/2, k))
\end{array}
$$

We now show that $T(n, k) \leq n(\log n + k)$. By induction, this inequality follows if

$$
n-1 + x(\log x + k - 1) + (n-x)[\log(n-x) + k - 1] \leq n(\log n + k)
$$

for $1 \leq x \leq n$. This inequality can be established by high-school calculus. Finally, since $k = \log n$, we have that the number of comparisons required to evaluate *ranktails* on a list of length n is at most $2n \log n$, and the total running time is $\Theta(n \log n)$ steps.

Experimental results

That was quite a lot of calculational effort to obtain the final algorithm, but is it actually better in practice than the naive one? We profiled three versions of the algorithm:

File	Size	Chars	AlgA1	AlgB1	AlgC1	AlgA2	AlgB2	AlgC2
dna	10424	5	0.08	0.10	0.08	**0.04**	0.08	0.16
ps	367639	87	2.76	10.96	**2.32**	3.18	22.50	3.54
txt	148480	72	**0.48**	3.08	0.72	0.86	6.06	1.28
ptt5	513216	159	–	136.38	8.70	611.3	37.78	**6.32**
alla	1000	1	2.96	0.10	**0.02**	0.18	0.06	**0.02**

Fig. 12.3 Running times of three versions for various files

(A) the specification of *ranktails* but with the definition of *rank* based on partition sorting;

(B) the improved algorithm that used repeated rerankings;

(C) the final program of Figure 12.2.

All algorithms were run with the implementation of *psort* described in Figure 12.1 (AlgA1, AlgB1 and AlgC1), and then with a guaranteed $\Theta(n \log n)$ algorithm based on mergesort (AlgA2, AlgB2 and AlgC2). The programs were compiled with GHC. Five different kinds of input were used: (i) a DNA file; (ii) a postscript file; (iii) the file `alice29.txt` from the Canterbury corpus and containing the text of Alice in Wonderland; (iv) a picture file `ptt5` from the same corpus; and (v) a text file containing 1000 occurrences of the letter "a". Running times in Figure 12.3 are in seconds. The second column gives the number of characters in the file and the third column the number of distinct characters. The entry for AlgA1 in the `ptt5` row is blank because the computation was abandoned after 12 hours. Highlighted entries show the best performance for each row.

The figures reveal a complicated picture. First, as expected, the AlgB1 and AlgB2 variants showed no advantage over either the naive or superior versions. But, apart from the last two rows, the naive algorithms performed about as well as the superior ones. Moreover, the algorithms based on ternary quicksort were roughly twice as fast as those based on mergesort. But the picture changes with `ptt5`, a file that mostly contains null characters, and with `alla`, the file that contains just the letter "a". Here, the superior algorithm is much better. Although not better than the others in all situations, AlgC1 seems to be the best overall.

Final remarks

Our final algorithm for *ranktails* is closely related to an algorithm for sorting the suffixes of a list proposed by Larsson and Sadakane (1999). Indeed, the whole pearl was inspired by their work. Ranking a list and sorting a list are closely related operations and each can be computed quickly from the other. In particular, the function *sorttails* that returns the unique permutation that sorts the tails of a list can be obtained from the final program for *ranktails* simply by replacing *resort · concat · label* in the first line of *ranktails* by *concat*. The function *sorttails* is needed as a preliminary step in the Burrows–Wheeler algorithm for data compression, a problem we will take up in the following pearl. The problem of sorting the suffixes of a string has been treated extensively in the literature because it has other applications in string matching and bioinformatics; a good source is Gusfield (1997).

This pearl was rewritten a number of times. Initially we started out with the idea of computing *perm*, a permutation that sorts a list. But *perm* is too specific in the way it treats duplicates: there is more than one permutation that sorts a list containing duplicate elements. One cannot get very far with *perm* unless one generalises to either *rank* or *partition*. We reformulated the problem in terms of *rank*, but ended up with the idea of partitioning a list rather than ranking it. Nevertheless, *rank* entered the picture again for the final optimisation step.

References

Larsson, N. J. and Sadakane, K. (1999). Faster suffix sorting. Research Report LU-CS-TR-99-214, Department of Computer Science, Lund University, Sweden.

Gusfield, D. (1997). *Algorithms on Strings, Trees and Sequences.* Cambridge, UK: Cambridge University Press.

13

The Burrows–Wheeler transform

Introduction

The Burrows–Wheeler transform (BWT) is a method for permuting a list with the aim of bringing repeated elements together. Its main use is as a preprocessing step in data compression. Lists with many repeated adjacent elements can be encoded compactly using simple schemes such as run length or move-to-front encoding. The result can then be fed into more advanced compressors, such as Huffman or arithmetic coding,[1] to compress the input even more.

Clearly, the best way of bringing repeated elements together is just to sort the list. But the idea has a major flaw as a preliminary to compression: there is no way to recover the original list unless the complete sorting permutation is also produced as part of the output. Without the ability to recover the original input, data compression is pointless; and if a permutation has to be produced as well, then compression is ineffective. Instead, the BWT achieves a more modest permutation, one that brings some but not all repeated elements into adjacent positions. The main advantage of the BWT is that the transform can be inverted using a single additional piece of information, namely an integer k in the range $0 \leq k < n$, where n is the length of the (nonempty) input list. In this pearl we describe the BWT, identify the fundamental reason why inversion is possible, and use it to derive the inverse transform from its specification.

Defining the BWT

Applied to a list xs the BWT sorts the rotations of xs, producing a matrix of rotated lists, and then returns the last column of the sorted matrix together with the position of xs in the matrix. As an illustration, consider the string yokohama. The rotations and the sorted rotations are pictured in

[1] Arithmetic coding is considered in two subsequent pearls; see Pearls 24 and 25.

```
0   y o k o h a m a          0   a m a y o k o h
1   o k o h a m a y          1   a y o k o h a m
2   k o h a m a y o          2   h a m a y o k o
3   o h a m a y o k          3   k o h a m a y o
4   h a m a y o k o          4   m a y o k o h a
5   a m a y o k o h          5   o h a m a y o k
6   m a y o k o h a          6   o k o h a m a y
7   a y o k o h a m          7   y o k o h a m a
```

Fig. 13.1 Rotations and sorted rotations

Figure 13.1. The output of the transform is the string `hmooakya`, the last column of the second matrix, and the number 7 because row 7 is the position of `yokohama` in the second matrix.

It is straightforward to specify the BWT:

$$transform \quad :: \quad Ord\ a \Rightarrow [a] \to ([a], Int)$$
$$transform\ xs \quad = \quad (map\ last\ xss, position\ xs\ xss)$$
$$\textbf{where}\ xss = sort\ (rots\ xs)$$

The position of row xs in the matrix xss is defined by

$$position\ xs\ xss \quad = \quad length\ (take While\ (\neq xs)\ xss)$$

and the rotations of a nonempty list by

$$rots \quad :: \quad [a] \to [[a]]$$
$$rots\ xs \quad = \quad take\ (length\ xs)\ (iterate\ lrot\ xs)$$
$$\textbf{where}\ lrot\ (x : xs) = xs \mathbin{+\!\!+} [x]$$

The subsidiary function *lrot* performs a single left rotation. The code for *transform* is not efficient, but we will ignore that problem for now.[2]

The function *transform* is helpful for compression because, applied to a text, it brings together characters with a common context. To give a brief illustration, an English text will contain many occurrences of words such as "this", "the", "that" and so on, as well as many occurrences of "where", "which", "when" and so on. Consequently, many of the rotations beginning with "h" will end with either a "t" or a "w". As a contrived example, transforming `"this, that or the other"` produces

$$(te, rshhhtttth\ \ oeia\ \ or, 22)$$

In this example all but one of the "t"s have been brought together.

---

[2] We will also ignore the fact that $transform\ [\,] = ([\,], 0)$ and consider only nonempty lists as valid arguments to *transform*.

The inverse $untransform :: Ord\ a \Rightarrow ([a], Int) \rightarrow [a]$ is, naturally enough, specified (over nonempty lists) by

$$untransform \cdot transform \quad = \quad id$$

The problem is how to compute *untransform*. The obvious method, if it can be made to work, is to use the first component of the result of *transform* to recreate the sorted matrix of rotations and then to use the second component to select the appropriate row. Fleshing out the idea, suppose $recreate :: Ord\ a \Rightarrow [a] \rightarrow [[a]]$ can be constructed to satisfy

$$recreate \cdot map\ last \cdot sort \cdot rots \quad = \quad sort \cdot rots$$

Then we can define $untransform\ (ys, k) = (recreate\ ys)\ !!\ k$, where $(!!)$ is the list-indexing operator. But can we really recreate the whole matrix of sorted rotations simply by knowing its last column? Yes we can, and the derivation of *recreate* is a fascinating exercise in program calculation.

Recreational calculation

Suppose in all that follows that the input to *recreate* is a list of length n, so *recreate* has to recreate an $n \times n$ matrix. The idea is to recreate the matrix column by column. Define *takeCols* by

$$\begin{aligned} takeCols \quad &:: \quad Int \rightarrow [[a]] \rightarrow [[a]] \\ takeCols\ j \quad &= \quad map\ (take\ j) \end{aligned}$$

Thus, $takeCols\ j$ takes the first j columns of an $n \times n$ matrix. In particular, $takeCols\ n$ is the identity function. We therefore replace *recreate* with the function $recreate\ n$, specified by the property

$$recreate\ j \cdot map\ last \cdot sort \cdot rots \quad = \quad takeCols\ j \cdot sort \cdot rots \qquad (13.1)$$

Thus, $recreate\ j$ recreates the first j columns of the sorted matrix of rotations from its last column.

The plan of attack is to construct an inductive definition of *recreate*. The base case is easy:

$$recreate\ 0 \quad = \quad map\ (const\ [\,])$$

Applied to a list ys of length n, the result of $recreate\ 0$ is a column of n empty lists. Since $takeCols\ 0$ applied to any $n \times n$ matrix also produces n empty lists, (13.1) is established for the case $j = 0$.

The fun begins with the inductive case. We will need three additional ingredients to make up the recipe. The first ingredient is a function *rrot* for performing a single right rotation:

$$rrot \quad :: \quad [a] \rightarrow [a]$$
$$rrot\ xs \quad = \quad [last\ xs] \mathbin{+\!\!+} init\ xs$$

Equivalently, $rrot\ (xs \mathbin{+\!\!+} [x]) = [x] \mathbin{+\!\!+} xs$. The crucial property of *rrot* is

$$map\ rrot \cdot rots \quad = \quad rrot \cdot rots \qquad (13.2)$$

Here is a proof:

$$map\ rrot\ (rots\ xs)$$
$$= \quad \{\text{definition of } rots\}$$
$$map\ rrot\ [xs, lrot\ xs, lrot^2\ xs, \ldots, lrot^{n-1}\ xs]$$
$$= \quad \{\text{definition of } map, \text{ using } rrot \cdot lrot = id\}$$
$$[rrot\ xs, xs, lrot\ xs, \ldots, lrot^{n-2}\ xs]$$
$$= \quad \{\text{definition of } rrot\}$$
$$rrot\ [xs, lrot\ xs, \ldots, lrot^{n-2}\ xs, rrot\ xs]$$
$$= \quad \{\text{since } rrot\ xs = lrot^{n-1}\ xs\}$$
$$rrot\ [xs, lrot\ xs, \ldots, lrot^{n-2}\ xs, lrot^{n-1}\ xs]$$
$$= \quad \{\text{definition of } rots\}$$
$$rrot\ (rots\ xs)$$

The second ingredient is a function *hdsort* that sorts a matrix on its first column. We can define *hdsort* using the Haskell function *sortBy*:

$$hdsort \quad :: \quad Ord\ a \Rightarrow [[a]] \rightarrow [[a]]$$
$$hdsort \quad = \quad sortBy\ cmp \quad \textbf{where } cmp\ (x : xs)\ (y : ys) = compare\ x\ y$$

The third ingredient is a function *consCol* that adds a new column to a matrix:

$$consCol \quad\quad :: \quad ([a], [[a]]) \rightarrow [[a]]$$
$$consCol\ (xs, xss) \quad = \quad zipWith\ (:)\ xs\ xss$$

The ingredients above satisfy various identities that we will need in cooking up a constructive definition of *recreate* to satisfy (13.1). First of all, for $j < n$ we have

$$takeCols\ (j+1) \cdot map\ rrot \quad = \quad consCol \cdot fork\ (map\ last, takeCols\ j) \qquad (13.3)$$

where $fork\ (f, g)\ x = (f\ x, g\ x)$. The right-hand side describes the operation of placing the last column of a matrix at the front of the first j columns; the left-hand side describes the operation of performing a single right rotation on each row and then taking the first $j+1$ columns. The identity expresses the fact that these two operations give the same result.

The second identity is

$$takeCols\ (j+1) \cdot hdsort\ =\ hdsort \cdot takeCols\ (j+1) \tag{13.4}$$

In words, sorting an $n \times n$ matrix on its first column and then taking a positive number of columns of the result yields exactly the same result as first taking the same number of columns and then sorting on the first column.

The third identity, the key one, is not so obvious:

$$hdsort \cdot map\ rrot \cdot sort \cdot rots\ =\ sort \cdot rots \tag{13.5}$$

In words, the following transformation on a matrix of sorted rotations is the identity: move the last column to the front and then resort the rows on the new first column. In fact, (13.5) is true only if $hdsort$ is a *stable* sorting algorithm, meaning that columns with the same first element appear in the output in the same order that they appeared in the input. Under this assumption we have, applied to an $n \times n$ matrix, that

$$sort\ =\ (hdsort \cdot map\ rrot)^n$$

This identity states that one can sort an $n \times n$ matrix (in fact, an arbitrary list of lists all of which have length n) by repeating n times the operation of rotating the last column into first position and then stably sorting according to the first column only. Since it captures essentially the operation of radix sort, we will call it the *radix sort property*. It can be proved by induction on n, but we omit details. It leads, with a little help, to the proof of (13.5):

$$hdsort \cdot map\ rrot \cdot sort \cdot rots$$

$=$ {radix sort property}

$$(hdsort \cdot map\ rrot)^{n+1} \cdot rots$$

$=$ {composition}

$$(hdsort \cdot map\ rrot)^n \cdot hdsort \cdot map\ rrot \cdot rots$$

$=$ {radix sort property}

$$sort \cdot hdsort \cdot map\ rrot \cdot rots$$

$=$ {identity (13.2)}

$$sort \cdot hdsort \cdot rrot \cdot rots$$

$=$ {since $sort \cdot hdsort = sort$}

$$sort \cdot rrot \cdot rots$$

$$= \quad \{\text{since } sort \cdot rrot = sort\}$$

$$sort \cdot rots$$

The two identities used in the last two steps generalise to $sort \cdot perm = sort$ for any permutation $perm$ of the input.

We are now ready to deal with $recreate$. Writing $sr = sort \cdot rots$ for brevity, we calculate:

$$recreate\ (j{+}1) \cdot map\ last \cdot sr$$

$$= \quad \{\text{specification (13.1)}\}$$

$$takeCols\ (j{+}1) \cdot sr$$

$$= \quad \{\text{property (13.5)}\}$$

$$takeCols\ (j{+}1) \cdot hdsort \cdot map\ rrot \cdot sr$$

$$= \quad \{\text{property (13.4)}\}$$

$$hdsort \cdot takeCols\ (j{+}1) \cdot map\ rrot \cdot sr$$

$$= \quad \{\text{property (13.3)}\}$$

$$hdsort \cdot consCol \cdot fork\ (map\ last, takeCols\ j) \cdot sr$$

$$= \quad \{\text{specification (13.1)}\}$$

$$hdsort \cdot consCol \cdot fork\ (map\ last, recreate\ j \cdot map\ last) \cdot sr$$

$$= \quad \{\text{since } fork\ (f \cdot h, g \cdot h) = fork\ (f, g) \cdot h\}$$

$$hdsort \cdot consCol \cdot fork\ (id, recreate\ j) \cdot map\ last \cdot sr$$

Hence, $recreate\ (j{+}1) = hdsort \cdot consCol \cdot fork\ (id, recreate\ j)$.

A faster algorithm

But, and it is a big but, the idea of recreating the complete matrix of sorted rotations before selecting one particular row leads to an unacceptably inefficient method for computing *untransform*. Recreating an $n \times n$ matrix takes $\Omega(n^2)$ steps and a quadratic time algorithm for *untransform* is simply no good. In fact, the above definition of *recreate n* takes $\Omega(n^2 \log n)$ steps because *hdsort* is computed a total of n times. In this section we show how to compute *untransform* in $\Theta(n \log n)$ steps.

In order to calculate a better algorithm for *untransform*, we need yet more ingredients. First of all, note that head-sorting a list of singletons is equivalent to sorting a list:

$$hdsort \cdot map\ wrap \quad = \quad map\ wrap \cdot sort$$

Here, *wrap x* = [*x*]. Second, it is not necessary to apply *hdsort* repeat-edly, since each sort involves one and the same permutation. More precisely, suppose

$$sort\ ys\ =\ apply\ p\ ys$$

where *p*, which depends on *ys*, is a permutation of [0 .. *n*−1] and *apply* applies a permutation to a list. The permutation *p* is defined by

$$p\ =\ map\ snd\ (sort\ (zip\ ys\ [0..n{-}1]))$$

and *apply* by

$$apply\ p\ xs\ =\ [xs \mathbin{!!} (p \mathbin{!!} i) \mid i \leftarrow [0..n{-}1]]$$

The first fact about *apply* is that for any permutation *p*

$$apply\ p \cdot consCol\ =\ consCol \cdot pair\ (apply\ p) \tag{13.6}$$

where *pair f* (*x, y*) = (*f x, f y*). More generally, if *beside* (*M, N*) denotes the operation of placing matrix *M* beside matrix *N*, then

$$apply\ p \cdot beside\ =\ beside \cdot pair\ (apply\ p)$$

Property (13.6) is the special case in which *M* is a $1 \times n$ matrix. Using (13.6), we reason:

$$\begin{aligned}
&recreate\ (j{+}1)\\
=\quad&\{\text{definition}\}\\
&hdsort \cdot consCol \cdot fork\ (id, recreate\ j)\\
=\quad&\{\text{taking } hdsort = apply\ p, \text{ where } p \text{ is as defined above}\}\\
&apply\ p \cdot consCol \cdot fork\ (id, recreate\ j)\\
=\quad&\{(13.6)\}\\
&consCol \cdot pair\ (apply\ p) \cdot fork\ (id, recreate\ j)\\
=\quad&\{\text{since } pair\ f \cdot fork\ (g, h) = fork\ (f \cdot g, f \cdot h)\}\\
&consCol \cdot fork\ (apply\ p, apply\ p \cdot recreate\ j)
\end{aligned}$$

Hence, *recreate* satisfies

$$\begin{aligned}
recreate\ 0\quad &=\quad map\ (const\ [\,])\\
recreate\ (j{+}1)\quad &=\quad consCol \cdot fork\ (apply\ p, apply\ p \cdot recreate\ j)
\end{aligned}$$

In this version of *recreate*, repeated applications of *hdsort* are replaced by repeated applications of *apply p*.

The next step is to use this recursive definition of *recreate* to find an alternative definition of *recreate*. In a word, we *solve* the recursion. We are going to show that

$$recreate\ j\ =\ tp \cdot take\ j \cdot tail \cdot iterate\ (apply\ p) \tag{13.7}$$

is just such a solution. The new ingredient is a function *tp*, short for *transpose*, a standard Haskell function that transposes a matrix. We will need three properties of *tp*:

$$tp \cdot take\ 0\ =\ map\ (const\ [\,]) \tag{13.8}$$
$$tp \cdot take\ (j{+}1)\ =\ consCol \cdot fork\ (head, tp \cdot take\ j \cdot tail) \tag{13.9}$$
$$apply\ p \cdot tp\ =\ tp \cdot map\ (apply\ p) \tag{13.10}$$

Property (13.8) says in effect that the transpose of a $0 \times n$ matrix is an $n \times 0$ matrix. The transpose of an empty list, a list containing no lists of length n, is a list of length n of empty lists. Property (13.9) says that to transpose a $(j{+}1) \times n$ matrix one can prefix the first row as a new first column to the transpose of a $j \times n$ matrix formed from the remaining rows. Finally, (13.10), which can be phrased in the equivalent form

$$apply\ p\ =\ tp \cdot map\ (apply\ p) \cdot tp$$

says that one can apply a permutation to the rows of a matrix by transposing the matrix, applying the permutation to each column and then transposing back again.

Property (13.8) immediately justifies (13.7) in the case $j\ =\ 0$. For the inductive step we start with

$$recreate\ (j{+}1)\ =\ consCol \cdot fork\ (apply\ p, apply\ p \cdot recreate\ j)$$

and reason:

> $fork\ (apply\ p, apply\ p \cdot recreate\ j)$
> $=$ {assuming (13.7)}
> $fork\ (apply\ p, apply\ p \cdot tp \cdot take\ j \cdot tail \cdot iterate\ (apply\ p))$
> $=$ {(13.10)}
> $fork\ (apply\ p, tp \cdot map\ (apply\ p) \cdot take\ j \cdot tail \cdot iterate\ (apply\ p))$
> $=$ {since $map\ f \cdot take\ j = take\ j \cdot map\ f$ and
> $\quad\quad map\ f \cdot tail = tail \cdot map\ f$}
> $fork\ (apply\ p, tp \cdot take\ j \cdot tail \cdot map\ (apply\ p) \cdot iterate\ (apply\ p))$
> $=$ {since $map\ f \cdot iterate\ f = tail \cdot iterate\ f$}
> $fork\ (apply\ p, tp \cdot take\ j \cdot tail \cdot tail \cdot iterate\ (apply\ p))$

$$= \quad \{\text{since } f = head \cdot tail \cdot iterate\ f \text{ and}$$
$$fork\ (f \cdot h, g \cdot h) = fork\ (f, g) \cdot h\}$$
$$fork\ (head, tp \cdot take\ j \cdot tail) \cdot tail \cdot iterate\ (apply\ p)$$

Now we use (13.9) to obtain

$$recreate\ (j{+}1) \quad = \quad tp \cdot take\ (j{+}1) \cdot tail \cdot iterate\ (apply\ p)$$

This completes the proof of (13.7).

We are ready for our last calculation. Recall that

$$untransform\ (ys, k) \quad = \quad (recreate\ n\ ys)\ !!\ k$$

where $n = length\ ys$. We reason:

$$(!!k) \cdot recreate\ n$$
$$= \quad \{(13.7)\}$$
$$(!!k) \cdot tp \cdot take\ n \cdot tail \cdot iterate\ (apply\ p)$$
$$= \quad \{\text{since } (!!k) \cdot tp = map\ (!!k)\}$$
$$map\ (!!k) \cdot take\ n \cdot tail \cdot iterate\ (apply\ p)$$
$$= \quad \{\text{since } map\ f \cdot take\ n = take\ n \cdot map\ f \text{ and}$$
$$map\ f \cdot tail = tail \cdot map\ f\}$$
$$take\ n \cdot tail \cdot map\ (!!k) \cdot iterate\ (apply\ p)$$

For the final step we need a law of *iterate*, namely

$$map\ (\oplus y)\ (iterate\ f\ x) \quad = \quad map\ (x\oplus)\ (iterate\ g\ y)$$

provided that $f\ x \oplus y = x \oplus g\ y$. The proof uses induction on n to show that $f^n\ x \oplus y = x \oplus g^n\ y$; details are left to the reader.

Since $(apply\ p\ ys)\ !!\ k = ys\ !!\ (p\ !!\ k)$, the above law gives

$$map\ (!!k)\ (iterate\ (apply\ p\ ys)) \quad = \quad map\ (ys!!)\ (iterate\ (p!!)\ k)$$

In summary, $untransform\ (ys, k)$ is computed by

$$take\ (length\ ys)\ (tail\ (map\ (ys!!)\ (iterate\ (p!!)\ k)))$$

If only $(!!)$ were a constant-time operation, this computation would take linear time. But $(!!)$ is not constant time, so the dish is not quite ready to leave the kitchen. The very last step is to bring in Haskell arrays:

$$untransform\ (ys, k) \quad = \quad take\ n\ (tail\ (map\ (ya!)\ (iterate\ (pa!)\ k)))$$
$$\textbf{where } n \quad = \quad length\ ys$$
$$ya \quad = \quad listArray\ (0, n{-}1)\ ys$$
$$pa \quad = \quad listArray\ (0, n{-}1)\ (map\ snd\ (sort\ (zip\ ys\ [0..])))$$

The revised definition of *untransform* makes use of the library *Data.Array* of Haskell arrays. The expression *listArray* $(0, n-1)$ *ys* builds an array with bounds 0 to $n-1$ whose values are the elements of *ys*. This function takes linear time. Unlike the list-indexing operation (!!), the array-indexing operation (!) takes constant time. The computation of *pa* takes $\Theta(n \log n)$ steps, but the rest of the computation takes $\Theta(n)$ steps.

Transform revisited

Finally, let us revisit *transform* to see whether we can improve its performance too. The key fact is that sorting the rotations of a list can be expressed in terms of sorting the suffixes of a related list. Suppose *tag xs* = *xs* ++ [*eof*], where *eof* (short for "end of file") is some element guaranteed not to be in the list *xs*. For example, when *xs* is a string, we can take *eof* to be the null character; and when *xs* is a list of natural numbers, we can take $x = -1$. Because *eof* is different from all other elements of *xs*, the permutation that sorts the first n suffixes of *tag xs* is the same permutation that sorts the n rotations of *xs*. Hence:

$$sort \ (rots \ xs) \ = \ apply \ p \ (rots \ xs)$$

where

$$p \ = \ map \ snd \ (sort \ (zip \ (tails \ (tag \ xs)) \ [0 \ .. \ n-1]))$$

The standard function *tails* returns the suffixes or tail segments of a list in decreasing order of length. Now we reason:

$$map \ last \cdot sort \cdot rots$$
$$= \quad \{\text{with above definition of } p\}$$
$$map \ last \cdot apply \ p \cdot rots$$
$$= \quad \{\text{since } map \ f \cdot apply \ p = apply \ p \cdot map \ f\}$$
$$apply \ p \cdot map \ last \cdot rots$$
$$= \quad \{\text{since } map \ last \cdot rots = rrot\}$$
$$apply \ p \cdot rrot$$

Hence, *map last · sort · rots* = *apply p · rrot*. Moreover:

$$position \ xs \ (sort \ (rots \ xs))$$
$$= \quad \{\text{with above definition of } p\}$$
$$position \ xs \ (apply \ p \ (rots \ xs))$$

$$= \quad \{\text{since } position \; xs \; (rots \; xs) = 0\}$$

$$position \; 0 \; p$$

Hence:

$$
\begin{aligned}
transform \; xs \;\; &= \;\; ([xa \,!\, (pa \,!\, i) \mid i \leftarrow [0 \cdots n{-}1]], k) \\
\textbf{where } n \;\; &= \;\; length \; ys \\
k \;\; &= \;\; length \; (take\,While \; (\neq 0) \; ps) \\
xa \;\; &= \;\; listArray \; (0, n{-}1) \; (rrot \; xs) \\
pa \;\; &= \;\; listArray \; (0, n{-}1) \; ps \\
ps \;\; &= \;\; map \; snd \; (sort \; (zip \; (tails \; (tag \; xs))[0 \,..\, n{-}1]))
\end{aligned}
$$

The bottleneck in this algorithm is the computation of ps; apart from that, the rest of the computation takes $\Theta(n)$ steps. As we saw in the previous pearl, finding the permutation that sorts the tails of a list of length n can be done in $\Theta(n \log n)$ steps. In fact, if the list is a list of elements over a fixed finite alphabet, then one can sort its suffixes in linear time by building a suffix tree; see Gusfield (1997).

Final remarks

The BWT was first described by Burrows and Wheeler (1994), though the algorithm was actually discovered by Wheeler in 1983. Nelson (1996), in writing the article that brought the BWT to the world's attention, showed that the resulting compression algorithm could outperform many commercial programs available at the time. The BWT has now been integrated into a high-performance utility `bzip2`, available from `www.bzip.org`. Radix sort is treated in Gibbons (1999), where it is derived using pointless calculation from tree sort.

References

Burrows, M. and Wheeler, D. J. (1994). A block-sorting lossless data compression algorithm. Research report 124, Digital Systems Research Center, Palo Alto, USA.

Gibbons, J. (1999). A pointless derivation of radix sort. *Journal of Functional Programming* **9** (3) 339–46.

Gusfield, D. (1997). *Algorithms on Strings, Trees and Sequences*. Cambridge University Press, Cambridge, UK.

Nelson, M. (1996). Data compression with the Burrows–Wheeler transform. *Dr. Dobb's Journal*, September.

14

The last tail

Introduction

Suppose the tails of a list are sorted into dictionary order. What tail comes last? For example, the last tail of "introduction" is "uction" but the last tail of "tomato" is "tomato" itself, since "to" precedes "tomato" in dictionary order. It follows from an earlier pearl on ranking and sorting suffixes (see Pearl 12) that this problem can be solved in $\Theta(n \log n)$ steps for a list of length n. But can we compute the last tail in $\Theta(n)$ steps? The answer turns out to be yes, but the algorithm is surprisingly complicated for such a simply stated problem, and its derivation seems to require substantial effort. So, be warned.

An inductive definition

Our problem is to compute

$$maxtail \quad :: \quad Ord\ a \Rightarrow [a] \rightarrow [a]$$
$$maxtail \quad = \quad maximum \cdot tails$$

Here, *tails* is the standard Haskell function that returns the possibly empty tails of a possibly empty list, so $maxtail\ [\ ] = [\ ]$. The function *maximum* returns the largest list in lexicographic order. Direct execution of *maxtail* takes quadratic time in the worst case, for example when the list consists of n repetitions of the same value.

Our strategy for doing better is to head for an inductive definition of *maxtail*. That is, we aim to express *maxtail* on a list of length $n+1$ in terms of *maxtail* on a list of length n. Since $maxtail\ [\ ] = [\ ]$, the base case is immediate. For the inductive case the two options are to express $maxtail\ (x : xs)$ in terms of x and $maxtail\ xs$, or to express $maxtail\ (xs \mathbin{+\!\!+} [x])$ in such terms. But, for instance, the maximum suffix of "zebra", namely "zebra" itself, cannot be expressed in terms of "z" and the maximum suffix of "ebra", namely "ra". Hence, we will look for an operation *op* such that

$$maxtail \ (xs + [x]) \quad = \quad op \ (maxtail \ xs) \ x \tag{14.1}$$

In other words, we seek an *op* so that *maxtail* = *foldl op* [ ].

To this end, let *maxtail xs* = *ys* and *maxtail* (*xs* + [*x*]) = *zs* + [*x*]. To satisfy (14.1) we have to show that *zs* ∈ *tails ys*. Since both *ys* and *zs* are tails of *xs* we have *zs* ≤ *ys* and *ys* + [*x*] ≤ *zs* + [*x*] by the definition of *maxtail*. But these inequalities imply that *zs* is a prefix of *ys*; in symbols, *zs* ⊑ *ys*. Suppose *zs* ≤ *ys* but *zs* is not a prefix of *ys*. Let *us* be the longest common prefix of *zs* and *ys*. Then *us* + [*z*] ⊑ *zs* and *us* + [*y*] ⊑ *ys*, where *z* < *y*. In such a case *zs* + [*x*] < *ys* + [*x*].

Thus, *zs* is a prefix of *ys*. But both are tails of *xs*, so *zs* is both a prefix and a suffix of *ys*. Consequently, *op* can be defined in two ways:

$$
\begin{aligned}
op \ ys \ x \quad &= \quad maximum \ [zs + [x] \mid zs \leftarrow tails \ ys] \\
op \ ys \ x \quad &= \quad maximum \ [zs + [x] \mid zs \leftarrow tails \ ys, \ zs \sqsubseteq ys]
\end{aligned}
\tag{14.2}
$$

The first step has been accomplished, though neither definition provides a linear-time algorithm.

Borders

Definition (14.2) of *op* has more structure than its companion and so merits further investigation. Consider the function *borders*, defined by

$$borders \ xs \quad = \quad [ys \mid ys \leftarrow tails \ xs, \ ys \sqsubseteq xs] \tag{14.3}$$

In "stringology" (Crochemore and Rytter, 2003), the *borders* of a list are those suffixes that are also prefixes. Two examples are

$$
\begin{aligned}
borders \ \text{``7412741274''} \quad &= \quad [\text{``7412741274''}, \text{``741274''}, \text{``74''}, \text{``''}] \\
borders \ \text{``mammam''} \quad &= \quad [\text{``mammam''}, \text{``mam''}, \text{``m''}, \text{``''}]
\end{aligned}
$$

Rather than define *border* by (14.3) we can also define

$$
\begin{aligned}
borders \ [\,] \quad &= \quad [[\,]] \\
borders \ xs \quad &= \quad xs : borders \ (border \ xs)
\end{aligned}
$$

where *border xs* is the longest proper common prefix and suffix of *xs*. The second definition has the same form as that of *tails*:

$$
\begin{aligned}
tails \ [\,] \quad &= \quad [[\,]] \\
tails \ xs \quad &= \quad xs : tails \ (tail \ ys)
\end{aligned}
$$

Restated in terms of *borders*, (14.2) now reads:

$$op \ ys \ x \quad = \quad maximum \ [zs + [x] \mid zs \leftarrow borders \ ys]$$

Suppose *borders* $ys = [zs_0, zs_1, \ldots, zs_n]$, so $zs_0 = ys$ and $zs_{i+1} = border\ zs_i$ for $0 \leq i < n$ and $zs_n = [\,]$. Let us see what information we can extract about the value of $op\ ys\ x$ from these ingredients.

First, for $0 \leq i < j \leq n$ we have

$$zs_i \mathbin{+\!\!+} [x] \geq zs_j \mathbin{+\!\!+} [x] \quad \equiv \quad head\ (zs_i \downarrow zs_j) \geq x \tag{14.4}$$

where $us \downarrow vs$ (pronounced "*us* after *vs*") is specified by $(xs \mathbin{+\!\!+} ys) \downarrow xs = ys$. The proof of (14.4) is:

$$\begin{aligned}
& zs_i \mathbin{+\!\!+} [x] \geq zs_j \mathbin{+\!\!+} [x] \\
\equiv\quad & \{\text{definition of lexicographic order since } zs_j \sqsubseteq zs_i\} \\
& (zs_i \downarrow zs_j) \mathbin{+\!\!+} [x] \geq [x] \\
\equiv\quad & \{\text{since } zs_i \downarrow zs_j \text{ is nonempty if } i < j\} \\
& head\ (zs_i \downarrow zs_j) \geq x
\end{aligned}$$

Second, in the case $ys = maxtail\ xs$ for some xs, we have, for $0 < i < j \leq n$, that

$$head\ (zs_{i-1} \downarrow zs_i) \leq head\ (zs_{j-1} \downarrow zs_j) \tag{14.5}$$

The proof is:

$$\begin{aligned}
& head\ (zs_{i-1} \downarrow zs_i) \leq head\ (zs_{j-1} \downarrow zs_j) \\
=\quad & \{\text{since } 0 < k \text{ implies } head\ (zs_{k-1} \downarrow zs_k) = head\ (ys \downarrow zs_k)\} \\
& head\ (ys \downarrow zs_i) \leq head\ (ys \downarrow zs_j) \\
\Leftarrow\quad & \{\text{lexicographic ordering}\} \\
& zs_j \mathbin{+\!\!+} (ys \downarrow zs_i) \leq zs_j \mathbin{+\!\!+} (ys \downarrow zs_j) \\
\equiv\quad & \{\text{since } ys = zs_k \mathbin{+\!\!+} (ys \downarrow zs_k) \text{ for any } k\} \\
& zs_j \mathbin{+\!\!+} (ys \downarrow zs_i) \leq ys \\
\Leftarrow\quad & \{\text{since } ys \text{ is a maximum suffix}\} \\
& zs_j \mathbin{+\!\!+} (ys \downarrow zs_i) \in tails\ ys \\
\equiv\quad & \{\text{since } ys = zs_i \mathbin{+\!\!+} (ys \downarrow zs_i) \text{ and } zs_j \in tails\ zs_i\} \\
& true
\end{aligned}$$

It follows from (14.4) and (14.5) that $op\ ys\ x = zs_i \mathbin{+\!\!+} [x]$, where i is the smallest i in the range $0 \leq i < n$ satisfying $head\ (zs_i \downarrow zs_{i+1}) \geq x$, if such an i exists. If it does not, then $op\ ys\ x = [x]$. A straightforward implementation of the search yields

$$op\ ys\ x\ \ \ |\ \ null\ ys\ \ \ \ \ \ \ \ \ \ \ \ \ \ \ \ =\ \ [x]$$
$$|\ \ head\ (ys \downarrow zs) \geq x\ \ =\ \ ys \mathbin{+\!\!+} [x]$$
$$|\ \ \textbf{otherwise}\ \ \ \ \ \ \ \ \ \ =\ \ op\ zs\ x$$
$$\textbf{where}\ zs = border\ ys$$

To complete this definition of *op* we need to derive a definition of *border*.

Border

Recall that *border ys* is the longest proper common prefix and suffix of *ys*. The value *border ys* is defined only for nonempty *ys*. Heading for an inductive definition, it is clear that $border\ [x] = [\,]$. For the inductive case, $border\ (ys \mathbin{+\!\!+} [x])$, we need the following property of the prefix ordering:

$$zs \mathbin{+\!\!+} [x] \sqsubseteq ys \mathbin{+\!\!+} [x]\ \ \equiv\ \ zs \sqsubseteq ys \wedge (zs \neq ys \Rightarrow x = head\ (ys \downarrow zs))$$

We now reason, for nonempty *ys*:

$$borders\ (ys \mathbin{+\!\!+} [x])$$
$$=\ \ \ \ \{(14.3)\}$$
$$[zs \mid zs \leftarrow tails\ (ys \mathbin{+\!\!+} [x]),\ zs \sqsubseteq ys \mathbin{+\!\!+} [x]]$$
$$=\ \ \ \ \{\text{since } tails\ (ys \mathbin{+\!\!+} [x]) = map\ (\mathbin{+\!\!+} [x])\ (tails\ ys) \mathbin{+\!\!+} [[\,]]\}$$
$$[zs \mathbin{+\!\!+} [x] \mid zs \leftarrow tails\ ys,\ zs \mathbin{+\!\!+} [x] \sqsubseteq ys \mathbin{+\!\!+} [x]] \mathbin{+\!\!+} [[\,]]$$
$$=\ \ \ \ \{\text{above property}\}$$
$$[zs \mathbin{+\!\!+} [x] \mid zs \leftarrow tails\ ys,\ zs \sqsubseteq ys,\ zs \neq ys \Rightarrow x = head\ (ys \downarrow zs)] \mathbin{+\!\!+}$$
$$[[\,]]$$
$$=\ \ \ \ \{(14.3)\}$$
$$[zs \mathbin{+\!\!+} [x] \mid zs \leftarrow borders\ ys,\ zs \neq ys \Rightarrow x = head\ (ys \downarrow zs)] \mathbin{+\!\!+} [[\,]]$$

Hence, since $border = head \cdot tail \cdot borders$ and $head \cdot borders = id$, we obtain

$$border\ (ys \mathbin{+\!\!+} [x])$$
$$=\ \ head\ ([zs \mathbin{+\!\!+} [x] \mid zs \leftarrow tail\ (borders\ ys),\ x = head\ (ys \downarrow zs)] \mathbin{+\!\!+} [[\,]])$$

This list comprehension can be replaced by an explicit search:

$$border\ (ys \mathbin{+\!\!+} [x])\ \ \ |\ \ head\ (ys \downarrow zs) \mathbin{==} x\ \ =\ \ zs \mathbin{+\!\!+} [x]$$
$$|\ \ \textbf{otherwise}\ \ \ \ \ \ \ \ \ \ \ =\ \ border\ (zs \mathbin{+\!\!+} [x])$$
$$\textbf{where}\ zs = border\ ys$$

Under the assumption that $ys = maxtail\ xs$ for some xs, we can appeal to (14.5) and optimize the search:

$$
\begin{array}{lll}
border\ (ys \mathbin{+\!\!+} [x]) & \mid\ head\ (ys \downarrow zs) < x & =\quad border\ (zs \mathbin{+\!\!+} [x]) \\
& \mid\ head\ (ys \downarrow zs) == x & =\quad zs \mathbin{+\!\!+} [x] \\
& \mid\ head\ (ys \downarrow zs) > x & =\quad [\,] \\
& \mathbf{where}\ zs = border\ ys &
\end{array}
$$

The recursive definitions of *maxtail* and *border* have turned out to be similar, so logically the next step is to combine them into one function.

Cocktail

Consider the function *cocktail* (a combination of two ingredients!) defined by

$$
\begin{array}{ll}
cocktail\ xs\ =\ & \mathbf{if}\ null\ xs\ \mathbf{then}\ ([\,],[\,])\ \mathbf{else} \\
& (border\ (maxtail\ xs),\ maxtail\ xs \downarrow border\ (maxtail\ xs))
\end{array}
$$

In particular, $maxtail = uncurry\ (\mathbin{+\!\!+}) \cdot cocktail$.

We now derive a recursive definition of *cocktail*, using the recursive definitions of *maxtail* and *border*. Setting $cocktail\ xs = (zs, ws)$, we compute $cocktail\ (xs \mathbin{+\!\!+} [x])$ by a case analysis.

Case $ws = [\,]$. In this case $xs = ys = zs = [\,]$, so

$$cocktail\ (xs \mathbin{+\!\!+} [x])\ =\ ([\,],[x])$$

In the remaining cases, where $ws \neq [\,]$, we have $ys = maxtail\ xs$, where $ys = zs \mathbin{+\!\!+} ws$, and $zs = border\ ys$, so $ws = ys \downarrow zs$.

Case $head\ ws < x$. In this case the definition *maxtail* gives

$$maxtail\ (xs \mathbin{+\!\!+} [x])\ =\ maxtail\ (zs \mathbin{+\!\!+} [x])$$

so $cocktail\ (xs \mathbin{+\!\!+} [x]) = cocktail\ (zs \mathbin{+\!\!+} [x])$.

Case $head\ ws = x$. In this case

$$
\begin{array}{lll}
maxtail\ (xs \mathbin{+\!\!+} [x]) & = & ys \mathbin{+\!\!+} [x] \\
border\ (ys \mathbin{+\!\!+} [x]) & = & zs \mathbin{+\!\!+} [x]
\end{array}
$$

Since $(ys \mathbin{+\!\!+} [x]) \downarrow (zs \mathbin{+\!\!+} [x]) = tail\ ws \mathbin{+\!\!+} [x]$, we have

$$cocktail\ (xs \mathbin{+\!\!+} [x])\ =\ (zs \mathbin{+\!\!+} [x],\ tail\ ws \mathbin{+\!\!+} [x])$$

Case $head\ ws > x$. In this case

$$
\begin{array}{lll}
maxtail\ (xs \mathbin{+\!\!+} [x]) & = & ys \mathbin{+\!\!+} [x] \\
border\ (ys \mathbin{+\!\!+} [x]) & = & [\,]
\end{array}
$$

so $cocktail\ (xs \mathbin{+\!\!+} [x]) = ([\,],\ ys \mathbin{+\!\!+} [x])$.

In summary, we have shown that

$$maxtail = uncurry \ (+\!\!+) \cdot cocktail$$
$$cocktail = foldl \ op \ ([\,],[\,])$$

$$
\begin{array}{llll}
op \ (zs, ws) \ x & | \ null \ ws & = & ([\,],[x]) \\
& | \ w < x & = & cocktail \ (zs +\!\!+ [x]) \\
& | \ w == x & = & (zs +\!\!+ [x], tail \ ws +\!\!+ [x]) \\
& | \ w > x & = & ([\,], zs +\!\!+ ws +\!\!+ [x]) \\
& \mathbf{where} \ w = head \ ws
\end{array}
$$

So far, so good, but the new version of *maxtail* still takes quadratic time. One reason is that $(+\!\!+)$ is not a constant-time operation. But even assuming it were, the computation would still be quadratic. Consider an input of the form $1^n 2$, where 1^n denotes n repetitions of 1. After n steps the computation of *cocktail* $1^n 2$ reduces to evaluation of $op \ (1^{n-1}, 1) \ 2$. Since $1 < 2$, the next step is to evaluate *cocktail* $1^{n-1} 2$. Hence, the total computation takes quadratic time.

The problem lies with the call *cocktail* $(zs +\!\!+ [x])$. If we could somehow restrict the length of zs to be at most half the length of the current maximum tail $ys = zs +\!\!+ ws$, then computation of *cocktail* would take linear time (ignoring the cost of the $+\!\!+$ operations). Spending a linear amount of time to reduce a problem to one of at most half the size leads to a linear-time algorithm. Fortunately, as we will now show, the length of zs can be so restricted.

Reducing the problem size

Let *cocktail* $xs = (zs, ws)$, so $ys = zs +\!\!+ ws$ is the maximum tail of xs and $zs = border \ ys$. Suppose $|zs| \geq |ws|$, where $|xs|$ denotes the length of xs. In this case ws is a tail of zs. For example, if $ys = $ "7412741274", then $zs = $ "741274" and $ws = $ "1274".

Define zs' by $zs = zs' +\!\!+ ws$. Then zs' is both a prefix and a tail of zs and hence also a prefix and tail of ys. In the example above, $zs' = $ "74". The reasoning can be repeated if $|zs'| \geq |ws|$. It follows that if we define q and r by

$$(q, r) = (|zs| \ \mathrm{div} \ |ws|, |zs| \ \mathrm{mod} \ |ws|)$$

and set $zs' = take \ r \ zs$, then $zs' \in borders \ ys$ and $zs = zs' +\!\!+ ws^q$, where ws^q is the concatenation of q copies of ws. Furthermore, since $|zs'| < |ws|$ we have that zs' is a tail of ws (so $zs' = drop \ (|ws| - r) \ ws$, a fact we will exploit below) and each of $zs' +\!\!+ ws^p$ for $1 \leq p < q$ are also borders of zs.

But $(zs' \mathbin{+\!\!+} ws^p) \downarrow (zs' \mathbin{+\!\!+} ws^{p-1}) = ws$, so in the case *head ws* $< x$ none of these borders need be inspected in the computation of *op* $(zs, ws)\ x$. It follows that we can replace *op* by

$$
\begin{array}{llll}
op\ (zs, ws)\ x & |\ \ null\ ws & = & ([\,], [x]) \\
 & |\ \ w < x & = & cocktail\ (take\ r\ zs \mathbin{+\!\!+} [x]) \\
 & |\ \ w == x & = & (zs \mathbin{+\!\!+} [x],\ tail\ ws \mathbin{+\!\!+} [x]) \\
 & |\ \ w > x & = & ([\,],\ zs \mathbin{+\!\!+} ws \mathbin{+\!\!+} [x]) \\
 & \mathbf{where}\ w & = & head\ ws \\
 & \qquad\quad r & = & (length\ zs)\ \mathrm{mod}\ (length\ ws)
\end{array}
$$

Moreover, $2r < |zs \mathbin{+\!\!+} ws|$, since $r \leq |zs|$ and $r < |ws|$. Armed with this fact we can show that computation of *cocktail xs* involves a total of at most $2n - m$ calls to *op*, where $n = |xs|$ and $m = |maxtail\ xs|$.

The proof is by induction. In the case $n = 0$ we have $m = 0$ and there are no calls to *op*. When $n = 1$ we have $m = 1$ and there is one call to *op*. This establishes the base cases.

For the inductive case, consider the computation of *cocktail* $(xs \mathbin{+\!\!+} [x])$, which first evaluates *cocktail xs* and then computes *op* $(cocktail\ xs)\ x$. Assume by induction that *cocktail xs* involves $2n - m$ calls of *op* and returns (zs, ws), where $|zs \mathbin{+\!\!+} ws| = m$ and *head ws* $= w$. If $w \geq x$ there are no more calls of *op*, so the total count is $2n - m + 1$. But in this case the resulting maximum tail has length $m+1$, and as $2n - m + 1 = 2(n+1) - (m+1)$ the case is established. If $w < x$, then we have to add in the count for *cocktail* $(take\ r\ zs \mathbin{+\!\!+} [x])$. By induction, this is $2(r+1) - m'$, where m' is the length of the final maximum tail. The total, therefore, is $2n - m + 1 + 2(r+1) - m'$, which is at most $2(n+1) - m'$ since $2r + 1 \leq m$.

Hence, ignoring the cost of *length* and $\mathbin{+\!\!+}$ operations, the computation of *cocktail* and *maxtail* take linear time. It remains to eliminate the *length* and $\mathbin{+\!\!+}$ operations.

Final optimisations

We first eliminate the length calculations in the definition of *op*, together with the first $\mathbin{+\!\!+}$ in the final clause. This is achieved by a data refinement in which the state (zs, ws) is replaced by a quadruple (p, q, ys, ws) in which $ys = zs \mathbin{+\!\!+} ws$ and $p = length\ zs$ and $q = length\ ws$. The reason we can drop the argument zs is that $take\ r\ zs = drop\ (q - r)\ ws$. We need, however, to retain the length of zs. Installing this change is easy and we omit details. It leads to the program of Figure 14.1, in which *cocktail* now names the refined version and *thd* selects the third component of a quadruple.

$$
\begin{aligned}
\textit{maxtail} &= \textit{thd} \cdot \textit{cocktail} \\
\textit{cocktail} &= \textit{foldl op} \, (0, 0, [\,], [\,])
\end{aligned}
$$

$$
\begin{aligned}
\textit{op} \, (p, q, ys, ws) \, x & \\
\mid \quad q == 0 \quad &= \quad (0, 1, [x], [x]) \\
\mid \quad w < x \quad &= \quad \textit{cocktail} \, (\textit{drop} \, (q - r) \, ws \mathbin{+\!\!+} [x]) \\
\mid \quad w == x \quad &= \quad (p{+}1, q, ys \mathbin{+\!\!+} [x], \textit{tail} \, ws \mathbin{+\!\!+} [x]) \\
\mid \quad \mathbf{otherwise} \quad &= \quad (0, p{+}q{+}1, ys \mathbin{+\!\!+} [x], ys \mathbin{+\!\!+} [x]) \\
\mathbf{where} \; w \quad &= \quad \textit{head ws} \\
r \quad &= \quad p \bmod q
\end{aligned}
$$

Fig. 14.1 The result of data refinement

Now we are left only with $(\mathbin{+\!\!+}[x])$ operations. One way to ensure that $(\mathbin{+\!\!+}[x])$ takes constant time is to convert all the lists into queues and to use an efficient implementation of queues that guarantees insertion at the rear of the queue as well as that removal from the front takes constant time. But another method is suggested by the observation that each of the lists ys and ws arising during the computation of *cocktail xs* is a tail of xs. The operation op constructs these tails step by step, but a more efficient method is to construct them all at once. The way to do this is to convert what we have into an iterative algorithm.

More precisely, suppose we define *step* by

$$
\textit{step} \, (p, q, ys', ws', xs) \quad = \quad \textit{thd} \, (\textit{foldl op} \, (p, q, ys' \uparrow xs, ws' \uparrow xs) \, xs)
$$

where $us \uparrow vs$ (pronounced "*us* before *vs*") is what remains when the tail vs of us is removed from us. Thus, $us = (us \uparrow vs) \mathbin{+\!\!+} vs$. In particular:

$$
\begin{aligned}
\textit{maxtail} \, (x : xs) \quad &= \quad \textit{thd} \, (\textit{foldl op} \, (0, 1, [x], [x]) \, xs) \\
&= \quad \textit{thd} \, (\textit{foldl op} \, (0, 1, (x : xs) \uparrow xs, (x : xs) \uparrow xs) \, xs) \\
&= \quad \textit{step} \, (0, 1, x : xs, x : xs, xs)
\end{aligned}
$$

Next we derive a recursion for *step* (p, q, ys', ws', xs). Since $us \uparrow [\,] = us$ we obtain

$$
\textit{step} \, (p, q, ys', ws', [\,]) \quad = \quad ys'
$$

In the case that xs is not empty (so neither of ys' or ws' is empty) we have

$$
\begin{aligned}
\textit{step} \, &(p, q, ys', ws', x : xs) \\
&= \quad \textit{thd} \, (\textit{foldl op} \, (p, q, ys' \uparrow (x : xs), ws' \uparrow (x : xs)) \, (x : xs)) \\
&= \quad \textit{thd} \, (\textit{foldl op} \, (op \, (p, q, ys' \uparrow (x : xs), ws' \uparrow (x : xs)) \, x) \, xs)
\end{aligned}
$$

Now we need a case analysis.

Case $head\ (ws' \uparrow (x : xs)) < x$. In this case

$$op\ (p, q, ys' \uparrow (x : xs), ws' \uparrow (x : xs))\ x =$$
$$cocktail'\ (drop\ (q{-}r)\ (ws' \uparrow (x : xs)) \mathbin{+\!\!+} [x])$$

where $r = p \bmod q$. Abbreviating $drop\ (q{-}r)\ (ws' \uparrow (x : xs))$ to vs, we argue

$$step\ (p, q, ys', ws', x : xs)$$
$=$ {definition and case assumption}
$$thd\ (foldl\ op\ (cocktail'\ (vs \mathbin{+\!\!+} [x])))\ xs)$$
$=$ {definition of $cocktail'$}
$$thd\ (foldl\ op\ (foldl\ op\ (0, 0, [\,], [\,], [\,])\ (vs \mathbin{+\!\!+} [x])))\ xs)$$
$=$ {since $foldl\ f\,(foldl\ f\ e\ xs)\ ys = foldl\ f\ e\ (xs \mathbin{+\!\!+} ys)$}
$$thd\ (foldl\ op\ ([\,], [\,], [\,])\ (vs \mathbin{+\!\!+} x : xs))$$
$=$ {since $drop\ (q{-}r)\ (ws' \uparrow (x : xs)) \mathbin{+\!\!+} x : xs = drop\ (q{-}r)\ ws'$}
$$thd\ (foldl\ op\ ([\,], [\,], [\,])\ (drop\ (q{-}r)\ ws'))$$
$=$ {definition of $maxtail$}
$$maxtail\ (drop\ (q{-}r)\ ws')$$

Case $head\ (ws' \uparrow (x : xs)) = x$. In this case

$$op\ (p, q, ys' \uparrow (x : xs), ws' \uparrow (x : xs))\ x =$$
$$(p{+}1, q, ys' \uparrow (x : xs) \mathbin{+\!\!+} [x], tail\ (ws' \uparrow (x : xs)) \mathbin{+\!\!+} [x])$$
$$=\ (p{+}1, q, ys' \uparrow xs, tail\ (ws' \uparrow xs))$$

Hence, $step\ (p, q, ys', ws', x : xs) = (p{+}1, q, ys', tail\ ws', xs)$.

Case $head\ (ws' \uparrow (x : xs)) > x$. In this case

$$op\ (p, q, ys' \uparrow (x : xs), ws' \uparrow (x : xs))\ x =$$
$$(0, p{+}q{+}1, ys' \uparrow (x : xs) \mathbin{+\!\!+} [x], ys' \uparrow (x : xs) \mathbin{+\!\!+} [x])$$
$$=\ (0, p{+}q{+}1, ys' \uparrow xs, ys' \uparrow xs)$$

Hence, $step\ (p, q, ys', ws', x : xs) = (0, p{+}q{+}1, ys', ys', xs)$.

Summarising all the above, we have arrived at our final program:

$$maxtail\ [\,] \qquad = \quad [\,]$$
$$maxtail\ (x : xs) \quad = \quad step\ (0, 1, x : xs, x : xs, xs)$$

$step\ (p, q, ys, ws, [\ ])\ =\ ys$

$step\ (p, q, ys, w : ws, x : xs)$

$\quad|\quad w < x\quad =\quad maxtail\ (drop\ (q{-}r)\ (w : ws))$

$\quad|\quad w == x\quad =\quad step\ (p{+}1, q, ys, ws, xs)$

$\quad|\quad w > x\quad =\quad step\ (0, p{+}q{+}1, ys, ys, xs)$

$\quad$**where** $r = p \bmod q$

Final remarks

It is very easy to turn the final version of *maxtail* into a simple while loop. Perhaps this is not surprising, because we set out with the intention of deriving an inductive definition, and the form we were led to, namely an instance of *foldl*, is essentially a while loop in functional clothing. Nevertheless, the final algorithm has a very imperative feel, and it would be interesting to see a derivation in a procedural style using loop invariants. Our derivation was quite long and involved some fairly subtle reasoning, basically because a good deal of underlying structure is inherent in the problem. But maybe there is a simpler solution to what must be the shortest specification in this book.

References

Crochemore, M. and Rytter, W. (2003). *Jewels of Stringology*. Hong Kong: World Scientific.

15

All the common prefixes

Introduction

Let *llcp xs ys* denote the length of the longest common prefix of two lists *xs* and *ys*. For example *llcp* "common" "computing" = 3. Now consider the function *allcp*, short for all the common prefixes, defined by

$$allcp\ xs\ =\ map\ (llcp\ xs)\ (tails\ xs)$$

where *tails xs* returns the nonempty tails of *xs*. For example:

xs	*a*	*b*	*a*	*c*	*a*	*b*	*a*	*c*	*a*	*b*
allcp xs	10	0	1	0	6	0	1	0	2	0

The first element of *allcp xs* is, of course, *length xs*. Executed directly, the definition of *allcp* gives a quadratic-time algorithm. But can it be done in linear time? Yes it can, and the aim of this pearl is to show how. The function *allcp* is an important component of the Boyer–Moore algorithm for string matching, a problem we will take up in the following pearl, so a linear-time solution is of practical as well as theoretical interest.

A key property

The key property of *llcp* on which the fast algorithm rests is the following one. Let *us*, *vs* and *ws* be any three lists. Then, with *llcp us vs* = *m* and *llcp vs ws* = *n*, we have

$$llcp\ us\ ws\ =\ \begin{cases} min\ m\ n & \text{if } m \neq n \\ m + llcp\ (drop\ m\ us)\ (drop\ m\ ws) & \text{if } m = n \end{cases} \quad (15.1)$$

For the proof, observe that the first *min m n* elements are common to all three lists. If *m* < *n*, then the next element of *us* (if any) is different from the next element of *vs*, while the next element of *vs* is the same as the next element of *ws*. Hence *llcp us ws* = *m*. The reasoning is dual if *m* > *n*. Finally, if *m* = *n*, then matching has to continue with *drop m us* and *drop m ws*.

To use (15.1), take i and j in the range $1 \leq i, j < n$, where $n = length\ xs$, and let

$$p = llcp\ xs\ (drop\ i\ xs)$$
$$q = llcp\ xs\ (drop\ j\ xs)$$

In other words, the elements at positions i and j in *allcp xs* are p and q respectively. Furthermore, suppose $j \leq p$. Then, by definition of *llcp*, we have

$$p = j + llcp\ (drop\ j\ xs)\ (drop\ (i+j)\ xs)$$

Setting $us = xs$, $vs = drop\ j\ xs$ and $ws = drop\ k\ xs$, where $k = i + j$, (15.1) now gives

$$llcp\ xs\ (drop\ k\ xs) = \begin{cases} min\ (p{-}j)\ q & \text{if } q \neq p{-}j \\ q + llcp\ (drop\ q\ xs)\ (drop\ (q{+}k)\ xs) & \text{if } q = p{-}j \end{cases}$$

In other words, we can determine the kth entry in *allcp xs* from the ith and jth entries with either no extra work (the first clause) or with maybe a little extra work (the second clause). Of course, work is avoided only if $1 < i < k$ and $j = k{-}i < p$ because the second clause gives no computational shortcut if $j = p$. In particular, the cases $k = 0$ and $k = 1$ have to be calculated directly.

Here is how we use this information to compute the kth entry of *allcp* in the order $k = 1, 2, \ldots, n$. Suppose at each step we choose i by the condition that $i + p$ is as large as possible subject to $1 \leq i < k$. If $k < i + p$, then the shortcut above applies with $j = k - i$. If $k \geq i + p$, then there is no alternative but to calculate *llcp xs* $(drop\ k\ xs)$ directly. We can start off with $(i, p) = (0, 0)$ to ensure the case $k = 1$ is computed directly, and thereafter update (i, p) whenever a better choice is found.

All that leads to the program of Figure 15.1, which takes the form of a simple loop. To check that i and p are updated correctly, observe in the first clause of *step* that $k \geq i{+}p \Rightarrow k{+}a \geq i{+}p$, and in the third clause that $k{+}b \geq k{+}q = k{+}r = i{+}p$.

We claim that this program takes linear time under the assumption that each *snoc*, !! and *drop* operation takes constant time. To prove the claim it suffices to show that the total number of equality comparisons in *llcp* is linear in n. Such comparisons result in *True* (a match) or *False* (a mismatch). Each call of *step* ends with at most one mismatch, so there are at most $n - 1$ mismatches. To bound the number of matches, observe that in any step in which m matches occur, so $a = m$ or $b = m$, the value of $i{+}p$ is increased by m at least. Since $i{+}p \leq n$, the total number of matches is at most n.

$$allcp \ xs \ = \ fst4 \ (until \ (done \ n) \ (step \ xs) \ ([n], 0, 0, 1))$$
$$\textbf{where} \ n = length \ xs$$

$$done \ n \ (as, i, p, k) \ = \ k \mathbin{==} n$$

$$step \ xs \ (as, i, p, k)$$
$$\begin{array}{rll}
\mid & k \geq i + p & = \ (snoc \ as \ a, k, a, k + 1) \\
\mid & q \neq r & = \ (snoc \ as \ (min \ q \ r), i, p, k + 1) \\
\mid & q \mathbin{==} r & = \ (snoc \ as \ b, k, b, k + 1) \\
& \textbf{where} \ q & = \ as \mathbin{!!} (k - i) \\
& r & = \ p - (k - i) \\
& a & = \ llcp \ xs \ (drop \ k \ xs) \\
& b & = \ q + llcp \ (drop \ q \ xs) \ (drop \ (q + k) \ xs)
\end{array}$$

$$\begin{array}{rl}
fst4 \ (a, b, c, d) & = \ a \\
snoc \ xs \ x & = \ xs \mathbin{+\!\!+} [x]
\end{array}$$

$$\begin{array}{rl}
llcp \ xs \ [\,] & = \ 0 \\
llcp \ [\,] \ ys & = \ 0 \\
llcp \ (x : xs) \ (y : ys) & = \ \textbf{if} \ x \mathbin{==} y \ \textbf{then} \ 1 + llcp \ xs \ ys \ \textbf{else} \ 0
\end{array}$$

Fig. 15.1 The initial program

Data refinement

However, *snoc*, (!!), and *drop* do not take constant time. The remainder of the development is just data refinement to ensure that they can be implemented by constant-time operations.

Let us deal with *drop* first. The idea is to bring in the library *Data.Array* of Haskell arrays and replace *llcp* by another version that uses index operations on a (global) array $xa = listArray \ (0, n - 1) \ xs$, where $n = length \ xs$:

$$llcp' \ j \ k \ \begin{array}[t]{ll}
\mid \ j \mathbin{==} n \lor k \mathbin{==} n & = \ 0 \\
\mid \ xa \mathbin{!} j \mathbin{==} xa \mathbin{!} k & = \ 1 + llcp' \ (j + 1) \ (k + 1) \\
\mid \ \textbf{otherwise} & = \ 0
\end{array}$$

That means we can replace the definitions of a and b in *step* by

$$\begin{array}{rl}
a & = \ llcp' \ 0 \ k \\
b & = \ q + llcp' \ q \ (q + k)
\end{array}$$

It remains to deal with the *snoc* and (!!) operations. The obvious step is again to use an array. However, adding an element to the end of an array is only a constant-time operation if we embed the whole computation in a suitable monad, and that is something we choose to avoid. Another option is to use Haskell's *Data.Sequence* library. This library provides a constant-time *snoc*, but only a logarithmic-time indexing operation. Good enough in

$$
\begin{array}{lll}
allcp\ xs & = & extract\ (until\ done\ step\ (as, empty, 0, 1)))
\end{array}
$$

where

$$
\begin{array}{lll}
extract\ (as, qs, h, k) & = & elems\ as \\
done\ (as, qs, h, k) & = & (k \mathrel{==} n) \\
n & = & length\ xs \\
as & = & insert\ empty\ n \\
xa & = & listArray\ (0, n{-}1)\ xs
\end{array}
$$

$$
\begin{array}{lll}
step\ (as, qs, h, k) & \mid & k \geq h\ = \ (insert\ as\ a, insert\ as'\ a, k + a, k + 1) \\
& \mid & q \neq r\ = \ (insert\ as\ m, insert\ qs'\ m, h, k + 1) \\
& \mid & q \mathrel{==} r\ = \ (insert\ as\ b, insert\ as'\ b, k + b, k + 1)
\end{array}
$$

$$
\begin{array}{lll}
\textbf{where}\ as' & = & snd\ (remove\ as) \\
(q, qs') & = & remove\ qs \\
r & = & h - k \\
m & = & min\ q\ r \\
a & = & llcp'\ 0\ k \\
b & = & q + llcp'\ q\ (q + k)
\end{array}
$$

$$
\begin{array}{lll}
llcp'\ j\ k & \mid & j \mathrel{==} n \vee k \mathrel{==} n = 0 \\
& \mid & xa\ !\ j \mathrel{==} xa\ !\ k = 1 + llcp\ (j + 1)\ (k + 1) \\
& \mid & \textbf{otherwise} = 0
\end{array}
$$

Fig. 15.2 The final program

---

practice, but we promised a linear-time solution, so we have to work a little harder.

Our solution is to use a queue, in fact two of them. Chris Okasaki's implementation of queues (Okasaki, 1995) provides a type *Queue a* with the following four operations:

$$
\begin{array}{lll}
insert & :: & Queue\ a \rightarrow a \rightarrow Queue\ a \\
remove & :: & Queue\ a \rightarrow (a, Queue\ a) \\
empty & :: & Queue\ a \\
elems & :: & Queue\ a \rightarrow [a]
\end{array}
$$

The function *insert* inserts a new element at the rear of the queue, *remove* returns the first element and the remaining elements of a nonempty queue, *empty* gives an empty queue, and *elems* returns the list of elements in a queue. The first three operations take constant time, while *elems* takes time proportional to the length of the queue.

We replace the component *as* in the argument of *step* with a queue, also called *as*, and add in a second queue *qs*, representing the suffix $drop\,(k{-}i)\,as$. Then $q = as\,!!\,(k - i)$ is the first element of *qs*. There is no need to maintain argument i, so we can remove it and replace p by $h = i + p$. Installing these changes is straightforward and leads to the final program of Figure 15.2.

Final remarks

The problem of computing *allcp* is identified as the fundamental preprocessing step of string matching by Gusfield (1997), where it is called "the
Z algorithm". The same problem is dealt with by Crochemore and Rytter,
under the name "table of prefixes". Our treatment follows Gusfield quite
closely, except for the identification of (15.1) as the key property of *llcp* that
enables everything to work, and the use of queues to make the *snoc* and !!
operations efficient.

References

Crochemore, M. and Rytter, W. (2003). *Jewels of Stringology*. Hong Kong: World
    Scientific.
Gusfield, D. (1997). *Algorithms on Strings, Trees and Sequences*. Cambridge, UK:
    Cambridge University Press.
Okasaki, C. (1995). Simple and efficient purely functional queues and deques. *Jour-
    nal of Functional Programming*, **5** (4), 583–92.

16

The Boyer–Moore algorithm

Introduction

The problem of string matching consists of finding all occurrences of one nonempty string, called the *pattern*, in another string, called the *text*. Here is the specification:

$$matches \quad :: \quad Eq \ a \Rightarrow [a] \rightarrow [a] \rightarrow [Int]$$
$$matches \ ws \quad = \quad map \ length \cdot filter \ (endswith \ ws) \cdot inits$$

The function *inits* returns a list of the prefixes of the text in order of increasing length. The expression *endswith ws xs* tests whether the pattern *ws* is a suffix of *xs*. The value *matches ws xs* is a list of integers p such that *ws* is a suffix of *take p xs*. For example:

$$matches \ \text{``abcab''} \ \text{``ababcabcab''} \quad = \quad [7, 10]$$

In other words, *matches ws xs* returns a list integers p such that *ws* appears in *xs* ending at position p (counting positions from 1).

The function *matches* is polymorphic, so any algorithm for the problem has to rely only on an equality test $(==) :: a \rightarrow a \rightarrow Bool$ for information about the elements of the two lists. Polymorphic string matching rules out any algorithm that depends upon a being finite. Assuming it takes constant time to carry out an equality test, the running time of *matches ws xs* is $\Theta(mn)$ steps in the worst case, where $m = length \ ws$ and $n = length \ xs$. Our aim in this pearl is to derive the famous Boyer–Moore (BM) algorithm for string matching, which reduces the time to $\Theta(m + n)$ steps. In the following pearl we will derive the equally famous Knuth–Morris–Pratt (KMP) algorithm for the same problem with the same complexity. And the trick is simply to apply appropriate efficiency-improving laws dictated by the form of the expression under manipulation.

The scan lemma

For string matching, indeed for any problem involving the function *inits*, the most important law is known as the *scan lemma*:

$$map\ (foldl\ op\ e) \cdot inits\ \ =\ \ scanl\ op\ e$$

The expression on the left is evaluated on a list of length n with $\Theta(n^2)$ evaluations of *op*, while the equivalent expression in terms of the standard Haskell function *scanl* requires only $\Theta(n)$ evaluations.

Although there is a *map* in the definition of *matches*, there is also a *filter*, so the first step in transforming *matches* is to rewrite the specification using another law:

$$map\ f \cdot filter\ p\ \ =\ \ map\ fst \cdot filter\ snd \cdot map\ (fork\ (f, p)) \qquad (16.1)$$

where *fork* $(f, p)\ x = (f\ x, p\ x)$. The law is used simply to bring a *map* next to *inits* in preparation for applying the scan lemma. Use of (16.1) leads to

$$\begin{aligned} &matches\ ws\\ &=\ \ map\ fst \cdot filter\ snd \cdot map\ (fork\ (length, endswith\ ws)) \cdot inits \end{aligned}$$

The next question to ask is: can *fork* (*length*, *endswith ws*) be cast as an instance of *foldl*? Certainly, *length* = *foldl count* 0 where *count* $n\ x = n + 1$. Suppose for the moment that we can also find e and *op*, both of which will depend on *ws*, so that

$$endswith\ ws\ \ =\ \ foldl\ op\ e \qquad (16.2)$$

Then we are in a position to apply another standard law: the tupling law for *foldl*. This law states that

$$fork\ (foldl\ op1\ e1, foldl\ op2\ e2)\ \ =\ \ foldl\ op\ (e1, e2)$$

where *op* $(a, b)\ x = (op1\ a\ x, op2\ b\ x)$. Use of the tupling law results in

$$\begin{aligned} fork\ (length, endswith\ ws)\ \ &=\ \ foldl\ step\ (0, e)\\ step\ (n, x)\ y\ \ &=\ \ (n + 1, op\ x\ y) \end{aligned}$$

Finally, we can apply the scan lemma to arrive at

$$matches\ ws\ \ =\ \ map\ fst \cdot filter\ snd \cdot scanl\ step\ (0, e)$$

If *op* takes constant time, or at least amortized constant time, then so does *step*, and the result is a linear-time program. That, in a nutshell, is the genesis of all efficient polymorphic string-matching algorithms.

The problem is that there is no *op* and e to satisfy (16.2). The function *endswith ws* returns a single Boolean value and this is insufficient information to express it as an instance of *foldl*. The next best thing is to express *endswith ws* as a composition

$$endswith\ ws\ \ =\ \ p \cdot foldl\ op\ e \qquad\qquad (16.3)$$

The form of (16.3) is dictated solely by the desire to apply the scan lemma. Instead of (16.1) we can use a slight generalisation:

$$map\ f \cdot filter\ (p \cdot g)\ \ =\ \ map\ fst \cdot filter\ (p \cdot snd) \cdot map\ (fork\ (f, g))\ \ (16.4)$$

Then we obtain

$$matches\ ws\ \ =\ \ map\ fst \cdot filter\ (p \cdot snd) \cdot scanl\ step\ (0,\ e)$$

Provided *p* and *op* take amortized constant time, *matches* will still take linear time.

What remains is to find *p*, *op* and *e* to satisfy (16.3). But we have not yet defined *endswith* formally. Here are two reasonable definitions:

$$endswith\ ws\ xs\ \ =\ \ reverse\ ws \sqsubseteq reverse\ xs$$
$$endswith\ ws\ xs\ \ =\ \ ws \in tails\ xs$$

In the first definition, $us \sqsubseteq vs$ if *us* is a prefix of *vs*. It is clear that *ws* is a suffix of *xs* if and only if the reverse of *ws* is a prefix of the reverse of *xs*. The prefix relation is easier to implement than the suffix relation:

$$[\,]\sqsubseteq vs \qquad\qquad =\ \ True$$
$$(u : us) \sqsubseteq [\,] \qquad =\ \ False$$
$$(u : us) \sqsubseteq (v : vs)\ \ =\ \ (u == v \wedge us \sqsubseteq vs)$$

Although both definitions of *endswith* define the same function, they have different forms. And, since it is form rather than function that dictates the course of development, we are at a crossroads. As we will see, taking the first path leads to the BM algorithm, while taking the second leads to the KMP algorithm. In the rest of this pearl we will take the first path. In the following pearl we will explore the second path.

The Boyer–Moore algorithm

The first definition of *endswith* can be restated as a composition:

$$endswith\ ws\ \ =\ \ (reverse\ ws \sqsubseteq\ ) \cdot reverse$$

Consequently, appeal to (16.4) leads to

$$
\begin{aligned}
&matches\ ws \\
&\quad = \quad map\ fst \cdot filter\ ((sw \sqsubseteq) \cdot snd) \cdot map\ (fork\ (length, reverse)) \cdot inits \\
&\quad \textbf{where}\ sw = reverse\ ws
\end{aligned}
$$

But $reverse = foldl\ (flip\ (:))\ [\,]$, so we can again make use of the tupling law of $foldl$, followed by the scan lemma, to obtain

$$
\begin{aligned}
matches\ ws \quad &= \quad map\ fst \cdot filter\ ((sw \sqsubseteq) \cdot snd) \cdot scanl\ step\ (0, [\,]) \\
&\quad\ \textbf{where}\ sw = reverse\ ws \\
step\ (n, sx)\ x \quad &= \quad (n + 1, x : sx)
\end{aligned}
$$

This is the basic form of the BM algorithm. Application of $scanl$ generates successive "windows" of the text together with their position. Each window contains the reversal of some initial segment of the text, with successive windows differing in just one position, so there is a "shift" of length one at each stage. The terms "window" and "shift" are from Lecroq (2003), which contains a very readable introduction to string matching. Each of these windows is processed by matching against the pattern ws from right to left.

Shifting

As it stands, the BM algorithm still takes $\Omega(mn)$ steps in the worst case because the test $(sw \sqsubseteq)$ can take $\Omega(m)$ steps (in all that follows we fix $m = length\ ws$ and assume $m \neq 0$). For example, one worst case arises when the pattern is a list of m repetitions of a single value and the text is a list of n repetitions of the same value. The way to make the worst case better is to see if we can shift over some windows because they cannot be candidates for matching. Such shifts depend on how much of a match there is at the current window.

Let $llcp\ sw\ sx$ denote the length of the longest common prefix of sw and sx. We encountered this function in the previous pearl. Clearly, $sw \sqsubseteq sx$ if and only if $m = llcp\ sw\ sx$. Given $i = llcp\ sw\ sx$ for the current window (n, sx), can we put a lower bound on the position $n + k$ of the next window at which there can be a match? Certainly, we must have $0 < k \leq m$ or we might miss a match. Suppose the next window has the form $(n + k, ys \mathbin{+\!\!+} sx)$, where $k = length\ ys$. If there is a match at this window, so $sw \sqsubseteq ys \mathbin{+\!\!+} sx$, then $take\ k\ sw = ys$ and $drop\ k\ sw \sqsubseteq sx$.

Using this information and setting $i = llcp\ sw\ sx$, we can now show that

$$
llcp\ sw\ (drop\ k\ sw) \quad = \quad min\ i\ (m - k) \tag{16.5}
$$

First, assume $i < m-k$. Then

$$take\ i\ (drop\ k\ sw)$$

$=$ {since $drop\ k\ sw \sqsubseteq sx$ implies $drop\ k\ sw = take\ (m-k)\ sx$}

$$take\ i\ (take\ (m-k)\ sx)$$

$=$ {since $i \leq m-k$}

$$take\ i\ sx$$

$=$ {since $i = llcp\ sw\ sx$}

$$take\ i\ sw$$

Similar reasoning gives

$$take\ (i+1)\ (drop\ k\ sw)\ \neq\ take\ (i+1)\ sw$$

In other words, if $i < m-k$, then $llcp\ sw\ (drop\ k\ sw) = i$. In the other case, $i \geq m-k$, we reason:

$$drop\ k\ sw$$

$=$ {since $length\ (drop\ k\ sw) = m-k \leq i$}

$$take\ i\ (drop\ k\ sw)$$

$\sqsubseteq$ {since $drop\ k\ sw \sqsubseteq sx$}

$$take\ i\ sx$$

$=$ {since $i = llcp\ sw\ sx$}

$$take\ i\ sw$$

$\sqsubseteq$ {definition of $\sqsubseteq$}

$$sw$$

But $drop\ k\ sw \sqsubseteq sw \equiv llcp\ sw\ (drop\ k\ sw) = m-k$, establishing (16.5).

Now, given any i in the range $0 \leq i \leq m$, let k be the *smallest positive* value in the range $1 \leq k \leq m$ satisfying (16.5). Provided $m \neq 0$, the value $k = m$ satisfies (16.5) if nothing smaller does. It follows that we can skip the next $k-1$ windows without missing a match. The value k is specified as $k = shift\ sw\ i$, where

$$shift\ sw\ i\ =\ head\ [k\ |\ k \leftarrow [1\,..\,m],\ llcp\ sw\ (drop\ k\ sw)\ ==\ min\ i\ (m-k)]$$

This is not a very good way to compute $shift\ sw\ i$, as the computation can take $\Omega(m^2)$ steps in the worst case. In the following section we will show how to compute $map\ (shift\ sw)\ [0\,..\,m]$ in $O(m)$ steps.

In summary, after a match of length i at the current window (n, sx), the next $shift\ sw\ i$ windows can safely be ignored without missing any additional matches. That means we can redefine *matches* to read

$$
\begin{array}{llll}
\textit{matches ws} & = & \textit{test} \cdot \textit{scanl step } (0, [\,]) \\
\textbf{where} & & \\
\textit{test } [\,] & = & [\,] \\
\textit{test } ((n, \textit{sx}) : \textit{nxs}) & = & \textbf{if } i \mathrel{==} m \\
& & \quad \textbf{then } n : \textit{test } (\textit{drop } (k{-}1)\ \textit{nxs}) \\
& & \quad \textbf{else } \textit{test } (\textit{drop } (k{-}1)\ \textit{nxs}) \\
& & \quad \textbf{where } i = \textit{llcp sw sx} \\
& & \qquad\qquad\ k = \textit{shift sw } i \\
(\textit{sw}, m) & = & (\textit{reverse ws}, \textit{length ws})
\end{array}
$$

Note that two versions of *matches* are equivalent only if $m \neq 0$.

A final improvement

There is one final improvement we can make. As before, let $i = llcp\,sw\,sx$ and $k = shift\,sw\,i$. Furthermore, suppose $m{-}k \leq i$, so $llcp\,sw\,(drop\,k\,sw) = m{-}k$. That means that $drop\,k\,sw$ is a prefix of sw. Since $m{-}k \leq i$, it follows that $llcp\,(drop\,k\,sw)\,sx = m{-}k$.

Now, the next window to be tried is $(n{+}k, ys \mathbin{+\mkern-10mu+} sx)$, where $length\,ys = k$. We reason:

$$
\begin{array}{cl}
 & llcp\,sw\,(ys \mathbin{+\mkern-10mu+} sx) \\
= & \{\text{setting } i' = llcp\,sw\,ys, \text{ so } i' \leq k\} \\
 & \textbf{if } i' \mathrel{==} k \textbf{ then } k + llcp\,(drop\,k\,sw)\,sx \textbf{ else } i' \\
= & \{\text{above, since } llcp\,(drop\,k\,sw)\,sx = m{-}k \text{ if } m{-}k \leq i\} \\
 & \textbf{if } i' \mathrel{==} k \textbf{ then } m \textbf{ else } i'
\end{array}
$$

Hence, provided $m{-}k \leq i$, the length of the longest common prefix of *sw* and the text at the next window can be computed by comparing only the first k elements. If $m{-}k > i$, then there is no saving and the next window may require up to m comparisons.

The improvement can be implemented by equipping the function *test* with an additional parameter j, indicating how much of the next candidate window to check. Installing this final refinement, we obtain the program of Figure 16.1, which is complete except for the definitions of *llcp* and *shift*. This program is Galil's (1979) version of the BM algorithm. Ignoring the time to compute *shift*, the running time of *matches* is $O(m + n)$ steps for a text of length n. For a proof of this claim, which is non-trivial, see Theorem 3.2.3 of Gusfield (1997).

$$
\begin{array}{lll}
\textit{matches ws} & = & \textit{test } m \cdot \textit{scanl step } (0, [\,]) \\
\textbf{where} \\
\textit{test } j \,[\,] & = & [\,] \\
\textit{test } j \,((n, sx) : nxs) & \mid & i == m \qquad\qquad = n : \textit{test } k \ (\textit{drop } (k{-}1) \, nxs) \\
& \mid & m{-}k \le i \qquad = \textit{test } k \ (\textit{drop } (k{-}1) \, nxs) \\
& \mid & \textbf{otherwise} \ \ = \textit{test } m \ (\textit{drop } (k{-}1) \, nxs) \\
& & \textbf{where } i' \ \ = \ \ \textit{llcp sw } (\textit{take } j \ sx) \\
& & \qquad\quad i \ \ = \ \ \textbf{if } i' == j \textbf{ then } m \textbf{ else } i' \\
& & \qquad\quad k \ \ = \ \ \textit{shift sw } i \\
(sw, m) & = & (\textit{reverse ws}, \textit{length ws})
\end{array}
$$

Fig. 16.1 The final program

Computing shifts

The definition of *shift sw* given in the previous section leads to a cubic-time algorithm for computing *shifts sw* $=$ *map* (*shift sw*) $[0 \mathinner{.\,.} m]$: computation of *shift sw i* can take quadratic time and there are $m{+}1$ values of i. If we can compute *shifts sw* in linear time and store the result in an array a, then replacing *shift sw i* by $a\,!\,i$ gives a linear-time algorithm for *matches*. The aim of this section is to show how to compute *shifts sw* in linear time. Arguably, this is the most subtle aspect of the BM algorithm.

First of all, set $f(k) = $ *llcp sw* (*drop k sw*) for brevity. Note that $f(m) = 0$ and $f(k) \le m{-}k$. We first reason, for any i in the range $0 \le i \le m$:

$$
\begin{array}{ll}
& \textit{shift sw } i \\
= & \{\text{definition}\} \\
& \textit{minimum } [k \mid k \leftarrow [1 \mathinner{.\,.} m], \ f(k) == \min i \ (m{-}k)] \\
= & \{\text{case analysis on } \min\} \\
& \textit{minimum } ([k \mid k \leftarrow [1 \mathinner{.\,.} m{-}i], \ f(k) == i] \mathbin{+\!\!+} \\
& \qquad\qquad\ \ [k \mid k \leftarrow [m{-}i{+}1 \mathinner{.\,.} m], \ f(k){+}k == m]) \\
= & \{\text{since } f(k) = i \Rightarrow k \le m{-}i\} \\
& \textit{minimum } ([k \mid k \leftarrow [1 \mathinner{.\,.} m], \ f(k) == i] \mathbin{+\!\!+} \\
& \qquad\qquad\ \ [k \mid k \leftarrow [m{-}i{+}1 \mathinner{.\,.} m], \ f(k){+}k == m])
\end{array}
$$

Next we bring in the Haskell library *Data.Array* and, in particular, the function *accumArray*. This function first made an appearance in Pearl 1. The following fact about *accumArray* is immediate from its definition:

$$
(\textit{accumArray op e } (0, m) \ vks) \,!\, i \ = \ \textit{foldl op e } [k \mid (v, k) \leftarrow vks, \ v == i]
$$

for all i in the range $0 \leq i \leq m$, provided $map\ fst\ vks \subseteq [0 .. m]$. The proviso is necessary because $accumArray$ is undefined if any index is out of the given range. In particular, with

$$a\quad =\quad accumArray\ min\ m\ (0, m)\ vks$$
$$vks\quad =\quad [(f(k), k)\ |\ k \leftarrow [1 .. m]]$$

we have

$$a\ !\ i\quad =\quad minimum\ ([k\ |\ k \leftarrow [1 .. m],\ f(k) == i] + [m])$$

for $0 \leq i \leq m$. That deals with the first term in the definition of $shift\ sw\ i$. We now have to factor in the second term. The idea is to replace a by

$$a\quad =\quad accumArray\ min\ m\ (0, m)\ (vks + vks')$$

where the list vks' is any convenient permutation of

$$[(i, minimum\ [k\ |\ k \leftarrow [m{-}i{+}1 .. m],\ f(k){+}k == m])\ |\ i \leftarrow [1 .. m]]$$

Then we have $shift\ sw\ i = a\ !\ i$.

We claim that the following definition of vks', which computes the list above in reverse order, does the job:

$$vks'\qquad\qquad =\quad zip\ [m, m{-}1 .. 1]\ (foldr\ op\ [\ ]\ vks)$$
$$vks\qquad\qquad =\quad [(f(k), k)\ |\ k \leftarrow [1 .. m]]$$
$$op\ (v, k)\ ks\quad =\quad \textbf{if}\ v + k == m\ \textbf{then}\ k : ks\ \textbf{else}\ head\ ks : ks$$

Note that $op\ (f(m), m)\ [\ ] = [m]$ because $f(m) = 0$ and so $f(m) + m = m$. For example, with $xs = foldr\ op\ [\ ]\ vks$ we have

f	2	4	0	5	2	3	0	2	0
k	1	2	3	4	5	6	7	8	9
xs	4	4	4	4	6	6	9	9	9

The ith element of xs (counting from 0) is the smallest $k > i$ such that $f(k){+}k = m$. In vks' the index $m{-}i$ is paired with $xs\ !!\ i$; equivalently, i is paired with $xs\ !!\ (m{-}i)$, which is just what is required.

As the final step, recall the function $allcp$ from the previous pearl:

$$allcp\ xs\quad =\quad [llcp\ xs\ (drop\ k\ xs)\ |\ k \leftarrow [0 .. length\ xs - 1]]$$

There we showed how to compute $allcp$ in linear time. For present purposes we need a variant of $allcp\ xs$ in which the first element is dropped and an additional element $llcp\ xs\ [\ ]$ is added at the end. This additional value is zero, so we define

$$allcp'\ xs\quad =\quad tail\ (allcp\ xs) + [0]$$

Finally, we can reason:

$$[(f(k), k) \mid k \leftarrow [1 \mathbin{..} m]]$$

$=$ {definition of f}

$$[(llcp\ sw\ (drop\ k\ sw), k) \mid k \leftarrow [1 \mathbin{..} m]]$$

$=$ {definition of zip}

$$zip\ [llcp\ sw\ (drop\ k\ sw) \mid k \leftarrow [1 \mathbin{..} m]]\ [1 \mathbin{..} m]$$

$=$ {definition of $allcp'$}

$$zip\ (allcp'\ sw)\ [1 \mathbin{..} m]$$

Putting these pieces together, we obtain

$$
\begin{aligned}
a &= accumArray\ min\ m\ (0, m)\ (vks \mathbin{+\!\!+} vks') \\
\textbf{where} & \\
m &= length\ sw \\
vks &= zip\ (allcp'\ sw)\ [1 \mathbin{..} m] \\
vks' &= zip\ [m, m{-}1 \mathbin{..} 1]\ (foldr\ op\ [\,]\ vks) \\
op\ (v, k)\ ks &= \textbf{if}\ v + k \mathbin{==} m\ \textbf{then}\ k : ks\ \textbf{else}\ head\ ks : ks
\end{aligned}
$$

Replacing *shift sw i* by $a\ !\ i$ in Figure 16.1 gives a linear-time algorithm for *matches*.

Final remarks

The BM algorithm was first described in Boyer and Moore (1977); see also Cormen *et al.* (2001), Crochemore and Rytter (2003) and Gusfield (1997) for further exploration and discussion of the method. Most often the algorithm is explained in terms of two rules, the *bad character* rule and the *good suffix* rule, neither of which appear explicitly above. Our derivation of the BM algorithm, at least in its basic form, was a simple exercise in symbolic manipulation, applying appropriate efficiency-improving laws dictated solely by the form of the expressions being considered. Chief among these laws were the scan lemma and the tupling law of *foldl*. Moreover, the key idea of the BM algorithm, namely the idea of matching the pattern to the text in right-to-left order, emerged simply as the consequence of one very reasonable way to define *endswith*. Subsequent optimisations depended more on the content of the expressions than their form, but this is to be expected in any algorithm containing subtle ideas.

References

Boyer, R. S. and Moore, J. S. (1977). A fast string searching algorithm. *Communications of the ACM* **20**, 762–72.

Cormen, T. H., Leiserson, C. E., Rivest, R. L. and Stein, C. (2001). *Introduction to Algorithms*, second edition. Cambridge, MA: The MIT Press.

Crochemore, M. and Rytter, W. (2003). *Jewels of Stringology*. Hong Kong: World Scientific.

Galil, Z. (1979). On improving the worst cast of the Boyer–Moore string matching algorithm. *Communications of the ACM* **22** (9), 505–8.

Gusfield, D. (1997). *Algorithms on Strings, Trees and Sequences*. Cambridge, UK: Cambridge University Press.

Lecroq, T. (2003). Experimental results on string matching algorithms. *Software – Practice and Experience* **25** (7), 727–65.

17

The Knuth–Morris–Pratt algorithm

Introduction

In this pearl we continue with the problem of string matching and take the other fork in the road, the one that begins with the following definition of *endswith*:

$$endswith\ ws\ xs\ =\ ws \in tails\ xs$$

The path turns out to lead to the KMP algorithm. Remember, the goal is to find functions p and op, and value e, so that $endswith\ ws = p \cdot foldl\ op\ e$. Then we have

$$
\begin{array}{lll}
matches & :: & Eq\ a \Rightarrow [a] \to [a] \to [Int] \\
matches\ ws & = & map\ fst \cdot filter\ (p \cdot snd) \cdot scanl\ step\ (0, e) \\
step\ (n, x)\ y & = & (n + 1, op\ x\ y)
\end{array}
$$

The value of *matches ws xs* is a list of integers n for which the pattern *ws* appears in the text *xs* ending at position n. Provided p and op take constant time, or at least amortized constant time, the computation of *matches* takes $\Theta(m + n)$ steps on a pattern of length m and a text of length n.

First steps

One way of writing *endswith ws* as a composition is

$$endswith\ ws\ =\ not \cdot null \cdot filter\ (= ws) \cdot tails$$

But $filter\ (= ws) \cdot tails$ cannot be defined as an instance of *foldl* because it returns either an empty list or $[ws]$, and this is insufficient information to define the function inductively. More promising is $filter\ (\sqsubseteq ws) \cdot tails$. Applied to *xs*, this function returns in decreasing order of length *all* tails of *xs* that are prefixes of *ws*. The first element of this list is *ws* if and only if *endswith ws xs*. Thus:

$$endswith\ ws\ =\ (= ws) \cdot head \cdot filter\ (\sqsubseteq ws) \cdot tails$$

Of course, the first function ($= ws$) is no longer a constant-time test. That problem is solved by generalising $filter \ (\sqsubseteq ws) \cdot tails$ to a function $split$, defined by

$$split \ ws \ xs \ = \ head \ [(us, ws \downarrow us) \mid us \leftarrow tails \ xs, \ us \sqsubseteq ws]$$

The operation $\downarrow$ is defined by $(us + \! \! \! + vs) \downarrow us = vs$. Hence, $split \ ws \ xs$ splits ws into two lists us and vs so that $us + \! \! \! + vs = ws$. The value of us is the longest suffix of xs that is a prefix of ws. For example:

$$split \ \text{``endnote''} \ \text{``append''} \ = \ (\text{``end''}, \text{``note''})$$

Now we have $endswith \ ws = null \cdot snd \cdot split \ ws$. It remains to find op and e so that $split \ ws = foldl \ op \ e$. Equivalently, we want e and op to satisfy

$$
\begin{aligned}
split \ ws \ [\,] &= e \\
split \ ws \ (xs + \! \! \! + [x]) &= op \ (split \ ws \ xs) \ x
\end{aligned}
$$

We have $split \ ws \ [\,] = ([\,], ws)$, which gives us e, so it remains to discover op. The crucial observation is that

$$split \ ws \ xs = (us, vs) \ \Rightarrow \ split \ ws \ (xs + \! \! \! + [x]) = split \ ws \ (us + \! \! \! + [x])$$

In words, the longest suffix of $xs + \! \! \! + [x]$ that is a prefix of ws is a suffix of $us + \! \! \! + [x]$. It cannot be a longer suffix, for that would mean there is a longer suffix of xs than us that is a prefix of ws, contradicting the definition of us as the longest such suffix.

To discover op we first express $split$ recursively:

$$split \ ws \ xs \ = \ \textbf{if} \ xs \sqsubseteq ws \ \textbf{then} \ (xs, ws \downarrow xs) \ \textbf{else} \ split \ ws \ (tail \ xs)$$

Now, setting $split \ ws \ xs = (us, vs)$, so $ws = us + \! \! \! + vs$, we reason:

$$
\begin{aligned}
& split \ ws \ (xs + \! \! \! + [x]) \\
= \quad & \{\text{observation above}\} \\
& split \ ws \ (us + \! \! \! + [x]) \\
= \quad & \{\text{recursive definition of } split\} \\
& \textbf{if} \ us + \! \! \! + [x] \sqsubseteq ws \ \textbf{then} \ (us + \! \! \! + [x], ws \downarrow (us + \! \! \! + [x])) \\
& \textbf{else} \ split \ ws \ (tail \ (us + \! \! \! + [x])) \\
= \quad & \{\text{since } ws = us + \! \! \! + vs \text{ and definitions of } \sqsubseteq \text{ and } \downarrow\} \\
& \textbf{if} \ [x] \sqsubseteq vs \ \textbf{then} \ (us + \! \! \! + [x], tail \ vs) \\
& \textbf{else} \ split \ ws \ (tail \ (us + \! \! \! + [x]))
\end{aligned}
$$

$$= \quad \{\text{case analysis on } us\}$$
$$\textbf{if } [x] \sqsubseteq vs \textbf{ then } (us + [x], tail \, vs)$$
$$\textbf{else if } null \, us \textbf{ then } ([\,], ws)$$
$$\textbf{else } split \, ws \, (tail \, us + [x])$$

This calculation gives us our definition of *op*:

$$op \, (us, vs) \, x \quad | \quad [x] \sqsubseteq vs \quad = \quad (us + [x], tail \, vs)$$
$$| \quad null \, us \quad = \quad ([\,], ws)$$
$$| \quad \textbf{otherwise} \quad = \quad op \, (split \, ws \, (tail \, us)) \, x$$

Summarising where we are at this point:

$$matches \, ws \quad = \quad map \, fst \cdot filter \, (null \cdot snd \cdot snd) \cdot$$
$$scanl \, step \, (0, ([\,], ws))$$
$$step \, (n, (us, vs)) \, x \quad = \quad (n + 1, op \, (us, vs) \, x)$$

This is the basic form of the KMP algorithm: each step maintains a current split (us, vs) of the pattern *ws* in which *us* is the longest prefix of *ws* matching some suffix of the current portion of the text. Positions for which $vs = [\,]$ are those where the pattern matches exactly and are recorded.

The problem with *op* is that it is inefficient: the third clause requires computation of $split \, ws \, (tail \, us)$, which in turn may involve computing and possibly recomputing $split \, ws \, zs$ for an arbitrary substring *zs* of *ws*. Clearly, *op* does too much work and we need something better.

Data refinement

One way to improve efficiency is to seek a change of representation of the first argument to *op*, namely the current split (us, vs) of the pattern *ws*. Specifically, suppose *abs* and *rep* are functions with types

$$abs \quad :: \quad Rep \, ([a], [a]) \rightarrow ([a], [a])$$
$$rep \quad :: \quad ([a], [a]) \rightarrow Rep \, ([a], [a])$$

for some data type *Rep*. The function *rep* is the representation function, while *abs* is the abstraction function. The terminology is standard in data refinement. We also want $abs \cdot rep = id$, so *abs* is left-inverse to *rep*. This condition states that the abstract value can be recovered from any representation of it. The other direction $rep \cdot abs = id$ will only hold if the change of representation is a bijection, which is not normally the case in data refinement.

If we can find the necessary ingredients to ensure

$$foldl \, op \, ([\,], ws) = abs \cdot foldl \, op' \, (rep \, ([\,], ws)) \tag{17.1}$$

as well as ensure that *abs* and *op′* take constant time, then we can redefine *matches* to read

$$matches\ ws\ =\ map\ fst \cdot filter\ (null \cdot snd \cdot abs \cdot snd) \cdot$$
$$scanl\ step\ (0, rep\ ([\,], ws))$$
$$step\ (n, r)\ x\ =\ (n + 1, op'\ r\ x)$$

To find *abs*, *op′* and *rep* satisfying (17.1) we appeal to the *fusion* law of *foldl*. This laws states the $f \cdot foldl\ g\ a = foldl\ h\ b$ provided three conditions are met: (i) f is a strict function; (ii) $f\ a = b$; and (iii) $f\ (g\ y\ x) = h\ (f\ y)\ x$ for all x and y. The first condition is not needed if we want to assert that the fusion law holds only for all finite lists. The twist here is that we want to apply the law in the anti-fusion or *fission* direction, splitting a fold into two parts.

The second fusion condition is immediate: $abs\ (rep\ ([\,], ws)) = ([\,], ws)$. And there is an obvious definition of *op′* that satisfies the third fusion condition, namely

$$op'\ r\ =\ rep \cdot op\ (abs\ r) \tag{17.2}$$

Then we have

$$abs\ (op'\ r\ x) = abs\ (rep\ (op\ (abs\ r)\ x)) = op\ (abs\ r)\ x$$

Installing the definition of *op* in (17.2) we obtain

$$
\begin{aligned}
op'\ r\ x\ \ |\ \ & [x] \sqsubseteq vs\ \ &=\ \ & rep\ (us \mathbin{+\!\!+} [x], tail\ vs) \\
|\ \ & null\ us\ \ &=\ \ & rep\ ([\,], ws) \\
|\ \ & \textbf{otherwise}\ \ &=\ \ & op'\ (rep\ (split\ ws\ (tail\ us)))\ x \\
& \textbf{where}\ (us, vs) = abs\ r
\end{aligned}
$$

It remains to choose *Rep* and the two functions *abs* and *rep*.

Trees

In functional programming, practically all efficient representations involve a tree of some kind, and this one is no different. We define

$$\textbf{data}\ Rep\ a\ =\ Null\ |\ Node\ a\ (Rep\ a)\ (Rep\ a)$$

So *Rep* is a binary tree. The function *abs* is defined by

$$abs\ (Node\ (us, vs)\ \ell\ r)\ =\ (us, vs) \tag{17.3}$$

and clearly takes constant time. The function *rep* is defined by

$$rep\ (us, vs)\ =\ Node\ (us, vs)\ (left\ us\ vs)\ (right\ us\ vs) \tag{17.4}$$

where

$$
\begin{aligned}
left\,[\,]\;vs &= Null \\
left\,(u:us)\;vs &= rep\,(split\;ws\;us) \\[4pt]
right\;us\,[\,] &= Null \\
right\;us\,(v:vs) &= rep\,(us \mathbin{+\!\!+} [v],\,vs)
\end{aligned}
$$

The reason for choosing *rep* in the above way is that *op′* takes the simple form

$$
op'\,(Node\,(us,vs)\;\ell\;r)\;x \quad
\begin{aligned}
&|\quad [x] \sqsubseteq vs &&= \; r \\
&|\quad null\;us &&= \; root \\
&|\quad \textbf{otherwise} &&= \; op'\;\ell\;x
\end{aligned}
$$

where $root = rep\,([\,],\,ws)$. For instance, the first clause is justified by

$$
\begin{aligned}
&op'\,(Node\,(us,vs)\;\ell\;r)\;x \\
=\quad &\{\text{definition of } op' \text{ in the case } [x] \sqsubseteq vs\} \\
&rep\,(us \mathbin{+\!\!+} [x],\,tail\;vs) \\
=\quad &\{\text{definition of } right \text{ and } x = head\;vs\} \\
&right\;us\;vs \\
=\quad &\{\text{definition of } rep\} \\
&r
\end{aligned}
$$

The other clauses are similar. If we also set $op'\;Null\;x = root$, then *op′* takes an even simpler form:

$$
\begin{aligned}
op'\;Null\;x &= root \\
op'\,(Node\,(us,vs)\;\ell\;r)\;x \quad &|\quad [x] \sqsubseteq vs &&= \; r \\
&|\quad \textbf{otherwise} &&= \; op'\;\ell\;x
\end{aligned}
$$

Although *op′* does not take constant time, it does take amortized constant time. The tree *root* has height m, the length of the pattern; taking a right branch decreases the height of the current tree by exactly one, while taking a left-branch increases the height, possibly by more than one. A standard amortization argument now shows that evaluating *foldl op′ root* on a list of length n involves at most $2m + n$ calls of *op′*.

What remains is to show how to compute *rep* efficiently. It is here that a final standard technique of program transformation enters the picture: use of an accumulating parameter. The idea is to specify a generalised version, *grep* say, of *rep* by

$$
rep\,(us,vs) \;=\; grep\,(left\;us\;vs)\,(us,vs)
$$

and then to derive a direct definition of *grep*. From (17.4) we have

$$grep \; \ell \; (us, vs) \;\; = \;\; Node \; (us, vs) \; \ell \; (right \; us \; vs)$$

Now, by the definition of *right*, we have *right us* [ ] = *Null* and

$$\begin{aligned} right \; us \; (v : vs) \;\; &= \;\; rep \; (us +\!\!+ [v], vs) \\ &= \;\; grep \; (left \; (us +\!\!+ [v]) \; vs) \; (us +\!\!+ [v], vs) \end{aligned}$$

To simplify *left* (*us* $+\!\!+$ [*v*]) *vs* we need a case analysis on *us*. In the case *us* = [ ] we reason:

$$\begin{aligned} & left \; ([\,] +\!\!+ [v]) \; vs \\ = \quad & \{\text{definition of } left\} \\ & rep \; (split \; ws \; [\,]) \\ = \quad & \{\text{definition of } split\} \\ & rep \; ([\,], ws) \\ = \quad & \{\text{definition of } root\} \\ & root \end{aligned}$$

In the inductive case *u* : *us* we reason:

$$\begin{aligned} & left \; (u : us +\!\!+ [v]) \; vs \\ = \quad & \{\text{definition of } left\} \\ & rep \; (split \; ws \; (us +\!\!+ [v])) \\ = \quad & \{\text{definition of } split\} \\ & rep \; (op \; (split \; ws \; us) \; v) \\ = \quad & \{\text{definition (17.2) of } op'\} \\ & op' \; (rep \; (split \; ws \; us)) \; v \\ = \quad & \{\text{definition of } left\} \\ & op' \; (left \; (u : us) \; vs) \; v \end{aligned}$$

Summarising this calculation:

$$left \; (us +\!\!+ [v]) \; vs = \textbf{if} \; null \; us \; \textbf{then} \; root \; \textbf{else} \; op' \; (left \; us \; vs) \; v$$

Hence, *grep* can be defined by

$$\begin{aligned} grep \; \ell \; (us, [\,]) \;\; &= \;\; Node \; (us, [\,]) \; \ell \; Null \\ grep \; \ell \; (us, v : vs) \;\; &= \;\; Node \; (us, v : vs) \; \ell \\ & \qquad (grep \; (op' \; \ell \; v) \; (us +\!\!+ [v], vs)) \end{aligned}$$

$$
\begin{array}{lcl}
matches\ ws & = & map\ fst \cdot filter\ (ok \cdot snd) \cdot scanl\ step\ (0, root) \\
\textbf{where} \\
ok\ (Node\ vs\ \ell\ r) & = & null\ vs \\
step\ (n, t)\ x & = & (n + 1, op\ t\ x) \\
op\ Null\ x & = & root \\
op\ (Node\ [\ ]\ \ell\ r)\ x & = & op\ \ell\ x \\
op\ (Node\ (v : vs)\ \ell\ r)\ x & = & \textbf{if}\ v == x\ \textbf{then}\ r\ \textbf{else}\ op\ \ell\ x \\
root & = & grep\ Null\ ws \\
grep\ \ell\ [\ ] & = & Node\ [\ ]\ \ell\ Null \\
grep\ \ell\ (v : vs) & = & Node\ (v : vs)\ \ell\ (grep\ (op\ \ell\ v)\ vs)
\end{array}
$$

Fig. 17.1 The final program for *matches*

Let us now put all the pieces together. We have

$$
matches\ ws\ =\ map\ fst \cdot filter\ (ok \cdot snd) \cdot scanl\ step\ (0, root)
$$

where

$$
\begin{array}{lcl}
ok\ (Node\ (us, vs)\ \ell\ r) & = & null\ vs \\
step\ (n, t)\ x & = & (n + 1, op\ t\ x) \\
root & = & grep\ Null\ ([\ ], ws)
\end{array}
$$

The function *op* (which is *op'* renamed) is defined by

$$
\begin{array}{lcl}
op\ Null\ x & = & root \\
op\ (Node\ (us, [\ ])\ \ell\ r)\ x & = & op\ \ell\ x \\
op\ (Node\ (us, v : vs)\ \ell\ r)\ x & = & \textbf{if}\ v == x\ \textbf{then}\ r\ \textbf{else}\ op\ \ell\ x
\end{array}
$$

and the function *grep* by

$$
\begin{array}{lcl}
grep\ \ell\ (us, [\ ]) & = & Node\ (us, [\ ])\ \ell\ Null \\
grep\ \ell\ (us, v : vs) & = & Node\ (us, v : vs)\ \ell\ (grep\ (op\ \ell\ v)\ (us \mathbin{+\!\!+} [v], vs))
\end{array}
$$

Inspection of the right-hand sides of these definitions shows that the first component *us* of the pair *(us, vs)* plays no part in the algorithm, as its value is never used. Hence, we simply drop *us* and obtain our final program, recorded in Figure 17.1.

The tree *root* is cyclic: left subtrees point backwards to earlier nodes in the tree, or to *Null*. This tree encapsulates the failure function of the KMP algorithm as a cyclic graph. The operation *op* takes amortized constant time, assuming the cost of an equality test is constant. The time to compute *root* is $\Theta(m)$ steps, where $m = length\ ws$. Hence, *matches* takes $\Theta(m)$ steps to build *root* and thereafter $\Theta(n)$ steps, where n is the length of the text, to compute the occurrences of the pattern in the text.

The program above is not quite the full KMP algorithm, but corresponds to what is known as the Morris–Pratt algorithm. The full KMP algorithm contains an extra wrinkle. Suppose we introduce a function *next*, defined by

$$
\begin{aligned}
next\ Null\ x &= Null \\
next\ (Node\ [\,]\ \ell\ r)\ x &= Node\ [\,]\ \ell\ r \\
next\ (Node\ (v : vs)\ \ell\ r)\ x &= \textbf{if}\ \ v == x\ \textbf{then}\ next\ \ell\ x \\
&\quad\ \textbf{else}\ \ Node\ (v : vs)\ \ell\ r
\end{aligned}
$$

Essentially, *next t x* replaces the tree *t* with the first tree on the list of left subtrees of *t* whose associated label does not begin with *x*. The point about *next* is that, as can be seen from the definition of *op*, we have

$$
op\ (Node\ (v : vs)\ \ell\ r)\ x \ \ = \ \ op\ (Node\ (v : vs)\ (next\ \ell\ v)\ r)\ x
$$

It follows that evaluation of *op* can be made more efficient by replacing each node *Node (v : vs) ℓ r* in the tree with a new node *Node (v : vs) (next ℓ v) r*. But we won't go into further details.

Final remarks

The KMP algorithm was first described in Knuth *et al.* (1977). However, many other descriptions of the algorithm exist (e.g. Gusfield, 1997; Cormen *et al.*, 2001; Crochemore and Rytter, 2002). In fact, there are over a hundred papers devoted to string matching in general, and the KMP and BM algorithms in particular. In fact, we have written two previous papers about the KMP ourselves (Bird, 1977; Bird *et al.*, 1989), one over 30 years ago, before the laws of functional programming were firmly established. The above presentation of the KMP algorithm is a more polished and revised version of the one contained in Bird *et al.* (1989). Recently, Olivier Danvy and his colleagues at BRICS have written a number of papers showing how to obtain the KMP and BM algorithms by partial evaluation. For example, Ager *et al.* (2003) uses similar ideas to those in Bird (1977) to solve a long-outstanding open problem in partial evaluation, namely how to obtain the KMP from a naive algorithm by a process of partial evaluation that takes linear time. And Danvy and Rohde (2005) present a derivation of the search phase of the BM algorithm using partial evaluation, by identifying the bad character rule as a binding-time improvement.

References

Ager, M. S., Danvy, O. and Rohde, H. K. (2003). Fast partial evaluation of pattern matching in strings. BRICS Report Series, RS-03-11, University of Aarhus, Denmark.

Bird, R. S. (1977). Improving programs by the introduction of recursion. *Communications of the ACM* **20** (11), 856–63.

Bird, R. S., Gibbons, J. and Jones, G. (1989). Formal derivation of a pattern matching algorithm. *Science of Computer Programming* **12**, 93–104.

Cormen, T. H., Leiserson, C. E., Rivest, R. L. and Stein, C. (2001). *Introduction to Algorithms*, second edition. Cambridge, MA: MIT Press.

Crochemore, M. and Rytter, W. (2002). *Jewels of Stringology*. Hong Kong: World Scientific.

Danvy, O. and Rohde, H. K. (2005). On obtaining the Boyer–Moore string-matching algorithm by partial evaluation. BRICS Research Report RS-05-14, University of Aarhus, Denmark.

Gusfield, D. (1997). *Algorithms on Strings, Trees and Sequences*. Cambridge, UK: Cambridge University Press.

Knuth, D. E., Morris, J. H. and Pratt, V. B. (1977). Fast pattern matching in strings. *SIAM Journal on Computing* **6**, 323–50.

18

Planning solves the Rush Hour problem

Introduction

Rush Hour is an intriguing sliding-block puzzle, invented some years ago by the celebrated puzzlist Nob Yoshigahara and marketed by Think Fun.[1] It is played on a 6×6 grid and can be solved in reasonable time by a brute-force breadth-first search. The generalised version – played on an $n \times n$ grid – is known to be PSPACE-complete, so a better than exponential-time solver is very unlikely. Still, with the help of a suitable planning algorithm, it is possible to improve significantly on the brute-force approach, and the aim of this pearl is to show how. Further details of how Rush Hour is played are postponed until later, because we want to start out with a more abstract formulation of puzzles, breadth-first search and planning.

Puzzles

Consider an abstract puzzle defined in terms of two finite sets, a set of states and a set of moves. Given are three functions

$$
\begin{array}{lll}
moves & :: & State \rightarrow [Move] \\
move & :: & State \rightarrow Move \rightarrow State \\
solved & :: & State \rightarrow Bool
\end{array}
$$

The function *moves* determines the legal moves that can be made in a given state and *move* returns the new state that results when a given move is made. The function *solved* determines which states are a solution to the puzzle. Described in this way, a puzzle is essentially a deterministic finite automaton. Solving the puzzle means finding some sequence of moves, preferably a shortest such sequence, that leads from a given initial state to some solved state:

$$
solve \quad :: \quad State \rightarrow Maybe\ [Move]
$$

---

[1] Rush Hour is obtainable from http://www.puzzles.com/products/rushhour.htm.

The value of *solve q* is *Nothing* if there is no sequence of moves beginning in state *q* that leads to a solved state and returns *Just ms* otherwise, where *ms* satisfies *solved* (*foldl move q ms*).

We can implement *solve* by carrying out either a breadth-first or a depth-first search. In either case the key idea is to introduce the synonyms

type *Path*   =   ([*Move*], *State*)
type *Frontier* =   [*Path*]

A path consists of a sequence of moves made in some given starting state, together with the resulting state. A frontier is a list of paths waiting to be explored further. Then, a breadth-first search can be defined by

bfsearch   :: [*State*] → *Frontier* → *Maybe* [*Move*]
bfsearch qs [ ]   =   *Nothing*
bfsearch qs (*p*@(*ms*, *q*) : *ps*)
              | *solved q*   =   *Just ms*
              | *q* ∈ *qs*   =   *bfsearch qs ps*
              | **otherwise** =   *bfsearch* (*q* : *qs*) (*ps* ++ *succs p*)

where

succs   :: *Path* → [*Path*]
succs (*ms*, *q*) =   [(*ms* ++ [*m*], *move q m*) | *m* ← *moves q*]

The first component *qs* of *bfsearch* represents the set of analysed states. In a breadth-first search the frontier is managed as a queue, so paths at the same distance from the starting state are analysed before their successors. Analysing a path means accepting it if the final state is a solved state, rejecting it if the final state has already been analysed, and otherwise adding its successors to the end of the current frontier for future exploration. A breadth-first search will find a shortest solution if a solution exists.

With one change, the definition of depth-first search is exactly the same as that of breadth-first search. The change is to replace the term *ps* ++ *succs p* by *succs p* ++ *ps*. In a depth-first search the frontier is maintained as a stack, so the successors of a path are analysed before any other path at the same level. A depth-first search will find a solution if one exists, but it probably won't be the shortest.

Under breadth-first search the current frontier can be exponentially longer than under depth-first search. Consequently, as defined above, *bfsearch* takes much more time than *dfsearch*. The reason is that evaluation of *ps* ++ *succs p* takes time proportional to the length of the frontier *ps*. One way to make the code faster, though it does not reduce the space complexity, is to introduce an accumulating parameter, defining *bfsearch'* by

$$bfsearch'\ qs\ pss\ ps = bfsearch\ qs\ (ps +\!\!+ concat\ (reverse\ pss))$$

Then, after some simple calculation which we omit, we obtain

$$bfsearch' :: [State] \rightarrow [Frontier] \rightarrow Frontier \rightarrow Maybe\ [Move]$$
$$bfsearch'\ qs\ [\,]\ [\,]\ =\ Nothing$$
$$bfsearch'\ qs\ pss\ [\,]\ =\ bfsearch'\ qs\ [\,]\ (concat\ (reverse\ pss))$$
$$bfsearch'\ qs\ pss\ (p@(ms, q) : ps)$$
$$\begin{array}{lll} |\quad solved\ q & = & Just\ ms \\ |\quad q \in qs & = & bfsearch'\ qs\ pss\ ps \\ |\quad \textbf{otherwise} & = & bfsearch'\ (q : qs)\ (succs\ p : pss)\ ps \end{array}$$

In fact, there is a simpler version of *bfsearch'* in which the accumulating parameter is of type *Frontier* rather than [*Frontier*]:

$$bfsearch' :: [State] \rightarrow Frontier \rightarrow Frontier \rightarrow Maybe\ [Move]$$
$$bfsearch'\ qs\ [\,]\ [\,]\ =\ Nothing$$
$$bfsearch'\ qs\ rs\ [\,]\ =\ bfsearch'\ qs\ [\,]\ rs$$
$$bfsearch'\ qs\ rs\ (p@(ms, q) : ps)$$
$$\begin{array}{lll} |\quad solved\ q & = & Just\ ms \\ |\quad q \in qs & = & bfsearch'\ qs\ rs\ ps \\ |\quad \textbf{otherwise} & = & bfsearch'\ (q : qs)\ (succs\ p +\!\!+ rs)\ ps \end{array}$$

This version of *bfsearch'* has a different behaviour than the previous one in that successive frontiers are traversed alternately from left to right and from right to left, but a shortest solution will still be found if a solution exists.

We can now define

$$bfsolve\ q\ =\ bfsearch'\ [\,]\ [\,]\ [([\,], q)]$$

The function *bfsolve* implements *solve* using a breadth-first search.

Planning

But what we have got so far is simply the strategy of trying every possible sequence of moves until finding one that works. That is not the way humans solve puzzles. Instead they make plans. For our purposes a plan is a sequence of moves that, if the moves can be carried out, leads to a solved state. Thus:

type *Plan* = [*Move*]

Plans have to consist of non-repeated moves, otherwise the plan cannot be carried out. If, in order to make move m, a plan requires move m to be made first, then clearly the plan cannot be implemented. An empty plan means success. Otherwise, suppose the first move in the current plan is move m. If move m can be carried out in the current state, then it is made. If it cannot, then we make use of a function *premoves* :: $State \rightarrow Move \rightarrow [[Move]]$ such that, for each alternative *pms* in *premoves q m*, the move m can be made provided the preparatory moves *pms* are made first. In turn, moves in *pms* may require further preparatory moves, so we have to form new, extended plans by iterating *premoves*:

$$newplans :: State \rightarrow Plan \rightarrow [Plan]$$
$$newplans\ q\ ms\ =\ mkplans\ ms$$
where
$$mkplans\ ms\ \ \ |\ \ null\ ms\ \ \ \ \ =\ \ [\,]$$
$$\ \ \ \ \ \ \ \ \ \ \ \ \ \ \ \ |\ \ m \in qms\ \ \ \ =\ \ [ms]$$
$$\ \ \ \ \ \ \ \ \ \ \ \ \ \ \ \ |\ \ \textbf{otherwise}\ =\ \ concat\ [mkplans\ (pms + ms)\ |$$
$$\ pms \leftarrow premoves\ q\ m,$$
$$\ all\ (\notin ms)\ pms]$$
$$\ \ \ \ \ \ \ \ \ \ \ \ \ \textbf{where}\ m = head\ ms;\ \ qms = moves\ q$$

The result of *newplans q ms* is a possibly empty list of nonempty plans, the first move of each of which can be made in state q. To kick-start the planning process we assume that a puzzle in state q can be solved by making the moves in *goalmoves q*, where *goalmoves* :: $State \rightarrow Plan$.

Using just the two new functions *goalmoves* and *premoves* we can now formulate an alternative search process based on the idea of an augmented path and frontier:

$$\textbf{type}\ APath\ \ \ \ \ \ =\ \ ([Move], State, Plan)$$
$$\textbf{type}\ AFrontier\ \ =\ \ [APath]$$

An augmented path consists of moves already made from some starting state, the state that results and a plan for the remaining moves. The search consists of exploring augmented paths in order until either one plan succeeds or all plans fail:

$$psearch\ ::\ [State] \rightarrow AFrontier \rightarrow Maybe\ [Move]$$
$$psearch\ qs\ [\,]\ =\ Nothing$$
$$psearch\ qs\ (p@(ms, q, plan) : ps)$$
$$\ \ \ |\ \ solved\ q\ \ \ \ \ \ =\ \ Just\ ms$$
$$\ \ \ |\ \ q \in qs\ \ \ \ \ \ \ =\ \ psearch\ qs\ ps$$
$$\ \ \ |\ \ \textbf{otherwise}\ =\ \ psearch\ (q : qs)\ (asuccs\ p + ps + bsuccs\ p)$$

where

$$asuccs, bsuccs :: APath \rightarrow [APath]$$

$$asuccs \ (ms, q, plan)$$
$$= \ [(ms\!+\!\![m], move \ q \ m, plan') \mid m : plan' \leftarrow newplans \ q \ plan]$$
$$bsuccs \ (ms, q, \_)$$
$$= \ [(ms\!+\!\![m], q', goalmoves \ q') \mid m \leftarrow moves \ q, \textbf{let} \ q' = move \ q \ m]$$

In *psearch qs ps* all the plans in the frontier *ps* are tried first in a depth-first manner. If all of them fail, then we add in further plans, each of which consists of making some legal move and starting over with a new goal. These additional plans, expressed by the term *bsuccs*, are necessary for completeness. Simple puzzles may be solvable by suitable planning, but plans may fail even though there is a solution. This is a consequence of the fact that plans are executed greedily and moves that can be made are made. To ensure a complete strategy we have to be willing to make additional plans at each stage.

As with a breadth-first search, we can make *psearch* faster by introducing an accumulating parameter:

$$psearch' :: [State] \rightarrow AFrontier \rightarrow AFrontier \rightarrow Maybe \ [Move]$$
$$psearch' \ qs \ [\,] \ [\,] \ = \ Nothing$$
$$psearch' \ qs \ rs \ [\,] \ = \ psearch' \ qs \ [\,] \ rs$$
$$psearch' \ qs \ rs \ (p@(ms, q, plan) : ps)$$
$$| \ solved \ q \quad = \ Just \ (reverse \ ms)$$
$$| \ q \in qs \quad\quad = \ psearch' \ qs \ rs \ ps$$
$$| \ \textbf{otherwise} \ = \ psearch' \ (q : qs) \ (bsuccs \ p \ +\!\!+ \ rs) \ (asuccs \ p \ +\!\!+ \ ps)$$

The function *psolve* can now be defined by

$$psolve \quad :: \quad State \rightarrow Maybe \ [Move]$$
$$psolve \ q \ = \ psearch' \ [\,] \ [\,] \ [([\,], q, goalmoves \ q)]$$

The function *psolve* implements *solve* using planning. It is possible to define a variation of *psearch* that explores plans in a breadth-first manner, but we will leave details to the reader. Note that *psearch* will find a solution if one exists, but not necessarily the shortest one.

Rush Hour

Let us now apply the above ideas to Rush Hour. As mentioned before, this is a puzzle consisting of a 6×6 grid of 36 cells. Covering some of these cells are vehicles. Each vehicle is either vertical or horizontal and occupies either two cells or three cells, depending on whether the vehicle is a car or truck.

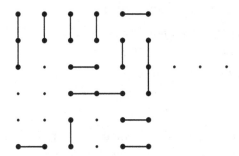

Fig. 18.1 A Rush Hour grid

Horizontal vehicles can move left or right, while vertical vehicles can move up or down. One fixed cell, three places down along the right vertical side of the grid, is special and is called the *exit* cell. One vehicle is special: it is horizontal and occupies cells to the left of the exit cell. The object of the puzzle is simply to move the special vehicle to the exit cell. An example starting grid is pictured in Figure 18.1.

There are various ways to represent the grid, of which the most obvious is to name each cell by a pair of Cartesian coordinates. A more space-efficient alternative (a useful consideration with breadth-first search) is to number the cells as follows:

1	2	3	4	5	6
8	9	10	11	12	13
15	16	17	18	19	20
22	23	24	25	26	27
29	30	31	32	33	34
36	37	38	39	40	41

The left and right borders are cells divisible by 7, the top border consists of cells with negative numbers and the bottom border has cells greater than 42. The exit cell is cell 20. A grid state can be defined as a list of pairs of cells, each pair being the rear and front cells occupied by a single vehicle. The vehicles in the grid are named implicitly by their positions in the list, with the special vehicle being vehicle 0, so the first pair represents the cells occupied by the special vehicle. For example, the grid of Figure 18.1 is represented by

$$g1 = [(17, 18), (1, 15), (2, 9), (3, 10), (4, 11), (5, 6), (12, 19),$$
$$(13, 27), (24, 26), (31, 38), (33, 34), (36, 37), (40, 41)]$$

This representation is captured by introducing the synonyms

$$
\begin{array}{lll}
\textbf{type } \textit{Cell}   & = & \textit{Int} \\
\textbf{type } \textit{Grid}   & = & [(\textit{Cell}, \textit{Cell})] \\
\textbf{type } \textit{Vehicle} & = & \textit{Int} \\
\textbf{type } \textit{Move}   & = & (\textit{Vehicle}, \textit{Cell}) \\
\textbf{type } \textit{State}   & = & \textit{Grid}
\end{array}
$$

The list of occupied cells can be constructed in increasing order by filling in the intervals associated with each vehicle and merging the results:

$$
\begin{array}{lll}
\textit{occupied} & :: & \textit{Grid} \rightarrow [\textit{Cell}] \\
\textit{occupied} & = & \textit{foldr } (\textit{merge} \cdot \textit{fillcells}) \, [\,] \\[4pt]
\textit{fillcells } (r, f) & = & \textbf{if } r > f{-}7 \textbf{ then } [r \mathbin{..} f] \textbf{ else } [r, r{+}7 \mathbin{..} f]
\end{array}
$$

A vehicle occupying the cells in the interval (r, f), where r is the rear and f is the front, is horizontal if $r > f-7$ and vertical if $r \leq f-7$. The free cells of a grid are now defined by

$$
\begin{array}{lll}
\textit{freecells}   & :: & \textit{Grid} \rightarrow [\textit{Cell}] \\
\textit{freecells } g & = & \textit{allcells} \setminus\!\setminus \textit{occupied } g
\end{array}
$$

where $\textit{allcells} = [c \mid c \leftarrow [1 \mathbin{..} 41], c \bmod 7 \neq 0]$. We omit the standard definitions of $\textit{merge}$ and the ordered list difference operator $\setminus\!\setminus$.

The function $\textit{moves}$ is implemented by

$$
\begin{array}{lll}
\textit{moves} & :: & \textit{Grid} \rightarrow [\textit{Move}] \\
\textit{moves } g & = & [(v, c) \mid (v, i) \leftarrow \textit{zip } [0..]\, g,\ c \leftarrow \textit{adjs } i,\ c \in \textit{fs}] \\
& & \textbf{where } \textit{fs} = \textit{freecells } g \\[4pt]
\textit{adjs } (r, f) & = & \textbf{if } r > f{-}7 \textbf{ then } [f{+}1, r{-}1] \textbf{ else } [f{+}7, r{-}7]
\end{array}
$$

A move (v, c) is legal if and only if cell c is unoccupied and adjacent, along the appropriate axis, to the cells currently occupied by v. Note that a move consists of moving a vehicle exactly one step on the grid.

The function $\textit{move}$ is implemented by

$$
\begin{array}{lll}
\textit{move } g \, (v, c) & = & g1 \mathbin{+\!\!+} \textit{adjust } i\, c : g2 \\
& & \textbf{where } (g1, i : g2) = \textit{splitAt } v \, g
\end{array}
$$

and $\textit{adjust}$ by

$$
\begin{array}{l}
\textit{adjust } (r, f)\, c \\
\quad \mid\ r > f{-}7 \quad = \ \textbf{if } c > f \textbf{ then } (r{+}1, c) \textbf{ else } (c, f{-}1) \\
\quad \mid\ \textbf{otherwise} \ = \ \textbf{if } c < r \textbf{ then } (c, f{-}7) \textbf{ else } (r{+}7, c)
\end{array}
$$

The arithmetic here is fairly self-explanatory and justification is omitted.

A grid is solved if the front of vehicle 0 is at the exit cell:

$$solved \quad :: \quad Grid \rightarrow Bool$$
$$solved\ g \quad = \quad snd\ (head\ g) = 20$$

We can now implement the breadth-first strategy by

$$bfsolve \quad :: \quad Grid \rightarrow Maybe\ [Move]$$
$$bfsolve\ g \quad = \quad bfsearch'\ [\,]\ [\,]\ [([\,], g)]$$

where *bfsearch'* is as defined in the previous section.

To implement *psearch* we need to define the two additional functions *goalmoves* and *premoves*. The former is easy:

$$goalmoves \quad :: \quad Grid \rightarrow Plan$$
$$goalmoves\ g \quad = \quad [(0, c)\ |\ c \leftarrow [snd\ (head\ g) + 1 .. 20]]$$

That is, *goalmoves* is the list of moves required to step the special vehicle 0 forward to the exit.

We need to define *premoves g m* only when m is a move with a target cell c that is currently occupied. In such a case there is a unique pair (v, i) in $zip\ [0..]\ g$ with interval i containing c. The function *blocker* discovers this pair:

$$blocker \quad :: \quad Grid \rightarrow Cell \rightarrow (Vehicle, (Cell, Cell))$$
$$blocker\ g\ c \quad = \quad search\ (zip\ [0..]\ g)\ c$$

$$search\ ((v, i) : vis)\ c \quad = \quad \textbf{if}\ covers\ c\ i\ \textbf{then}\ (v, i)\ \textbf{else}\ search\ vis\ c$$

$$covers\ c\ (r, f) \quad = \quad r \leq c \wedge c \leq f \wedge (r > f - 7 \vee (c - r)\ mod\ 7 = 0)$$

The blocking vehicle v, occupying the interval $i = (r, f)$, has to be moved out of the way so as to free the cell c; this is achieved by moving v left or right if horizontal, or down or up if vertical, an appropriate number of moves. These moves are computed with the function *freeingmoves*:

$$freeingmoves :: Cell \rightarrow (Vehicle, (Cell, Cell)) \rightarrow [[Move]]$$
$$freeingmoves\ c\ (v, (r, f))$$

$$\begin{aligned}
|\quad r > f - 7 \quad &= \quad [[(v, j)\ |\ j \leftarrow [f+1 .. c+n]]\ |\ c+n < k+7]\ \texttt{++}\\
&\qquad [[(v, j)\ |\ j \leftarrow [r-1, r-2 .. c-n]]\ |\ c-n > k]\\
|\quad \textbf{otherwise} \quad &= \quad [[(v, j)\ |\ j \leftarrow [r-7, r-14 .. c-m]]\ |\ c-m > 0]\ \texttt{++}\\
&\qquad [[(v, j)\ |\ j \leftarrow [f+7, f+14 .. c+m]]\ |\ c+m < 42]\\
\textbf{where}\ (k, m, n) &= (f - f\ mod\ 7, f - r + 7, f - r + 1)
\end{aligned}$$

If v is horizontal, so $r > f - 7$, then its length is $n = f - r + 1$ and, in order to free the cell c, we have to move v either rightwards to cell $c + n$ or leftwards to cell $c - n$, provided these cells are on the grid. If v is vertical, then its length is $n = (f - r) \operatorname{div} 7 + 1$ and we have to move v either upwards to cell $c - 7n$ or downwards to cell $c + 7n$, again provided these cells are on the grid. The value of m in this case is $m = 7 \times n$.

Now we can define *premoves* by

$$
\begin{array}{lcl}
\textit{premoves} & :: & \textit{Grid} \rightarrow \textit{Move} \rightarrow [[\textit{Move}]] \\
\textit{premoves } g\,(v, c) & = & \textit{freeingmoves } c\,(\textit{blocker } g\,c)
\end{array}
$$

However, the definition of *newplans* given in the previous section needs to be modified in order to work with Rush Hour. To see why, imagine the current plan consists of the goal moves $[(0, 19), (0, 20)]$ where vehicle 0 occupies the cells $[17, 18]$ on the opening grid. Suppose the first move $(0, 19)$ is not possible until the preparatory moves *pms* are made. Now it is perfectly possible that one of the moves in *pms* is $(0, 16)$, moving vehicle 0 one place to the left. After executing *pms* in preparation for the move $(0, 19)$ we see that $(0, 19)$ is no longer a well-defined move in the resulting grid because it requires 0 to move two steps forward, and so has first to be expanded to the single-step moves $[(0, 18), (0, 19)]$. Hence, we need to modify *newplans* to read

$$
\begin{array}{lcl}
\textit{newplans} & :: & \textit{Grid} \rightarrow \textit{Plan} \rightarrow [\textit{Plan}] \\
\textit{newplans } g\,[\,] & = & [\,] \\
\textit{newplans } g\,(m : ms) & = & \textit{mkplans } (\textit{expand } g\,m \mathbin{+\!\!+} ms) \\
\textbf{where } \textit{mkplans } ms & = & \textbf{if } m \in \textit{gms } \textbf{then } [ms] \textbf{ else} \\
& & \quad \textit{concat } [\textit{mkplans } (\textit{pms} \mathbin{+\!\!+} ms) \mid \\
& & \qquad \textit{pms} \leftarrow \textit{premoves } g\,m, \\
& & \qquad \textit{all } (\notin ms)\,\textit{pms}] \\
& & \quad \textbf{where } m = \textit{head } ms; \; \textit{gms} = \textit{moves } g
\end{array}
$$

The new function *expand*, which expands a possibly invalid move into a sequence of valid moves, is defined by

$$
\begin{array}{l}
\textit{expand } :: \textit{Grid} \rightarrow \textit{Move} \rightarrow [\textit{Move}] \\
\textit{expand } g\,(v, c) \\
\quad \mid \; r > f - 7 \;\;\; = \;\; \textbf{if } c > f \textbf{ then } [(v, p) \mid p \leftarrow [f{+}1 \mathbin{..} c]] \\
\qquad\qquad\qquad\qquad\quad \textbf{else } [(v, p) \mid p \leftarrow [r{-}1, r{-}2 \mathbin{..} c]] \\
\quad \mid \; \textbf{otherwise} \;\; = \;\; \textbf{if } c > f \textbf{ then } [(v, p) \mid p \leftarrow [f{+}7, f{+}14 \mathbin{..} c]] \\
\qquad\qquad\qquad\qquad\quad \textbf{else } [(v, p) \mid p \leftarrow [r{-}7, r{-}14 \mathbin{..} c]] \\
\quad \textbf{where } (r, f) = g \,!!\, v
\end{array}
$$

We can now implement the planning algorithm by

$$
\begin{array}{lcl}
\textit{psolve} & :: & \textit{Grid} \rightarrow \textit{Maybe } [\textit{Move}] \\
\textit{psolve } g & = & \textit{psearch}'\,[\,]\,[\,]\,[([\,], g, \textit{goalmoves } g)]
\end{array}
$$

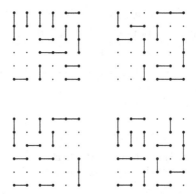

Fig. 18.2 Four Rush Hour problems

Table 18.1. *Solution times to solve four Rush Hour problems*

Puzzle	*bfsolve*	Moves	*psolve*	Moves	*dfsolve*	Moves
1	9.11	34	0.23	38	3.96	1228
2	4.71	18	0.04	27	3.75	2126
3	1.70	55	0.91	75	0.97	812
4	9.84	81	2.36	93	2.25	1305

where *psearch'* is as defined in the previous section except for the revised definition of *newplans*.

Results

So, how much better is *psolve* than *bfsolve*? We took four Rush Hour puzzles from Nick Baxter's puzzleworld site www.puzzleworld.org/SlidingBlock Puzzles/rushhour.htm, pictured in Figure 18.2. These were solved on a Pentium 3, 1000MHz computer, using GHCi. The results (times are in seconds) are shown in Table 18.1. As can be seen from Table 18.1, *psolve* is significantly faster than *bfsolve*, varying from a factor of 100 to a factor of 2. On the other hand, *psolve* may make unnecessary moves. For comparison, the times and move counts for *dfsolve* are also included in the table.

Final remarks

The PSPACE-completeness result for Rush Hour can be found in Flake and Baum (2002). I learned about Rush Hour at the 2008 Advanced Functional

Programming Summer School (Jones, 2008), where Mark Jones presented a series of lectures about the benefits of thinking functionally about problems. He gave a breadth-first solution, but he also challenged participants at the summer school to come up with a faster solution. This pearl was composed in response to Jones' challenge.

References

Flake, G. W. and Baum, E. B. (2002). Rush Hour is PSPACE-complete, or "Why you should generously tip parking lot attendants". *Theoretical Computer Science* **270** (1), 895–911.

Jones, M. P. (2008). Functional thinking. *Advanced Functional Programming Summer School*, Boxmeer, The Netherlands.

19

A simple Sudoku solver

HOW TO PLAY: Fill in the grid so that every row, every column and every 3×3 box contains the digits 1–9. There's no maths involved. You solve the puzzle with reasoning and logic.

Advice on how to play Sudoku, The Independent Newspaper

Introduction

The game of Sudoku is played on a 9×9 grid. Given a matrix, such as that in Figure 19.1, the idea is to fill in the empty cells with the digits 1 to 9 so that each row, column and 3×3 box contains the numbers 1 to 9. In general there may be one, none or many solutions, though in a good Sudoku puzzle there should always be a unique solution. Our aim in this pearl is to construct a Haskell program to solve Sudoku puzzles. Specifically, we will define a function *solve* for computing all the ways a given grid may be completed. If only one solution is wanted, then we can take the head of the list. Lazy evaluation means that only the first result will then be computed. We begin with a specification, then use equational reasoning to calculate a more efficient version. There is no maths involved, just reasoning and logic!

Specification

We begin with some basic data types, starting with matrices:

```
type Matrix a  =  [Row a]
type Row a     =  [a]
```

An $m \times n$ matrix is a list of m rows in which each row has the same length n. A grid is a 9×9 matrix of digits:

```
type Grid   =   Matrix Digit
type Digit  =   Char
```

147

		4		5	7			
				9	4			
3	6						8	
7	2			6				
		4		2				
			8			9	3	
4							5	6
		5	3					
		6	1			9		

Fig. 19.1 A Sudoku grid

The valid digits are 1 to 9 with 0 standing for a blank:

$$digits \; = \; [`1' .. `9']$$
$$blank \; = \; (== `0')$$

We suppose that a given grid contains only digits and blanks. We also suppose that the input grid is valid, meaning that no digit is repeated in any row, column or box.

Now for the specification. The aim is to write down the simplest and clearest specification of *solve* without regard to how efficient the result might be. One possibility is first to construct a list of all correctly completed grids, and then to test the given grid against them to identify those whose non-blank entries match the given ones. Another possibility, and the one we will adopt, is to start with the given grid and to install all possible choices for the blank entries. Then we compute all the grids that arise from making every possible choice and filter the result for the valid ones. This specification is formalised by

$$solve \; = \; filter \; valid \cdot expand \cdot choices$$

The subsidiary functions have types

$$
\begin{aligned}
choices \;\; &:: \;\; Grid \rightarrow Matrix \; Choices \\
expand \;\; &:: \;\; Matrix \; Choices \rightarrow [Grid] \\
valid \;\; &:: \;\; Grid \rightarrow Bool
\end{aligned}
$$

The simplest choice of *Choices* is **type** $Choices = [Digit]$. Then we have

$$
\begin{aligned}
choices \;\; &:: \;\; Grid \rightarrow Matrix \; Choices \\
choices \;\; &= \;\; map \; (map \; choice) \\
choice \; d \;\; &= \;\; \textbf{if} \; blank \; d \; \textbf{then} \; digits \; \textbf{else} \; [d]
\end{aligned}
$$

If the cell is blank, then all digits are installed as possible choices; otherwise there is no choice and a singleton is returned.

Next, expansion is just matrix Cartesian product:

$$
\begin{array}{lll}
expand & :: & Matrix\ Choices \rightarrow [Grid] \\
expand & :: & cp \cdot map\ cp
\end{array}
$$

The Cartesian product of a list of lists is given by

$$
\begin{array}{lll}
cp & :: & [[a]] \rightarrow [[a]] \\
cp\ [\,] & = & [[\,]] \\
cp\ (xs : xss) & = & [x : ys \mid x \leftarrow xs,\ ys \leftarrow cp\ xss]
\end{array}
$$

For example, $cp\ [[1, 2], [3], [4, 5]] = [[1, 3, 4], [1, 3, 5], [2, 3, 4], [2, 3, 5]]$. Thus, *map cp* returns a list of all possible choices for each row and $cp \cdot map\ cp$ installs each choice for the rows in all possible ways.

Finally, we deal with *valid*. A valid grid is one in which no row, column or box contains duplicates:

$$
\begin{array}{lll}
valid & :: & Grid \rightarrow Bool \\
valid\ g & = & all\ nodups\ (rows\ g)\ \wedge \\
& & all\ nodups\ (cols\ g)\ \wedge \\
& & all\ nodups\ (boxs\ g)
\end{array}
$$

The standard function *all p* applied to a finite list *xs* returns *True* if all elements of *xs* satisfy *p* and *False* otherwise. The function *nodups* can be defined by

$$
\begin{array}{lll}
nodups & :: & Eq\ a \Rightarrow [a] \rightarrow Bool \\
nodups\ [\,] & = & True \\
nodups\ (x : xs) & = & all\ (\neq x)\ xs\ \wedge\ nodups\ xs
\end{array}
$$

The function *nodups* takes quadratic time. As an alternative we could sort the list of digits and check that it is strictly increasing. Sorting can be done in $\Theta(n \log n)$ steps. However, with $n = 9$ it is not clear that sorting the digits is worthwhile. What would you prefer: $2n^2$ steps or $100n \log_2 n$ steps?

It remains to define *rows*, *cols* and *boxs*. If a matrix is given by a list of its rows, then *rows* is just the identity function on matrices:

$$
\begin{array}{lll}
rows & :: & Matrix\ a \rightarrow Matrix\ a \\
rows & = & id
\end{array}
$$

The function *cols* computes the transpose of a matrix. One possible definition is

$$
\begin{array}{lll}
cols & :: & Matrix\ a \to Matrix\ a \\
cols\ [xs] & = & [[x]\mid x \leftarrow xs] \\
cols\ (xs : xss) & = & zipWith\ (:)\ xs\ (cols\ xss)
\end{array}
$$

The function *boxs* is a little more interesting:

$$
\begin{array}{lll}
boxs & :: & Matrix\ a \to Matrix\ a \\
boxs & = & map\ ungroup \cdot ungroup \cdot map\ cols \cdot group \cdot map\ group
\end{array}
$$

The function *group* splits a list into groups of three:

$$
\begin{array}{lll}
group & :: & [a] \to [[a]] \\
group\ [\,] & = & [\,] \\
group\ xs & = & take\ 3\ xs : group\ (drop\ 3\ xs)
\end{array}
$$

The function *ungroup* takes a grouped list and ungroups it:

$$
\begin{array}{lll}
ungroup & :: & [[a]] \to [a] \\
ungroup & = & concat
\end{array}
$$

The action of *boxs* in the 4×4 case, when *group* splits a list into groups of two, is illustrated by

$$
\begin{pmatrix} a & b & c & d \\ e & f & g & h \\ i & j & k & l \\ m & n & o & p \end{pmatrix}
\longrightarrow
\begin{pmatrix} \begin{pmatrix} ab & cd \\ ef & gh \end{pmatrix} \\ \begin{pmatrix} ij & kl \\ mn & op \end{pmatrix} \end{pmatrix}
\longrightarrow
\begin{pmatrix} \begin{pmatrix} ab & ef \\ cd & gh \end{pmatrix} \\ \begin{pmatrix} ij & mn \\ kl & op \end{pmatrix} \end{pmatrix}
$$

The function *group · map group* produces a list of matrices; transposing each matrix and ungrouping yields the boxes.

Observe that instead of thinking about matrices in terms of indices, and doing arithmetic on indices to identify the rows, columns, and boxes, we have gone for definitions of these functions that treat the matrix as a complete entity in itself. Geraint Jones has aptly called this style *wholemeal programming*. Wholemeal programming is good for you: it helps to prevent a disease called indexitis and encourages lawful program construction.

For example, here are three laws that are valid on 9×9 Sudoku grids, in fact on arbitrary $N^2 \times N^2$ matrices:

$$
\begin{array}{lll}
rows \cdot rows & = & id \\
cols \cdot cols & = & id \\
boxs \cdot boxs & = & id
\end{array}
$$

Equivalently, all three functions are involutions. Two are easy to prove, but one is more difficult. The difficult law is not the one about *boxs*, as you might expect, but the involution property of *cols*. Though intuitively obvious, proving it from the definition of *cols* is slightly tricky. The involution property of *boxs* is an easy calculation using the involution property of *cols*, simple properties of *map* and the fact that *group* · *ungroup* = *id*.

Here are three more laws, valid on $N^2 \times N^2$ matrices of choices:

$$map\ rows \cdot expand\ =\ expand \cdot rows \qquad (19.1)$$

$$map\ cols \cdot expand\ =\ expand \cdot cols \qquad (19.2)$$

$$map\ boxs \cdot expand\ =\ expand \cdot boxs \qquad (19.3)$$

We will make use of these laws in a short while.

Pruning the matrix of choices

Though executable in theory, the specification of *solve* is hopeless in practice. Assuming about a half of the 81 entries are fixed initially (a generous estimate), there are about 9^{40}, or

147 808 829 414 345 923 316 083 210 206 383 297 601

grids to check! We therefore need a better approach. To make a more efficient solver, a good idea is to remove any choices from a cell c that already occur as singleton entries in the row, column and box containing c. A singleton entry corresponds to a fixed choice. We therefore seek a function

$$prune\ \ ::\ \ Matrix\ Choices \rightarrow Matrix\ Choices$$

so that

$$filter\ valid \cdot expand\ =\ filter\ valid \cdot expand \cdot prune$$

How can we define *prune*? Well, since a matrix is a list of rows, a good place to start is by pruning a single row. The function *pruneRow* is defined by

$$pruneRow \qquad ::\ \ Row\ Choices \rightarrow Row\ Choices$$
$$pruneRow\ row\ =\ map\ (remove\ fixed)\ row$$
$$\textbf{where}\ fixed = [d\ |\ [d] \leftarrow row]$$

The function *remove* removes choices from any choice that is not fixed:

$$remove\ xs\ ds\ \ =\ \ \textbf{if}\ singleton\ ds\ \textbf{then}\ ds\ \textbf{else}\ ds \setminus\!\setminus xs$$

The function *pruneRow* satisfies

$$filter\ nodups \cdot cp\ =\ filter\ nodups \cdot cp \cdot pruneRow \qquad (19.4)$$

The proof is left as an exercise.

We are now nearly ready for a calculation that will determine the function *prune*. Nearly, but not quite, because we are going to need two laws about *filter*. The first is that if $f \cdot f = id$, then

$$filter\ (p \cdot f) \quad = \quad map\ f \cdot filter\ p \cdot map\ f \tag{19.5}$$

Equivalently, $filter\ (p \cdot f) \cdot map\ f = map\ f \cdot filter\ p$. The second law is that

$$filter\ (all\ p) \cdot cp \quad = \quad cp \cdot map\ (filter\ p) \tag{19.6}$$

Proofs of (19.5) and (19.6) are again left as exercises.

Now for the calculation. The starting point is to rewrite $filter\ valid \cdot expand$:

$$
\begin{aligned}
filter\ valid \cdot expand \quad = \quad & filter\ (all\ nodups \cdot boxs) \cdot \\
& filter\ (all\ nodups \cdot cols) \cdot \\
& filter\ (all\ nodups \cdot rows) \cdot expand
\end{aligned}
$$

The order in which the filters appear on the right is not important. The plan of attack is to send each of these filters into battle with *expand*. For example, in the *boxs* case we argue:

$$
\begin{aligned}
& filter\ (all\ nodups \cdot boxs) \cdot expand \\
= \quad & \{(19.5),\ \text{since}\ boxs \cdot boxs = id\} \\
& map\ boxs \cdot filter\ (all\ nodups) \cdot map\ boxs \cdot expand \\
= \quad & \{(19.3)\} \\
& map\ boxs \cdot filter\ (all\ nodups) \cdot expand \cdot boxs \\
= \quad & \{\text{definition of}\ expand\} \\
& map\ boxs \cdot filter\ (all\ nodups) \cdot cp \cdot map\ cp \cdot boxs \\
= \quad & \{(19.6)\ \text{and}\ map\ f \cdot map\ g = map\ (f \cdot g)\} \\
& map\ boxs \cdot cp \cdot map\ (filter\ nodups \cdot cp) \cdot boxs \\
= \quad & \{(19.4)\} \\
& map\ boxs \cdot cp \cdot map\ (filter\ nodups \cdot cp \cdot pruneRow) \cdot boxs \\
= \quad & \{(19.6)\} \\
& map\ boxs \cdot filter\ (all\ nodups) \cdot cp \cdot map\ cp \cdot map\ pruneRow \cdot boxs \\
= \quad & \{\text{definition of}\ expand\} \\
& map\ boxs \cdot filter\ (all\ nodups) \cdot expand \cdot map\ pruneRow \cdot boxs \\
= \quad & \{(19.5)\ \text{in the form}\ map\ f \cdot filter\ p = filter\ (p \cdot f) \cdot map\ f\} \\
& filter\ (all\ nodups \cdot boxs) \cdot map\ boxs \cdot expand \cdot map\ pruneRow \cdot boxs \\
= \quad & \{(19.3)\} \\
& filter\ (all\ nodups \cdot boxs) \cdot expand \cdot boxs \cdot map\ pruneRow \cdot boxs
\end{aligned}
$$

We have shown that

$$filter\ (all\ nodups \cdot boxs) \cdot expand$$
$$= \quad filter\ (all\ nodups \cdot boxs) \cdot expand \cdot pruneBy\ boxs$$

where $pruneBy\ f = f \cdot map\ pruneRow \cdot f$. Repeating the same calculation for *rows* and *cols*, we obtain

$$filter\ valid \cdot expand \quad = \quad filter\ valid \cdot expand \cdot prune$$

where

$$prune \quad = \quad pruneBy\ boxs \cdot pruneBy\ cols \cdot pruneBy\ rows$$

In conclusion, the previous definition of *solve* can be replaced with a new one:

$$solve \quad = \quad filter\ valid \cdot expand \cdot prune \cdot choices$$

In fact, rather than just one *prune*, we can have as many *prunes* as we like. This is sensible, because after one round of pruning some choices may be resolved into singleton choices and another round of pruning may remove still more impossible choices. The simplest Sudoku problems are solved just by repeatedly pruning the matrix of choices until only singleton choices are left.

Single-cell expansion

For more devious puzzles we can combine pruning with another idea: expanding the choices for a single cell only. While *expand* installed all possible choices in all cells on the grid in one go, single-cell expansion picks on one cell and installs all the choices for that cell only. The hope is that mixing *prunes* with single-cell expansions can lead to a solution more quickly.

Therefore, we construct a function *expand1* that expands the choices for one cell only. This function is required to satisfy the property that, up to some permutation of the answer:

$$expand \quad = \quad concat \cdot map\ expand \cdot expand1 \tag{19.7}$$

A good choice of cell on which to perform expansion is one with the smallest number of choices (not equal to one of course). A cell with no choices means that the puzzle is unsolvable, so identifying such a cell quickly is a good idea. Think of cell containing cs choices as sitting in the middle of a row *row*, so $row = row1 \mathbin{+\!\!+} [cs] \mathbin{+\!\!+} row2$, in the matrix of choices, with rows *rows1* above this row and rows *rows2* below it. Then we can define

$$
\begin{aligned}
\textit{expand1} \quad &:: \quad \textit{Matrix Choices} \rightarrow [\textit{Matrix Choices}] \\
\textit{expand1 rows} \;=\; & [\textit{rows1} +\!\!+ [\textit{row1} +\!\!+ [c] : \textit{row2}] +\!\!+ \textit{rows2} \mid c \leftarrow \textit{cs}] \\
\textbf{where } (\textit{rows1}, \textit{row} : \textit{rows2}) \;=\; & \textit{break } (\textit{any smallest}) \textit{ rows} \\
(\textit{row1}, \textit{cs} : \textit{row2}) \;=\; & \textit{break smallest row} \\
\textit{smallest cs} \;=\; & \textit{length cs} == n \\
n \;=\; & \textit{minimum } (\textit{counts rows}) \\
\textit{counts} \;=\; & \textit{filter } (\neq 1) \cdot \textit{map length} \cdot \textit{concat}
\end{aligned}
$$

The value n is the smallest number of choices, not equal to one, in any cell of the matrix of choices. If the matrix of choices contains only singleton choices, then n is the minimum of the empty list, which is not defined. The standard function *break p* splits a list into two:

$$
\textit{break p xs} \;=\; (\textit{takeWhile } (\textit{not} \cdot p) \textit{ xs}, \textit{dropWhile } (\textit{not} \cdot p) \textit{ xs})
$$

Thus, *break* (*any smallest*) *rows* breaks the matrix into two lists of rows with the head of the second list being some row that contains a cell with the smallest number of choices. A second appeal to *break* then breaks this row into two sub-rows, with the head of the second being the element *cs* with the smallest number of choices. Each possible choice is installed and the matrix reconstructed. If there are zero choices, then *expand1* returns an empty list.

It follows from the definition of n that (19.7) holds only when applied to matrices with at least one non-singleton choice. Say a matrix is *complete* if all choices are singletons and *unsafe* if the singleton choices in any row, column or box contain duplicates. Incomplete and unsafe matrices can never lead to valid grids. A complete and safe matrix of choices determines a unique valid grid. These two tests can be implemented by

$$
\textit{complete} \;=\; \textit{all } (\textit{all single})
$$

where *single* is the test for a singleton list, and

$$
\textit{safe m} \;=\; \textit{all ok } (\textit{rows m}) \wedge \textit{all ok } (\textit{cols m}) \wedge \textit{all ok } (\textit{boxs m})
$$

where *ok row* = *nodups* $[d \mid [d] \leftarrow \textit{row}]$.

Assuming a matrix is safe but incomplete, we can calculate:

$$
\begin{aligned}
& \textit{filter valid} \cdot \textit{expand} \\
=\; & \{\text{since } \textit{expand} = \textit{concat} \cdot \textit{map expand} \cdot \textit{expand1} \\
& \quad \text{on incomplete matrices}\}
\end{aligned}
$$

$$filter\ valid \cdot concat \cdot map\ expand \cdot expand\,1$$
$$=\quad \{\text{since } filter\ p \cdot concat = concat \cdot map\ (filter\ p)\}$$
$$concat \cdot map\ (filter\ valid \cdot expand) \cdot expand\,1$$
$$=\quad \{\text{since } filter\ valid \cdot expand = filter\ valid \cdot expand \cdot prune\}$$
$$concat \cdot map(filter\ valid \cdot expand \cdot prune) \cdot expand\,1$$

Introducing $search = filter\ valid \cdot expand \cdot prune$, we therefore have, on safe but incomplete matrices, that

$$search \cdot prune = concat \cdot map\ search \cdot expand\,1$$

And now we can replace *solve* by a third version:

$$
\begin{array}{lll}
solve & = & search \cdot choices \\
search\ m & | \quad not\ (safe\ m) & = \quad [\,] \\
 & | \quad complete\ m' & = \quad [map\ (map\ head)\ m'] \\
 & | \quad \textbf{otherwise} & = \quad concat\ (map\ search\ (expand\,1\ m')) \\
 & | \quad \textbf{where}\ m' = prune\ m &
\end{array}
$$

This is our final simple Sudoku solver.

Final remarks

We tested the solver on 36 puzzles recorded at the website http://haskell.org/haskellwiki/Sudoku. It solved them in 8.8 s (on a 1GHz Pentium 3 PC). We also tested them on six minimal puzzles (each with 17 non-blank entries) chosen randomly from the 32 000 given at the site. It solved them in 111.4 s. There are about a dozen different Haskell Sudoku solvers at the site. All of these, including a very nice solver by Lennart Augustsson, deploy coordinate calculations. Many use arrays and most use monads. Ours is about twice as slow as Augustsson's on the nefarious puzzle (a particularly hard puzzle with the minimum 17 non-blank entries), but about 30 times faster than Yitz Gale's solver on easy puzzles. We also know of solvers that reduce the problem to Boolean satisfiability, constraint satisfaction, model checking and so on. I would argue that the one presented above is certainly one of the simplest and shortest. And at least it was derived, in part, by equational reasoning.

20

The *Countdown* problem

Introduction

Countdown is the name of a game from a popular British television programme; in France it is called *Le Conte est Bon*. Contestants are given six source numbers, not necessarily all different, and a target number, all of which are positive integers. The aim is to use some of the source numbers to build an arithmetic expression whose value is as close to the target as possible. Expressions are constructed using only the four basic operations of addition, subtraction, multiplication and division. Contestants are allowed 30 s thinking time. For example, with source numbers $[1, 3, 7, 10, 25, 50]$ and target 831 there is no exact solution; one expression that comes closest is $7 + (1 + 10) \times (25 + 50) = 832$. Our aim in this pearl is to describe various programs for solving *Countdown*, all based in one way or another on exhaustive search. *Countdown* is attractive as a case study in exhaustive search because the problem is simply stated and the different solutions illustrate the space and time trade-offs that have to be taken into account in comparing functional programs.

A simple program

Here is a straightforward program for *Countdown*:

$$countdown1 \quad :: \quad Int \to [Int] \to (Expr, Value)$$
$$countdown1\ n \quad = \quad nearest\ n \cdot concatMap\ mkExprs \cdot subseqs$$

First of all, the source numbers are given as a list; the order of the elements is unimportant, but duplicates do matter. We will suppose that the list is in ascending order, a fact that is exploited later on. Each selection is therefore represented by a nonempty subsequence. For each subsequence xs, all possible arithmetic expressions that can be constructed from xs are determined, along with their values.[1] The results are concatenated and one nearest the target is selected.

The ingredients making up *countdown*1 are defined as follows. First, *subseqs* returns a list of all the nonempty subsequences of a nonempty list:

$$
\begin{aligned}
subseqs\ [x] \quad &= \quad [[x]] \\
subseqs\ (x : xs) \quad &= \quad xss \mathbin{+\!\!+} [x] : map\ (x\ :)\ xss \\
&\qquad \textbf{where}\ xss = subseqs\ xs
\end{aligned}
$$

Next, the data types of expressions and values can be declared by

$$
\begin{aligned}
\textbf{data}\ Expr \quad &= \quad Num\ Int \mid App\ Op\ Expr\ Expr \\
\textbf{data}\ Op \quad &= \quad Add \mid Sub \mid Mul \mid Div \\
\textbf{type}\ Value \quad &= \quad Int
\end{aligned}
$$

The value of an expression is computed by

$$
\begin{aligned}
value \quad &:: \quad Expr \rightarrow Value \\
value\ (Num\ x) \quad &= \quad x \\
value\ (App\ op\ e1\ e2) \quad &= \quad apply\ op\ (value\ e1)\ (value\ e2)
\end{aligned}
$$

where *apply Add* = (+), *apply Sub* = (−) and so on. However, not all possible expressions are valid in *Countdown*. For instance, the result of a subtraction should be a positive integer, and division is valid only when the divisor divides the dividend exactly. An expression is valid if its subexpressions are, and if the operation at the root passes the test *legal*, where

$$
\begin{aligned}
legal \quad &:: \quad Op \rightarrow Value \rightarrow Value \rightarrow Bool \\
legal\ Add\ v1\ v2 \quad &= \quad True \\
legal\ Sub\ v1\ v2 \quad &= \quad (v2 < v1) \\
legal\ Mul\ v1\ v2 \quad &= \quad True \\
legal\ Div\ v1\ v2 \quad &= \quad (v1 \bmod v2 \mathbin{==} 0)
\end{aligned}
$$

The next ingredient is *mkExpr*, which creates a list of all legal expressions that can be built using the given subsequence:

$$
\begin{aligned}
mkExprs \quad &:: \quad [Int] \rightarrow [(Expr,\ Value)] \\
mkExprs\ [x] \quad &= \quad [(Num\ x,\ x)] \\
mkExprs\ xs \quad &= \quad [ev \mid (ys, zs) \leftarrow unmerges\ xs, \\
&\qquad\qquad ev1 \leftarrow mkExprs\ ys, \\
&\qquad\qquad ev2 \leftarrow mkExprs\ zs, \\
&\qquad\qquad ev \leftarrow combine\ ev1\ ev2]
\end{aligned}
$$

---

[1] Logically there is no need to return both expressions and values as the latter can be determined from the former. But, as we have seen in the pearl "Making a century" (Pearl 6), it is a good idea to avoid computing values more than once, so this optimisation has been incorporated from the outset.

Given an ordered list xs of length greater than one, *unmerges* xs is a list of all pairs (ys, zs) of nonempty lists such that *merge* ys zs = xs, where *merge* merges two ordered lists into one (it is in the specification of *unmerges* that we exploit the fact that inputs are ordered). One way of defining *unmerges* is as follows:

$$
\begin{aligned}
unmerges \quad&::\quad [a] \to [([a], [a])] \\
unmerges\ [x, y] \quad&=\quad [(([x], [y]), ([y], [x]))] \\
unmerges\ (x : xs) \quad&=\quad [([x], xs), (xs, [x])] \mathbin{+\!\!+} \\
&\qquad concatMap\ (add\ x)\ (unmerges\ xss) \\
&\qquad \textbf{where}\ add\ x\ (ys, zs) = [(x : ys, zs), (ys, x : zs)]
\end{aligned}
$$

It is an instructive exercise to calculate this definition of *unmerges* from its specification, but we will leave that pleasure to the reader.

The function *combine* is defined by

$$
\begin{aligned}
&combine :: (Expr, Value) \to (Expr, Value) \to [(Expr, Value)] \\
&combine\ (e1, v1)\ (e2, v2) \\
&\quad = \quad [(App\ op\ e1\ e2, apply\ op\ v1\ v2) \mid op \leftarrow ops,\ legal\ op\ v1\ v2]
\end{aligned}
$$

where $ops = [Add, Sub, Mul, Div]$.

Finally, the function *nearest* n takes a nonempty list of expressions and returns some expression in the list whose value is nearest the target n. We also want to stop searching the list if and when an expression is found whose value matches the target exactly:

$$
\begin{aligned}
nearest\ n\ ((e, v) : evs) \quad&=\quad \textbf{if}\ d == 0\ \textbf{then}\ (e, v) \\
&\qquad \textbf{else}\ search\ n\ d\ (e, v)\ evs \\
&\qquad \textbf{where}\ d = abs\ (n - v) \\[4pt]
search\ n\ d\ ev\ [\,] \quad&=\quad ev \\
search\ n\ d\ ev\ ((e, v) : evs) \quad&\mid\ d' == 0 \quad=\quad (e, v) \\
&\mid\ d' < d \quad=\quad search\ n\ d'\ (e, v)\ evs \\
&\mid\ d' \ge d \quad=\quad search\ n\ d\ ev\ evs \\
&\quad \textbf{where}\ d' = abs\ (n - v)
\end{aligned}
$$

For example, under GHCi (version 6.8.3 running on a 2394MHz laptop under Windows XP) we have

```
> display (countdown1 831 [1,3,7,10,25,50])
(7+((1+10)*(25+50))) = 832
(42.28 secs, 4198816144 bytes)
> length $ concatMap mkExprs $ subseqs [1,3,7,10,25,50]
4672540
```

So *countdown*1 takes about 42 s to determine and analyse about 4.5 million expressions, about 100 000 expressions per second. This is not within the 30 s limit, so is not good enough.

Two optimisations

There are two simple optimisations that can help improve matters. The first concerns the legality test. There are about 33 million expressions that can be built from six numbers, of which, depending on the input, between 4 million and 5 million are legal. But there is a great deal of redundancy. For example, each of the following pairs of expressions is essentially the same:

$$x + y \text{ and } y + x, \quad x * y \text{ and } y * x, \quad (x - y) + z \text{ and } (x + z) - y$$

A stronger legality test is provided by

$$
\begin{aligned}
legal \; Add \; v1 \; v2 &= (v1 \leq v2) \\
legal \; Sub \; v1 \; v2 &= (v2 < v1) \\
legal \; Mul \; v1 \; v2 &= (1 < v1) \wedge (v1 \leq v2) \\
legal \; Div \; v1 \; v2 &= (1 < v2) \wedge (v1 \bmod v2 \mathrel{==} 0)
\end{aligned}
$$

This stronger test takes account of the commutativity of $+$ and $*$ by requiring that arguments be in numerical order, and the identity properties of $*$ and $/$ by requiring that their arguments be non-unitary. This test reduces the number of legal expressions to about 300 000. One can go further and strengthen the legality test yet more, but we will leave that to the next section.

The second optimisation concerns *unmerges* and *combine*. As defined above, *unmerges* xs returns all pairs (ys, zs) such that *merge* $ys \; zs = xs$, and that means each pair is generated twice, once in the form (ys, zs) and once in the form (zs, ys). There is no need to double the work, and we can redefine *unmerges* so that it returns only the essentially distinct pairs:

$$
\begin{aligned}
unmerges \; [x, y] &= [([x], [y])] \\
unmerges \; (x : xs) &= [([x], xs)] \mathbin{+\!\!+} concatMap \; (add \; x) \; (unmerges \; xss) \\
&\quad \textbf{where} \; add \; x \; (ys, zs) = [(x : ys, zs), (ys, x : zs)]
\end{aligned}
$$

The function *combine* can be easily modified to take account of the new *unmerges*:

$$
\begin{aligned}
&combine \; (e1, v1) \; (e2, v2) \\
&\quad = [(App \; op \; e1 \; e2, apply \; op \; v1 \; v2) \mid op \leftarrow ops, \; legal \; op \; v1 \; v2] \mathbin{+\!\!+} \\
&\qquad [(App \; op \; e2 \; e1, apply \; op \; v2 \; v1) \mid op \leftarrow ops, \; legal \; op \; v2 \; v1]
\end{aligned}
$$

$comb1\ (e1, v1)\ (e2, v2)$
$$= \ [(App\ Add\ e1\ e2, v1 + v2), (App\ Sub\ e2\ e1, v2 - v1)] \mathbin{+\!\!+}$$
      if $1 < v1$ **then**
      $[(App\ Mul\ e1\ e2, v1 * v2)] \mathbin{+\!\!+} [(App\ Div\ e2\ e1, q) \mid r = 0]$
      else $[\,]$
      where $(q, r) = divMod\ v2\ v1$

$comb2\ (e1, v1)\ (e2, v2)$
$$= \ [(App\ Add\ e1\ e2, v1 + v2)] \mathbin{+\!\!+}$$
      if $1 < v1$ **then**
      $[(App\ Mul\ e1\ e2, v1 * v2), (App\ Div\ e1\ e2, 1)]$
      else $[\,]$

Fig. 20.1 Definitions of $comb1$ and $comb2$

However, a faster method is to incorporate the stronger legality test directly into the definition of *combine*:

$combine\ (e1, v1)\ (e2, v2)$
    $\mid\ \ v1 < v2 \ \ = \ \ comb1\ (e1, v1)\ (e2, v2)$
    $\mid\ \ v1 == v2 \ \ = \ \ comb2\ (e1, v1)\ (e2, v2)$
    $\mid\ \ v1 > v2 \ \ = \ \ comb1\ (e2, v2)\ (e1, v1)$

The function $comb1$ is used when the first expression has a value strictly less than the second, and $comb2$ when the two values are equal. Their definitions are given in Figure 20.1. Installing these changes leads to *countdown2*, whose definition is otherwise the same as *countdown1*. For example:

```
> display (countdown2 831 [1,3,7,10,25,50])
(7+((1+10)*(25+50))) = 832
(1.77 secs, 168447772 bytes)
> length $ concatMap mkExprs $ subseqs [1,3,7,10,25,50]
240436
```

This is better, in that it takes only about 2 s to determine and analyse about 250 000 expressions, but there is still room for improvement.

An even stronger legality test

In an attempt to restrict still further the number of expressions that have to be considered, let us say that an expression is in *normal form* if it is a sum of the form

$$[(e_1 + e_2) + \cdots + e_m] - [(f_1 + f_2) + \cdots + f_n]$$

where $m \geq 1$ and $n \geq 0$, both $e_1, e_2, \ldots$ and $f_1, f_2, \ldots$ are in ascending order of value, and each e_j and f_j is a product of the form

$$[(g_1 * g_2) * \cdots * g_p]/[(h_1 * h_2) * \cdots * h_q]$$

where $p \geq 1$ and $q \geq 0$, both $g_1, g_2, \ldots$ and $h_1, h_2, \ldots$ are in ascending order of value and each g_j and h_j is either a single number or an expression in normal form.

Up to rearrangements of subexpressions with equal values, each expression has a unique normal form. Of the 300 000 expressions over six numbers that are legal according to the earlier definition, only about 30 000 to 70 000 are in normal form. However, normal form does not eliminate redundancy completely. For example, the expressions $2 + 5 + 7$ and $2 * 7$ have the same value, but the latter is built out of numbers that are a subsequence of the former. There is, therefore, no need to build the former. But we will not explore the additional optimisation of "thinning" a list of expressions to retain only the really essential ones. Experiments show that thinning turns out to be not worth the candle: the savings made in analysing only the really essential expressions are outweighed by the amount of effort needed to determine them.

We can capture normal forms by strengthening the legality test, but this time we have to consider expressions as well as values. First let us define *non* by

$$
\begin{array}{lll}
non & :: & Op \rightarrow Expr \rightarrow Bool \\
non\ op\ (Num\ x) & = & True \\
non\ op1\ (App\ op2\ e1\ e2) & = & op1 \neq op2
\end{array}
$$

Then the stronger legality test is implemented by

$$
\begin{array}{ll}
legal & :: \quad Op \rightarrow (Expr,\ Value) \rightarrow (Expr,\ Value) \rightarrow Bool \\
\multicolumn{2}{l}{legal\ Add\ (e1, v1)\ (e2, v2)} \\
\quad = & (v1 \leq v2) \wedge non\ Sub\ e1 \wedge non\ Add\ e2 \wedge non\ Sub\ e2 \\
\multicolumn{2}{l}{legal\ Sub\ (e1, v1)\ (e2, v2)} \\
\quad = & (v2 < v1) \wedge non\ Sub\ e1 \wedge non\ Sub\ e2 \\
\multicolumn{2}{l}{legal\ Mul\ (e1, v1)\ (e2, v2)} \\
\quad = & (1 < v1 \wedge v1 \leq v2) \wedge non\ Div\ e1 \wedge non\ Mul\ e2 \wedge non\ Div\ e2 \\
\multicolumn{2}{l}{legal\ Div\ (e1, v1)\ (e2, v2)} \\
\quad = & (1 < v2 \wedge v1\ mod\ v2 = 0) \wedge non\ Div\ e1 \wedge non\ Div\ e2
\end{array}
$$

Just as before, we can incorporate the above legality test into a modified definition of *combine*. It is necessary only to change *comb1* and *comb2*. The revised definitions are given in Figure 20.2.

$comb1\ (e1, v1)\ (e2, v2)$
$=\ (\textbf{if}\ non\ Sub\ e1 \wedge non\ Sub\ e2\ \textbf{then}$
$\qquad [(App\ Add\ e1\ e2, v1 + v2)\ |\ non\ Add\ e2] \mathbin{+\!\!+} [(App\ Sub\ e2\ e1, v2 - v1)]$
$\qquad \textbf{else}\ [\ ])\ \mathbin{+\!\!+}$
$\quad (\textbf{if}\ 1 < v1 \wedge non\ Div\ e1 \wedge non\ Div\ e2\ \textbf{then}$
$\qquad [(App\ Mul\ e1\ e2, v1 * v2)\ |\ non\ Mul\ e2] \mathbin{+\!\!+} [(App\ Div\ e2\ e1, q)\ |\ r == 0]$
$\qquad \textbf{else}\ [\ ])$
$\quad \textbf{where}\ (q, r) = divMod\ v2\ v1$
$comb2\ (e1, v1)\ (e2, v2)$
$=\ [(App\ Add\ e1\ e2, v1 + v2)\ |\ non\ Sub\ e1,\ non\ Add\ e2,\ non\ Sub\ e2] \mathbin{+\!\!+}$
$\quad (\textbf{if}\ 1 < v1 \wedge non\ Div\ e1 \wedge non\ Div\ e2\ \textbf{then}$
$\qquad [(App\ Mul\ e1\ e2, v1 * v2)\ |\ non\ Mul\ e2] \mathbin{+\!\!+} [(App\ Div\ e1\ e2, 1)]$
$\qquad \textbf{else}\ [\ ])$

Fig. 20.2 New definitions of *comb1* and *comb2*

Calling the result of installing these changes *countdown3*, we have

```
> display (countdown3 831 [1,3,7,10,25,50])
(7+((1+10)*(25+50))) = 832
(1.06 secs, 88697284 bytes)
> length $ concatMap mkExprs $ subseqs [1,3,7,10,25,50]
36539
```

Now it takes only 1 s to determine and analyse about 36 000 expressions, which is roughly double the speed of *countdown2*.

Memoisation

Even ignoring the redundancy in the set of expressions being determined, computations are repeated because every subsequence is treated as an independent problem. For instance, given the source numbers [1 .. 6], expressions with basis [1 .. 5] will be computed twice, once for the subsequence [1 .. 5] and once for [1 .. 6]. Expressions with basis [1 .. 4] will be computed four times, once for each of the subsequences

$$[1, 2, 3, 4], \quad [1, 2, 3, 4, 5], \quad [1, 2, 3, 4, 6], \quad [1, 2, 3, 4, 5, 6]$$

In fact, expressions with a basis of k numbers out of n source numbers will be computed 2^{n-k} times.

One way to avoid repeated computations is to memoise the computation of *mkExprs*. In memoisation, the top-down structure of *mkExprs* is preserved but computed results are remembered and stored in a memo table for subsequent retrieval. To implement memoisation we need a data type *Memo* on which the following operations are supported:

$$
\begin{array}{lcl}
empty & :: & Memo \\
fetch & :: & Memo \rightarrow [Int] \rightarrow [(Expr, Value)] \\
store & :: & [Int] \rightarrow [(Expr, Value)] \rightarrow Memo \rightarrow Memo
\end{array}
$$

The value *empty* defines an empty memo table, *fetch* takes a list of source numbers and looks up the computed expressions for the list, while *store* takes a similar list together with the expressions that can be built from them, and stores the result in the memo table.

We can now rewrite *mkExprs* to read

$$
\begin{array}{lcl}
mkExprs & :: & Memo \rightarrow [Int] \rightarrow [(Expr, Value)] \\
mkExprs\ memo\ [x] & = & [(Num\ x, x)] \\
mkExprs\ memo\ xs & = & [ev \mid (ys, zs) \leftarrow unmerges\ xs, \\
& & \qquad ev1 \leftarrow fetch\ memo\ ys, \\
& & \qquad ev2 \leftarrow fetch\ memo\ zs, \\
& & \qquad ev \leftarrow combine\ ev1\ ev2]
\end{array}
$$

This code assumes that for any given subsequence *xs* of the input, all the arithmetic expressions for *ys* and *zs* for each possible split of *xs* have already been computed and stored in the memo table. This assumption is valid if we list and process the subsequences of the source numbers in such a way that if *xs* and *ys* are both subsequences of these numbers, and *xs* is a subsequence of *ys*, then *xs* appears before *ys* in the list of subsequences. Fortunately, the given definition of *subseqs* does possess exactly this property. We can now define

$$
\begin{array}{lcl}
countdown4 & :: & Int \rightarrow [Int] \rightarrow (Expr, Value) \\
countdown4\ n & = & nearest\ n \cdot extract \cdot memoise \cdot subseqs
\end{array}
$$

where *memoise* is defined by

$$
\begin{array}{lcl}
memoise & :: & [[Int]] \rightarrow Memo \\
memoise & = & foldl\ insert\ empty \\
insert\ memo\ xs & = & store\ xs\ (mkExprs\ memo\ xs)\ memo
\end{array}
$$

The function *extract* flattens a memo table, returning a list of all the expressions in it. This function is defined below when we fix on the structure of *Memo*.

One possible structure for *Memo* is a trie:

$$
\begin{array}{lcl}
\textbf{data}\ Trie\ a & = & Node\ a\ [(Int, Trie\ a)] \\
\textbf{type}\ Memo & = & Trie\ [(Expr, Value)]
\end{array}
$$

A trie is a Rose tree whose branches are labelled, in this case with an integer. The empty memo table is defined by *empty* = *Node* [ ] [ ]. We search a memo table by following the labels on the branches:

$$
\begin{array}{lll}
fetch & :: & Memo \to [Int] \to [(Expr,\ Value)] \\
fetch\ (Node\ es\ xms)\ [\,] & = & es \\
fetch\ (Node\ es\ xms)\ (x : xs) & = & fetch\ (follow\ x\ xms)\ xs \\
\\
follow & :: & Int \to [(Int,\ Memo)] \to Memo \\
follow\ x\ xms & = & head\ [m \mid (x',\ m) \leftarrow xms,\ x \mathbin{==} x']
\end{array}
$$

Note that searching a table for an entry with label xs returns an undefined result (the head of an empty list) if there is no path in the trie whose branches are labelled with xs. But this is not a problem, because the definition of *subseqs* guarantees that entries are computed in the right order, so all necessary entries will be present.

Here is how we store new entries:

$$
\begin{array}{l}
store :: [Int] \to [(Expr,\ Value)] \to Memo \to Memo \\
store\ [x]\ es\ (Node\ fs\ xms) = Node\ fs\ ((x,\ Node\ es\ [\,]) : xms) \\
store\ (x : xs)\ es\ (Node\ fs\ xms) \\
\quad = Node\ fs\ (yms + (x,\ store\ xs\ es\ m) : zms) \\
\qquad \textbf{where}\ (yms, (z, m) : zms) = break\ (equals\ x)\ xms \\
\qquad\qquad\quad equals\ x\ (z, m) = (x \mathbin{==} z)
\end{array}
$$

The definition of *store* assumes that if an entry for $xs + [x]$ is new, then the entries for xs are already present in the table. The Haskell function *break p* was defined in the previous pearl.

Finally, we can extract all entries from a memo table by

$$
\begin{array}{lll}
extract & :: & Memo \to [(Expr,\ Value)] \\
extract\ (Node\ es\ xms) & = & es + concatMap\ (extract \cdot snd)\ xms
\end{array}
$$

Now we have, for example:

```
> display (countdown4 831 [1,3,7,10,25,50])
(10*((1+7)+(3*25))) = 830
(0.66 secs, 55798164 bytes)
```

The computation returns a different expression, owing to the different order in which expressions are analysed, but at a cost of about half that of *countdown3*.

Skeleton trees

Memoisation of *countdown* comes at a cost: building the memo table makes heavy demands on the heap and much time is spent in garbage collection. How can we keep the advantage of memoisation while reducing space requirements?

Suppose we ignore the operators in an expression, focusing only on the parenthesis structure. How many different oriented binary trees can we build? In an oriented tree the order of the subtrees is not taken into account. We exploited this idea in an "oriented" definition of *unmerges*. It turns out that there are only 1881 oriented binary trees with a basis included in six given numbers. An oriented binary tree may also be called a *skeleton* tree. For an algorithm that is economical in its use of space we could, therefore, build these trees first, and only afterwards insert the operators.

Pursuing this idea, consider the following type of tip-labelled binary tree:

data *Tree* = *Tip Int* | *Bin Tree Tree*

Instead of memoising expressions we can memoise trees:

type *Memo* = *Trie* [*Tree*]

We can build trees in exactly the same way as we built expressions:

$$
\begin{array}{lll}
mkTrees & :: & Memo \rightarrow [Int] \rightarrow [Tree] \\
mkTrees\ memo\ [x] & = & [Tip\ x] \\
mkTrees\ memo\ xs & = & [Bin\ t1\ t2 \mid (ys, zs) \leftarrow unmerges\ xs, \\
& & \quad\quad t1 \leftarrow fetch\ memo\ ys, \\
& & \quad\quad t2 \leftarrow fetch\ memo\ zs]
\end{array}
$$

We can convert a tree into a list of expressions by inserting operators in all legal ways:

$$
\begin{array}{lll}
toExprs & :: & Tree \rightarrow [(Expr, Value)] \\
toExprs\ (Tip\ x) & = & [(Num\ x, x)] \\
toExprs\ (Bin\ t1\ t2) & = & [ev \mid ev1 \leftarrow toExprs\ t1,\ ev2 \leftarrow toExprs\ t2, \\
& & \quad\quad ev \leftarrow combine\ ev1\ ev2]
\end{array}
$$

Now we have

$$
\begin{array}{l}
countdown5\ n \\
\quad = \quad nearest\ n \cdot concatMap\ toExprs \cdot extract \cdot memoise \cdot subseqs
\end{array}
$$

| File | countdown1 | | countdown2 | | countdown3 | | countdown4 | | countdown5 | |
	Total	GC	Total	GC	Total	GC	Total	GC	Total	GC
d6	1.56	0.78	0.19	0.08	0.09	0.05	0.08	0.02	0.05	0.00
d7	77.6	36.9	2.03	1.19	0.44	0.09	0.53	0.30	0.33	0.02
d8	–	–	99.8	57.2	13.8	7.30	16.9	9.02	7.22	0.31

Fig. 20.3 Running times of *countdown* for inputs of six, seven and eight source numbers

where *memoise* is defined by

$$memoise \quad :: \quad [[Int]] \to Memo$$
$$memoise \quad = \quad foldl\ insert\ empty$$
$$insert\ memo\ xs \quad = \quad store\ xs\ (mkTrees\ memo\ xs)\ memo$$

Running our standard example yields

```
> display (countdown5 831 [1,3,7,10,25,50])
(10*((1+7)+(3*25))) = 830
(1.06 secs, 88272332 bytes)
```

So it seems on the evidence of this single test that memoising skeleton trees rather than expressions may not have been such a good idea. But the situation merits a closer look.

A further experiment

Let us see how the five versions of *countdown* described above perform with an optimising compiler. We compiled the five programs under GHC, version 6.8.3, with the $-O2$ flag set. The statistics were gathered using GHC's run-time system with the $-s$ flag. There were three files, $d6$, $d7$ and $d8$ containing six, seven and eight source numbers respectively. In each case we ensured there was no exact match, so the full space of possible expressions was explored. The statistics are provided in Figure 20.3. Shown are the total time and the time spent in garbage collection; all times are in seconds. The program *countdown*1 was not run on $d8$.

Three main conclusions can be drawn from the experiment. First and most obviously, compilation gives a substantial improvement over interpretation. Second, for six or seven source numbers, there is not much difference between *countdown*3 (the version with the strong legality test), *countdown*4 (the version with both the strong legality test and memoisation) and *countdown*5 (the version with the strong legality test and memoisation of skeleton trees rather than expressions). But for eight source numbers, the final version *countdown*5 has begun to pull away, running about twice as fast as the others, mostly owing to the reduced time spent in garbage collection, in fact about 5% of the total time, compared with about 50% for *countdown*3 and *countdown*4.

Final remarks

This pearl has been based on material extracted and modified from Bird and Mu (2005), which presents the specification of *Countdown* in a relational setting, and goes on to calculate a number of programs using the algebraic laws of fold and unfold. None of these calculations has been recorded above. *Countdown* was first studied in an earlier pearl (Hutton, 2002) as an illustration of how to prove that functional programs meet their specification. Hutton's aim was not to derive the best possible algorithm, but to present one whose correctness proof required only simple induction. Essentially, Hutton's proof dealt with the correctness of *countdown*2.

References

Bird, R. S. and Mu, S.-C. (2005). *Countdown*: a case study in origami programming. *Journal of Functional Programming* **15** (6), 679–702.

Hutton, G. (2002). The *Countdown* problem. *Journal of Functional Programming* **12** (6), 609–16.

21

Hylomorphisms and nexuses

Introduction

It was Erik Meijer who coined the name *hylomorphism* to describe a computation that consists of a fold after an unfold. The unfold produces a data structure and the fold consumes it. The intermediate data structure can be eliminated from the computation, a process called *deforestation*. The result is a pattern of recursion that fits most of the recursive definitions one is likely to meet in practice. Nevertheless, the intermediate data structure has its uses. It defines the *call-tree* of the hylomorphism, and can be made the workhorse of an alternative, and sometimes faster, implementation of the hylomorphism. Improvements in speed are possible when the call-tree contains *shared* nodes, nodes with more than one incoming edge. A tree with shared nodes is called a *nexus* and a nexus arises with any recursion whose recursive subproblems overlap, as is typical with dynamic programming. Our aim in this pearl is to illustrate how to build nexuses by considering two or three particularly interesting examples.

Folds, unfolds and hylomorphisms

Rather than discuss ideas in an abstract setting, we will consider just one example of an intermediate data structure, namely the following kind of leaf-labelled tree:

$$\textbf{data } \textit{Tree } a \;=\; \textit{Leaf } a \mid \textit{Node } [\textit{Tree } a]$$

The fold and unfold functions for *Tree a* depend on the isomorphism

$$\textit{Tree } a \;\approx\; \textit{Either } a \; [\textit{Tree } a]$$

To fold over a tree one has to supply an accumulating function with type *Either a* $[b] \rightarrow b$, and to unfold into a tree one has to supply a function with type $b \rightarrow$ *Either a* $[b]$. More precisely:

$$
\begin{aligned}
fold & \quad :: \quad (\mathit{Either}\; a\; [b] \to b) \to \mathit{Tree}\; a \to b \\
fold\; f\; t & \quad = \quad \textbf{case}\; t\; \textbf{of} \\
& \qquad\qquad \mathit{Leaf}\; x \quad \to \quad f\; (\mathit{Left}\; x) \\
& \qquad\qquad \mathit{Node}\; ts \quad \to \quad f\; (\mathit{Right}\; (\mathit{map}\; (fold\; f)\; ts)) \\
unfold & \quad :: \quad (b \to \mathit{Either}\; a\; [b]) \to b \to \mathit{Tree}\; a \\
unfold\; g\; x & \quad = \quad \textbf{case}\; g\; x\; \textbf{of} \\
& \qquad\qquad \mathit{Left}\; y \quad\;\; \to \quad \mathit{Leaf}\; y \\
& \qquad\qquad \mathit{Right}\; xs \quad \to \quad \mathit{Node}\; (\mathit{map}\; (unfold\; g)\; xs)
\end{aligned}
$$

Defining $hylo\; f\; g = fold\; f \cdot unfold\; g$ and deforesting, we obtain

$$
\begin{aligned}
hylo\; f\; g\; x \quad = \quad & \textbf{case}\; g\; x\; \textbf{of} \\
& \mathit{Left}\; y \quad\;\; \to \quad f\; (\mathit{Left}\; y) \\
& \mathit{Right}\; xs \quad \to \quad f\; (\mathit{Right}\; (\mathit{map}\; (hylo\; f\; g)\; xs))
\end{aligned}
$$

The pattern of this recursive definition is less familiar than it might be, mostly because the presence of the type *Either* obscures what is going on. So, let us simplify a little, while maintaining full generality. A function with type *Either a [b] → b* can be unpacked into two component functions and *fold* can be expressed in the alternative form

$$
\begin{aligned}
fold & \quad :: \quad (a \to b) \to ([b] \to b) \to \mathit{Tree}\; a \to b \\
fold\; f\; g\; (\mathit{Leaf}\; x) & \quad = \quad f\; x \\
fold\; f\; g\; (\mathit{Node}\; ts) & \quad = \quad g\; (\mathit{map}\; (fold\; f\; g)\; ts)
\end{aligned}
$$

Similarly, a function with type $b \to \mathit{Either}\; a\; [b]$ can be unpacked into three simpler functions, and *unfold* can be expressed in the alternative form

$$
\begin{aligned}
unfold & \quad :: \quad (b \to \mathit{Bool}) \to (b \to a) \to (b \to [b]) \to b \to \mathit{Tree}\; a \\
unfold\; p\; v\; h\; x & \quad = \quad \textbf{if}\; p\; x\; \textbf{then}\; \mathit{Leaf}\; (v\; x)\; \textbf{else} \\
& \qquad\quad \mathit{Node}\; (\mathit{map}\; (unfold\; p\; v\; h)\; (h\; x))
\end{aligned}
$$

With these new definitions, $hylo = fold\; f\; g \cdot unfold\; p\; v\; h$ can be deforested to read

$$
hylo\; x \quad = \quad \textbf{if}\; p\; x\; \textbf{then}\; f\; (v\; x)\; \textbf{else}\; g\; (\mathit{map}\; hylo\; (h\; x))
$$

This is better than before, but now we see that the function v is redundant since its effect can be absorbed into a modified definition of f. Removing it gives

$$
hylo\; x \quad = \quad \textbf{if}\; p\; x\; \textbf{then}\; f\; x\; \textbf{else}\; g\; (\mathit{map}\; hylo\; (h\; x)) \tag{21.1}
$$

as the general form of a hylomorphism over *Tree a*. In words, if the argument x is basic $(p\; x)$, then compute the result $f\; x$ directly; otherwise decompose x into subproblems $(h\; x)$, compute the result of each subproblem

($map\ hylo\ (h\ x)$) and assemble the results with g. At last, this seems a very familiar form of recursion.

Definition (21.1) is the deforested version of $fold\ f\ g \cdot unfold\ p\ id\ h$. As the opposite of deforestation there is the idea of *annotation*, in which the tree structure is maintained to the end of the computation, but labels are attached to each node that carries the value of the hylomorphism for the subtree defined by the node. More precisely, define the labelled variant *LTree* of *Tree* by

data $LTree\ a\ =\ LLeaf\ a\ |\ LNode\ a\ [LTree\ a]$

Now define *fill* by

$$
\begin{array}{ll}
fill & ::\ (a \to b) \to ([b] \to b) \to Tree\ a \to LTree\ b \\
fill\ f\ g & =\ fold\ (lleaf\ f)\ (lnode\ g)
\end{array}
$$

where the smart constructors *lleaf* and *lnode* are defined by

$$
\begin{array}{ll}
lleaf\ f\ x & =\ LLeaf\ (f\ x) \\
lnode\ g\ ts & =\ LNode\ (g\ (map\ label\ ts))\ ts
\end{array}
$$

and *label* by

$$
\begin{array}{ll}
label\ (LLeaf\ x) & =\ x \\
label\ (LNode\ x\ ts) & =\ x
\end{array}
$$

The function *fill* consumes a tree, but it produces a labelled tree with exactly the same structure in which each label is the result of folding the subtree rooted there. The label at the root of the tree gives the value of the hylomorphism, so

$$hylo\ =\ label \cdot fill\ f\ g \cdot unfold\ p\ id\ h$$

With this definition we have arrived at the central idea of the pearl. Suppose that the tree $unfold\ p\ id\ h$ is a genuine nexus, and suppose we can apply *fill* $f\ g$ to it without destroying sharing. Then *hylo* can be computed more efficiently than by the recursive method of (21.1).

It remains to see how the idea works out in practice. In all the examples to come we are going to restrict (21.1) to the case where x is a nonempty list and p is the test for a singleton list. Thus, our examples are all hylomorphisms of the form

$$
\begin{array}{ll}
hylo & ::\ ([a] \to b) \to ([b] \to b) \to ([a] \to [[a]]) \to [a] \to b \\
hylo\ f\ g\ h & =\ fold\ f\ g \cdot mkTree\ h
\end{array}
$$

where $mkTree\ h\ =\ unfold\ single\ id\ h$ and *single* is the test for singletons. In particular, h takes a list of length at least two as argument and returns a list of nonempty lists.

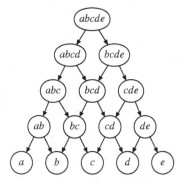

Fig. 21.1 A nexus

Three examples

For our first example, take $h = split$, where

$$split\ xs\ =\ [take\ n\ xs, drop\ n\ xs]\quad \textbf{where}\ \ n = length\ xs\ \text{div}\ 2$$

Restricted to lists xs of length 2^n, the result of $mkTree\ split\ xs$ is a perfect binary tree with $2^n - 1$ nodes and 2^n leaves, each labelled with singleton lists, one for each element of xs. There is no sharing, so the nexus also has this number of nodes and leaves. As a concrete instance, $hylo\ id\ merge\ split$ is the standard divide and conquer algorithm for mergesort restricted to lists whose lengths are a power of 2. Contrast this with our second example, in which we take $h = isegs$, where

$$isegs\ xs\ =\ [init\ xs, tail\ xs]$$

For example, $isegs$ "abcde" = ["abcd", "bcde"]. The function $isegs$ is so named because it returns the two *immediate segments* of a list of length at least 2. The result of $mkTree\ isegs\ xs$ is a perfect binary tree whose leaves are again labelled with singletons. The tree has size $2^n - 1$ nodes where $n = length\ xs$, so it takes at least this time to build it. However, unlike our first example, subtrees can be shared, giving us a genuine nexus. An example is pictured in Figure 21.1. The nexus has been labelled with the distinct nonempty segments of $abcde$. More precisely, it has been filled with $fill\ id\ recover$, where

$$
\begin{aligned}
recover\qquad &::\ \ [[a]] \rightarrow [a]\\
recover\ xss\ &=\ \ head\ (head\ xss) : last\ xss
\end{aligned}
$$

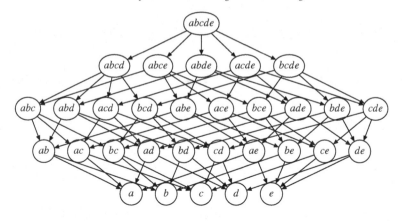

Fig. 21.2 Another nexus

The function *recover* satisfies *recover · isegs* = *id*. The nexus has $n(n+1)/2$ nodes for an input of length n, so sharing gives a significant reduction in size.

For our third example, take $h = minors$, where

$$minors\ [x, y] \quad = \quad [[x], [y]]$$
$$minors\ (x : xs) \quad = \quad map\ (x\ :)\ (minors\ xs) \mathbin{+\!\!+} [xs]$$

For example, *minors* "abcde" = ["abcd", "abce", "abde", "acde", "bcde"]. The function *minors* returns those subsequences of its argument in which just one element is dropped.[1] The result returned by *mkTree minors xs*, where *xs* is a nonempty list, is once again a tree labelled with singletons. For an input of length n the tree has size $S(n)$, where $S(0) = 0$ and $S(n+1) = 1 + (n+1)S(n)$. Solving this recurrence gives

$$S(n) \quad = \quad n! \sum_{k=1}^{n} \frac{1}{k!}$$

so $S(n)$ is between $n!$ and $en!$.[2] Again, there is potential for sharing, and one nexus is pictured in Figure 21.2. The nexus has been labelled with the distinct nonempty subsequences of *abcde*; more precisely, it has been filled by *fill id recover*, where *recover* is the same as in our second example. The nexus has only $2^n - 1$ nodes, which is a substantial reduction over the tree.

---

[1] The function *minors* appears again in the following two pearls in connection with matrices.
[2] The sequence appears as A002627 in Sloane's integer sequences, which gives $S(n) = \lfloor (e-1)n! \rfloor$.

Building a nexus

We now turn to the problem of how to build a nexus and how to fill it without destroying sharing. In all our examples the nexus has its leaves at the same depth, so one obvious idea is to build the nexus *fill f g · mkTree h* layer by layer from bottom to top. Building stops when we have a singleton layer. It also seems obvious that each layer should be a list of labelled trees, i.e. [*LTree a*], but this decision is premature. Instead, we postulate a type *Layer a*, so that each layer is an element of *Layer* (*LTree a*). The general bottom-up scheme for constructing the nexus of *fill f g · mkTree h* for various *h* is then implemented by

$$mkNexus\ f\ g\ =\ label \cdot extractL \cdot until\ singleL\ (stepL\ g) \cdot initialL\ f$$

where the subsidiary functions have the following types:

$$
\begin{array}{lll}
initialL & :: & ([a] \rightarrow b) \rightarrow [a] \rightarrow Layer\ (LTree\ b) \\
stepL & :: & ([b] \rightarrow b) \rightarrow Layer\ (LTree\ b) \rightarrow Layer\ (LTree\ b) \\
singleL & :: & Layer\ (LTree\ b) \rightarrow Bool \\
extractL & :: & Layer\ (LTree\ b) \rightarrow LTree\ b
\end{array}
$$

Our aim is to find implementations of these four functions for each of the three instantiations, *h = split*, *h = isegs* and *h = minors*.

The first two, *h = split* and *h = isegs*, are easy because we can get away with choosing *Layer a = [a]* and defining

$$
\begin{array}{lll}
initialL\ f & = & map\ (lleaf\ f \cdot wrap) \\
singleL & = & single \\
extractL & = & head
\end{array}
$$

where *wrap x = [x]*. Thus, the initial layer is a list of leaves. The definition of *stepL* for *h = split* is

$$stepL\ g\ =\ map\ (lnode\ g) \cdot group$$

where *group* :: [a] → [[a]] groups a list into pairs and is defined by

$$
\begin{array}{lll}
group\ [\,] & = & [\,] \\
group\ (x : y : xs) & = & [x, y] : group\ xs
\end{array}
$$

With these definitions we have, for example, that *mkNexus id merge xs*, where *xs* is a list whose length is a power of 2, is a bottom-up definition of mergesort in which elements are merged in pairs, then merged in fourths, and so on.

For $h = isegs$ we just have to change the definition of *group* to read

$$group\ [x] \qquad\quad = \quad []$$
$$group\ (x : y : xs) \quad = \quad [x, y] : group\ (y : xs)$$

Thus, *group xs* now returns a list of the adjacent pairs of elements of *xs*. This choice is a fairly obvious one, as can be appreciated by referring to Figure 21.1, and we omit a formal proof.

As might be expected, the case $h = minors$ is considerably more difficult. We have to find some way of grouping the trees at one level for assembly into the trees at the next level. Let us begin slowly by seeing what happens to the bottom layer, a list of leaves. We have to pair up the leaves, and one way of doing so is illustrated for five leaves a, b, c, d and e by

$$(ab \quad ac \quad ad \quad ae) \quad (bc \quad bd \quad be) \quad (cd \quad ce) \quad (de)$$

Here, *ab* abbreviates $[a, b]$ and so on. Ignoring the parenthetical information, the second layer is obtained by redefining *group* to read

$$group\ [x] \qquad = \quad []$$
$$group\ (x : xs) \quad = \quad map(bind\ x)\ xs + group\ xs$$
$$\mathbf{where}\ bind\ x\ y = [x, y]$$

At the next level we have to combine pairs into triples, and the way to do this is to exploit the grouping structure implicit in the second layer: pair up the elements in the first group and combine each pair with the corresponding element in the remaining groups. Then carry out the tripling procedure with the remaining groups. This leads to the third layer

$$((abc \quad abd \quad abc) \quad (acd \quad acc) \quad (adc)) \quad ((bcd \quad bce) \quad (bde)) \quad ((cde))$$

in which *abc* abbreviates $[[a, b], [a, c], [b, c]]$, and so on. The fourth layer, namely a grouping of quadruples,

$$(((abcd \quad abce) \quad (abde)) \quad ((acde))) \quad (((bcde)))$$

can be computed in the same fashion: this time triple up the first group and combine each triple with the corresponding triple in the remaining groups and then repeat the quadrupling for the remaining groups.

The necessary grouping information can be captured by representing each layer as a list of trees; in other words, a forest. The forest has shape constraints and is determined by two numbers, its length n and the common depth d of its component trees. A forest with depth 0 consists of a list of n leaves. A forest of length n and depth $d+1$ consists of a list of n trees in which the children of the first tree are a forest of length n and depth d, the children of the second tree are a forest of length $n-1$ and depth d, and so on, down to the final tree whose children are a forest of length 1 and depth d. The bottom layer of our nexus is a forest of length n and depth 0, the next layer a forest of length $n-1$ and depth 1, and so on, with the top layer being a forest of length n and depth $n-1$. As a data type, a forest is an element of [*Tree a*], so we define *Layer a* = [*Tree a*]. The fact that we started out the pearl with the type *Tree a* is purely fortuitous; we would have had to declare the type *Tree a* anyway to define forests.

Here are the implementations of *initialL*, *singleL* and *extractL* for building a nexus with $h = minors$:

$$
\begin{aligned}
initialL\ f\ &=\ map\ (Leaf \cdot lleaf\ f \cdot wrap) \\
singleL\ &=\ single \\
extractL\ &=\ extract \cdot head \\
&\quad \textbf{where}\ extract\ (Leaf\ x)\ \ =\ x \\
&\qquad\qquad\quad extract\ (Node\ [t])\ =\ extract\ t
\end{aligned}
$$

The function *initialL* constructs a forest of depth 0 whose labels are the leaves of a labelled tree (an element of *LTree a*). The function *extractL* takes a forest of length 1 and some depth d and extracts its label. It is a bit mind-boggling that the computation of *mkNexus* is carried out in terms of a data structure of type [*Tree (LTree a)*], a list of trees of labelled trees.

It remains to define *stepL*, which is given by

$$stepL\ g\ =\ map\ (mapTree\ (lnode\ g)) \cdot group$$

where *mapTree* is the map function for *Tree a* and

$$
\begin{aligned}
&group\ ::\ [Tree\ a] \rightarrow [Tree\ [a]] \\
&group\ [t]\ =\ [\ ] \\
&group\ (Leaf\ x : vs) \\
&\quad =\ Node\ [Leaf\ [x, y]\ |\ Leaf\ y \leftarrow vs] : group\ vs \\
&group\ (Node\ us : vs) \\
&\quad =\ Node\ (zipWith\ combine\ (group\ us)\ vs) : group\ vs
\end{aligned}
$$

$$
\begin{aligned}
combine\ (Leaf\ xs)\ (Leaf\ x)\ &=\ Leaf\ (xs \mathbin{+\!\!+} [x]) \\
combine\ (Node\ us)\ (Node\ vs)\ &=\ Node\ (zipWith\ combine\ us\ vs)
\end{aligned}
$$

These definitions formalise the verbal description of the process given earlier. To justify them we have to prove that

$$mkNexus\ f\ g\ =\ fill\ f\ g \cdot mkTree\ minors$$

However, the proof is rather long and we omit it.

Why build the nexus?

A good question. Everything we have said above about building a nexus bottom up and layer by layer applies equally well if we throw away the nexus and just retain the labelling information. Take the case $h = isegs$ and consider *solve*, where

$$solve \quad :: \quad [a] \to b) \to ([b] \to b) \to [a] \to b$$
$$solve\ f\ g \quad = \quad head \cdot until\ single\ (map\ g \cdot group) \cdot map\ (f \cdot wrap)$$

and *group* is the function associated with *isegs*. The function *solve f g* implements the hylomorphism *hylo f g isegs* without building a nexus. Similarly, consider *solve*, where

$$solve\ f\ g \quad = \quad extractL \cdot until\ singleL\ (step\ g) \cdot map\ (Leaf \cdot f \cdot wrap)$$
$$step\ g \quad = \quad map\ (mapTree\ g) \cdot group$$

and *extractL*, *singleL* and *group* are the functions associated with *minors*. Again, *solve f g* implements the hylomorphism *hylo f g minors* without building a nexus.

The answer to the question is that the nexus is useful when we want to consider problems that are variants of the ones discussed above. For example, a standard problem involving segments is the problem of *optimal bracketing*, in which one seeks to bracket an expression $x_1 \oplus x_2 \oplus \cdots \oplus x_n$ in the best possible way. It is assumed that $\oplus$ is an associative operation, so the way in which the brackets are inserted does not affect the value. However, different bracketings may have different costs. The cost of computing $x \oplus y$ depends on the sizes of x and y, and the recursive solution makes use not of *isegs* but the function *uncats*, where

$$uncats\ [x, y] \quad = \quad [([x], [y])]$$
$$uncats\ (x : xs) \quad = \quad ([x], xs) : map\ (cons\ x)\ (uncats\ xs)$$
$$\mathbf{where}\ cons\ x\ (ys, zs) = (x : ys, zs)$$

For example, *uncats* "abcde" is

$$[(\text{``a''}, \text{``bcde''}), (\text{``ab''}, \text{``cde''}), (\text{``abc''}, \text{``de''}), (\text{``abcd''}, \text{``e''})]$$

Each of these pairs represents a possible initial bracketing, and a minimum cost solution is obtained by recursively computing the cost and sizes of each component in each pair and then taking a minimum of the costs of combining them.

Using *uncats* in place of *isegs* does not give us an element of *Tree a* but a more complicated kind of tree in which each "subtree" is a list of pairs of subtrees. Nevertheless, we can solve the bracketing problem by computing the nexus for *isegs*, provided we replace the definition of the smart constructor *lnode* with another one:

$$lnode\ g\ [u, v] \quad = \quad LNode\ (g\ (zip\ (lspine\ u)\ (rspine\ v)))\ [u, v]$$

The functions $lspine, rspine :: LTree\ a \to [a]$ are defined by

$$
\begin{aligned}
lspine\ (LLeaf\ x) \quad &= \quad [x] \\
lspine\ (LNode\ x\ [u, v]) \quad &= \quad lspine\ u \mathbin{+\!\!+} [x] \\
rspine\ (LLeaf\ x) \quad &= \quad [x] \\
rspine\ (LNode\ x\ [u, v]) \quad &= \quad [x] \mathbin{+\!\!+} rspine\ r
\end{aligned}
$$

For example, the left and right spines of the two subtrees of the tree of Figure 21.1 are $[a, ab, abc, abcd]$ and $[bcde, cde, de, e]$. Zipping them together gives *uncats abcde*. The definition of *lspine* takes quadratic time, but it is easy to make it take linear time with the help of an accumulating parameter.

As a second example, consider the nexus of subsequences in Figure 21.2. One example of a problem involving subsequences is the *Countdown* example considered in the previous pearl. In that problem we made use of a function *unmerges* defined by

$$
\begin{aligned}
unmerges\ [x, y] \quad &= \quad [([x], [y])] \\
unmerges\ (x : xs) \quad &= \quad [([x], xs)] \mathbin{+\!\!+} concatMap\ (add\ x)\ (unmerges\ xss) \\
&\quad\ \textbf{where}\ add\ x\ (ys, zs) = [(x : ys, zs), (ys, x : zs)]
\end{aligned}
$$

For example, *unmerges* "abcd" is

$$
\begin{aligned}
&[(\text{``a''}, \text{``bcd''}), (\text{``ab''}, \text{``cd''}), (\text{``b''}, \text{``acd''}), (\text{``abc''}, \text{``d''}), \\
&\ (\text{``bc''}, \text{``ad''}), (\text{``ac''}, \text{``bd''}), (\text{``c''}, \text{``abd''})]
\end{aligned}
$$

The order in which the pairs of subsequences appear in this list is not important, and neither is the order within each pair. What is important is that each subsequence is paired with its complement. In *Countdown*, the set of possible expressions one can build from a list *xs* of integers in ascending order is computed by recursively building the expressions for each list in each component of *unmerges xs* and then combining results.

Using *unmerges* in place of *minors* does not give us an element of *Tree a*, but rather a more complicated data structure. Nevertheless, just as before, we can solve *Countdown* by computing the nexus for *minors* provided we replace the definition of the smart constructor *lnode* with another one. What we have to do, in effect, is to find some way of extracting *unmerges* from the labels of the nexus associated with a node. That means retrieving every

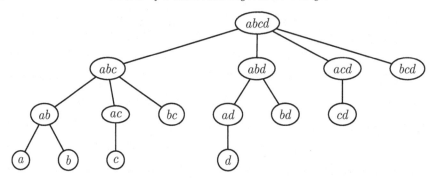

Fig. 21.3 A binomial spanning tree

label of the nexus. In principle this can be done by carrying out a *breadth-first* traversal of the nexus. For example, the breadth-first traversal of the nexus associated with *abcd* in Figure 21.2, minus its first element, is

  abc, abd, acd, bcd, ab, ac, bc, ad, bd, cd, a, b, c, d

If we split this list into two halves and zip the first half with the reverse of the second half, we arrive at *unmerges* "abcd", though the pairs appear in a different order, as do the components of each pair.

   However, any traversal of a graph requires us to keep track of nodes visited, and this is not possible with a nexus because two nodes cannot be checked for equality. The alternative is first to construct a *spanning tree* of the nexus and then to traverse its subtrees in breadth-first order. Traversing a forest is implemented by

```
traverse  :: [LTree a] → [a]
traverse [ ]  =  [ ]
traverse ts   =  map label ts ++ traverse (concatMap subtrees ts)

subtrees (LLeaf x)     =  [ ]
subtrees (LNode x ts)  =  ts
```

One spanning tree of the nexus associated with *abcd* in Figure 21.2 is pictured in Figure 21.3. This tree is a *binomial tree* of rank 4. Binomial trees are close cousins of the trees in the forest used to construct the nexus. A binomial tree of rank n has n children, which are, in order, binomial trees of ranks $n-1, n-2, \ldots, 0$. To construct the binomial spanning tree of the nexus, we have to drop children, none from the first subtree, one from the second subtree and so on. The same recipe has to be applied recursively to the children. Thus, for the kth child we have to drop k children from its first child, $k + 1$ children from its second child and so on. The function *forest k*, defined by

$$forest\ k\ (LLeaf\ x : ts)\ =\ LLeaf\ x : ts$$
$$forest\ k\ (LNode\ x\ us : vs)$$
$$=\ LNode\ x\ (forest\ k\ (drop\ k\ us)) : forest\ (k + 1)\ vs$$

carries out this pruning. Now we can define

$$lnode\ g\ ts\ =\ LNode\ (g\ (zip\ xs)\ (reverse\ ys))\ ts$$
$$\textbf{where}\ (xs, ys) = halve\ (traverse\ (forest\ 0\ ts))$$

where *halve xs = splitAt (length xs* div 2) *xs*.

Final remarks

The name hylomorphism first appeared in Meijer (1992); see also Meijer *et al.* (1991). The material in this pearl has been drawn from two main sources. Nexus building was described first in Bird and Hinze (2003), where another way of building the nexus for *minors* was given, one that used a cyclic tree with up and down pointers. Later on, in Bird (2008), it was shown that for some problems, admittedly of a fairly restricted class, the essential function *group* for building each layer of the nexus could be expressed as the transpose of the decomposition function *h* of the hylomorphism.

References

Bird, R. S. and Hinze, R. (2003). Trouble shared is trouble halved. *ACM SIGPLAN Haskell Workshop*, Uppsala, Sweden.

Bird, R. S. (2008). Zippy tabulations of recursive functions. In *LNCS 5133: Proceedings of the Ninth International Conference on the Mathematics of Program Construction*, ed. P. Audebaud and C. Paulin-Mohring. pp. 92–109.

Meijer, E. (1992). Calculating compilers. PhD thesis, Nijmegen University, The Netherlands.

Meijer, E., Fokkinga, M. and Paterson, R. (1991). Functional programming with bananas, lenses, envelopes and barbed wire. *Proceedings of the 5th ACM Conference on Functional Programming Languages and Computer Architecture*. New York, NY: Springer-Verlag, pp. 124–44.

22

Three ways of computing determinants

Introduction

The determinant, $\det(A)$, or $|A|$, of an $n \times n$ matrix $A = (a_{ij})$ can be defined by the Leibniz formula

$$|A| = \sum_{\pi} \text{sign}\,(\pi) \prod_{1 \leq j \leq n} a_{j\pi(j)}$$

The sum is taken over all permutations π of $[1 .. n]$ and $\text{sign}\,(\pi) = 1$ for even permutations (those that have an even number of inversions), and -1 for odd ones. Executed directly, the computation of $|A|$ takes $\Theta(n \times n!)$ steps. One way to reduce the time to $\Theta(n^3)$ is to convert the matrix to upper triangular form using Gaussian elimination. Gaussian elimination brings in division as an additional operation, so if A is an integer matrix and the determinant has to be computed exactly, then the result of each division has to be exact. That means using rational division. Rational division involves normalising numerators and denominators, so time is spent computing the greatest common divisor of two integers.

One method that avoids rational division is known as *Chió's pivotal condensation* algorithm. This is essentially a variant of Gaussian elimination that uses integer division only. Chió's method requires $\Theta(n^3)$ multiplications but only $\Theta(n)$ divisions (and exponentiations). The downside is that the size of the intermediate results grows exponentially. However, there is a variant of the algorithm in which the intermediate results are kept reasonably small, but the number of integer divisions goes up to $\Theta(n^3)$.

Finally, there are methods for computing the determinant reasonably quickly that avoid division altogether. One is based on iterated matrix multiplication. The size of the intermediate results is small, but the operation count goes up to $\Theta(n^4)$. Since we will need to calculate determinants in the following pearl, we devote this pearl to describing and comparing these three kinds of algorithm.

The school-book method

As a warm-up let us first implement the school-book method of computing determinants. This involves recursively computing the determinant of the *minors* of the matrix. For example:

$$
\begin{vmatrix} a_{11} & a_{12} & a_{13} \\ a_{21} & a_{22} & a_{23} \\ a_{31} & a_{32} & a_{33} \end{vmatrix} = a_{11} \begin{vmatrix} a_{22} & a_{23} \\ a_{32} & a_{33} \end{vmatrix} - a_{21} \begin{vmatrix} a_{12} & a_{13} \\ a_{32} & a_{33} \end{vmatrix} + a_{31} \begin{vmatrix} a_{12} & a_{13} \\ a_{22} & a_{23} \end{vmatrix}
$$

With matrices represented as a list of rows, the school-book method is implemented by

```
det        :: [[Integer]] → Integer
det [[x]]  = x
det xss    = foldr1 (−) (zipWith (∗) col1 (map det (minors cols)))
             where col1 = map head xss
                   cols = map tail xss
```

The 1×1 case is computed directly. Otherwise, each element of the first column is multiplied by the determinant of the corresponding minor of the remaining columns and the results are combined with an alternating sum. The function *minors*, which made an appearance in the previous pearl, is defined by

```
minors          :: [a] → [[a]]
minors []       = []
minors (x : xs) = xs : map (x :) (minors xs)
```

For example, *minors* "abcd" = ["bcd", "acd", "abd", "abc"].

Although the definition of *det* is short and sweet, the associated computation takes exponential time. The recurrence relation for $T(n)$, the number of steps needed to compute the determinant of an $n \times n$ matrix, satisfies $T(n) = nT(n-1) + \Theta(n)$, with solution $T(n) = \Theta(n!)$. Nevertheless, it is good enough when $n = 2$ or $n = 3$.

Using rational division

Gaussian elimination depends on the fact that adding any multiple of one row to any other row does not change the value of the determinant. Assuming the leading entry of the first row is not zero, we can add suitable multiples of the first row to the other rows to reduce the elements in the first column to zero. Repeating this process on the submatrix formed by eliminating the first row and column reduces the matrix to upper triangular form. The determinant of an upper triangular matrix is the product of the elements on the diagonal.

The process is complicated by the fact that the leading entry of the matrix may be zero. In such a case we have to find an appropriate row whose first entry, the *pivot*, is not zero. The function *det* is defined by

$$
\begin{aligned}
&det \qquad :: \quad [[\textit{Ratio Integer}]] \rightarrow \textit{Ratio Integer} \\
&det\ [[x]] \ = \ x \\
&det\ xss \ = \\
&\quad \textbf{case}\ \ break\ ((\neq 0) \cdot head)\ xss\ \textbf{of} \\
&\quad (yss, [\,]) \qquad\qquad \rightarrow \quad 0 \\
&\quad (yss, zs : zss) \quad \rightarrow \quad \textbf{let}\ x = head\ zs * det\ (reduce\ zs\ (yss \mathbin{+\!\!+} zss)) \\
&\qquad\qquad\qquad\qquad\qquad\quad \textbf{in if}\ \ even\ (length\ yss)\ \textbf{then}\ x\ \textbf{else}\ -x
\end{aligned}
$$

The expression *break* $((\neq 0) \cdot head)\ xss$ breaks a matrix into two parts (yss, zss) in which either zss is empty or the head of its first row zs is not zero. In the former case the matrix is singular and its determinant is zero. In the latter case the remaining rows $(yss \mathbin{+\!\!+} zss)$ are reduced to an $(n-1) \times (n-1)$ matrix by adding a suitable multiple of zs to each row and discarding the first column:

$$
\begin{aligned}
reduce\ xs\ yss \qquad &= \quad map\ (reduce1\ xs)\ yss \\
reduce1\ (x : xs)\ (y : ys) \ &= \quad zipWith(\lambda a\ b \rightarrow b - d * a)\ xs\ ys \\
&\qquad \textbf{where}\ d = y/x
\end{aligned}
$$

Finally, the determinant of the reduced matrix is negated if the parity of the position of the pivotal row in the matrix is odd. Division ($/$) is implemented as rational division.

Using integer division

Another way to compute $|A|$ is based on the following fact. Define the matrix X by setting $x_{jk} = a_{11} * a_{jk} - a_{1k} * a_{j1}$ for $2 \leq j, k \leq n$. Equivalently,

$$
x_{jk} \quad = \quad \begin{vmatrix} a_{11} & a_{1k} \\ a_{j1} & a_{jk} \end{vmatrix}
$$

So X is an $(n-1) \times (n-1)$ matrix. Then $|A| = |X|/a_{11}^{n-2}$ provided $a_{11} \neq 0$. This is Chió's identity. The determinant of an $n \times n$ matrix is expressed in terms of the determinant of a "condensed" $(n-1) \times (n-1)$ whose entries are the determinants of 2×2 matrices. Although Chió's identity also makes use of division, the division is exact and can be implemented as integer division. Note the assumption that the leading entry a_{11} is not zero. If it is, then, just as in Gaussian elimination, we have to look for a suitable non-zero pivot. The row containing the pivot can be swapped with the first row. Swapping two rows changes the sign of the determinant if the pivotal row is moved an odd number of places. That leads to the following algorithm for *det*:

$$
\begin{aligned}
det \quad & :: \quad [[\mathit{Integer}]] \to \mathit{Integer} \\
det\,[[x]] \quad = \quad & x \\
det\,xss \quad = \quad &
\end{aligned}
$$

$$
\begin{aligned}
&\textbf{case } break\,((\neq 0) \cdot head)\,xss \textbf{ of} \\
&(yss, [\,]) \quad\qquad \to \quad 0 \\
&(yss, zs : zss) \quad \to \quad \textbf{let } x \;=\; det\,(condense\,(zs : yss +\!\!+ zss)) \\
&\qquad\qquad\qquad\qquad\qquad\; d \;=\; head\,zs \uparrow (length\,xss - 2) \\
&\qquad\qquad\qquad\qquad\qquad\; y \;=\; x \text{ div } d \\
&\qquad\qquad\qquad\qquad \textbf{in if } even\,(length\,yss) \textbf{ then } y \textbf{ else } -y
\end{aligned}
$$

Here, $(\uparrow)$ denotes exponentiation. The function *condense* is defined by

$$
\begin{aligned}
condense \;=\; & map\,(map\,det \cdot pair \cdot uncurry\,zip) \cdot pair \\
& \textbf{where } pair\,(x : xs) \qquad\quad = \quad map\,((,)\,x)\,xs \\
& \qquad\;\; det\,((a, b), (c, d)) \;=\; a * d - b * c
\end{aligned}
$$

The first row of the matrix is paired with each other row. Each pair of rows, say $([a_1, a_2, \ldots, a_n], [b_1, b_2, \ldots, b_n])$, is then zipped and paired, yielding

$$
[((a_1, b_1), (a_2, b_2)), ((a_1, b_1), (a_3, b_3)), \ldots ((a_1, b_1), (a_n, b_n))]
$$

Finally, the 2×2 determinant of each pair of pairs is computed.

As to the complexity, condensing an $n \times n$ matrix takes $\Theta(n^2)$ steps, so the recurrence relation for $T(n)$ satisfies $T(n) = T(n-1) + \Theta(n^2)$, with solution $T(n) = \Theta(n^3)$. Although rational division is avoided, the integers get big very quickly. It would be much better if the divisions were not all performed at the end of the process, but interleaved with each condensation step.

Interleaving

Interleaving of condensation and division is possible owing to one of the many curious properties of determinants. Let X be the condensed matrix obtained from A and let Y be the condensed matrix obtained from X. Thus, Y is an $(n{-}2) \times (n{-}2)$ matrix. Then, assuming $a_{11} \neq 0$, each element of Y is divisible by a_{11}. We leave the proof as an exercise. That means we can eliminate the factor $1/a_{11}^{n-2}$ in Chió's method by dividing each element of the doubly condensed matrix by a_{11}. That leads to the implementation $det = det' \, 1$, where

$$
\begin{aligned}
det' & \quad :: \quad Integer \to [[Integer]] \to Integer \\
det' \, k \, [[x]] & \quad = \quad x \\
det' \, k \, xss & \quad =
\end{aligned}
$$

$\quad$ **case** $break \, ((\neq 0) \cdot head) \, xss$ **of**

$\quad\quad (yss, [\,]) \quad\quad\quad\quad \to \quad 0$

$\quad\quad (yss, zs : zss) \quad \to \quad$ **let** $x = det' \, (head \, zs) \, (cd \, k \, (zs : yss \mathbin{+\!\!+} zss))$

$\quad\quad\quad\quad\quad\quad\quad\quad\quad\quad$ **in if** $even \, (length \, yss)$ **then** x **else** $-x$

where cd (short for condense and divide) is defined by

$$
\begin{aligned}
cd \, k \quad = \quad & map \, (map \, det \cdot pair \cdot uncurry \, zip) \cdot pair \\
& \textbf{where} \; pair \, (x : xs) \quad\quad\quad = \quad map \, ((,) \, x) \, xs \\
& \quad\quad\quad det \, ((a, b), (c, d)) \quad = \quad (a * d - b * c) \operatorname{div} k
\end{aligned}
$$

Of course, in this version the number of integer divisions goes up to $\Theta(n^3)$.

Using no division

Finally, we present one other method of computing det that avoids division altogether. The method appears somewhat magical and we are not going to justify it. For an $n \times n$ matrix $X = (x_{ij})$ define $\mathrm{MUT}(X)$ (short for make upper triangular) by

$$
\mathrm{MUT}(X) = \begin{pmatrix} -\sum_{j=2}^{n} x_{jj} & x_{12} & \cdots & x_{1n} \\ 0 & -\sum_{j=3}^{n} x_{jj} & \cdots & x_{2n} \\ \cdots & & & \\ 0 & 0 & \cdots & -\sum_{j=n+1}^{n} x_{jj} \end{pmatrix}
$$

Thus, the entries of X below the diagonal are made zero, those above the diagonal are left unchanged and each diagonal entry is replaced by the negated sum of the elements of the diagonal below it. Note that $\sum_{j=n+1}^{n} x_{jj} = 0$.

Next, let $F_A(X) = \mathrm{MUT}(X) \times A$ and set $B = F_A^{n-1} \, A'$, where $A' = A$ if n is odd and $A' = -A$ if n is even. In words, apply F_A to A' a total of $(n-1)$ times. Then B is the everywhere zero matrix except for its first entry b_{11}, which equals $|A|$. Computing $\mathrm{MUT}(X) \times A$ takes $\Theta(n^3)$ steps and, since this computation is repeated $n - 1$ times, the total time for computing $|A|$ is $\Theta(n^4)$ steps.

The following implementation follows the prescription faithfully:

$$
\begin{array}{lll}
det & :: & [[Integer]] \rightarrow Integer \\
det\ ass & = & head\ (head\ bss)
\end{array}
$$

> **where**
> $$
> \begin{array}{lll}
> bss & = & foldl\ (matmult \cdot mut)\ ass'\ (replicate\ (n-1)\ ass) \\
> ass' & = & \textbf{if}\ odd\ n\ \textbf{then}\ ass\ \textbf{else}\ map\ (map\ negate)\ ass \\
> n & = & length\ ass
> \end{array}
> $$

The function *mut* implements MUT:

$$
\begin{array}{l}
mut\ xss \\
\quad =\ zipWith\ (+\!\!+)\ zeros\ (zipWith\ (:)\ ys\ (zipWith\ drop\ [1..]\ xss)) \\
\qquad \textbf{where}\ ys = map\ negate\ (tail\ (scanr\ (+)\ 0\ (diagonal\ xss)))
\end{array}
$$

The value *zeros* is an infinite lower triangular matrix of zeros, beginning with an empty row:

$$
zeros\ =\ [take\ j\ (repeat\ 0)\ |\ j \leftarrow [0..]]
$$

The function *diagonal* returns the elements along the diagonal:

$$
\begin{array}{lll}
diagonal\ [\,] & = & [\,] \\
diagonal\ (xs : xss) & = & head\ xs : diagonal\ (map\ tail\ xss)
\end{array}
$$

Finally, *matmult* implements matrix multiplication:

$$
\begin{array}{lll}
matmult\ xss\ yss & = & zipWith\ (map \cdot dp)\ xss\ (repeat\ (transpose\ yss)) \\
dp\ xs\ ys & = & sum\ (zipWith\ (*)\ xs\ ys)
\end{array}
$$

The function *dp* implements the dot product of two vectors.

However, note that MUT(X) does not depend on the entries below the diagonal of X. Under lazy evaluation they are never computed by *mut*. Nevertheless, it is more efficient to recast the definition of *mut* in terms of a special matrix multiplication operation *trimult* that multiplies an upper triangular matrix with an arbitrary matrix to give another upper triangular matrix. Suppose *xss* is the list of rows of an upper triangular matrix and *yss* is an arbitrary matrix. Then

$$
trimult\ xss\ yss\ =\ zipWith\ (map \cdot dp)\ xss\ (submats\ (transpose\ yss))
$$

produces an upper triangular matrix. The function *submats* returns a list of the principal submatrices:

$$
\begin{array}{lll}
submats & :: & [[a]] \rightarrow [[[a]]] \\
submats\ [[x]] & = & [[[x]]] \\
submats\ xss & = & xss : submats\ (map\ tail\ (tail\ xss))
\end{array}
$$

For upper triangular matrices xss the definition of $mut\ xss$ simplifies to

$$mut\ xss\ =\ zipWith\ (:)\ ys\ (map\ tail\ xss))$$
$$\textbf{where}\ ys = map\ negate\ (tail\ (scanr\ (+)\ 0\ (map\ head\ xss)))$$

The diagonal of an upper triangular matrix xss is $map\ head\ xss$ and the elements above the diagonal are $map\ tail\ xs$.

We can now rewrite det in the form

$$
\begin{aligned}
det &\quad :: \quad [[Integer]] \rightarrow Integer \\
det\ ass &\quad = \quad head\ (head\ bss) \\
\textbf{where} & \\
bss &\quad = \quad foldl\ (trimult \cdot mut)\ ass'\ (replicate\ (n-1)\ ass) \\
ass' &\quad = \quad \textbf{if}\ odd\ n\ \textbf{then}\ upper\ ass \\
&\qquad\quad \textbf{else}\ map\ (map\ negate)\ (upper\ ass) \\
n &\quad = \quad length\ ass
\end{aligned}
$$

where $upper = zipWith\ drop\ [0..]$.

A brief comparison

So, which of the three methods described above is best? Rational division (Gaussian elimination), integer division (two versions, one using Chió's identity and one using condense and divide) or no division (by iterated matrix multiplication)?

We carried out a brief comparison of the methods, using random matrices for various sizes of n, each with entries in the range $(-20, 20)$. As might be expected, the original Chió version was hopeless, but the second version that combined condensation steps and division was the clear winner. For $n = 150$, Gaussian elimination took about 30 s, the modified Chió version took 10 s and the iterated multiplication method took 40 s.

Final remarks

Chió's method, which goes back 150 years, is described at http://math world.wolfram.com/ChioPivotalCondensation.html. The modified version is really due to Bareiss (1968), who based its justification on Sylvester's identity, a more general version of Chió's identity. However, the history of the iterated multiplication method is more obscure. The main fact on which it depends still awaits a purely algebraic proof. We extracted it from an algorithm of Mahajan and Vinay (1997) that was based on the idea of *clow* sequences. The word clow is an acronym for "closed walk", and a clow sequence is a generalisation of the cycle decomposition of a permutation in which each cycle can contain repetitions of intermediate elements; hence, a closed walk. Mahajan and Vinay showed that all the signed matrix terms for clow sequences that do not correspond to permutations cancel each other out, leaving just those terms $a_{1\pi(1)} a_{2\pi(2)} \cdots a_{n\pi(n)}$ that do correspond to permutations. But their proof is not trivial. The signed matrix term corresponding to a clow sequence can be expressed as a path in a layered directed acyclic graph to one of two endpoints and the computation of the sum of such factors computed as a path problem. By recasting the associated recursive definition directly back into matrix operations, the identity described above was discovered. Although we cannot find any reference to it in the literature, it is almost certainly not new.

One point not emphasised in the narrative was that no Haskell arrays were harmed in the description of the algorithms, immutable or otherwise. Instead, each matrix was quietly represented as a list of its rows. That enabled each algorithm to be expressed fairly concisely. But perhaps a better alternative is to define a suitable abstract type for matrices in which the necessary operations, first column, first row, diagonal, principal submatrices and so on, are provided as primitives.

References

Bareiss, E. H. (1968). Sylvester's identity and multi-step integer preserving Gaussian elimination. *Mathematics of Computation* **22** (103), 565–78.

Mahajan, M. and Vinay, V. (1997). Determinant: combinatorics, algorithms and complexity. *Chicago Journal of Theoretical Computer Science*, Article 5.

23

Inside the convex hull

Introduction

The problem of computing the convex hull of a set of points is central to many tasks in computational geometry and has been much studied. Finding the hull makes sense in any finite dimension d, but most textbooks focus primarily on the cases $d = 2$ and $d = 3$. Our aim in this pearl is simply to specify the d dimensional form of the problem and then to describe a straightforward incremental algorithm for computing the hull. The incremental algorithm is well known and a number of sophisticated improvements have been proposed, but we deal only with the basic idea. We will not derive the algorithm, but instead show how to test it using the Claessen and Hughes QuickCheck library. In fact, testing revealed an error in the code, an error we have deliberately left in to see if the reader can spot it.

Background

Many geometric algorithms fall apart when the arithmetic is not exact, so it is a good idea to stay within the realm of integer arithmetic and confine attention to the subset $Q(d)$ of d-dimensional Euclidean space $E(d)$ consisting of those points whose Cartesian coordinates are rational numbers. A point in $Q(d)$ can be represented by a list of $d+1$ integers $[x_0, x_1, \ldots, x_d]$ in which $x_d \neq 0$; this list represents the d rational Cartesian coordinates $[x_0/x_d, x_1/x_d, \ldots, x_{d-1}/x_d]$. Hence, we define $Point = [Integer]$. The dimension of a point is given by

$$
\begin{aligned}
dimension \quad &:: \quad Point \to Int \\
dimension\ ps \quad &= \quad length\ ps - 1
\end{aligned}
$$

By definition, a d-simplex is a list of $d+1$ points in $Q(d)$ together with a value, $+1$ or -1, indicating the orientation of the simplex that arises from the way the points are listed:

$$
\textbf{type}\ Simplex \quad = \quad ([Point], Int)
$$

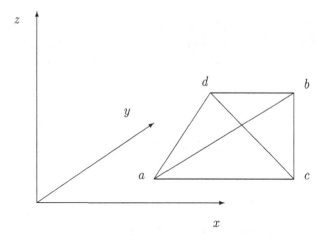

Fig. 23.1 A positively oriented tetrahedron, with a, b and c in the (x, y) plane and d above.

The points, or vertices, of a d-simplex have to be in "general position", meaning that no two points are identical, no three points are collinear, no four points are coplanar and so on. A 1-simplex in $Q(1)$ is an edge, a 2-simplex in $Q(2)$ is a triangle, and a 3-simplex in $Q(3)$ is a tetrahedron. Formally, points $[v_0, v_1, \ldots, v_d]$, where v_j has coordinates $[x_{j0}, x_{j1}, \ldots, x_{jd}]$, are in general position if the determinant of the matrix $X = (x_{ij})$ is non-zero. The value of the determinant is proportional to the signed volume of the simplex and the orientation is, by definition, the sign of the determinant:[1]

$$
\begin{aligned}
orientation &\quad :: \quad [Point] \rightarrow Int \\
orientation &\quad = \quad fromIntegral \cdot signum \cdot det
\end{aligned}
$$

Even permutations of the points leave the orientation unchanged, while odd permutations invert it. In $Q(1)$, an edge $[a, b]$ has positive orientation if $a > b$, negative orientation if $a < b$ and zero orientation if $a = b$. In $Q(2)$, a triangle $[a, b, c]$ has positive orientation if the order $[a, b, c]$ is anticlockwise round the triangle, negative orientation if the order goes clockwise and zero orientation if a, b and c are collinear. In $Q(3)$, and with the standard right-handed orientation of the x, y and z axes, a tetrahedron $[a, b, c, d]$ has positive orientation if the triangle $[b, c, d]$ when viewed from point a has positive orientation. Such a tetrahedron is pictured in Figure 23.1.

Each d-simplex smp determines a convex region $CS(smp)$ of space in $Q(d)$, namely the rational points inside smp or on its boundary. To determine whether a point lies in $CS(smp)$ we first compute the *facets* of smp.

[1] Definitions of det were given in the previous pearl.

A facet of a d-simplex is a list of d points, together with an associated orientation derived from the simplex. The facets of an edge are its two endpoint vertices, the facets of a triangle are its three edges and so on. The facets of a simplex and the associated orientations are defined by

$$
\begin{aligned}
&\textit{facets} &&::&& \textit{Simplex} \rightarrow [\textit{Facet}] \\
&\textit{facets}\,(\textit{us}, b) &&=&& \textit{zip}\,(\textit{minors us})\,(\textit{cycle}\,[b, -b]) \\
\\
&\textit{minors} &&::&& [a] \rightarrow [[a]] \\
&\textit{minors}\,[\,] &&=&& [\,] \\
&\textit{minors}\,(x:xs) &&=&& xs:\textit{map}\,(x:)\,(\textit{minors xs})
\end{aligned}
$$

where $\textit{Facet} = ([\textit{Point}], \textit{Int})$. The minors of a list is a list of subsequences. For example, $\textit{minors}$ "abcd" $=$ ["bcd", "acd", "abd", "abc"]. We met this function in the two previous pearls. For an edge $[a, b]$ in $Q(1)$ with positive orientation the facets are the 0-simplexes $[b]$ and $[a]$ with associated orientations $+1$ and -1 respectively. A point p is strictly inside the region of the simplex $[a, b]$ if the simplex $[p, b]$ has the same orientation as $[b]$ has, namely $+1$, and $[p, a]$ has the same orientation as $[a]$, namely -1. In other words, $b < p < a$. The same reasoning holds in higher dimensions. Thus, in $Q(2)$, a triangle $[a, b, c]$ with positive orientation has the three facets

$$([b, c], +1), \quad ([a, c], -1), \quad ([a, b], +1)$$

and a point p is strictly inside $[a, b, c]$ if the three simplexes $[p, b, c]$, $[p, a, c]$ and $[p, a, b]$ have orientations $+1$, -1 and $+1$, implying that p is to the left of the edge from b to c, to the right of the edge from a to c and to the left of the edge from a to b.

The region $CS(\textit{smp})$ of those points strictly inside $\textit{smp}$ or on its boundary is defined by a predicate:

$$
\begin{aligned}
&\textit{insideCS} :: \textit{Simplex} \rightarrow \textit{Point} \rightarrow \textit{Bool} \\
&\textit{insideCS smp p} \\
&\quad = \quad \textit{and}\,[0 \leq b * \textit{orientation}\,(p:us) \mid (\textit{us}, b) \leftarrow \textit{facets smp}]
\end{aligned}
$$

A point p is strictly inside $CS(\textit{smp})$ if $b = \textit{orientation}\,(p:us)$ for each facet $(\textit{us}, b)$ of $\textit{smp}$ and on the boundary of $\textit{smp}$ if $\textit{orientation}\,(p:us) = 0$ for at least one facet $(\textit{us}, b)$ of $\textit{smp}$.

Convex hulls

The convex hull $CH(\textit{vs})$ of a set of points $\textit{vs}$ in $Q(d)$ is a region of $Q(d)$. It can be defined in a number of mathematically equivalent ways, including the following: $CH(\textit{vs})$ is the union of the sets $CS(\textit{smp})$ for all d-simplexes *smp* determined by points of *vs*. For example, in $Q(2)$ the convex hull of *vs* is the union of the regions determined by all triangles whose vertices are in *vs*. The set $CH(vs)$ can therefore be characterised by a predicate:

$$insideCH \quad :: \quad [Point] \rightarrow Point \rightarrow Bool$$
$$insideCH \; vs \; p \quad = \quad or \; [insideCS \; smp \; p \; | \; smp \leftarrow simplexes \; vs]$$

where *simplexes vs* lists the simplexes of *vs*:

$$simplexes \quad :: \quad [Point] \rightarrow [Simplex]$$
$$simplexes \; vs \quad = \quad [(us, b) \; | \; us \leftarrow tuples \; (d+1) \; vs,$$
$$\textbf{let} \; b = orientation \; us, \; b \neq 0]$$
$$\textbf{where} \; d = dimension \; (head \; vs)$$

The value of *tuples n vs* is a list of all n-tuples of *vs*; that is, all subsequences of *vs* of length n. The definition of *tuples* is left as an exercise.

According to the above definition of *insideCH*, the set $CH(vs)$ is empty if *vs* has no simplexes. A set of points *vs* in $Q(1)$ has no 1-simplexes if the points are coincident, in $Q(2)$ if they are collinear and in $Q(3)$ if they are coplanar. It is possible to define the convex hull for such sets of points by reducing the dimension, but we will leave the specification as it is.

An incremental algorithm

There are $\Omega(n^{d+1})$ possible d-simplexes among n points, so evaluating the expression *insideCH vs p* takes $\Omega(n^{d+1})$ steps. Most of these simplexes overlap, indeed some may coincide, and it is necessary only to consider some subset that covers the hull without overlap. Therefore, a more efficient algorithm is obtained by replacing *simplexes* with another function *partition*, with the same type, that partitions the hull. Then we can replace *insideCH* by *insideCH'*, where

$$insideCH' \quad :: \quad [Point] \rightarrow Point \rightarrow Bool$$
$$insideCH' \; vs \; p \quad = \quad or \; [insideCS \; smp \; p \; | \; smp \leftarrow partition \; vs]$$

The function *partition* can be defined by a process that starts with a single simplex and then adds new simplexes as each additional point outside the current hull is inspected:

$$partition :: [Point] \rightarrow [Simplex]$$
$$partition \; vs$$
$$= \; \textbf{case} \; findSimplex \; vs \; \textbf{of}$$
$$Nothing \quad \rightarrow \quad []$$
$$Just \; [smp] \quad \rightarrow \quad foldl \; update \; [smp] \; (vs \setminus\setminus vertices \; smp)$$

The vertices of a simplex are listed by

$$vertices \quad :: \quad Simplex \rightarrow [Point]$$
$$vertices \quad = \quad sort \cdot fst$$

The vertices are listed in order; so, if vs is maintained as a sorted list, then \\ can be implemented efficiently as ordered list difference. The function *findSimplex* finds a simplex if there is one. If there is not one, then there is no partition and an empty hull. Otherwise the simplex is used as a starting point and its vertices are removed from the list of additional points that need to be considered. It remains to define *findSimplex* and *update*. We deal with these functions separately.

Finding a simplex

One obvious way of defining *findSimplex* is

$$findSimplex\ vs \quad = \quad \textbf{if }\ null\ smps\ \textbf{then }\ Nothing\ \textbf{else }\ Just\ (head\ smps)$$
$$\textbf{where }\ smps = simplexes\ vs$$

But in the worst case the cost of *findSimplex vs* is $\Omega(n^{d+1})$ steps, which rather undercuts the aim of finding a more efficient algorithm. The worst case is unlikely in practice, so the above definition is probably good enough, but there is an alternative method. The idea is to start with the first point v_0 of vs and then to carry out a single search of the rest of vs to find the remaining points. First, a second point v_1 is found so that v_0 and v_1 are not coincident. Then the search continues with the elements of vs after v_1 to find a third point v_2 that is not collinear with v_0 and v_1, and so on until $d+1$ points are found that are in general position. The tricky aspect is not the search but the fact that the non-degeneracy of $k+1$ points in $Q(d)$ cannot be determined by a simple determinant test: the associated matrix of point coordinates has size $(k+1) \times (d+1)$, which is not square if $k < d$.

Instead we need to consider square submatrices. Consider the matrix X of size $(k+1) \times (d+1)$ obtained from the first $k+1$ vertices and the submatrices of size $(k+1) \times (k+1)$ formed by taking every possible combination of k columns from the first d columns, together with the last column (the denominators of the rational coordinates of the vertices). Then the $k+1$ points are degenerate if the determinants of all these square submatrices are zero. The degeneracy test is implemented by

$$degenerate\ k \quad = \quad all\ (== 0) \cdot map\ det \cdot submatrices\ k \cdot transpose$$
$$submatrices\ k\ vs \quad = \quad map\ (\mathbin{+\!\!+} [last\ vs])\ (tuples\ k\ (init\ vs))$$

The function *transpose* transposes a matrix, so *submatrices* selects columns of a matrix by selecting rows of the transposed matrix. The determinant of a matrix is the determinant of its transpose. Since there are $O(d^k)$ submatrices of the transposed matrix, and computing the determinant takes $O(k^3)$ steps, the computation of *degenerate k vs* for a list of $k+1$ points *vs* in $Q(d)$, where $k \leq d$, takes $O(k^3 d^k) = O(d^{d+3})$ steps.

The function *findSimplex* is now implemented by

$$
\begin{array}{lcl}
\textit{findSimplex} & :: & [\textit{Point}] \rightarrow \textit{Maybe Simplex} \\
\textit{findSimplex} \; [\,] & = & \textit{Nothing} \\
\textit{findSimplex} \; (v : vs) & = & \textit{search} \; (\textit{length} \; v - 1) \; 1 \; [v] \; vs
\end{array}
$$

where the function *search* is defined by

$$
\begin{array}{llll}
\textit{search} \; d \; k \; us \; vs \\
\quad | \quad k == d + 1 & = & \textit{Just} \; (us, \textit{orientation} \; us) \\
\quad | \quad \textit{null} \; vs & = & \textit{Nothing} \\
\quad | \quad \textit{degenerate} \; k \; (v : us) & = & \textit{search} \; d \; k \; us \; (\textit{tail} \; vs) \\
\quad | \quad \textbf{otherwise} & = & \textit{search} \; d \; (k + 1) \; (v : us) \; (\textit{tail} \; vs) \\
\qquad \textbf{where} \; v = \textit{head} \; vs
\end{array}
$$

The running time of *findSimplex vs*, where *vs* has n points, is $O(d^{d+3}n)$ steps, which is linear in n, though with a large constant factor.

Update

In order to define the remaining function *update*, consider a set *smps* of simplexes that partition the convex hull for the points considered so far. The facets of these simplexes are of two kinds: the internal facets – those that occur exactly twice (with opposite orientations); and the external facets – those that occur exactly once. For example, take the vertices of a square $[a, b, c, d]$ in $Q(2)$. There are two possible triangulations: the triangles $[a, b, c]$ and $[c, d, a]$, or $[a, b, d]$ and $[b, c, d]$. In the first triangulation the edge $[a, c]$ is internal and in the second the edge $[b, d]$ is internal. The external facets are computed by

$$
\begin{array}{lcl}
\textit{external} & :: & [\textit{Simplex}] \rightarrow [\textit{Facet}] \\
\textit{external} & = & \textit{foldr} \; op \; [\,] \cdot \textit{sort} \cdot \textit{concatMap} \; \textit{facets}
\end{array}
$$

where

$$
\begin{array}{lcl}
op \; smp \; [\,] & = & [\,] \\
op \; smp \; (smp' : smps) & = & \textbf{if} \; \textit{vertices} \; smp == \textit{vertices} \; smp' \; \textbf{then} \; smps \\
& & \textbf{else} \; smp : smp' : smps
\end{array}
$$

The cost of computing *external smps* is $O(dS \log dS)$, where S is size of *smps*, since the dominating time is the time to sort the facets of *smps* and there are $O(dS)$ of them.

Each new point v splits the external facets into two: the *visible* facets and the *invisible* ones. Imagine a light-bulb situated at v; this light-bulb illuminates just the visible facets. A facet (us, b) is visible to v if v is strictly outside it, meaning that *orientation* $(v : us)$ has opposite sign to b:

> *visible*   :: $Point \rightarrow [Facet] \rightarrow [Facet]$
> *visible v fs* = $[(us, b) \mid (us, b) \leftarrow fs,\ b * orientation\ (v : us) < 0]$

There are no visible facets if v is inside or on the current hull. In particular, if v is a copy of one of the vertices processed so far, then the current hull will be unchanged, so it does not matter if *vs* contains repeated points (and it does not matter if we do not remove the vertices of the starting simplex from the starting points).

To update the hull we add to *smps* a new simplex for each visible facet:

> *newSimplex*   :: $Point \rightarrow Facet \rightarrow Simplex$
> *newSimplex v* (us, b) = $(v : us, -b)$

The orientation assigned to the new simplex is correct because if (us, b) is visible to v, then $b * orientation(v : us) < 0$, and so $orientation(v : us) = -b$.

Now we can define *update* by

> *update* :: $[Simplex] \rightarrow Point \rightarrow [Simplex]$
> *update smps v*
>   = $smps \mathbin{+\!\!+} map\ (newSimplex\ v)\ (visible\ v\ (external\ smps))$

The time to compute *update smps* is dominated by the time to compute the visible facets, and this takes $O(dS \log dS)$ steps, where S is the size of *smps*. The complexity of *insideCH'* as a function of n, the number of points in *vs*, is therefore $O(dnS \log dS)$, where S is the maximum number of simplexes maintained at each stage. It is known that $S = O(n^e)$, where $e = \lfloor d/2 \rfloor$, so evaluating *insideCH' vs* takes $O(n^{e+1} \log n)$ steps. This is better than *insideCH*, but we can improve *insideCH'* yet further.

An improvement

As described above, the incremental algorithm computes a set of simplexes that partition the hull. At each stage the external facets of the hull are determined in order to discover those that are visible to a new point, and new simplexes are then added to the hull. It is clearly more sensible to maintain the external facets of the simplexes rather than the simplexes themselves. If we set *faces* = *external · partition*, then we can replace *insideCH′* by *insideCH″*, where

$$insideCH''\ vs\ p\ =\ and\ [0 \leq b * orientation\ (p : us)\ |\ (us, b) \leftarrow faces\ vs]$$

The function *faces* has type $[Point] \rightarrow [Facet]$. In computational geometry one of the usual ways of describing a convex hull is by listing its external facets.

An efficient computation of *faces* can be derived by appealing to the fusion law of *foldl*. We need to find $update' :: [Facet] \rightarrow Point \rightarrow [Facet]$, so that

$$external\ (update\ smps\ v)\ =\ update'\ (external\ smps)\ v$$

Since the external facets of a single simplex are all its facets we then obtain

$$
\begin{aligned}
&faces\ vs \\
&=\ \textbf{case}\ findSimplex\ vs\ \textbf{of} \\
&\qquad Nothing\quad \rightarrow\ [\,] \\
&\qquad Just\ [smp]\ \rightarrow\ foldl\ update'\ (facets\ smp)\ (vs \setminus\!\setminus vertices\ vs)
\end{aligned}
$$

We will not go into the derivation of *update′* but just state the result:

$$
\begin{aligned}
update'\ fs\ v\quad &=\ (fs \setminus\!\setminus fs') + map\ (newFacet\ v)\ (external\ fs') \\
&\quad \textbf{where}\ fs' = visible\ v\ fs \\[4pt]
newFacet\ v\ (us, b)\ &=\ (v : us, b)
\end{aligned}
$$

In words, the facets visible to the new point are removed from the current set of facets and new facets are added. The visible facets form a connected set and their boundary is the set of their external sub-facets, namely a set of $(d-2)$-simplexes that occur exactly once. For example, in $Q(3)$ the facets are triangles and the external sub-facets of a visible set of connected triangles are the set of edges that form its boundary. The orientation assigned to each new facet is just the orientation of the associated sub-facet. To appreciate this last point, consider an edge $([a, b], +1)$ in $Q(2)$ that is visible to a point c and in which b is a boundary point (so the following edge beginning with b is not visible). The 0-simplex associated with b has positive orientation and the new edge $[c, b]$ has to be directed towards b, so also has positive orientation.

The running time of *faces* is dominated by the time to discover the facets visible to a new point. In order to find these facets, every single facet of the hull is inspected; that is clearly an inefficient method, since the visible facets form a small locally connected set. It is here that more sophisticated algorithms, such as the *Bulldozer* algorithm of Blelloch *et al.* (2001), enter the picture, but we will not go into further details.

QuickCheck

Koen Claessen and John Hughes have produced a very useful suite of functions, called *QuickCheck*, for testing Haskell programs; see Claessen and Hughes (2000). It would take up too much space to explain the details of *QuickCheck*, but we briefly show how to use the functions in the suite to check the two versions of the convex hull algorithm described above.

First we need a generator for generating a point in $Q(d)$:

$$
\begin{aligned}
point & \;::\; Int \to Gen\,[Integer] \\
point\ d & \;=\; \mathbf{do}\,\{xs \leftarrow vector\ d;\ return\ (xs \mathbin{+\!\!+} [1])\}
\end{aligned}
$$

The utility *vector d* returns a randomly generated list of *d* values, here integers. The result of *point d* is a generator that returns a list of $d+1$ integers in which the last integer is 1.

Next we need a generator for generating a list of *n* points:

$$
\begin{aligned}
points & \;::\; Int \to Int \to Gen\,[[Integer]] \\
points\ d\ 0 & \;=\; return\,[\,] \\
points\ d\ (n+1) & \;=\; \mathbf{do}\,\{p \leftarrow point\ d;\ ps \leftarrow points\ d\ n; \\
& \qquad\qquad return\ (p : ps)\}
\end{aligned}
$$

Now we can define a property *prop_Hull* that checks the incremental algorithm against the specification:

$$
\begin{aligned}
prop\_Hull & \;::\; Int \to Int \to Property \\
prop\_Hull\ d\ n & \;=\; forAll\,(points\ d\ n)\ \$\ \lambda vs \to \\
& \qquad forAll\,(point\ d)\ \$\ \lambda v \to \\
& \qquad insideCH\ vs\ v \;\mathbf{==}\; insideCH'\ vs\ v
\end{aligned}
$$

For example, evaluating *quickCheck* (*prop_Hull* 3 10) produces the output

```
OK, passed 100 tests.
```

However, replacing *insideCH'* by *insideCH''* in *prop_Hull* reveals an error:

```
Main> quickCheck (prop_Hull 2 4)
Falsifiable, after 2 tests:
[[0,0,1],[0,0,1],[0,0,1],[-1,-1,1]]
[1,0,1]
```

Oh dear, what has gone wrong? Well, the problem is that the four points are collinear, so there is no partition and no faces. While *insideCH vs* correctly returns *False* when *vs* are collinear points in $Q(2)$, the test *insideCH″ vs* returns *True*. We need to rewrite *insideCH″* to read

$$insideCH″\ vs\ v\ =\ \textbf{if}\ null\ fs\ \textbf{then}\ False\ \textbf{else}$$
$$and\ [0 \leq b * orientation\ (v : us)\ |\ (us, b) \leftarrow fs]$$
$$\textbf{where}\ fs = faces\ vs$$

Then *QuickCheck* is happy. Did you spot the error?

Final remarks

There are numerous textbooks on computational geometry that deal with convex-hull algorithms; O'Rourke (1998) and Preparata and Shamos (1985) are just two of them. In particular, O'Rourke's excellent book devotes two carefully crafted chapters to the topic, and his bibliography contains references to most of the literature, though Dijkstra's (1976) treatment of the three-dimensional case is missing. This particular pearl arose as a result of trying to come to grips with the details of Karimipour and Frank (2009), but the details differ significantly. I would like to thank Irina Voiculescu for a number of profitable discussions about the convex hull and how to compute it.

References

Claessen, K. and Hughes, J. (2000). QuickCheck: a lightweight tool for random testing of Haskell programs. *ACM SIGPLAN International Conference of Functional Programming*, Montreal, Canada, pp. 268–79. See also http://www.cs.chalmers.se/~rjmh/QuickCheck/.

Blelloch, G., Burch, H., Crary, K., *et al.* (2001). Persistent triangulations. *Journal of Functional Programming* **11** (5), 441–66.

Dijkstra, E. W. (1976). *A Discipline of Programming*. Englewood Cliffs, NJ: Prentice-Hall.

Karimipour, F. and Frank, A. U. (2009). A dimension independent convex hull algorithm. Unpublished.

O'Rourke, J. (1998). *Computational Geometry*, second edition. Cambridge, UK: Cambridge University Press.

Preparata, F. P. and Shamos, M. I. (1985). *Computational Geometry*. New York, NY: Springer-Verlag.

24

Rational arithmetic coding

Introduction

This pearl, and the one following, is all about arithmetic coding, a way of doing data compression. Unlike other methods, arithmetic coding does not represent each individual symbol of the text as an integral number of bits; instead, the text as a whole is encoded as a binary fraction in the unit interval. Although the idea can be traced back much earlier, it was not until the publication of an "accessible implementation" by Witten, Neal and Cleary in 1987 that arithmetic coding became a serious competitor in the world of data compression. Over the past two decades the method has been refined and its advantages and disadvantages over rival schemes have been elucidated. Arithmetic coding can be more effective at compression than rivals such as Huffman coding, or Shannon–Fano coding, and is well suited to take account of the statistical properties of the symbols in a text. On the other hand, coding and decoding times are longer than with other methods.

Arithmetic coding has a well-deserved reputation for being tricky to implement; nevertheless, our aim in these two pearls is to give a formal development of the basic algorithms. In the present pearl, coding and decoding are implemented in terms of arbitrary-precision rational arithmetic. This implementation is simple and elegant, though expensive in time and space. In the following pearl, coding and decoding are reimplemented in terms of finite-precision integers. This is where most of the subtleties of the problem reside.

Arithmetic coding with rational arithmetic

The basic idea behind arithmetic coding is to:

(i) Break the source text into *symbols*, where a symbol is some logical grouping of characters such as a word, or perhaps just a single character. For simplicity, we assume that the number of possible symbols is finite.

(ii) Associate each distinct symbol with a semi-open *interval* of the unit interval $[0, 1)$. Such an association is provided by a *model*.

(iii) Successively *narrow* the unit interval by an amount determined by the interval associated with each symbol in the text.

(iv) Choose some suitably short *fraction* in the final interval.

We can capture the basic data types in Haskell by defining

type *Fraction* $=$ *Ratio Integer*
type *Interval* $=$ (*Fraction*, *Fraction*)

A fraction is represented by the ratio of two arbitrary-precision integers (elements of *Integer*) and an interval by two fractions. A proper fraction f is one in which $0 \le f < 1$. The unit interval is represented by $(0, 1)$ and we write $f \in (\ell, r)$ to mean $\ell \le f < r$, so intervals are closed on the left and open on the right. We also write $i \subseteq j$ to mean that i is a subinterval of j.

Narrowing

The value $i \triangleright j$ narrows an interval i by an interval j, returning a subinterval k of i such that k is in the same relationship to i as j is to the unit interval:

$$(\triangleright) \qquad :: \quad Interval \rightarrow Interval \rightarrow Interval$$
$$(\ell_1, r_1) \triangleright (\ell_2, r_2) \;=\; (\ell_1 + (r_1 - \ell_1) * \ell_2, \ell_1 + (r_1 - \ell_1) * r_2)$$

The operation $\triangleright$ is associative with $(0, 1)$ as unit, a good reason to denote it with an infix symbol. It is easy to check that if $f \in i \triangleright j$, then $f \in i$. Hence, $i \triangleright j \subseteq i$. Also, if $f \in i \triangleright j$ then $(f \triangleleft i) \in j$, where the operation $(\triangleleft)$ widens a fraction:

$$(\triangleleft) \qquad :: \quad Fraction \rightarrow Interval \rightarrow Fraction$$
$$f \triangleleft (\ell, r) \;=\; (f - \ell)/(r - \ell)$$

In summary:

$$f \in i \triangleright j \;\Rightarrow\; f \in i \wedge (f \triangleleft i) \in j \tag{24.1}$$

In fact, (24.1) is an equivalence. Furthermore, if we extend $\triangleleft$ to an operation on intervals by defining $(\ell, r) \triangleleft j = (\ell \triangleleft j, r \triangleleft j)$, then $(i \triangleright j) \triangleleft i = j$, so $\triangleright$ has all the properties of a mathematical group.

Models

In order to encode a text, each possible symbol has to be associated with a given interval. For our purposes, *Model* is an abstract type representing a finite mapping from a finite set of *Symbols* to *Intervals* with associated functions:

$$\begin{aligned} interval &:: Model \rightarrow Symbol \rightarrow Interval \\ symbol &:: Model \rightarrow Fraction \rightarrow Symbol \end{aligned}$$

Thus, $interval\,m\,x$ is the interval associated with symbol x in model m, while $symbol\,m\,f$ is the symbol associated with the unique interval containing the proper fraction f. We suppose that the intervals associated with symbols partition the unit interval, so

$$x = symbol\,m\,f \;\equiv\; f \in interval\,m\,x \tag{24.2}$$

for every model m and proper fraction f.

As an important practical refinement on the basic idea, the model is allowed to change as each symbol of the text is read. Such a scheme is called *adaptive* encoding. For instance, one can begin with a simple model in which all symbols are associated with intervals of the same width and then let the model adapt by widening the intervals associated with the more frequently occurring symbols in the text. The wider an interval is, the more scope there is for finding a short fraction within it. More sophisticated adaptations are also possible. For example, in English the letter "q" is nearly always followed by a "u". Therefore, on encountering a symbol "q", the interval for "u" can be widened in the expectation that the next symbol is a "u".

It is not our purpose to study model adaptation in detail. Instead, we will just suppose the existence of an additional function

$$adapt \;::\; Model \rightarrow Symbol \rightarrow Model$$

The function $intervals :: Model \rightarrow [Symbol] \rightarrow [Interval]$ is now defined by

$$\begin{aligned} intervals\,m\,[\,] &= [\,] \\ intervals\,m\,(x:xs) &= interval\,m\,x : intervals\,(adapt\,m\,x)\,xs \end{aligned}$$

Each symbol of the text is converted into an interval by applying *interval* to a succession of models. As long as the decoder knows the initial model and *adapt*, it can perform the necessary adaptations to the model as each symbol is reconstructed. Crucially, there is no need to transmit the various models along with the text.

Encoding

Having defined the relevant data types and auxiliary operations, we can now specify the function *encode*:

$$encode \quad :: \quad Model \rightarrow [Symbol] \rightarrow Fraction$$
$$encode\ m \quad = \quad pick \cdot foldl\ (\triangleright)\ (0,1) \cdot intervals\ m$$

where $pick\ i \in i$. The intervals associated with the symbols of the text are used to narrow the unit interval to some final interval, from which some fraction is chosen.

Here is a simple example. Suppose m is a static model that contains five symbols with intervals given by

$$[(e,(0,3/8)),(g,(3/8,1/2)),(n,(1/2,5/8)),(r,(5/8,7/8)),(v,(7/8,1))]$$

Then

$$encode\ m\ \text{"evergreen"}$$
$$= \quad pick((0,1) \triangleright (0,3/8) \triangleright (7/8,1) \cdots \triangleright (1/2,5/8))$$
$$= \quad pick(11445828/2^{25}, 11445909/2^{25})$$

The best choice for *pick* returns $(89\,421/2^{18})$, the unique fraction in this interval with the shortest binary expansion, namely 010101110101001101. So the nine characters of "evergreen" can be encoded as 18 bits, or three characters. In fact, since the numerator of a shortest fraction has to be odd, the last bit is always 1 and can be omitted, so only the first 17 bits need be output. The best that Huffman encoding can achieve is 19 bits. We will return to an appropriate choice of *pick* later on; for now we assume only that $pick\ i \in i$.

Decoding

The obvious way to specify *decode* is by the condition

$$xs \quad = \quad decode\ m\ (encode\ m\ xs)$$

for all finite lists of symbols xs. However, for reasons given in a moment, the specification is weakened to require only that

$$xs \quad \sqsubseteq \quad decode\ m\ (encode\ m\ xs) \tag{24.3}$$

where $\sqsubseteq$ is the prefix relation on lists, so $xs \sqsubseteq ys$ if $ys = xs \mathbin{+\!\!+} zs$ for some zs. Thus, *decode* is left-inverse to *encode*, in that it is required to produce the sequence of symbols that *encode* encodes but is not required to stop after producing them.

To define *decode*, let the input to *encode* be $xs = [x_0, x_1, \ldots, x_{n-1}]$. Let m_0 be the initial model and $j_0 = (0,1)$ the initial interval. Define

$$m_{k+1} \quad = \quad adapt\ m_k\ x_k$$
$$i_k \quad = \quad interval\ m_k\ x_k$$
$$j_{k+1} \quad = \quad j_k \triangleright i_{k+1}$$

for $0 \le k < n$. Thus, by definition of *encode*, if $f = encode\ m_0\ xs$ then $f \in j_n$. Now we can reason for $n > 0$:

$$f \in j_n$$
$$\equiv \quad \{\text{definition of } j_n\}$$
$$f \in (j_{n-1} \triangleright i_n)$$
$$\Rightarrow \quad \{(24.1)\}$$
$$f \in j_{n-1} \wedge (f \triangleleft j_{n-1}) \in i_n$$
$$\equiv \quad \{\text{definition of } i_n\}$$
$$f \in j_{n-1} \wedge (f \triangleleft j_{n-1}) \in interval\ m_n\ x_n$$
$$\equiv \quad \{(24.2)\}$$
$$f \in j_{n-1} \wedge x_n = symbol\ m_n\ (f \triangleleft j_{n-1})$$

Hence, by induction, we can compute

$$x_k \;=\; symbol\ m_k\ (f \triangleleft j_{k-1}) \tag{24.4}$$

in the order $k = n{-}1, n{-}2, \ldots, 0$. Equally well, (24.4) can used to compute the symbols in the order $k = 0, 1, \ldots, n{-}1$. However, since the decoder does not know the number of symbols, it will continue to produce more symbols indefinitely. Note that the associativity of $\triangleright$ was not exploited in the reasoning above.

We implement decoding using the Haskell function *unfoldr*, defined by

```
unfoldr     ::  (b → Maybe (a, b)) → b → [a]
unfoldr f b  =  case f b of
                   Just (a, b')  →   a : unfoldr f b'
                   Nothing       →   [ ]
```

The function *decode* is defined by

```
decode       ::  Model → Fraction → [Symbol]
decode m f    =  unfoldr step (m, (0, 1), f)
step (m, i, f) =  Just (x, (adapt m x, i ▷ interval m x, f))
                  where x = symbol m (f ◁ i)
```

The proof that this definition of *decode* satisfies (24.3) is by induction on *xs*. The details add nothing to the informal description above and we omit them.

That leaves the problem of termination. There are two possible methods for dealing with termination. Provided the number of symbols in the text is known beforehand, this number can be transmitted prior to encoding. Then *decode* can be stopped after producing the required number of symbols.

The second method is to use a special end-of-file symbol EOF, appended to the end of each text. Then *decode* is stopped when this special symbol is generated. The second method is the one usually adopted in practice, but has the disadvantage of forcing each model to allocate an interval, however small, for EOF, thereby restricting the total width of the intervals available for the other symbols.

Incremental encoding and decoding

Simple and elegant as the above definitions of *encode* and *decode* are, they produce and consume fractions. And the denominators of fractions get big very quickly. We would prefer coding and decoding to produce and consume lists of bits, not least because it opens up the possibility of producing some output before consuming all the input and reducing denominator size.

To this end we decompose *pick* into two functions, *toBits* :: *Interval* → [*Bit*] and *toFrac* :: [*Bit*] → *Fraction*, so that *pick* = *toFrac* · *toBits*. The definitions of *encode* and *decode* are revised to read:

$$
\begin{array}{lll}
encode & :: & Model \rightarrow [Symbol] \rightarrow [Bit] \\
encode\ m & = & toBits \cdot foldl\ (\rhd)\ (0,1) \cdot intervals\ m \\
\\
decode & :: & Model \rightarrow [Bit] \rightarrow [Symbol] \\
decode\ m\ bs & = & unfoldr\ step\ (m,(0,1),toFrac\ bs) \\
step\ (m,i,f) & = & Just\ (x,(adapt\ m\ x,i \rhd interval\ m\ x,f)) \\
& & \textbf{where}\ x = symbol\ m\ (f \lhd i)
\end{array}
$$

The new version of *encode* consumes symbols and produces bits, while *decode* consumes bits and produces symbols. The functions *toBits* and *toFrac* have yet to be determined, but as long as *toFrac* (*toBits* i) ∈ i for all intervals i we are guaranteed that (24.3) is satisfied.

The new definition of *encode* consumes all its input before delivering any output. We first show how to make *encode* incremental, because it will suggest appropriate definitions of *toBits* and *toFrac*.

Streaming

Consider the function *stream* defined by

$$
\begin{array}{l}
stream\ f\ g\ s\ xs\ =\ unfoldr\ step\ (s,xs) \\
\textbf{where}\ step\ (s,xs) = \textbf{case}\ f\ s\ \textbf{of} \\
\qquad\qquad\qquad\qquad Just\ (y,s')\ \rightarrow\ Just\ (y,(s',xs)) \\
\qquad\qquad\qquad\qquad Nothing\ \quad \rightarrow\ \textbf{case}\ xs\ \textbf{of} \\
\qquad\qquad\qquad\qquad\qquad\qquad\qquad x:xs'\ \rightarrow\ step\ (g\ s\ x,xs') \\
\qquad\qquad\qquad\qquad\qquad\qquad\qquad [\ ]\qquad \rightarrow\ Nothing
\end{array}
$$

This function describes a process that alternates between producing output and consuming input. Starting in state s, control is initially passed to the producer function f, which delivers output until no more can be produced. Control is then passed to the consumer process g, which consumes the next input x and delivers a new state. The cycle then continues until the input is exhausted.

The following theorem, called the *streaming theorem*, relates *stream* to the composition of an *unfoldr* with a *foldl*.

Theorem 24.1 *Suppose f and g satisfy the streaming condition*

$$f\ s = Just\ (y, s') \quad \Rightarrow \quad f\ (g\ s\ x) = Just\ (y, g\ s'\ x)$$

for all s and x. Then unfoldr f (foldl g s xs) = stream f g s xs for all s and all finite lists xs.

The proof of the streaming theorem is postponed to the Appendix. To apply it to *encode*, suppose $toBits = unfoldr\ bit$ for some function bit satisfying

$$bit\ i = Just\ (b, i_b) \quad \Rightarrow \quad bit\ (i \triangleright j) = Just\ (b, i_b \triangleright j) \tag{24.5}$$

Then we have

$$encode\ m \quad = \quad stream\ bit\ (\triangleright)\ (0, 1) \cdot intervals\ m$$

The result is an incremental algorithm for *encode*.

In order to satisfy (24.5) we need a suitable definition of *bit*. We also have to satisfy *toFrac* (*toBits* i) $\in i$. Observe that (24.5) demands that, whenever *bit* i produces a bit b, the same bit has to be produced by *bit* i' for any subinterval i' of i. This severely constrains the definition of *bit*. One possibility is to take

$$
\begin{array}{lll}
bit\ (\ell, r) & |\ \ r \leq 1/2 & = \quad Just\ (0, (2{*}\ell, 2{*}r)) \\
& |\ \ 1/2 \leq \ell & = \quad Just\ (1, (2{*}\ell{-}1, 2{*}r{-}1)) \\
& |\ \ \textbf{otherwise} & = \quad Nothing
\end{array}
$$

Thus, *bit* i produces nothing if i strictly straddles $1/2$; otherwise it produces a 0 if $i \subseteq (0, 1/2)$ and a 1 if $i \subseteq (1/2, 1)$. This choice is reasonable, since fractions in $(0, 1/2)$ have binary expansions that begin with a zero, while fractions in $(1/2, 1)$ have expansions that begin with a one.

If *bit* i does produce a bit b, then so does *bit* i' for any subinterval i' of i, including $i \triangleright j$. Furthermore:

$$
\begin{array}{lll}
(2{*}\ell, 2{*}r) & = & (0, 2) \triangleright (\ell, r) \\
(2{*}\ell{-}1, 2{*}r{-}1) & = & (-1, 1) \triangleright (\ell, r)
\end{array}
$$

Hence, if *bit i* does produce a bit b, then $bit\ i = Just\ (b, j_b \triangleright i)$, where $j_0 = (0, 2)$ and $j_1 = (-1, 1)$. And $j_b \triangleright (i \triangleright j) = (j_b \triangleright i) \triangleright j$ since $\triangleright$ is associative. Therefore, (24.5) is satisfied with $i_b = j_b \triangleright i$.

The length of *toBits i* is finite; in fact

$$length\ (toBits\ (\ell, r)) \;\leq\; \lfloor \log_2 1/(r - \ell) \rfloor$$

For the proof, note that *toBits* applied to an interval of width greater than $1/2$ yields the empty sequence of bits, since such an interval strictly straddles $1/2$. Moreover, each evaluation of *bit* is on an interval of double the width of its predecessor. Hence, if $1/2^{k+1} < r - \ell \leq 1/2^k$, equivalently if $k = \lfloor \log_2[1/(r - \ell)] \rfloor$, then termination is guaranteed after at most k bits have been produced.

With the above choice of *toBits* the companion function *toFrac* is defined by

$$toFrac \;=\; foldr\ (\lambda\, b\, f \to (b + f)/2)\ (1/2)$$

Equivalently, $toFrac\ bs = foldr\ (\lambda b f \to (b + f)/2)\, 0\, (bs + \!\!+ [1])$. Thus, *toFrac bs* in effect appends a 1 bit to the end of *bs* and converts the result into a fraction in the usual way. It is easy to check that $toFrac\ bs = (2n + 1)/2^{k+1}$, where $k = length\ bs$ and $n = toInt\ bs$, the binary integer represented by *bs*.

To show that $pick\ i \in i$, where $pick = toFrac \cdot toBits$, observe that *pick* is the composition of a function that consumes a list with a function that produces a list. The intermediate list can be eliminated, giving a direct definition

$$
\begin{aligned}
pick\ (\ell, r) \quad | \quad & r \leq 1/2 & = \quad & pick\ (2{*}\ell, 2{*}r)/2 \\
| \quad & 1/2 \leq \ell & = \quad & (1 + pick\ (2{*}\ell - 1, 2{*}r - 1))/2 \\
| \quad & \textbf{otherwise} & = \quad & 1/2
\end{aligned}
$$

The proof that $pick\ i \in i$ (indeed, *pick i* is strictly contained in i) now follows by fixpoint induction. In a fixpoint induction the hypothesis is assumed and then shown to hold under recursive calls. Thus, a fixpoint induction proof is essentially a proof by induction on the depth of recursion. Further details are left as an exercise.

That leaves the problem of how to implement decoding incrementally. It is possible to get *decode* to work incrementally, but we will not go into details because the work would be wasted: the reimplementation of *encode* and *decode* in terms of finite-precision integers to come in the next pearl requires a completely different approach.

Final remarks

The material in these two pearls is drawn from Bird and Gibbons (2003) and Stratford (2005). Witten *et al.* (1987) described "accessible implementation". For details of Huffman and Shannon–Fano coding, see Huffman (1952) and Fano (1961). For recent perspectives on the subject of arithmetic coding, see Moffat *et al.* (1998) and Mackay (2003). The streaming theorem is new, and was created specifically for the purposes of formulating an incremental version of encoding, but it has other applications; see Gibbons (2007). A good example of practice leading to new theory.

References

Bird, R. S. and Gibbons, J. (2003). Arithmetic coding with folds and unfolds. *Advanced Functional Programming 4, Volume 2638 of Lecture Notes in Computer Science*, ed. J. Jeuring and S. Peyton Jones. Springer-Verlag, pp. 1–26.

Fano, R. M. (1961). *Transmission of Information*. Cambridge, MA/New York, NY: MIT Press/Wiley.

Gibbons, J. (2007). Metamorphisms: streaming representation-changers. *Science of Computer Programming* **65**, 108–39.

Huffman, D. A. (1952). A method for the construction of minimum-redundancy codes. *Proceedings of the Institute of Radio Engineers* **40** (9), 1098–101.

Mackay, D. (2003). *Information Theory, Learning and Inference Algorithms*. Cambridge, UK: Cambridge University Press.

Moffat, A., Neal, R. M. and Witten, I. H. (1998). Arithmetic coding revisited. *ACM Transactions on Information Systems* **16** (3), 256–94.

Stratford, B. (2005). *A formal treatment of lossless data compression*. DPhil thesis, Oxford University Computing Laboratory, Oxford, UK.

Witten, I. H., Neal, R. M. and Cleary, J. G. (1987). Arithmetic coding for data compression. *Communications of the ACM* **30** (6), 520–40.

Appendix

The streaming theorem can be proved by appealing to a more general theorem about *unfoldr*. This theorem states that $unfoldr\ f \cdot g = unfoldr\ h$ provided two conditions are satisfied:

$$
\begin{aligned}
h\ x = Nothing &\Rightarrow f\ (g\ x) = Nothing \\
h\ x = Just\ (y, x') &\Rightarrow f\ (g\ x) = Just\ (y, g\ x')
\end{aligned}
$$

This result is known as the *fusion law* of *unfoldr*. In particular, the fusion conditions for

$$unfoldr\ step\ (s, xs) = unfoldr\ f\ (foldl\ g\ s\ xs)$$

where xs is restricted to be a finite list and

$$step\ (s, xs)\ =\ \textbf{case}\ f\ s\ \textbf{of}$$
$$Just\ (y, s')\ \rightarrow\ Just\ (y, (s', xs))$$
$$Nothing\ \rightarrow\ \textbf{case}\ xs\ \textbf{of}$$
$$x : xs\ \rightarrow\ step\ (g\ s\ x, xs)$$
$$[\,]\ \rightarrow\ Nothing$$

come down to

$$step\ (s, xs) = Nothing\ \Rightarrow\ f\ (foldl\ g\ s\ xs) = Nothing$$

and

$$step\ (s, xs) = Just\ (y, (s', xs'))$$
$$\Rightarrow\ f\ (foldl\ g\ s\ xs) = Just\ (y, foldl\ g\ s'\ xs')$$

for all finite lists xs. The first condition is easy to verify and the second condition follows from

$$f\ s = Just\ (y, s')\ \Rightarrow\ f\ (foldl\ g\ s\ xs) = Just\ (y, foldl\ g\ s'\ xs)$$

for all finite lists xs, which can be proved by induction on xs, given that the streaming condition holds for f and g.

25

Integer arithmetic coding

Introduction

This pearl continues the study of arithmetic coding begun in the previous one. The aim is to replace rational arithmetic with integer arithmetic. The basic idea is to represent the interval being narrowed by a pair of limited-precision integers (ℓ, r), where $0 \leq \ell < r \leq 2^e$ and e is a fixed integer; this pair represents the subinterval $(\ell/2^e, r/2^e)$ of the unit interval. The intervals supplied by models are represented in exactly the same way but with a different integer d. As we will see below, d and e have to satisfy $d \leq e-2$, so they cannot be the same. The values of e and d, assumed to be global constants in what follows, are chosen to be sufficiently small that all calculations can be done with limited-precision integers, for example with the Haskell type Int.

New definitions

We now take $Interval = (Int, Int)$, so $interval\,m\,x$ returns a pair (p, q) of limited-precision integers, representing the interval $(p/2^d, q/2^d)$. The function $symbol\,m$ takes an integer n in the range $0 \leq n < 2^d$ and returns a symbol x. As before, $x = symbol\,m\,n$ if and only if $n \in interval\,m\,x$, except that n is now an integer.

Next, we change the definition of narrowing by replacing $\triangleright$ with $\blacktriangleright$, defined by

$$(\blacktriangleright) \qquad :: \quad Interval \rightarrow Interval \rightarrow Interval$$
$$(\ell, r) \blacktriangleright (p, q) = (\ell + \lfloor (r-\ell)*p/2^d \rfloor, \ell + \lfloor (r-\ell)*q/2^d \rfloor)$$

The largest integer that can arise in evaluations of $\blacktriangleright$ is 2^{e+d} (because $(r-\ell)*q$ can be that big) and, provided this integer is in Int, all interval calculations can now be done with Int.

Next, recall the function $toBits$ of the previous pearl. This function converted a fractional interval into a list of bits. We have $toBits = unfoldr\,bit$, where

208

$$bit\ (\ell, r)\ \ |\ \ r \leq {}^1\!/_2\ \ \ \ \ \ \ = \ \ Just\ (0, (2*\ell, 2*r))$$
$$|\ \ {}^1\!/_2 \leq \ell\ \ \ \ \ \ = \ \ Just\ (1, (2*\ell-1, 2*r-1))$$
$$|\ \ \textbf{otherwise}\ \ = \ \ Nothing$$

For integer encoding, *bit* is replaced by *ibit*, so that *ibit* too uses limited-precision integer arithmetic:

$$ibit\ (\ell, r)\ \ |\ \ r \leq 2^{e-1}\ \ \ \ = \ \ Just\ (0, (2*\ell, 2*r))$$
$$|\ \ 2^{e-1} \leq \ell\ \ \ \ = \ \ Just\ (1, (2*\ell-2^e, 2*r-2^e))$$
$$|\ \ \textbf{otherwise}\ \ = \ \ Nothing$$

The function *ibit* is a version of *bit* that works on intervals scaled by 2^e, so satisfies $2^e * toFrac\ (unfoldr\ ibit\ i) \in i$.

Installing the above revisions leads to a new definition of *encode*, namely

$$encode_1\ m\ \ = \ \ unfoldr\ ibit \cdot foldl\ (\blacktriangleright)\ (0, 2^e) \cdot intervals\ m \tag{25.1}$$

In words, symbols of the text are converted into intervals which are then used to narrow the interval $(0, 2^e)$ to some final interval i from which a bit string is produced that, when converted to a fraction and scaled by 2^e, gives a number in i. It all seems straightforward.

The problem with (25.1), however, is that it just simply does not work! Narrowing with $\blacktriangleright$ will eventually collapse an interval to the empty interval, something that cannot happen with $\triangleright$. To illustrate, take $e = 5$, $d = 3$ and suppose m associates the interval $(3, 5)$ with the letter "a" and $(5, 6)$ with the letter "b". With *adapt* $m\ x = m$, so m is a static model, we have

$$encode_1\ m\ \text{"bba"}$$
$$= \ \ foldl\ (\blacktriangleright)\ (0, 32)\ [(5, 6), (5, 6), (3, 5)]$$
$$= \ \ foldl\ (\blacktriangleright)\ (20, 24)\ [(5, 6), (3, 5)]$$
$$= \ \ foldl\ (\blacktriangleright)\ (22, 23)\ [(3, 5)]$$
$$= \ \ (22, 22)$$

Moreover, *unfoldr ibit* $(22, 22)$ generates infinite garbage. Whoops!

Incremental encoding and interval expansion

What saves the day is a combination of two ideas: incremental encoding and interval expansion. First, suppose we replace (25.1) by

$$encode_2\ m\ \ = \ \ stream\ ibit\ (\blacktriangleright)\ (0, 2^e) \cdot intervals\ m \tag{25.2}$$

The operations *ibit* and $\blacktriangleright$ do not satisfy the streaming condition because $\blacktriangleright$ is not an associative operation and $encode_2 \neq encode_1$. Indeed, revisiting the example above, we have

$$encode_2 \; m \; \text{``bba''}$$

$$
\begin{aligned}
&= \quad stream \; ibit \; (\blacktriangleright) \; (0, 32) \; [(5, 6), (5, 6), (3, 5)] \\
&= \quad stream \; ibit \; (\blacktriangleright) \; (20, 24) \; [(5, 6), (3, 5)] \\
&= \quad 101 : stream \; ibit \; (\blacktriangleright) \; (0, 32) \; [(5, 6), (3, 5)] \\
&= \quad 101101 : stream \; ibit \; (\blacktriangleright) \; (0, 32) \; [(3, 5)] \\
&= \quad 101101 : stream \; ibit \; (\blacktriangleright) \; (12, 20) \; [\,] \\
&= \quad 101101
\end{aligned}
$$

Interval collapse is avoided. That is the good news. On the other hand:

$$encode_2 \; m \; \text{``aab''}$$

$$
\begin{aligned}
&= \quad stream \; ibit \; (\blacktriangleright) \; (0, 32) \; [(3, 5), (3, 5), (5, 6)] \\
&= \quad stream \; ibit \; (\blacktriangleright) \; (12, 20) \; [(3, 5), (5, 6)] \\
&= \quad stream \; ibit \; (\blacktriangleright) \; (15, 17) \; [(5, 6)] \\
&= \quad stream \; ibit \; (\blacktriangleright) \; (16, 16) \; [\,] \\
&= \quad 0111 \ldots
\end{aligned}
$$

Interval collapse is not avoided because each intermediate interval straddles 16, the midpoint, and *ibit* returns *Nothing* on such intervals.

The conclusion is that incremental encoding alone is not quite enough to avoid interval collapse. The problem is with intervals straddling 2^{e-1}, and the purpose of the second idea, interval expansion, is to increase the width of such intervals to at least 2^{e-2}. A narrowed interval $(\ell, r) \blacktriangleright (p, q)$ will not collapse if

$$\lfloor (r-\ell) * p/2^d \rfloor < \lfloor (r-\ell) * q/2^d \rfloor$$

for all $p < q$, equivalently if $\lfloor (r-\ell) * p/2^d \rfloor < \lfloor (r-\ell) * (p+1)/2^d \rfloor$ for all p. Since $\lfloor x \rfloor < \lfloor y \rfloor$ provided $x + 1 \leq y$, this condition is satisfied if $2^d \leq r-\ell$. Hence, collapse is avoided provided $r-\ell \leq 2^{e-2}$ and so if $d \leq e-2$.

Interval expansion

Interval expansion is a data refinement in which an interval (ℓ, r) is represented by a triple of the form $(n, (\ell', r'))$, where $\ell' = widen \; n \; \ell$ and $r' = widen \; n \; r$ and

$$widen \; n \; x \quad = \quad 2^n(x - 2^{e-1}) + 2^{e-1}$$

A *fully expanded* interval is one in which n is as large as possible, subject to the bounds $0 \leq \ell' < r' \leq 2^e$. For example, taking $e = 5$, the interval $(13, 17)$ of width 4 can be represented by the fully expanded interval $(2, (4, 20))$ of width 16.

The function *expand* takes an interval and fully expands it. To define *expand*, and to avoid writing fractions and exponentials in what follows, define the four integers e_i for $1 \leq i \leq 4$ by $e_i = (i/4)2^e$. Observe that

$$0 \leq 2 * (\ell - e_2) + e_2 \quad \equiv \quad e_1 \leq \ell$$
$$2 * (r - e_2) + e_2 \leq e_4 \quad \equiv \quad r \leq e_3$$

Hence, we can further expand $(n, (\ell, r))$ if $e_1 \leq \ell$ and $r \leq e_3$. This leads to the definition of *expand* in terms of a subsidiary function *extend*:

$$expand\ i \ = \ extend\ (0, i)$$
$$extend\ (n, (\ell, r))$$
$$| \quad e_1 \leq \ell \wedge r \leq e_3 \quad = \quad extend\ (n{+}1, 2*\ell{-}e_2, 2*r{-}e_2)$$
$$| \quad \textbf{otherwise} \qquad = \quad (n, (\ell, r))$$

The converse of *expand* is *contract*, defined by

$$contract\ (n, (\ell, r)) \quad = \quad (shorten\ n\ \ell, shorten\ n\ r)$$

where $shorten\ n\ x = (x - e_2)/2^n + e_2$. We have $shorten\ n \cdot widen\ n = id$, from which follows $contract \cdot expand = id$, but, in general, $expand \cdot contract \neq id$. This is the usual situation with the abstraction and representation functions of a data refinement.

Next, define *enarrow*, short for extend and narrow, by

$$enarrow \qquad :: \quad (Int, Interval) \rightarrow Interval \rightarrow (Int, Interval)$$
$$enarrow\ ei\ j \ = \ (n, i \blacktriangleright j) \quad \textbf{where}\ (n, i) = extend\ ei$$

Thus, *enarrow* takes a partially expanded interval, fully expands it and then narrows the result with $\blacktriangleright$. Consequently, (ℓ, r) is narrowed only when $\ell < e_1$ or $e_3 < r$. If, in addition, $\ell < e_2 < r$, then either $\ell < e_1$ and $e_2 < r$, or $\ell < e_2$ and $e_3 < r$. In either case, $e_1 < r-\ell$, which is exactly what is required.

A new definition

We now replace (25.2) by yet a third, completely new definition:

$$encode_3\ m \ = \ stream\ ebit\ enarrow\ (0, (0, 2^e)) \cdot intervals\ m \qquad (25.3)$$

The function *ebit* is a counterpart to *ibit* that works on expanded intervals, and is specified by the property

$$unfoldr\ ebit \ = \ unfoldr\ ibit \cdot contract \qquad (25.4)$$

where *ibit* was defined above. An explicit definition of *ebit* is developed below. The function *ebit* will return *Nothing* on intervals that straddle e_2, so *encode₃* ensures that an interval is narrowed by ▶ only if its width is at least e_1, thereby avoiding interval collapse if $d \leq e-2$.

The function *encode₃* is different from all previous versions of *encode*. That means we are back to square one with the problem of how to define *decode*. We postpone discussion of the relationship between *encode₃ m xs* and *xs* until after constructing an explicit definition of *ebit*.

Equation (25.4) suggests appeal to the fusion law of *unfoldr*. This law (which was used in the Appendix of the previous pearl) states that

$$unfoldr\ h\ =\ unfoldr\ f \cdot g$$

provided the following two fusion conditions are satisfied:

$$h\ x = Nothing \quad \Rightarrow \quad f\ (g\ x) = Nothing$$
$$h\ x = Just\ (y, x') \quad \Rightarrow \quad f\ (g\ x) = Just\ (y, g\ x')$$

Taking $h = ebit$, $f = ibit$ and $g = contract$, we have to show

$$ebit\ x = Nothing \quad \Rightarrow \quad ibit\ (contract\ x) = Nothing$$
$$ebit\ x = Just\ (y, x') \quad \Rightarrow \quad ibit\ (contract\ x) = Just\ (y, contract\ x')$$

Here is the definition of *ebit* that satisfies these conditions:

$$
\begin{aligned}
&ebit\ (0, (\ell, r)) \\
&\quad |\quad r \leq e_2 \qquad = \quad Just\ (0, (0, (2*\ell, 2*r))) \\
&\quad |\quad e_2 \leq \ell \qquad = \quad Just\ (1, (0, (2*\ell - e_4, 2*r - e_4))) \\
&\quad |\quad \textbf{otherwise} \quad = \quad Nothing \\
&ebit\ (n+1, (\ell, r)) \\
&\quad |\quad r \leq e_2 \qquad = \quad Just\ (0, (n, (\ell + 2^n * e_2, r + 2^n * e_2))) \\
&\quad |\quad e_2 \leq \ell \qquad = \quad Just\ (1, (n, (\ell - 2^n * e_2, r - 2^n * e_2))) \\
&\quad |\quad \textbf{otherwise} \quad = \quad Nothing
\end{aligned}
$$

This definition will be simplified shortly. Setting $contract\ (n, (\ell, r)) = (\ell', r')$ it is easy to check that $r \leq e_2 \equiv r' \leq e_2$ and $e_2 \leq \ell \equiv e_2 \leq \ell'$, so the first fusion condition is satisfied. The second condition is immediate in the case $n = 0$, since $contract\ (0, i) = i$. The remaining case comes down to the identity

$$2*shorten\ (n+1)\ x - e_4 * b\ =\ shorten\ n\ (x + (1-2b)*2^n * e_2)$$

for $b = 0$ and $b = 1$, and is easily verified.

The definition of *ebit* is inefficient as well as clumsy, but it can be improved. Observe that $e_2 \leq \ell + 2^n e_2$ and $r - 2^n e_2 \leq e_2$ for all $n \geq 0$. Thus, in the case $r \leq e_2$ the computation of $unfoldr\ ebit\ (n, (\ell, r))$ proceeds

$$unfoldr \ ebit \ (n, (\ell, r))$$
$$= \quad 0 : unfoldr \ ebit \ (n-1, (\ell+2^{n-1}e_2, r+2^{n-1}e_2))$$
$$= \quad 01 : unfoldr \ ebit \ (n-2, (\ell+2^{n-2}e_2, r+2^{n-2}e_2))$$
$$= \quad \ldots$$
$$= \quad 01^{n-1} : unfoldr \ ebit \ (0, (\ell+e_2, r+e_2))$$
$$= \quad 01^{n} : unfoldr \ ebit \ (0, (2\ell, 2r))$$

where 01^n denotes a zero followed by n ones. Similarly, if $e_2 \leq \ell$, then

$$unfoldr \ ebit \ (n, (\ell, r)) \quad = \quad 10^n : unfoldr \ ebit \ (0, (2\ell - e_4, 2r - e_4))$$

Hence, $unfoldr \ ebit = concat \cdot unfoldr \ ebits$, where

$$ebits \ (n, (\ell, r))$$
$$\begin{array}{llll} | & r \leq e_2 & = & Just \ (bits \ n \ 0, (0, (2*\ell, 2*r))) \\ | & e_2 \leq \ell & = & Just \ (bits \ n \ 1, (0, (2*\ell - e_4, 2*r - e_4))) \\ | & \textbf{otherwise} & = & Nothing \end{array}$$

and $bits \ n \ b = b : replicate \ n \ (1 - b)$ returns a b followed by n copies of $1 - b$. It follows that we can replace (25.3) by the equivalent but more efficient version

$$encode_3 \ m$$
$$= \quad concat \cdot stream \ ebits \ enarrow \ (0, (0, 2^e)) \cdot intervals \ m \qquad (25.5)$$

Definition (25.5) is our final program for *encode*.

A crucial question

But, what does $encode_3$ actually do? How is its output related to its input? The version of *encode* in the previous pearl satisfied

$$toFrac \ (encode \ m \ xs) \quad \in \quad foldl \ (\triangleright) \ (0, 1) \ (intervals \ m \ xs)$$

But this cannot be the case with $encode_3$.

To answer this crucial question, define the variant $encode_3'$ of $encode_3$ that includes the starting interval as an extra argument, something we could have done from the outset:

$$encode_3' \ m \ ei \quad = \quad concat \cdot stream \ ebits \ enarrow \ ei \cdot intervals \ m$$

Then we have

$$2^e * toFrac \ (encode_3' \ m \ ei \ xs) \quad \in \quad contract \ ei \qquad (25.6)$$

for all models m, expanded intervals ei and lists of symbols xs. Property (25.6), whose proof is given in the Appendix, is crucial for implementing *decode*.

A final problem

Unfortunately, (25.5) is not guaranteed to give a version of *encode* that works with limited-precision arithmetic in all cases. The problem is with the number n in a fully expanded interval (n, i). It is conceivable that n can be very large, so large that it is not representable by an element of *Int*. For example, imagine narrowing $(0, e_4)$ a very large number of times with an interval such as $(3/8, 5/8)$. The narrowed interval strictly straddles e_2, so the output of *encode* is the empty list of bits. But interval expansion applied at each step will produce an expanded interval of the form $(n, (0, e_4))$, where n can exceed the upper limit of a limited-precision integer. Of course, the situation is extremely unlikely in practice, but it is logically possible. The plain fact of the matter is that no version of arithmetic coding is guaranteed to work with any form of limited-precision arithmetic. If the situation above does arise, then the two options are either to abort encoding with a suitable error message or to switch back to rational arithmetic coding.

Inverting streams

Now we tackle the problem of decoding. The function *decode* is specified by the condition $xs \sqsubseteq decode\ m\ (encode\ m\ xs)$. With (25.3), or the equivalent (25.5), as the definition of *encode*, the only way to satisfy this condition is to show how to invert streams. To this end we will make use of a function *destream* defined by

$$
\begin{aligned}
destream\ f\ g\ h\ s\ ys\ &=\ unfoldr\ step\ (s, ys) \\
\textbf{where}\ step\ (s, ys)\ &=\ \textbf{case}\ f\ s\ \textbf{of} \\
&\qquad Just\ (y, s')\ \rightarrow\ step\ (s', ys \downarrow [y]) \\
&\qquad Nothing\ \quad\ \rightarrow\ Just\ (x, (g\ s\ x, ys)) \\
&\qquad \textbf{where}\ x = h\ s\ ys
\end{aligned}
$$

The operation $\downarrow$ is defined by $(us \mathbin{+\!\!+} vs) \downarrow us = vs$. The function *destream* is dual to *stream*: when $f\ s$ produces some output y, then y is removed from the head of the input ys; when $f\ s$ returns nothing, an element of the output is produced using the "helper" function h.

The relationship between *stream* and *destream* is given by the following theorem, called the *destreaming theorem*, whose proof is also given in the Appendix.

Theorem 25.1 *Suppose stream $f\ g\ s\ xs$ returns a finite list and h satisfies $h\ s\ (stream\ f\ g\ s\ (x : xs)) = x$ if $f\ s = Nothing$. Under these assumptions we have $xs \sqsubseteq destream\ f\ g\ h\ s\ (stream\ f\ g\ s\ xs)$*

To apply the destreaming theorem to *encode*, take $f = ebit$, $g = enarrow$ and $s = ei$. Then we have

$$decode\ m \quad = \quad destream\ ebit\ enarrow\ h\ (m, (0, (0, e_4)))$$

provided that the helper function h satisfies

$$h\ (m, ei)\ (encode_3'\ m\ ei\ (x : xs)) \quad = \quad x \qquad\qquad (25.7)$$

for all intervals ei that straddle e_2.

Just as (25.3) can be improved to (25.5) by replacing *ebit* with *ebits*, so can the above definition of *decode*. The result is

$$decode\ m\ bs = unfoldr\ step\ (m, (0, (0, e_4)), bs)$$
$$step\ (m, (n, (\ell, r)), bs)$$

$\mid\ \ r \le e_2$	$=$	$step\ (m, (0, (2{*}\ell, 2{*}r)), bs \downarrow bits\ n\ 0)$
$\mid\ \ e_2 \le \ell$	$=$	$step\ (m, (0, (2{*}\ell{-}e_4, 2{*}r{-}e_4)), bs \downarrow bits\ n\ 1)$
$\mid\ $ **otherwise**	$=$	$Just\ (x, (adapt\ m\ x,$
		$enarrow\ (n, (\ell, r))\ (interval\ m\ x), bs))$

$$\textbf{where}\ x = h\ (m, (n, (\ell, r)))\ bs$$

It remains to discover the helper function h.

The helper function

We begin with a calculation that produces a definition of ◄, the operation that plays the same role for ► as ◄ did for ▷. Recall that

$$f \triangleleft (\ell, r) \quad = \quad (f - \ell)/(r - \ell)$$

and $f \in i \triangleright j \equiv (f \triangleleft i) \in j$. The calculation exploits an important property known as the *rule of floors*: $n \le f \equiv n \le \lfloor f \rfloor$ for all integers n and reals f. Let k, ℓ, r, p and q be any numbers. We calculate:

$$k \in (\ell, r) \blacktriangleright (p, q)$$
$\equiv$ {definition of ►}
$$\ell + \lfloor (r{-}\ell){*}p/2^d \rfloor \le k < \ell + \lfloor (r{-}\ell){*}q/2^d \rfloor$$
$\equiv$ {arithmetic}
$$\lfloor (r{-}\ell){*}p/2^d \rfloor < k - \ell + 1 \le \lfloor (r{-}\ell){*}q/2^d \rfloor$$
$\equiv$ {rule of floors}
$$(r{-}\ell){*}p/2^d < k - \ell + 1 \le (r{-}\ell){*}q/2^d$$
$\equiv$ {arithmetic}
$$p \le ((k - \ell + 1){*}2^d - 1)/(r - \ell) < q$$

$\equiv$ {rule of floors}
$$p \leq \lfloor ((k - \ell + 1)*2^d - 1)/(r - \ell) \rfloor < q$$

Hence, $k \in (i \blacktriangleright j) \equiv (k \blacktriangleleft i) \in j$, where

$$
\begin{aligned}
(\blacktriangleleft) &\quad :: \quad Int \rightarrow Interval \rightarrow Int \\
k \blacktriangleleft (\ell, r) &\quad = \quad ((k - \ell + 1)*2^d - 1) \operatorname{div} (r - \ell)
\end{aligned}
$$

Next, recall property (25.6) from the previous section: for all ei and xs

$$2^e * toFrac\,(encode_3'\, m\ ei\ xs) \quad \in \quad contract\ ei$$

Equivalently, using the definition of *contract* and *widen*, we have

$$widen\ n\ (2^e * toFrac\,(encode_3'\ m\ (n, i)\ xs)) \in i$$

Assuming the interval i has integer bounds and using the rule of floors again, the above is equivalent to

$$\lfloor widen\ n\ (2^e * toFrac\,(encode_3'\ m\ (n, i)\ xs)) \rfloor \in i$$

Next, take (n, i) to be a fully expanded interval straddling e_2, so

$$
\begin{aligned}
&encode_3'\ m\ (n, i)\ (x : xs) \\
&\quad = \quad encode_3'\,(adapt\ m\ x)\ (n, i \blacktriangleright interval\ m\ x)\ xs
\end{aligned}
$$

Then we obtain

$$\lfloor widen\ n\ (2^e * toFrac\,(encode_3'\ m\ (n, i)\ (x : xs))) \rfloor \in i \blacktriangleright interval\ m\ xs$$

Finally, recall the relationship between *symbol* and *interval*, namely that $x = symbol\ m\ n$ if and only if $n \in interval\ m\ x$. It follows that h can be defined by

$$
\begin{aligned}
h\,(m, ei)\ bs \quad &= \quad symbol\ m\,(\lfloor widen\ n\ (2^e * toFrac\ bs) \rfloor \blacktriangleleft i) \\
&\mathbf{where}\ (n, i) = extend\ ei
\end{aligned}
$$

Incremental decoding

The current definition of *decode* has a number of deficiencies: it uses rational arithmetic (in the computation of h, since *toFrac bs* is a fraction), it is not incremental and it is very inefficient. The computation of *extend* is duplicated both in evaluation of h and *enarrow*, the function *toFrac* is re-evaluated for every output symbol and *widen n* involves exponentiation, an expensive operation. All in all, *decode* sucks. But by making *decode* incremental we can overcome all these deficiencies.

We make *decode* incremental in three stages. First, we eliminate all dependency on the function *extend* by including the relevant computation in a revision to *step*:

$$
\begin{array}{ll}
step\,(m,(n,(\ell,r)),bs) & \\
\quad |\ \ r \le e_2 & =\ \ step\,(m,(0,(2{*}\ell,2{*}r)),bs \downarrow bits\ n\ 0) \\
\quad |\ \ e_2 \le \ell & =\ \ step\,(m,(0,(2{*}\ell{-}e_4,2{*}r{-}e_4)),bs \downarrow bits\ n\ 1) \\
\quad |\ \ e_1 \le \ell \wedge r \le e_3 & =\ \ step\,(m,(n{+}1,(2{*}\ell{-}e_2,2{*}r{-}e_2)),bs) \\
\quad |\ \ \textbf{otherwise} & =\ \ Just\,(x, \\
& \qquad (adapt\ m\ x,(n,(\ell,r) \blacktriangleright interval\ m\ x),bs)) \\
\quad\ \textbf{where}\ x = symbol\ m\ (\lfloor widen\ n\ (e_4{*}toFrac\ bs)\rfloor \blacktriangleleft (\ell,r))
\end{array}
$$

The point is that, when *step* (m, ei, bs) returns something, ei will now be a fully expanded interval, so *enarrow* can be replaced by $\blacktriangleright$.

Next, we show how to avoid repeated computations of *toFrac*. Define f and *step'* by

$$
\begin{array}{ll}
f\ n\ bs & =\ \ widen\ n\ (e_4{*}toFrac\ bs) \\
step'\,(m,(n,i),f\ n\ bs) & =\ \ step\,(m,(n,i),bs)
\end{array}
$$

Here the idea is to maintain $f\ n\ bs$ rather than bs as the third argument of *step*, where n is the expansion factor in the second argument. We leave it as an exercise to show that

$$
\begin{array}{ll}
f\ 0\ (bs \downarrow bits\ n\ b) & =\ \ 2{*}f\ n\ bs - e_4{*}b \\
f\ (n{+}1)\ bs & =\ \ 2{*}f\ n\ bs - e_2
\end{array}
$$

This leads to the following version of *decode*, in which *step'* is renamed *step* again:

$$
decode\ m\ bs\ =\ \ unfoldr\ step\,(m,(0,(0,e_4)),e_4{*}toFrac\ bs) \tag{25.8}
$$

where

$$
\begin{array}{ll}
step\,(m,(n,(\ell,r)),f) & \\
\quad |\ \ r \le e_2 & =\ \ step\,(m,(0,(2{*}\ell,2{*}r)),2{*}f) \\
\quad |\ \ e_2 \le \ell & =\ \ step\,(m,(0,(2{*}\ell{-}e_4,2{*}r{-}e_4)),2{*}f{-}e_4) \\
\quad |\ \ e_1 \le \ell \wedge r \le e_3 & =\ \ step\,(m,(n{+}1,(2{*}\ell{-}e_2,2{*}r{-}e_2)),2{*}f{-}e_2) \\
\quad |\ \ \textbf{otherwise} & =\ \ Just\,(x, \\
& \qquad (adapt\ m\ x,(n,(\ell,r) \blacktriangleright interval\ m\ x),f)) \\
\quad\ \textbf{where}\ x = symbol\ m\ (\lfloor f \rfloor \blacktriangleleft (\ell,r))
\end{array}
$$

$$decode\ m\ bs\ =\ unfoldr\ step\ (m, (0, e_4), toInt\ (take\ e\ bs'), drop\ e\ bs')$$
$$\mathbf{where}\ bs' = bs \mathbin{+\!\!+} 1 : repeat\ 0$$

$$
\begin{aligned}
step\ &(m, (\ell, r), n, b : bs) \\
&\mid\quad r \le e_2 &=&\quad step\ (m, (2{*}\ell, 2{*}r), 2{*}n{+}b, bs) \\
&\mid\quad e_2 \le \ell &=&\quad step\ (m, (2{*}\ell{-}e_4, 2{*}r{-}e_4), 2{*}n{-}e_4 + b, bs) \\
&\mid\quad e_1 \le \ell \wedge r \le e_3 &=&\quad step\ (m, (2{*}\ell{-}e_2, 2{*}r{-}e_2), 2{*}n{-}e_2 + b, bs) \\
&\mid\quad \mathbf{otherwise} &=&\quad Just\ (x, \\
&&&\quad\ (adapt\ m\ x, (\ell, r) \blacktriangleright interval\ m\ x, n, b : bs)) \\
&\mathbf{where}\ x = symbol\ m\ (n \blacktriangleleft (\ell, r))
\end{aligned}
$$

Fig. 25.1 The final version of *decode*

Now we see that n is a redundant variable, so we can drop it:

$$
\begin{aligned}
step\ &(m, (\ell, r), f) \\
&\mid\quad r \le e_2 &=&\quad step\ (m, (2{*}\ell, 2{*}r), 2{*}f) \\
&\mid\quad e_2 \le \ell &=&\quad step\ (m, (2{*}\ell{-}e_4, 2{*}r{-}e_4), 2{*}f{-}e_4) \\
&\mid\quad e_1 \le \ell \wedge r \le e_3 &=&\quad step\ (m, (2{*}\ell{-}e_2, 2{*}r{-}e_2), 2{*}f{-}e_2) \\
&\mid\quad \mathbf{otherwise} &=&\quad Just\ (x, \\
&&&\quad\ (adapt\ m\ x, (\ell, r) \blacktriangleright interval\ m\ x, f)) \\
&\mathbf{where}\ x = symbol\ m\ (\lfloor f \rfloor \blacktriangleleft (\ell, r))
\end{aligned}
$$

Finally, we are ready for incremental computation. Observe in (25.8) that, because $e_4 = 2^e$, the term $\lfloor e_4 {*} toFrac\ bs \rfloor$ depends only on the first e elements of bs. In fact

$$\lfloor e_4 {*} toFrac\ bs \rfloor\ =\ toInt\ (take\ e\ (bs \mathbin{+\!\!+} 1 : repeat\ 0))$$

where $toInt = foldl\ (\lambda n\ b \rightarrow 2{*}n + b)\ 0$ converts a bit string into an integer. The string bs has to be extended with sufficient elements of $1 : repeat\ 0$ to ensure that the total length of the result is a least e. Moreover, with $bs' = bs \mathbin{+\!\!+} 1 : repeat\ 0$ we have

$$
\begin{aligned}
\lfloor 2{*}e_4{*}toFrac\ bs \rfloor\ &=\ toInt\ (take\ (e{+}1)\ bs') \\
&=\ 2{*}toInt\ (take\ e\ bs') + head\ (drop\ e\ bs')
\end{aligned}
$$

That means we can replace the third argument f in the definition of *step* by a pair (n, ds), where $n = toInt\ (take\ e\ bs')$ and $ds = drop\ e\ bs'$ and $bs' = bs \mathbin{+\!\!+} 1 : repeat\ 0$. And this leads to our final version of *decode* recorded in Figure 25.1

Final remarks

The reader who has followed us to the bitter end will appreciate that there is rather a lot of arithmetic in arithmetic coding, and that includes the arithmetic of folds and unfolds as well as numbers. As we said in the previous pearl, arithmetic coding is a simple idea, but one that requires care to implement with limited-precision integer arithmetic.

Appendix

The proof of Theorem 25.1 depends on the following two properties, both of which are easy consequences of the definitions of *stream* and *destream*:

$$f\ s = Nothing \Rightarrow$$
$$stream\ f\ g\ s\ (x:xs) = stream\ f\ g\ (g\ s\ x)\ xs \wedge$$
$$destream\ f\ g\ h\ s\ ys = x : destream\ f\ g\ h\ (g\ s\ x)\ ys$$
$$f\ s = Just\ (y, s') \Rightarrow$$
$$stream\ f\ g\ s\ xs = y : stream\ f\ g\ s'\ xs \wedge$$
$$destream\ f\ g\ h\ s\ (y:ys) = destream\ f\ g\ h\ s'\ ys$$

In the first property x is defined by $x = h\ s\ ys$. We now prove

$$xs \sqsubseteq destream\ f\ g\ h\ s\ (stream\ f\ g\ s\ xs)$$

by a double induction on xs and n, where n is the length of $stream\ f\ g\ s\ xs$.

Case [ ]: Immediate since [ ] is a prefix of every list.

Case $x : xs$: First consider the subcase $f\ s = Nothing$. The first property above gives

$$destream\ f\ g\ h\ s\ (stream\ f\ g\ s\ (x:xs))$$
$$=\quad x : destream\ f\ g\ h\ (g\ z\ x)\ (stream\ f\ g\ (g\ z\ x)\ xs)$$

Since $x : xs \sqsubseteq x : xs'$ if and only if $xs \sqsubseteq xs'$, an appeal to induction establishes the case.

In the case $f\ s = Just\ (y, s')$ the second property above gives

$$destream\ f\ g\ h\ s\ (stream\ f\ g\ s\ (x:xs))$$
$$=\quad destream\ f\ g\ h\ s'\ (stream\ f\ g\ s'\ (x:xs))$$

But since $length\ (stream\ f\ g\ z'\ (x:xs)) = n - 1$ in this case, we can again appeal to induction to establish the case and complete the proof.

The final task is to prove that $e_4 * toFrac\ (encode_3'\ m\ ei\ xs) \in contract\ ei$.

The proof is by a double induction on xs and n, where n is the length of $encode'_3 \, m \, ei \, xs$.

Case [ ]: In this case $encode'_3 \, m \, ei \, [\,] = concat \, (unfoldr \, ebits \, ei)$. Now

$$e_4 * (toFrac \, (concat \, (unfoldr \, ebits \, ei))) \in contract \, ei$$

$\equiv \qquad$ {definition of $ebit$}

$$e_4 * (toFrac \, (unfoldr \, ebit \, ei)) \in contract \, ei$$

$\equiv \qquad$ {since $unfoldr \, ebit = unfoldr \, ibit \cdot contract$}

$$e_4 * (toFrac \, (unfoldr \, ibit \, (contract \, ei))) \in contract \, ei$$

$\Leftarrow \qquad$ {definition of $ibit$}

$$true$$

This establishes the case.

Case $x : xs$: In this case we need the following alternative definition of $encode'_3$:

$encode'_3 \, m \, (n, (\ell, r)) \, (x : xs)$
$\quad | \quad r \leq e_2 \qquad = \quad bits \, n \, 0 \mathbin{+\!\!+} encode'_3 \, m \, (0, (2\ell, 2r)) \, (x : xs)$
$\quad | \quad e_2 \leq \ell \qquad = \quad bits \, n \, 1 \mathbin{+\!\!+} encode'_3 \, m \, (0, (2\ell - e_4, 2r - e_4)) \, (x : xs)$
$\quad | \quad \textbf{otherwise} \; = \quad encode'_3 \, (adapt \, m \, x) \, ej \, xs$
$\quad \quad \textbf{where} \; ej = enarrow \, (n, (\ell, r)) \, (interval \, m \, x)$

By induction we have $encode'_3 \, (adapt \, m \, x) \, ej \, xs \in contract \, ej$. But

$$contract \, (enarrow \, ei \, j) \subseteq contract \, (extend \, ei) = contract \, ei$$

This establishes the case for the third clause of $encode'_3$.
    For the remaining two clauses, observe that the length of

$$encode'_3 \, m \, (0, (2\ell - be_4, 2r - be_4)) \, (x : xs)$$

is less than n. Hence, by induction, we have

$$e_4 * toFrac \, (encode'_3 \, m \, (0, (2\ell - be_4, 2r - be_4)) \, (x : xs))$$
$$\in \; (2\ell - b * e_4, 2r - be_4)$$

Finally, since $toFrac \, (bits \, n \, b \mathbin{+\!\!+} bs) = (2^n + (b-1) + toFrac \, bs)/2^{n+1}$, an easy calculation shows that $e_4 * toFrac \, bs \in (2\ell - be_4, 2r - be_4)$ if and only if

$$e_4 * toFrac \, (bits \, n \, b \mathbin{+\!\!+} bs) \in contract \, (n, (\ell, r))$$

establishing the case and completing the proof.

26

The Schorr–Waite algorithm

Introduction

The Schorr–Waite algorithm is a method for marking the nodes of a directed graph reachable from a given starting node. The graph is restricted to have out-degree 2. The algorithm consists of an iterative loop that carries out a depth-first traversal of the graph, but does not use an explicit stack to control the traversal. Instead, it simulates the stack by modifying the graph, taking care to restore the graph to its initial state at the end of the marking process. The algorithm is fairly subtle. Morris (1982) described it as "that most recalcitrant algorithm" and Bornat (2000) as "the first mountain that any formalism for pointer aliasing should climb".

The aim of this pearl is to present the Schorr–Waite algorithm as an exercise in explaining an algorithm by program transformation. We begin with a simple version of the marking algorithm and then describe three transformations that result in the final algorithm. Each transformation describes a different representation of the stack, culminating in a representation as a linked list embedded in the graph.

Specification

In Schorr and Waite's formulation of the problem, the graph represents a McCarthy S-expression McCarthy (1960) and so has out-degree 2. Nodes are represented by positive integers. Thus, we declare

type $Node$ = Int
type $Graph$ = $Node \rightarrow (Node, Node)$

The operations $left, right :: Graph \rightarrow Node \rightarrow Node$ extract the information associated with a given node and

$setl, setr$ :: $Graph \rightarrow Node \rightarrow Node \rightarrow Graph$

update the information associated with a node. So $left\,(setl\ g\ x\ y)\ x = y$, and similarly for $setr$.

The marking function *mark* takes a graph *g* and a starting node *root* and returns a Boolean-valued function *m* so that $m\ x = True$ if and only if node *x* is reachable from *root*. We will implement *mark g* as a function that returns both *g* and *m*. The reason is that the final algorithm modifies *g* during the course of execution; so, by showing that the various versions of *mark* are equivalent, we guarantee that not only is the final value of *m* the same for each version, but also the final value of *g*. Thus, *mark* has type

$$mark\ ::\ Graph \rightarrow Node \rightarrow (Graph, Node \rightarrow Bool)$$

A perfectly reasonable alternative is to embed the marking function in the graph, so that a graph becomes a mapping from nodes to triples. Then *mark* needs only return the final graph. But the present arrangement of keeping the marking function separate is both clearer and easier to reason about.

The function *mark* is implemented with a standard stack-based algorithm that carries out a depth-first search of the graph:

$$mark\ g\ root\ =\ seek0\ (g, const\ False)\ [root]$$

$$seek0\ (g, m)\ [\,]\ =\ (g, m)$$
$$seek0\ (g, m)\ (x : xs)$$
$$\quad |\quad not\ (m\ x)\quad =\quad seek0\ (g, set\ m\ x)\ (left\ g\ x : right\ g\ x : xs)$$
$$\quad |\quad \textbf{otherwise}\quad =\quad seek0\ (g, m)\ xs$$

The functions *set* and *unset* (needed later) are defined by

$$set, unset\ ::\ (Node \rightarrow Bool) \rightarrow Node \rightarrow (Node \rightarrow Bool)$$
$$set\ f\ x\quad =\quad \lambda y \rightarrow \textbf{if}\ y == x\ \textbf{then}\ True\ \textbf{else}\ f\ y$$
$$unset\ f\ x\quad =\quad \lambda y \rightarrow \textbf{if}\ y == x\ \textbf{then}\ False\ \textbf{else}\ f\ y$$

This definition of *mark* is our starting point.

Safe replacement

When reasoning about any algorithm that involves the manipulation of pointers, one sooner or later comes up against the problem of *safe replacement*. To illustrate, define the function *replace* by

$$replace\quad ::\quad Eq\ a \rightarrow (a \rightarrow b) \rightarrow a \rightarrow b \rightarrow (a \rightarrow b)$$
$$replace\ f\ x\ y\quad =\quad \lambda z \rightarrow \textbf{if}\ z = x\ \textbf{then}\ y\ \textbf{else}\ f\ z$$

Thus, *replace* is a generalised version of the function *set* introduced above. When is it safe to use *replace*? For instance, when do the identities

$$map\ f\ xs\quad =\quad map\ (replace\ f\ x\ y)\ xs$$
$$filter\ p\ xs\quad =\quad filter\ (replace\ p\ x\ y)\ xs$$

hold? The answer is not surprising: it is when x is not on the list xs. The other answer, when $y = f\,x$ or $y = p\,x$, is also correct but not interesting. Also not interesting is the proof of the correctness of the first answer. We will see a number of appeals to safe replacement below, all signified with the hint "safe replacement".

Eliminating duplicate entries

Returning to the problem in hand, the stack is eliminated in stages by transforming *mark* into successively different but equivalent versions. The aim of the first transformation is to eliminate duplicate entries on the stack by using it to store only those nodes that have been marked. This transformation sets things up for later appeals to safe replacements. The function *seek*0 is converted into a new function *seek*1, defined by

$$seek1\ (g, m)\ x\ xs \quad = \quad seek0\ (g, m)\ (x : map\ (right\ g)\ xs)$$

and subject to the invariant *clean m xs = all m xs ∧ nodups xs*. Synthesizing a direct definition of *seek*1 is straightforward and leads to the following replacement for *mark*:

$$
\begin{aligned}
&mark\ g\ root = seek1\ (g, const\ False)\ root\ [\,] \\
&seek1\ (g, m)\ x\ xs \\
&\quad |\quad not\ (m\ x) \quad = \quad seek1\ (g, set\ m\ x)\ (left\ g\ x)\ (x : xs) \\
&\quad |\quad null\ xs \quad\quad = \quad (g, m) \\
&\quad |\quad \textbf{otherwise} \quad = \quad seek1\ (g, m)\ (right\ g\ (head\ xs))\ (tail\ xs)
\end{aligned}
$$

Since x is added to the stack only when x is marked, and nodes are marked at most once, the new version of the stack is a clean one.

Threading the stack

The second transformation is designed to ensure that, in addition to being clean, the stack is *threaded*, meaning that for each pair x, y of adjacent entries, either $x = left\ g\ y$ or $x = right\ g\ y$. This is not the case with *seek*1. Consider the expression $seek1\ (g, m)\ (left\ g\ x)\ (x : y : xs)$, in which $left\ g\ x$ is marked but $right\ g\ x$ is not. Then *seek*1 replaces x on the stack with $right\ g\ x$, which is not in general the *left*-value or *right*-value of y. If, however, we can contrive to leave x on the stack, flagging it in some way to avoid processing it twice, then adding $right\ g\ x$ to the top will maintain the constraint. The element x is removed later when all of its offspring have been marked.

This effect is achieved with the help of a second marking function p. Define *seek2* by

$$seek2\ (g, m)\ p\ x\ xs\ =\ seek1\ (g, m)\ x\ (filter\ p\ xs)$$

subject to the invariant *threaded g m p x xs* on the arguments of *seek2*, where

$$\begin{aligned} threaded\ g\ m\ p\ x\ xs\ =\ \ & clean\ m\ xs\ \wedge \\ & and\ [link\ u\ v\ |\ (u, v) \leftarrow zip\ (x : xs)\ xs] \end{aligned}$$
$$\textbf{where}\ link\ u\ v = \textbf{if}\ p\ v\ \textbf{then}\ u = left\ g\ v\ \textbf{else}\ u = right\ g\ v$$

Below we refer to the following fact with the hint "threadedness": provided $m\ x$ and $x \notin xs$, we have

$$\begin{aligned} threaded\ g\ m\ p\ x\ xs\ \Rightarrow\ \ & threaded\ g\ m\ (set\ p\ x)\ (left\ g\ x)\ (x : xs)\ \wedge \\ & threaded\ g\ m\ (unset\ p\ x)\ (right\ g\ x)\ (x : xs) \end{aligned}$$

We now synthesise a new version of *mark* based on *seek2*. It is clear that

$$mark\ g\ x\ =\ seek2\ (g, const\ False)\ (const\ False)\ x\ [\ ]$$

so it remains to calculate a direct definition of *seek2*. In the case *not* $(m\ x)$ we reason:

$$\begin{aligned} & seek2\ (g, m)\ p\ x\ xs \\ =\quad & \{\text{definition}\} \\ & seek1\ (g, m)\ x\ (filter\ p\ xs) \\ =\quad & \{\text{case assumption } not\ (m\ x)\} \\ & seek1\ (g, set\ m\ x)\ (left\ g\ x)\ (x : filter\ p\ xs) \\ =\quad & \{\text{safe replacement, since } x \notin xs\} \\ & seek1\ (g, set\ m\ x)\ (left\ g\ x)\ (x : filter\ (set\ p\ x)\ xs) \\ =\quad & \{\text{since } set\ p\ x\ x\ =\ True\} \\ & seek1\ (g, set\ m\ x)\ (left\ g\ x)\ (filter\ (set\ p\ x)\ (x : xs)) \\ =\quad & \{\text{definition of } seek2, \text{ and threadedness}\} \\ & seek2\ (g, set\ m\ x)\ (set\ p\ x)\ (left\ g\ x)\ (x : xs) \end{aligned}$$

Hence, $seek2\ (g, m)\ p\ x\ xs = seek2\ (g, set\ m\ x)\ (set\ p\ x)\ (left\ g\ x)\ (x : xs)$.

In the case $m\ x$ we have to search for the first element on the stack satisfying p because that is the next element to be processed. We therefore introduce a function *find2*, defined by

$$find2\ (g, m)\ p\ xs\ =\ seek1\ (g, m)\ x\ (filter\ p\ xs)$$

for any marked node x and then derive a direct definition of *find2* that does not depend on *seek1*. In the case xs is empty we have

$$find2\,(g, m)\,p\,[\,] \;\; = \;\; (g, m)$$

In the case $xs = y : ys$ and *not* $(p\,y)$, we have

$$find2\,(g, m)\,p\,(y : ys) \;\; = \;\; find2\,(g, m)\,p\,ys$$

In the remaining case $p\,y$, we reason:

$$find2\,(g, m)\,p\,(y : ys)$$
$$= \quad \{\text{definition of } find2 \text{ and } seek1 \text{ in the case } p\,y\}$$
$$seek1\,(g, m)\,(right\,g\,y)\,(filter\,p\,ys)$$
$$= \quad \{\text{safe replacement since } y \notin ys\}$$
$$seek1\,(g, m)\,(right\,g\,y)\,(filter\,(unset\,p\,y)\,ys)$$
$$= \quad \{\text{since } unset\,p\,v\,v = False\}$$
$$seek1\,(g, m)\,(right\,g\,y)\,(filter\,(unset\,p\,y)\,(y : ys))$$
$$= \quad \{\text{definition of } seek2, \text{ and threadedness}\}$$
$$seek2\,(g, m)\,(unset\,p\,y)\,(right\,g\,y)\,(y : ys)$$

We have shown that

$$mark\,g\,root \;=\; seek2\,(g, const\,False)\,(const\,False)\,root\,[\,]$$
$$seek2\,(g, m)\,p\,x\,xs$$
$$\mid \quad not\,(m\,x) \quad = \quad seek2\,(g, set\,m\,x)\,(set\,p\,x)\,(left\,g\,x)\,(x : xs)$$
$$\mid \quad \textbf{otherwise} \quad = \quad find2\,(g, m)\,p\,xs$$
$$find2\,(g, m)\,p\,[\,] = (g, m)$$
$$find2\,(g, m)\,p\,(y : ys)$$
$$\mid \quad not\,(p\,y) \quad = \quad find2\,(g, m)\,p\,ys$$
$$\mid \quad \textbf{otherwise} \quad = \quad seek2\,(g, m)\,(unset\,p\,y)\,(right\,g\,y)\,(y : ys)$$

The two mutually recursive functions *seek2* and *find2* are both tail-recursive and can be implemented in an imperative style as a simple loop.

Representing the stack by a linked list

The final transformation is to represent the stack by a linked list. The cunning idea of Schorr and Waite is to store the links in the graph. Although the result is no faster than the initial version, it does use less space. The linked representation of the stack uses no separate linking function. Instead, there is an additional marking function p which, along with m, occupies just 2 bits of storage for each node in the graph.

To prepare for the final transformation, we need two pieces of information. The first is the abstraction function *stack* that extracts the stack from its linked representation:

$$
\begin{aligned}
&stack \qquad\quad :: \quad Graph \rightarrow (Node \rightarrow Bool) \rightarrow Node \rightarrow [Node] \\
&stack\ g\ p\ x \quad | \quad x == 0 \qquad = \quad [\,] \\
&\qquad\qquad\quad | \quad p\ x \qquad\qquad = \quad x : stack\ g\ p\ (left\ g\ x) \\
&\qquad\qquad\quad | \quad not\ (p\ x) \quad = \quad x : stack\ g\ p\ (right\ g\ x)
\end{aligned}
$$

The node 0 is a new, special node that acts as a list terminator. Here is how to add a new node $x \neq 0$ to the stack:

$$
x : stack\ g\ p\ y \quad = \quad stack\ (setl\ g\ x\ y)\ (set\ p\ x)\ x \tag{26.1}
$$

The proof of (26.1) is

$$
\begin{aligned}
&\quad stack\ (setl\ g\ x\ y)\ (set\ p\ x)\ x \\
&= \quad \{\text{definition of } stack \text{ since } set\ p\ x\ x = True\} \\
&\quad x : stack\ (setl\ g\ x\ y)\ (set\ p\ x)\ (left\ (setl\ g\ x\ y)\ x) \\
&= \quad \{\text{since } left\ (setl\ g\ x\ y)\ x = y\} \\
&\quad x : stack\ (setl\ g\ x\ y)\ (set\ p\ x)\ y \\
&= \quad \{\text{safe replacement, as } x \notin stack\ (setl\ g\ x\ y)\ (set\ p\ x)\ y\} \\
&\quad x : stack\ g\ p\ y
\end{aligned}
$$

The second piece of information is a function *restore*, defined by

$$
\begin{aligned}
&restore :: Graph \rightarrow (Node \rightarrow Bool) \rightarrow Node \rightarrow [Node] \rightarrow Graph \\
&restore\ g\ p\ x\ [\,] \qquad\quad = \quad g \\
&restore\ g\ p\ x\ (y : ys) \quad | \quad p\ y \qquad\quad = \quad restore\ (setl\ g\ y\ x)\ p\ y\ ys \\
&\qquad\qquad\qquad\qquad\quad | \quad not\ (p\ y) \quad = \quad restore\ (setr\ g\ y\ x)\ p\ y\ ys
\end{aligned}
$$

The function *restore* is used to restore the graph to its initial state at the end of the marking process. The motivation for the definition is that *restore g p x xs = g* if *threaded g p x xs*, a claim we will leave as an exercise.

Having defined *stack* and *restore*, we can now define *seek3* and *find3*:

$$
\begin{aligned}
&seek3\ (g, m)\ p\ x\ y \quad = \quad seek2\ (restore\ g\ p\ x\ xs, m)\ p\ x\ xs \\
&\qquad\qquad\qquad\qquad\quad \textbf{where } xs = stack\ g\ p\ y \\
&find3\ (g, m)\ p\ x\ y \quad = \quad find2\ (restore\ g\ p\ x\ xs, m)\ p\ xs \\
&\qquad\qquad\qquad\qquad\quad \textbf{where } xs = stack\ g\ p\ y
\end{aligned}
$$

Synthesising a definition of *mark* in terms of *seek3* and *find3* is where the hard work begins. The first step is easy enough:

$$mark\ g\ root$$

$=$ {current definition of $mark$}

$$seek2\ (g,\ const\ False)\ (const\ False)\ root\ [\,]$$

$=$ {since $restore\ g\ p\ x\ [\,] = g$}

$$seek2\ (restore\ g\ p\ root\ [\,],\ const\ False)\ (const\ False)\ root\ [\,]$$

$=$ {definition of $seek3$ and $stack$}

$$seek3\ (g,\ const\ False)\ (const\ False)\ root\ 0$$

Hence, $mark\ g\ root = seek3\ (g,\ const\ False)\ (const\ False)\ root\ 0$.

Now to define $seek3\ (g, m)\ p\ x\ y$ directly. Suppose first that $not\ (m\ x)$. We reason:

$$seek3\ (g, m)\ p\ x\ y$$

$=$ {setting $xs = stack\ g\ p\ y$ and $g' = restore\ g\ p\ x\ xs$}

$$seek2\ (g', m)\ p\ x\ xs$$

$=$ {case $not\ (m\ x)$}

$$seek2\ (g',\ set\ m\ x)\ (set\ p\ x)\ (left\ g'\ x)\ (x : xs)$$

$=$ {safe replacement as $x \notin xs$}

$$seek2\ (g',\ set\ m\ x)\ (set\ p\ x)\ (left\ g\ x)\ (x : xs)$$

$=$ {claim: see below}

$$seek2\ (restore\ (setl\ g\ x\ y)\ (set\ p\ x)(left\ g\ x)\ (x : xs),\ set\ m\ x)$$
$$(set\ p\ x)\ (left\ g\ x)\ (x : xs)$$

$=$ {(26.1) and definition of $seek3$}

$$seek3\ (setl\ g\ x\ y,\ set\ m\ x)\ (set\ p\ x)\ (left\ g\ x)\ x$$

Hence, $seek3\ (g, m)\ p\ x\ y = seek3\ (setl\ g\ x\ y,\ set\ m\ x)\ (set\ p\ x)\ (left\ g\ x)\ x$. The claim is that

$$restore\ g\ p\ x\ xs\ =\ restore\ (setl\ g\ x\ y)\ (set\ p\ x)\ (left\ g\ x)\ (x : xs)$$

For the proof we reason:

$$restore\ (setl\ g\ x\ y)\ (set\ p\ x)\ (left\ g\ x)\ (x : xs)$$

$=$ {definition of $restore$ since $set\ p\ x\ x = True$}

$$restore\ (setl\ (setl\ g\ x\ y)\ x\ (left\ g\ x))\ (set\ p\ x)\ x\ xs$$

$=$ {definition of $setl$}

$$restore\ g\ (set\ p\ x)\ x\ xs$$

$=$ {safe replacement as $x \notin xs$}

$$restore\ g\ p\ x\ xs$$

In the case $m\ x$ we have

$$seek3\ (g, m)\ p\ x\ y$$
$$=\quad \{\text{as above, with } xs = stack\ g\ p\ y \text{ and } g' = restore\ g\ p\ x\ xs\}$$
$$seek2\ (g', m)\ p\ x\ xs$$
$$=\quad \{\text{case } m\ x\}$$
$$find2\ (g', m)\ p\ xs$$
$$=\quad \{\text{definition of } find3\}$$
$$find3\ (g, m)\ p\ x\ y$$

We tackle $find3$ by cases. First, $find3\ (g, m)\ p\ x\ 0 = (g, m)$. In the case $y \neq 0$ and $not\ (p\ y)$, we argue:

$$find3\ (g, m)\ p\ x\ y$$
$$=\quad \{\text{definition of } find3 \text{ and } stack, \text{ with } ys = stack\ g\ p\ (right\ g\ y)\}$$
$$find2\ (restore\ g\ p\ x\ (y : ys), m)\ p\ (y : ys)$$
$$=\quad \{\text{definition of } restore \text{ in case } not\ (p\ y)\}$$
$$find2\ (restore\ (setr\ g\ y\ x)\ p\ y\ ys, m)\ p\ (y : ys)$$
$$=\quad \{\text{definition of } find2 \text{ in the case } not\ (p\ y)\}$$
$$find2\ (restore\ (setr\ g\ y\ x)\ p\ y\ ys, m)\ p\ ys$$
$$=\quad \{\text{safe replacement: } ys = stack\ (setr\ g\ y\ x)\ p\ (right\ g\ y)\}$$
$$find3\ (setr\ g\ y\ x, m)\ p\ y\ (right\ g\ y)$$

Hence, $find3\ (g, m)\ p\ x\ y = find3\ (setr\ g\ y\ x, m)\ p\ y\ (right\ g\ y)$.

Finally, in the most complicated case $y \neq 0$ and $p\ y$, we argue:

$$find3\ (g, m)\ p\ x\ y$$
$$=\quad \{\text{definition of } find3 \text{ and } stack, \text{ with } ys = stack\ g\ p\ (left\ g\ y)\}$$
$$find2\ (restore\ g\ p\ x\ (y : ys), m)\ p\ (y : ys)$$
$$=\quad \{\text{definition of } restore \text{ in case } p\ y\}$$
$$find2\ (restore\ (setl\ g\ y\ x)\ p\ y\ ys, m)\ p\ (y : ys)$$
$$=\quad \{\text{definition of } find2 \text{ in the case } p\ y\}$$
$$seek2\ (restore\ (setl\ g\ y\ x)\ p\ y\ ys, m)\ (unset\ p\ y)\ (right\ g\ y)\ (y : ys)$$
$$=\quad \{\text{claim (see below): with}$$
$$\qquad swing\ g\ y\ x = setr\ (setl\ g\ y\ x)\ y\ (left\ g\ y)\}$$
$$seek2\ (restore\ (swing\ g\ y\ x)\ (unset\ p\ y)\ (right\ g\ y)\ (y : ys), m)$$
$$\qquad (unset\ p\ y)\ (right\ g\ y)\ (y : ys)$$

$=$ {safe replacement: $y : ys = stack\ (swing\ g\ y\ x)\ (unset\ p\ y)\ y$}

   $seek3\ (swing\ g\ y\ x, m)\ (unset\ p\ y)\ (right\ g\ y)\ y$

Hence, $find3\ (g, m)\ p\ x\ y = seek3\ (swing\ g\ y\ x, m)\ (unset\ p\ y)\ (right\ g\ y)\ y$. The claim in the penultimate step is that

$restore\ (setl\ g\ y\ x)\ p\ y\ ys$
   $=\ restore\ (swing\ g\ y\ x)\ (unset\ p\ y)\ (right\ g\ y)\ (y : ys)$

where $swing\ g\ y\ x = setr\ (setl\ g\ y\ x)\ y\ (left\ g\ y)$. Here is the proof:

   $restore\ (swing\ g\ y\ x)\ (unset\ p\ y)\ (right\ g\ y)\ (y : ys)$

$=$ {definition of *restore* since $unset\ p\ y\ y = False$}

   $restore\ (setr\ (swing\ g\ y\ x)\ y\ (right\ g\ y))\ (unset\ p\ y)\ y\ ys$

$=$ {since $setr\ (swing\ g\ y\ x)\ y\ (right\ g\ y) = setl\ g\ y\ x$}

   $restore\ (setl\ g\ y\ x)\ (unset\ p\ y)\ y\ ys$

$=$ {safe replacement as $y \notin ys$}

   $restore\ (setl\ g\ y\ x)\ p\ y\ ys$

In summary:

$mark\ g\ root = seek3\ (g, const\ False)\ (const\ False)\ root\ 0$
$seek3\ (g, m)\ p\ x\ y$
   | $\ \ not\ (m\ x)$ $=$ $seek3\ (setl\ g\ x\ y, set\ m\ x)\ (set\ p\ x)\ (left\ g\ x)\ x$
   | **otherwise** $=$ $find3\ (g, m)\ p\ x\ y$
$find3\ (g, m)\ p\ x\ y$
   | $\ \ y == 0$ $=$ (g, m)
   | $\ \ p\ y$ $=$ $seek3\ (swing\ g\ y\ x, m)\ (unset\ p\ y)\ (right\ g\ y)\ y$
   | **otherwise** $=$ $find3\ (setr\ g\ y\ x, m)\ p\ y\ (right\ g\ y)$
   where $swing\ g\ y\ x = setr\ (setl\ g\ y\ x)\ y\ (left\ g\ y)$

This is the Schorr–Waite marking algorithm.

Final remarks

The Schorr–Waite algorithm was first described in Schorr and Waite (1967). Formal reasoning about the algorithm using loop invariants includes Bornat (2000), Butler (1999), Gries (1979), Morris (1982) and Topor (1979), but this list is not exhaustive. Möller (1997, 1999) used relations and relational algebras to reason about the algorithm, while Mason (1988) used *Lisp* and mutable update functions.

   Any treatment of the Schorr–Waite algorithm is bound to be fairly detailed, and the present one is no different. Particularly important is the need for various safe replacement properties. An alternative approach to safe replacement using separation logic is presented by O'Hearn *et al.* (2004). We do claim, however, that each definition of *seek* in terms of previous versions has a coherent motivation, is reasonably simple to understand and is a good way to present the algorithm.

References

Bornat, R. (2000). Proving pointer programs in Hoare logic. *LNCS 1837: 5th Mathematics of Program Construction Conference*, pp. 102–26.

Butler, M. (1999). Calculational derivation of pointer algorithms from tree operations. *Science of Computer Programming* **33** (3), 221–60.

Gries, D. (1979). The Schorr–Waite graph marking algorithm. *Acta Informatica* **11**, 223–32.

McCarthy, J. (1960). Recursive functions of symbolic expressions and their computation by machine. *Communications of the ACM* **3**, 184.

Mason, I. A. (1988). Verification of programs that destructively manipulate data. *Science of Computer Programming* **10** (2), 177–210.

Möller, B. (1997). Calculating with pointer structures. *IFIP TC2/WG2.1 Working Conference on Algorithmic Languages and Calculi*. Chapman and Hall, pp. 24–48.

Möller, B. (1999). Calculating with acyclic and cyclic lists. *Information Sciences* **119**, 135–54.

Morris, J. M. (1982). A proof of the Schorr–Waite algorithm. *Proceedings of the 1981 Marktoberdorf Summer School*, ed. M. Broy and G. Schmidt. Reidel, pp. 25–51.

O'Hearn, P. W., Yang, H. and Reynolds, J. C. (2004). Separation and information hiding. *31st Principles of Programming Languages Conference*. ACM Publications, pp. 268–80.

Schorr, H. and Waite, W. M. (1967). An efficient machine-independent procedure for garbage collection in various list structures. *Communications of the ACM* **10**, 501–6.

Topor, R. W. (1979). The correctness of the Schorr–Waite marking algorithm. *Acta Informatica* **11**, 211–21.

27

Orderly insertion

Introduction

Consider the problem of inserting the elements of a list of N distinct elements of some ordered type A one by one into an initially empty array of size N in such a way that at each stage the inserted elements are in increasing order, though possibly with gaps between them. If you like, think of the list as a big pile of books on the floor in some jumbled order and the array as a bookshelf divided into slots. At each stage the books on the shelf have to be in alphabetical order. You pick up the topmost book on the pile and place it on the shelf. In general, that can only be done by moving some of the books already on the shelf to make room. The object of the exercise is to minimise the total number of moves – the distance of the move is not relevant. For example, with $A = Char$, one way of inserting the elements of the string "PEARLS" into an array of size 6 is given by

1	2	3	4	5	6	Moves
–	–	–	P	–	–	0
–	E	–	P	–	–	0
A	–	–	E	–	P	2
A	–	–	E	P	R	1
A	E	L	–	P	R	1
A	E	L	P	R	S	2

with a total number of six moves. Our aim in this pearl is to construct a function that does the job with a total of $\Theta(N \log^3 N)$ moves, which has been conjectured to be the best possible. The algorithm is not derived, but establishing the time bound involves some subtle calculation.

231

A naive algorithm

Let us begin by recording the minimum number $m(N)$ of moves necessary to insert any list of N elements into an array of size N for $1 \le N \le 12$:

$$N \quad = \quad 1 \ \ 2 \ \ 3 \ \ 4 \ \ 5 \ \ 6 \ \ \ 7 \ \ \ 8 \ \ \ 9 \ \ 10 \ \ 11 \ \ 12$$
$$m(N) \ = \ 0 \ \ 1 \ \ 2 \ \ 4 \ \ 6 \ \ 8 \ \ 11 \ \ 14 \ \ 17 \ \ 21 \ \ 24 \ \ 29$$

It is an interesting diversion to find a strategy which guarantees that any list of six elements can be inserted in an array of size six with at most eight moves (just because PEARLS can be inserted with six moves does not mean that all six-letter words can be). No asymptotic formula for $m(N)$ is known, though there is strong evidence that $m(N) = \Theta(N \log^3 N)$.

There is one obvious algorithm for the problem, though it has a poor worst-case performance. Insert the first element in the first position and insert subsequent elements by shifting previously inserted elements just enough spaces to make room. So, if the kth element is smaller than all previous values, the $k-1$ previously inserted elements have each to be shifted up one position. This naive algorithm requires $N(N-1)/2$ moves in the worst case.

Slightly better, but not by much, is the strategy of inserting each element in the middle of the available free slots, if any. The first $\lfloor \log N \rfloor$ elements can then be inserted without any moves. However, after half the elements have been inserted, the moves begin to build up, leading once again to a quadratic-time worst-case performance.

One reasonable refinement on the basic strategy is periodically to insert some elements in such a way as to leave an even distribution of free slots for those that follow. Suppose we choose some integer M and call elements numbered iM, where $1 \le i \le k$ and $kM \le N < (k+1)M$, the *special* elements. A special element iM is inserted by moving every inserted element to leave an even spread, and therefore may require $iM - 1$ moves. This gives a total cost of at most

$$\sum_{i=1}^{k} (iM - 1) = \Theta(N^2/M)$$

moves for inserting all special elements.

When special element iM has been inserted, suppose the $N - iM$ free slots are evenly distributed with, roughly, $C_i = iM/(N - iM)$ elements on either side of each free slot. The naive algorithm for inserting the next $M-1$ (or fewer if $i = k$) non-special elements can then force at most

$$\sum_{j=1}^{M-1} (jC_i + j - 1) = \Theta(C_i M^2)$$

moves. The total number of moves for inserting all the non-special elements is then

$$\Theta\left(\sum_{i=1}^{N/M} C_i M^2\right) = \Theta\left(M^2 \sum_{i=1}^{N/M} \frac{iM}{N - iM}\right) = \Theta(MN \log N)$$

Now, if we choose M so that $N^2/M \approx MN \log N$ so $M \approx \sqrt{N/\log N}$, the total number of moves is $\Theta(\sqrt{N^3 \log N})$, which is a little worse than $\Theta(N^{1.5})$.

An improved algorithm

The strategy of the previous section can be improved in two ways: we can choose a different sequence of special elements and we can choose a better method for inserting the non-special ones. The two improvements are independent, but we will need both in order to meet the required asymptotic bound.

Instead of having special elements evenly spaced, suppose we allow more of them as the slots fill up. More specifically, let the special elements be those numbered $n_1, n_2, \ldots, n_k$, where $n_1 = \lfloor N/2 \rfloor$, $n_2 = \lfloor 3N/4 \rfloor$, $n_3 = \lfloor 7N/8 \rfloor$ and so on up to $n_k = \lfloor (2^k-1)N/2^k \rfloor$, where $2^{k-1} < N \leq 2^k$, so $k = \lceil \log N \rceil$. For example, when $N = 1000$ the special elements are

500, 750, 875, 937, 968, 984, 992, 996, 998, 999

The final element is inserted with at most $N-1$ moves. Since $k = \lceil \log N \rceil$, the total cost for inserting special elements is at most

$$\sum_{i=1}^{k} (n_i - 1) \leq \sum_{i=1}^{k} N = \Theta(N \log N)$$

Now we must deal with the non-special elements. Consider non-special element numbered n in *phase i*, meaning $n_{i-1} < n < n_i$, where $n_0 = 0$. Suppose this element needs to be inserted after the element at position $p - 1$ but before the element at position q; in other words, in the interval $[p, q)$. If $p < q$, so there are free slots, the element can be inserted at index $\lfloor (p + q)/2 \rfloor$. If $p = q$, so there are no free slots, the elements in some region surrounding p have to be moved to make room. The crunch question is: what region should be selected?

The answer, reasonably enough, is in a region that is not too densely occupied. Imagine the N slots are arranged as the leaves of a size-balanced tree. For example, with $N = 11$ one possible tree is

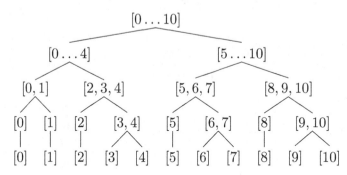

Each insertion point p determines a unique sequence $v_0, v_1, \ldots, v_k$ of intervals, where $v_0 = [p]$, along the path from p to the root of the tree. Let $L(v_j)$ be the length of interval v_j and $S(v_j)$ the number of currently occupied slots. The method for inserting element n in phase i is to insert n in the interval v_j, where j is the smallest integer satisfying the *density condition*

$$S(v_j) < \delta(i,j)L(v_j)$$

where

$$\delta(i,j) = \left(\frac{2^i - 1}{2^i}\right)^{j/k}$$

Moreover, element n and the $S(v_j)$ inserted elements are redistributed evenly across v_j, for a cost of $S(v_j)$ moves. Note that $1 = \delta(i,0)$ and $\delta(i,j) > \delta(i,k)$ for $j < k$. Note also that the density condition holds at the root:

$$S(v_k) < n_i \le \left(\frac{2^i - 1}{2^i}\right)N = \delta(i,k)L(v_k)$$

So there is always an interval that satisfies the density condition. If the density condition is satisfied, then $S(v_j) < L(v_j)$, since $\delta(i,j) \le 1$. So there is always an empty slot in v_j. Finally, note that the density condition holds for a leaf v_0 whenever $S(v_0) = 0$, so the slot at the desired insertion point is unoccupied.

As a specific example, the result of inserting the nine letters of DANGER-OUS into an array of size 9 is pictured in Figure 27.1.

As to the analysis of the total cost, suppose C elements are inserted during phase i, so $C \le N/2^i$. In the worst case, each of these elements has the same insertion point, so require insertion in some interval along some

1	2	3	4	5	6	7	8	9	Moves
–	–	–	–	D	–	–	–	–	0
–	–	A	–	D	–	–	–	–	0
–	–	A	–	D	–	–	N	–	0
–	A	–	D	–	G	–	N	–	2
–	A	–	D	E	G	–	N	–	0
–	A	D	E	–	G	N	–	R	3
–	A	D	E	G	N	O	–	R	2
A	D	E	G	N	O	R	–	U	7
A	D	E	G	N	O	R	S	U	0

Fig. 27.1 A DANGEROUS insertion

fixed path $v_0, v_1, \ldots, v_k$ from the insertion point to the root. Say element p, where $1 \leq p \leq C$, forces a shuffle in interval v_{j_p}. Let $S_0(v_{j_p})$ be the number of occupied slots just after the last redistribution involving the whole of v_{j_p} (which may have been when the last special element was inserted), and let $\Delta(v_{j_p}) = S(v_{j_p}) - S_0(v_{j_p})$, so $\Delta(v_{j_p}) \geq 0$.

The proofs of the following two estimates are given in the next section:

$$S(v_{j_p}) \quad < \quad 4k2^i(\Delta(v_{j_p}) + 1) \qquad (27.1)$$

$$\sum_{p=1}^{C} \Delta(v_{j_p}) \quad \leq \quad kC \qquad (27.2)$$

Since $C \leq N/2^i$, properties (27.1) and (27.2) give

$$\sum_{p=1}^{C} S(v_{j_p}) < \sum_{p=1}^{C} 4k2^i(\Delta(v_{j_p}) + 1) \leq 4k2^i(k+1)C \leq 4k(k+1)N$$

The total cost for seating all non-special elements is then at most

$$\sum_{i=1}^{k} 4k(k+1)N = 4k^2(k+1)N = \Theta(N \log^3 N)$$

Recalling that the total cost for inserting the special elements is $\Theta(N \log N)$, we obtain the bound $\Theta(N \log^3 N)$ for the total cost. In fact, the analysis proves somewhat more: the first $N/2$ elements can be inserted with at most $4N \log^2 N$ moves, the first $3N/4$ elements with at most $8N \log^2 N$ moves and so on. Putting it another way, if the array had size $(1 + \epsilon)N$ rather than exactly N, then N elements can be inserted with $\Theta((N \log^2 N)/\epsilon)$ moves.

Proofs

Abbreviating j_p to j, claim (27.1) is that $S(v_j) < 4k2^i(\Delta(v_j) + 1)$. Recall that $\Delta(v_j) = S(v_j) - S_0(v_j)$, that $S(v_j)$ is the number of currently occupied slots in the interval v_j and $S_0(v_j)$ was the number of occupied slots in interval v_j just after the previous distribution of some interval containing v_j. Here are the relevant properties on which the proof depends:

(i) $S(v_j) < \delta(i,j)L(v_j)$ and $S(v_{j-1}) \geq \delta(i,j-1)L(v_{j-1})$, because v_j is the smallest interval satisfying the density condition.

(ii) $2L(v_{j-1}) \geq L(v_j) - 1$, because the tree is balanced.

(iii) $2S_0(v_{j-1}) \leq S_0(v_j)+1$, because the previous distribution of an interval containing v_j resulted in an even spread.

(iv) $\Delta(v_j) \geq \Delta(v_{j-1})$, because v_{j-1} is a subinterval of v_j.

Using these facts we calculate:

$$2\Delta(v_j)$$
$$\geq \quad \{\text{since } \Delta(v_j) \geq \Delta(v_{j-1}) \text{ and definition of } \Delta\}$$
$$2S(v_{j-1}) - 2S_0(v_{j-1})$$
$$\geq \quad \{\text{since } 2S_0(v_{j-1}) \leq S_0(v_j) + 1 \leq S(v_j) + 1\}$$
$$2S(v_{j-1}) - S(v_j) - 1$$
$$\geq \quad \{\text{since } S(v_{j-1}) \geq \delta(i,j-1)L(v_{j-1})\}$$
$$2\delta(i,j-1)L(v_{j-1}) - S(v_j) - 1$$
$$\geq \quad \{\text{since } 2L(v_{j-1}) \geq L(v_j) - 1\}$$
$$\delta(i,j-1)(L(v_j) - 1) - S(v_j) - 1$$
$$> \quad \{\text{since } \delta(i,j)L(v_j) > S(v_j) \text{ and } \delta(i,j) \leq 1\}$$
$$(\delta(i,j-1)/\delta(i,j) - 1)S(v_j) - 2$$

Hence:

$$\Delta(v_j) + 1 > \frac{1}{2}\left(\frac{\delta(i,j-1)}{\delta(i,j)} - 1\right)S(v_j)$$

From the definition of $\delta(i,j)$ we obtain

$$\frac{\delta(i,j-1)}{\delta(i,j)} - 1 = \left(\frac{2^i}{2^i - 1}\right)^{1/k} - 1$$

Since $x^{1/k} = 2^{(1/k)\log x}$ and $2^y - 1 \geq y/2$ for $0 < y < 1$, we then obtain

$$\frac{\delta(i,j-1)}{\delta(i,j)} - 1 \geq \frac{1}{2k}\log\left(\frac{2^i}{2^i - 1}\right)$$

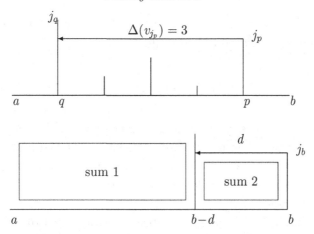

Fig. 27.2 Decomposition of $P(a, b, k)$ into two sums

Finally, since $2^i \log[2^i/(2^i - 1)] \geq 1$, we get $4k2^i(\Delta(v_j) + 1) > S(v_j)$, which is (27.1).

Claim (27.2) is that $\sum_{p=1}^{C} \Delta(v_{j_p}) \leq kC$. More generally, we show that

$$\sum_{p=a}^{b} \Delta(v_{j_p}) \leq k(b-a+1)$$

for $1 \leq a \leq b \leq C$. Let $P(a, b, k)$ denote the sum on the left, where we have made the dependency on k, the height of the tree, explicit. Consider the sequence of points $j_a, \ldots, j_b$, where $0 \leq j_p \leq k$. Each point denotes the interval in which an element is inserted. The value $\Delta(v_{j_p})$ is the number of elements in the interval v_{j_p} that have been inserted since the last redistribution at an interval containing v_{j_p}, say at j_q, and is therefore equal to the number of points between q and p. The situation is depicted in the first diagram of Figure 27.2.

To estimate $P(a, b, k)$, suppose $\Delta(v_{j_b}) = d$, so $0 \leq d \leq b-a$. Then P can be decomposed into two sums, as shown in Figure 27.2: the sum from a up to $b-d-1$ and the sum from $b-d$ to $b-1$, where we know in the second sum that the maximum j value is $j_b - 1$. This leads to the estimate that $P(a, b, k)$ is at most

$$(\max d : 0 \leq d \leq b-a : P(a, b-d-1, k) + P(b-d, b-1, j_b-1) + d)$$

Since $j_b \leq k$ and P is monotonic in its third argument, we have that $P(a, b, k)$ is at most

$$(\max d : 0 \leq d \leq b-a : P(a, b-d-1, k) + P(b-d, b-1, k-1) + d)$$

Now $P(a, b, k) = 0$ if $b - a \leq 1$ or if $k = 0$, and a simple induction argument yields $P(a, b, k) \leq k(b - a + 1)$ as required.

Implementation

Implementing the algorithm in Haskell is mostly straightforward; the only complicating factor is that various values have to be carried around. In particular, the phase number i and the size n of the array are needed in a number of calculations. The former is handled by labelling elements with their phase numbers and the latter by including n as an additional argument to certain functions.

An array is implemented as a simple association list of index–value pairs:

$$\textbf{type } \textit{Array a } = \; [(\textit{Int}, a)]$$

The invariant on *Array a* is that each index i is in the range $0 \leq i < n$ and the values are stored in increasing order. The main insertion function is defined by

$$\textit{insertAll n } = \; \textit{scanl } (\textit{insert n}) \, [\,] \cdot \textit{label n}$$

The function *insert n* carries out one insertion and *label n* labels elements with phase numbers. The result of *insertAll n* is a list of arrays, which can be used subsequently for display purposes and for counting moves.

The code for *label* involves determining the special elements. Special elements are assigned a phase number 0 and non-special elements a phase number i, where $i > 0$. The special elements are given by *specials n*, where

$$
\begin{aligned}
\textit{specials} \quad &:: \quad \textit{Int} \rightarrow [\textit{Int}] \\
\textit{specials n} \; &= \quad \textit{scanl1} \, (+) \, (\textit{halves n}) \\
\textit{halves n} \; &= \quad \textbf{if } n == 1 \textbf{ then } [\,] \textbf{ else } m : \textit{halves}(n - m) \\
&\quad\;\; \textbf{where } m = n \textbf{ div } 2
\end{aligned}
$$

For example, *specials* $11 = [5, 8, 9, 10]$. The function *label* is then defined by

$$
\begin{aligned}
\textit{label} \quad &:: \quad \textit{Int} \rightarrow [a] \rightarrow [(\textit{Int}, a)] \\
\textit{label n xs} \; &= \quad \textit{replace } 1 \, (\textit{zip} \, [1..] \, \textit{xs}) \, (\textit{specials n})
\end{aligned}
$$

where *replace* replaces positions by phase numbers:

$$
\begin{aligned}
&\textit{replace i} \, [\,] \, \textit{ns} \; = \; [\,] \\
&\textit{replace i} \, ((k, x) : \textit{kxs}) \, \textit{ns} \\
&\quad | \quad \textit{null ns} \; = \quad [(0, x)] \\
&\quad | \quad k < n \; = \quad (i, x) : \textit{replace i kxs ns} \\
&\quad | \quad k == n \; = \quad (0, x) : \textit{replace } (i{+}1) \, \textit{kxs} \, (\textit{tail ns}) \\
&\quad\;\; \textbf{where } n = \textit{head ns}
\end{aligned}
$$

For example, *label* 11 [1 .. 11] produces the list

$$[(1,1), (1,2), (1,3), (1,4), (0,5), (2,6), (2,7), (0,8), (0,9), (0,10), (0,11)]$$

Next we deal with *insert n*, which is implemented by

$$
\begin{array}{lll}
insert & :: & Ord\ a \Rightarrow Int \rightarrow Array\ a \rightarrow (Int, a) \rightarrow Array\ a \\
insert\ n\ as\ (i, x) & = & \textbf{if}\ \ i == 0 \\
& & \textbf{then}\ \ relocate\ (0, n)\ x\ as \\
& & \textbf{else}\ \ relocate\ (\ell, r)\ x\ as \\
& & \textbf{where}\ (\ell, r) = ipick\ n\ as\ (i, x)
\end{array}
$$

If element x is special, so its phase number is 0, then x is inserted by relocating x and all the elements in the array in the interval $(0, n)$. If x is not special, then *ipick* selects the interval (ℓ, r) in which the relocation takes place.

The function *relocate* is defined by

$$
\begin{array}{lll}
relocate & :: & Ord\ a \Rightarrow (Int, Int) \rightarrow a \rightarrow Array\ a \rightarrow Array\ a \\
relocate\ (\ell, r)\ x\ as & = & distribute\ (add\ x\ (entries\ (\ell, r)\ as))\ (\ell, r)\ as
\end{array}
$$

where *entries* returns the (ordered) list of entries in the specified interval and *add* inserts x in this list. These two functions are defined by

$$
\begin{array}{lll}
entries\ (\ell, r)\ as & = & [x \mid (i, x) \leftarrow as,\ l \leq i \wedge i < r] \\
add\ x\ xs & = & takeWhile\ (< x)\ xs \mathbin{+\!\!+} [x] \mathbin{+\!\!+} dropWhile\ (< x)\ xs
\end{array}
$$

The function *distribute* takes an ordered list, an interval and an array and distributes the elements of the list evenly across the interval:

$$
\begin{array}{lll}
distribute & :: & [a] \rightarrow (Int, Int) \rightarrow Array\ a \rightarrow Array\ a \\
distribute\ xs\ (\ell, r)\ as & = & takeWhile\ (\lambda(i, x) \rightarrow i < \ell)\ as \mathbin{+\!\!+} \\
& & spread\ xs\ (\ell, r) \mathbin{+\!\!+} \\
& & dropWhile\ (\lambda(i, x) \rightarrow i < r)\ as
\end{array}
$$

One way of defining *spread* is to divide both the list and interval into equal halves and recursively distribute the left half across the left interval and the right half across the right interval:

$$
\begin{array}{llll}
spread & :: & [a] \rightarrow (Int, Int) \rightarrow Array\ a \\
spread\ xs\ (\ell, r) & \mid & null\ xs & = & [\,] \\
& \mid & n == 0 & = & [(m, head\ xs)] \\
& \mid & n > 0 & = & spread\ ys\ (\ell, m) \mathbin{+\!\!+} spread\ zs\ (m, r) \\
& & \textbf{where}\ (n, m) & = & (length\ xs\ \text{div}\ 2, (\ell + r)\ \text{div}\ 2) \\
& & (ys, zs) & = & splitAt\ n\ xs
\end{array}
$$

The next function to tackle is *ipick*. The definition is

$$
\begin{aligned}
&ipick &&::\quad Ord\ a \Rightarrow Int \to Array\ a \to (Int, a) \to (Int, Int)\\
&ipick\ n\ as\ (i, x) &&=\quad \textbf{if}\ p < q\ \textbf{then}\ (p, q)\ \textbf{else}\\
&&&\quad\ head\ [(\ell, r)\ |\ (j, (\ell, r)) \leftarrow zip\ [0..]\ (ipath\ n\ p),\\
&&&\qquad\qquad\quad \textbf{let}\ s = length\ (entries\ (\ell, r)\ as),\\
&&&\qquad\qquad\quad densityTest\ i\ j\ n\ s\ (r - \ell)]\\
&&&\quad \textbf{where}\ (p, q) = ipoint\ n\ x\ as
\end{aligned}
$$

First, the insertion point for element x is determined by *ipoint*. The result is an interval (p, q) containing no elements. If $p < q$, so the interval is not empty, then the result of *ipick* is (p, q). Subsequent relocation with (p, q) will ensure that x is placed in the middle of the interval. If $p = q$, so the interval is empty, then the path of intervals from the insertion point p to the root of the virtual tree is computed by *ipath*. The first interval satisfying the density test *densityTest* is then selected.

The function *ipoint* is implemented by

$$
\begin{aligned}
&ipoint &&::\quad Ord\ a \Rightarrow Int \to a \to Array\ a \to (Int, Int)\\
&ipoint\ n\ x\ as &&=\quad search\ (0, n)\ as\\
&\textbf{where}\ search\ (p, q)\ [\,] &&=\quad (p, q)\\
&\qquad\quad\ search\ (p, q)\ ((i, y) : as) &&=\quad \textbf{if}\ x < y\ \textbf{then}\ (p, i)\\
&&&\qquad \textbf{else}\ \ search\ (i{+}1, q)\ as
\end{aligned}
$$

The value *ipath* $n\ p$ is computed by reversing the path from the root $(0, n)$ to p:

$$
ipath\ n\ p\ =\ reverse\ (intervals\ (0, n)\ p)
$$

where

$$
\begin{aligned}
&intervals\ (\ell, r)\ p\ \ |\ \ \ell + 1 == r\ &&=\quad [(\ell, r)]\\
&\qquad\qquad\qquad\quad |\ \ p < m\ &&=\quad (\ell, r) : intervals\ (\ell, m)\ p\\
&\qquad\qquad\qquad\quad |\ \ m \leq p\ &&=\quad (\ell, r) : intervals\ (m, r)\ p\\
&\qquad\qquad\qquad \textbf{where}\ m = (l + r)\ \text{div}\ 2
\end{aligned}
$$

It remains to deal with the density test, for which we use arbitrary-precision integer arithmetic rather than real arithmetic. All five arguments of the function *densityTest* are limited-precision integers, so they have to be converted to arbitrary precision:

$$
\begin{aligned}
&densityTest\ i'\ j'\ n\ s'\ w'\ &&=\quad 2 \uparrow (i * j) * s \uparrow k < (2 \uparrow i - 1) \uparrow j * w \uparrow k\\
&\textbf{where}\ (i, j, s, w)\ &&=\quad convert\ toInteger\ (i', j', s', w')\\
&\qquad\quad\ k\ &&=\quad toInteger\ (ceiling\ (logBase\ 2\ (fromIntegral\ n)))
\end{aligned}
$$

The function *convert* is defined by *convert* $f\ (a, b, c, d) = (f\ a, f\ b, f\ c, f\ d)$.

Final remarks

The problem of inserting elements of an ordered list of length N into an array of size N is a restricted version of a more general problem known as *online list labelling* (Bender *et al.*, 2002), in which the aim is to maintain a mapping from a dynamic set of M elements (so elements can be deleted as well as inserted in the array) from some linearly ordered set to integers in the range 0 to $N-1$ such that the order of the labels matches the order of the corresponding elements. The primary use of online list labelling is in a related problem known as *order maintenance*. This problem involves maintaining a list, initially consisting of a single base element, subject to insertions, deletions and order queries. Insertions take the form *insert*(x, y), meaning inserting a new element x into the list immediately after the (existing) element y. The *delete*(x) operation deletes x from the list and *query*(x, y) returns true or false, depending on whether x precedes y in the list. Although order maintenance does not require that labels be attached to each element, most solutions do indeed use online labelling as a component.

The interest in the algorithm lies not, of course, in the Haskell implementation, but in the intriguing choice of density function and the analysis of why the $\Theta(N \log^3 N)$ behaviour is obtained. No-one knows whether $\Omega(N \log^3 N)$ is a lower bound on the problem, although Zhang (1993) proves that this is a lower bound for any algorithm that restricts movements to result always in a position in which the free slots are evenly spaced. The algorithm above is "smooth" in this sense, and it seems unlikely that a non-smooth algorithm could achieve fewer movements, but it appears difficult to rule such an algorithm out.

Finally, this pearl has been adapted from Bird and Sadnicki (2007), where further references to the literature of the problem can be found.

References

Bender, M. A., Cole, R., Demaine, E. D., Frach-Colton, M. and Zito, J. (2002). Two simplified algorithms for maintaining order in a list. *Lecture Notes in Computer Science, Volume 2461*. Springer-Verlag, pp. 139–51.

Bird, R. S. and Sadnicki, S. (2007). Minimal on-line labelling. *Information Processing Letters* **101** (1), 41–5.

Zhang, J. (1993). Density control and on-line labeling problems. Technical Report 481 and PhD thesis, Computer Science Department, University of Rochester, New York, USA.

28

Loopless functional algorithms

Introduction

Imagine a program for generating combinatorial patterns of some kind, patterns such as the subsequences or permutations of a list. Suppose that each pattern is obtained from its predecessor by a single *transition*. For subsequences a transition i could mean "insert or delete the element at position i". For permutations a transition i could mean "swap the item in position i with the one in position $i - 1$". An algorithm for generating all patterns is called *loopless* if the first transition is produced in linear time and each subsequent transition in constant time. Note that it is the transitions that are produced in constant time, not the patterns; writing out a pattern is not usually possible in constant time.

Loopless algorithms were formulated in a procedural setting, and many clever tricks, such as the use of focus pointers, doubly linked lists and coroutines, have been used to construct them. This pearl and the following two explore what a purely functional approach can bring to the subject. We will calculate loopless functional versions of the Johnson–Trotter algorithm for producing permutations, the Koda–Ruskey algorithm for generating all prefixes of a forest and its generalisation to Knuth's *spider spinning* algorithm for generating all bit strings satisfying given inequality constraints. These novel functional algorithms rely on nothing more fancy than lists, trees and queues. The present pearl is mostly devoted to exploring the topic and giving some warm-up exercises. Bear in mind, though, that loopless algorithms are not necessarily faster than their non-loopless counterparts. To quote from Knuth (2001):

The extra contortions that we need to go through in order to achieve looplessness are usually ill-advised, because they actually cause the total execution time to be longer than it would be with a more straightforward algorithm. But hey, looplessness carries an academic cachet. So we might as well treat this task as a challenging exercise that might help us to sharpen our algorithmic wits.

Change the penultimate word to "calculational" and you will appreciate the real point of the exercise.

Loopless algorithms

We formulate the idea of a loopless algorithm in terms of the standard function *unfoldr*, defined by

$$
\begin{array}{ll}
unfoldr & :: \ (b \rightarrow Maybe\,(a,b)) \rightarrow b \rightarrow [a] \\
unfoldr\ step\ b & = \ \textbf{case}\ step\ b\ \textbf{of} \\
& \qquad Just\,(a,b') \ \rightarrow \ a : unfoldr\ step\ b' \\
& \qquad Nothing \qquad \rightarrow \ [\,] \\
\end{array}
$$

By definition a loopless algorithm is one that is expressed in the form

$$unfoldr\ step \cdot prolog$$

where *step* takes constant time and *prolog x* takes $O(n)$ steps, where n is some suitable measure of the size of x. Every loopless algorithm has to be of the above form, with these constraints on the ingredients.

There is a slightly tricky problem about our formulation of looplessness. In the framework of a *lazy* functional language such as Haskell our definition of a loopless program will not, in general, give a loopless computation with constant delay between each output. In a lazy language, the work done by *prolog* is distributed throughout the computation, not concentrated all at once at the beginning. Therefore, we should really interpret the composition operator ($\cdot$) between *unfoldr step* and *prolog* as being fully strict, meaning that *prolog* is evaluated fully before the unfolding begins. Although it is not possible to define a general fully strict composition operator in Haskell, we will take pains to ensure that *prolog* and *step* take linear and constant time under a strict as well as a lazy semantics.

Four warm-up exercises

The simplest warm-up exercise is the identity function on lists. Following the required recipe to the letter, we have

$$
\begin{array}{ll}
id & :: \ [a] \rightarrow [a] \\
id & = \ unfoldr\ uncons \cdot prolog \\
\\
prolog & :: \ [a] \rightarrow [a] \\
prolog & = \ id \\
\end{array}
$$

$$uncons \qquad\qquad :: \quad [a] \rightarrow Maybe\,(a,[a])$$
$$uncons\,[\,] \qquad\quad = \quad Nothing$$
$$uncons\,(x:xs) \quad = \quad Just\,(x,xs)$$

That was very easy, so now let us consider the function *reverse* that reverses a finite list. In Haskell this function is defined by

$$reverse \quad :: \quad [a] \rightarrow [a]$$
$$reverse \quad = \quad foldl\,(flip\,(:))\,[\,]$$

The combinator *flip* is defined by *flip f x y = f y x*. The above definition reverses a finite list in linear time. A loopless program for reversing a list is now given by

$$reverse \quad = \quad unfoldr\,uncons \cdot foldl\,(flip\,(:))\,[\,]$$

Of course, all the real work is done in the prologue.

For the next warm-up exercise, consider the function *concat* that concatenates a list of lists. Here is a loopless version, discussed below:

$$concat \qquad\qquad\qquad :: \quad [[a]] \rightarrow [a]$$
$$concat \qquad\qquad\qquad = \quad unfoldr\,step \cdot filter\,(not \cdot null)$$

$$step \qquad\qquad\qquad\quad :: \quad [[a]] \rightarrow Maybe\,(a,[[a]])$$
$$step\,[\,] \qquad\qquad\qquad = \quad Nothing$$
$$step\,((x:xs):xss) \quad = \quad Just\,(x,consList\,xs\,xss)$$

$$consList \qquad\qquad\quad :: \quad [a] \rightarrow [[a]] \rightarrow [[a]]$$
$$consList\,xs\,xss \qquad = \quad \textbf{if}\,\,null\,xs\,\,\textbf{then}\,\,xss\,\,\textbf{else}\,\,xs:xss$$

The prologue filters out nonempty lists from the input and takes linear time in the length of the list. The function *step* maintains the invariant that it takes and returns a list of *nonempty* lists. Empty lists have to be filtered out of the input, otherwise *step* would not take constant time. For example, consider an input of the form $[[1],[\,],[\,],\ldots,[\,],[2]]$ in which there are n empty sequences between the first and last singleton lists. After producing the first element 1, it takes n steps to produce the second element 2 of the final list.

Eagle-eyed readers might complain that this definition of *concat* is overkill, since the alternative

$$concat \quad = \quad unfoldr\,uncons \cdot foldr\,(+\!\!+)\,[\,]$$

is also loopless. Here, the real work is done in the prologue, which takes linear time in the total *size* of the input, namely the sum of the lengths of the component lists. At issue here is the precise measure of size being used.

Since we are not going to go as far as coding every conceivable input as a string in some finite alphabet, we leave the definition of size informal and accept both definitions of *concat* as being loopless.

For the fourth and final warm-up consider the preorder traversal of a forest of rose trees:

$$
\begin{aligned}
\textbf{type}\ \textit{Forest a} \ &=\ [\textit{Rose a}] \\
\textbf{data}\ \textit{Rose a} \ &=\ \textit{Node a} \,(\textit{Forest a})
\end{aligned}
$$

The preorder traversal of a forest can be defined by

$$
\begin{aligned}
\textit{preorder} \ &::\ \textit{Forest a} \to [a] \\
\textit{preorder}\,[\,] \ &=\ [\,] \\
\textit{preorder}\,(\textit{Node x xs} : \textit{ys}) \ &=\ x : \textit{preorder}\,(\textit{xs} + \!\!\!+ \,\textit{ys})
\end{aligned}
$$

Furthermore, *preorder = unfoldr step*, where

$$
\begin{aligned}
\textit{step} \ &::\ \textit{Forest a} \to \textit{Maybe}\,(a, \textit{Forest a}) \\
\textit{step}\,[\,] \ &=\ \textit{Nothing} \\
\textit{step}\,(\textit{Node x xs} : \textit{ys}) \ &=\ \textit{Just}\,(x, \textit{xs} + \!\!\!+ \,\textit{ys})
\end{aligned}
$$

The function *step* is not constant time because $+\!\!\!+$ is not, but we can make it so with a change of type. Instead of taking a forest as argument, we can make *step* take a list of forests, revising its definition to read

$$
\begin{aligned}
\textit{step} \ &::\ [\textit{Forest a}] \to \textit{Maybe}\,(a, [\textit{Forest a}]) \\
\textit{step}\,[\,] \ &=\ \textit{Nothing} \\
\textit{step}\,((\textit{Node x xs} : \textit{ys}) : \textit{zss}) \ &=\ \textit{Just}\,(x, \textit{consList xs}\,(\textit{consList ys zss}))
\end{aligned}
$$

This is essentially the same trick as we performed for *concat*. Now we have

$$
\textit{preorder} \ =\ \textit{unfoldr step} \cdot \textit{wrapList}
$$

where *wrapList xs = consList xs* [ ]. This is a loopless algorithm for *preorder*. Of course, it suffers from the same defect as *concat*; since the length of the output is proportional to the size of the input, we could equally well have done all the work in the prologue.

Boustrophedon product

Many combinatorial generation algorithms involve running up and down one list in between generating successive elements of another list, rather like the shuttle on a loom or an ox ploughing a field. Indeed, Knuth uses the name *boustrophedon product* for essentially this operation. We will call it *box*, and denote it with an infix symbol $\square$, because the name is short, pronounceable, and contains an "ox". Here is the definition:

$$
\begin{array}{lll}
(\square) & :: & [a] \rightarrow [a] \rightarrow [a] \\
[\,] \mathbin{\square} ys & = & ys \\
(x : xs) \mathbin{\square} ys & = & ys +\!\!+ [x] +\!\!+ (xs \mathbin{\square} reverse\ ys)
\end{array}
$$

For example:

$$
[3, 4] \mathbin{\square} [0, 1, 2] \;=\; [0, 1, 2, 3, 2, 1, 0, 4, 0, 1, 2]
$$

The definition of $\square$ leads to an inefficient computation, since ys is reversed at each step. Better is the following version, which reverses ys only once:

$$
\begin{array}{lll}
xs \mathbin{\square} ys & = & mix\ xs\ (ys,\ reverse\ ys) \\
mix\ [\,]\ (ys, sy) & = & ys \\
mix\ (x : xs)\ (ys, sy) & = & ys +\!\!+ [x] +\!\!+ mix\ xs\ (sy, ys)
\end{array}
$$

The operation $\square$ is associative with the empty list as identity element, a good reason to denote it with an infix symbol. We leave the proof of associativity to the reader, but it depends on two subsidiary identities that we will spell out now, as they are used later on:

$$
(xs +\!\!+ [y] +\!\!+ ys) \mathbin{\square} zs \;=\; (xs \mathbin{\square} zs) +\!\!+ [y] +\!\!+ (ys \mathbin{\square} zs') \tag{28.1}
$$

$$
reverse\ (xs \mathbin{\square} ys) \;=\; (reverse\ xs) \mathbin{\square} ys' \tag{28.2}
$$

where zs' and ys' are defined by

$$
\begin{array}{lll}
zs' & = & \textbf{if}\ even\ (length\ xs)\ \textbf{then}\ reverse\ zs\ \textbf{else}\ zs \\
ys' & = & \textbf{if}\ even\ (length\ xs)\ \textbf{then}\ reverse\ ys\ \textbf{else}\ ys
\end{array}
$$

Thus, both (28.1) and (28.2) depend on parity information about the length of xs.

Just as *concat* distributes $+\!\!+$ over a list of lists, so *boxall* distributes $\square$ over a list of lists:

$$
\begin{array}{lll}
boxall & :: & [[a]] \rightarrow [a] \\
boxall & = & foldr\ (\square)\ [\,]
\end{array}
$$

For a list of length n of lists each of length m the output of *boxall* has length $(m+1)^n - 1$, which is exponential in mn, the total length of the input. Now we can state our final exercise, which is to make *boxall* loopless.

Tupling

Since $boxall\ (xs : xss) = xs \mathbin{\square} (boxall\ xss)$ and the definition of $xs \mathbin{\square} ys$ involves $reverse\ ys$, it is clear that as well as computing *boxall* we also need to compute *reverse · boxall*. That suggests it is sensible to construct both *boxall* and *reverse · boxall* at the same time. To do so we make use of the tupling law of *foldr*. This law states that

$$(foldr\ f\ a\ xs, foldr\ g\ b\ xs) \quad = \quad foldr\ h\ (a, b)\ xs$$

where $h\ x\ (y, z) = (f\ x\ y, g\ x\ z)$.

Suppose we can find an operation ⊠ so that

$$reverse · boxall = foldr\ (⊠)\ [\ ]$$

Then the tupling law of *foldr* gives

$$(boxall\ xs, reverse\ (boxall\ xs)) \quad = \quad foldr\ op\ ([\ ], [\ ])\ xs$$

where

$$op\ xs\ (ys, sy) \quad = \quad (xs\ \square\ ys, xs\ ⊠\ sy) \tag{28.3}$$

The sequences *ys* and *sy* are each the reverse of the other, hence their names.

To discover ⊠ we appeal to the fusion law of *foldr*. This law states that $f\ (foldr\ g\ a\ xs) = foldr\ h\ b\ xs$ for all finite lists *xs* provided $f\ a = b$ and $f\ (g\ x\ y) = h\ x\ (f\ y)$ for all x and y. We have *reverse* $[\ ] = [\ ]$, so it remains to find a definition of ⊠ satisfying

$$reverse\ (xs\ \square\ ys) \quad = \quad xs\ ⊠\ (reverse\ ys)$$

Since *reverse* (*reverse xs*) = *xs* for all finite lists *xs*, we can define

$$xs\ ⊠\ sy \quad = \quad reverse\ (xs\ \square\ (reverse\ sy))$$

We can also give a direct, recursive definition of ⊠:

$$
\begin{aligned}
[\ ]\ ⊠\ sy \quad &= \quad sy \\
(x : xs)\ ⊠\ sy \quad &= \quad (xs\ ⊠\ (reverse\ sy)) \mathbin{+\!\!+} [x] \mathbin{+\!\!+} sy
\end{aligned}
$$

Alternatively, we can express ⊠ by appealing to (28.2):

$$
\begin{aligned}
xs\ ⊠\ sy \quad = \quad &\textbf{if}\ even\ (length\ xs)\ \textbf{then}\ (reverse\ xs)\ \square\ (reverse\ sy) \\
&\textbf{else}\ (reverse\ xs)\ \square\ sy
\end{aligned}
$$

Using (28.3) and the definition of □, the first recursive definition of ⊠ leads to the following definition of *op*, renamed as *op*1:

$$
\begin{aligned}
op1\ [\ ]\ (ys, sy) \quad &= \quad (ys, sy) \\
op1\ (x : xs)\ (ys, sy) \quad &= \quad (ys \mathbin{+\!\!+} [x] \mathbin{+\!\!+} zs, sz \mathbin{+\!\!+} [x] \mathbin{+\!\!+} sy) \\
&\qquad \textbf{where}\ (zs, sz) = op1\ xs\ (sy, ys)
\end{aligned}
$$

Using (28.3) and the definition of $\square$ in terms of *mix*, the second definition of $\boxtimes$ leads to the following definition of *op*, renamed as *op2*:

$$op2\ xs\ (ys, sy) \quad = \quad \textbf{if}\ even\ (length\ xs)$$
$$\textbf{then}\ (mix\ xs\ (ys, sy), mix\ (reverse\ xs)\ (sy, ys))$$
$$\textbf{else}\ (mix\ xs\ (ys, sy), mix\ (reverse\ xs)\ (ys, sy))$$

The difference between *op1* and *op2* is that the latter uses *reverse* explicitly while the former does not. Ignoring the cost of $+\!\!+$ operations, evaluation of either *op1 xs* or *op2 xs* takes time proportional to the length of *xs*, so both *foldr op1* $([\,],[\,])$ and *foldr op2* $([\,],[\,])$ take time proportional to the total size of the input. We keep both definitions, *op1* and *op2*, in play because they lead to two different loopless versions of *boxall*.

Trees and queues

The final step is to eliminate the expensive $+\!\!+$ operations. This is achieved in two stages, the first of which is to represent lists by forests of rose trees under the abstraction function *preorder*. Then we have

$$boxall \quad = \quad preorder \cdot fst \cdot foldr\ op1'\ ([\,],[\,])$$
$$boxall \quad = \quad preorder \cdot fst \cdot foldr\ op2'\ ([\,],[\,])$$

where *op1'* is specified by

$$pair\ preorder\ (op1'\ xs\ (ys, sy)) \quad = \quad op1\ xs\ (preorder\ ys, preorder\ sy)$$

and *pair f* $(x, y) = (f\ x, f\ y)$. Similarly for *op2'* and *op2*. We know from the warm-ups how to make *preorder* loopless, so provided *op1' xs* and *op2' xs* take time proportional to the length of *xs*, either of the above is a loopless program for *boxall*.

The definitions of *op1'* and *op2'* can be calculated formally, but the results are sufficiently clear that we will not go into details. First:

$$op1' \ ::\ [a] \rightarrow (Forest\ a, Forest\ a) \rightarrow (Forest\ a, Forest\ a)$$
$$op1'\ [\,]\ (ys, sy) \qquad = \quad (ys, sy)$$
$$op1'\ (x:xs)\ (ys, sy) \quad = \quad (ys +\!\!+ [Node\ x\ zs], sz +\!\!+ [Node\ x\ sy])$$
$$\textbf{where}\ (zs, sz) = op1'\ xs\ (sy, ys)$$

Second, with a new version of *mix*:

$$op2'\ xs\ (ys, sy) \quad = \quad \textbf{if}\ even\ (length\ xs)$$
$$\textbf{then}\ (mix\ xs\ (ys, sy), mix\ (reverse\ xs)\ (sy, ys))$$
$$\textbf{else}\ (mix\ xs\ (ys, sy), mix\ (reverse\ xs)\ (ys, sy))$$

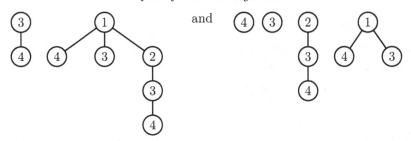

Fig. 28.1 Two forests produced by *foldr op1'* ([ ], [ ]) [[1, 2], [3, 4]]

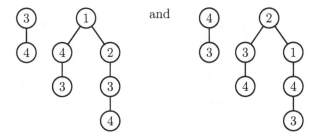

Fig. 28.2 Two forests produced by *foldr op2'* ([ ], [ ]) [[1, 2], [3, 4]]

$$
\begin{aligned}
mix\ [\,]\ (ys, sy) \quad &=\quad ys \\
mix\ (x : xs)\ (ys, sy) \quad &=\quad ys \mathbin{+\!\!+} [Node\ x\ (mix\ xs\ (sy, ys))]
\end{aligned}
$$

The definitions of *op1'* and *op2'* lead to different pairs of forests. For example, see Figures 28.1 and 28.2. In each case the preorders of the pair of forests are the same, so either definition will serve.

We are still not quite out of the wood yet, for appending a tree to the end of a forest is not a constant-time operation. Obvious ideas for solving this problem, such as turning appends into cons operations by reversing the forest, or bringing in an accumulating parameter, do not work. The most direct method, and one we will exploit for other purposes in subsequent pearls, is to introduce *queues*, redefining a forest to be a *queue* of trees rather than a list. Okasaki's implementation of queues provides a type *Queue a*, for which the following operations all take constant time:

$$
\begin{aligned}
insert \quad &::\quad Queue\ a \to a \to Queue\ a \\
remove \quad &::\quad Queue\ a \to (a, Queue\ a) \\
empty \quad &::\quad Queue\ a \\
isempty \quad &::\quad Queue\ a \to Bool
\end{aligned}
$$

To install queues, we redeclare the type *Forest* to read

type *Forest a* = *Queue* (*Rose a*)
data *Rose a* = *Node a* (*Forest a*)

The functions $op1'$ and $op2'$ are the same as before except that expressions of the form $as + [Node\ x\ bs]$ are replaced by $insert\ as\ (Node\ x\ bs)$. Now we have

$boxall$ = $unfoldr\ step \cdot wrapQueue \cdot fst \cdot foldr\ op1'\ (empty, empty)$
$boxall$ = $unfoldr\ step \cdot wrapQueue \cdot fst \cdot foldr\ op2'\ (empty, empty)$

where

$step$ :: $[Forest\ a] \rightarrow Maybe\ (a, [Forest\ a])$
$step\ [\,]$ = $Nothing$
$step\ (zs : zss)$ = $Just\ (x, consQueue\ xs\ (consQueue\ ys\ zss))$
  where $(Node\ x\ xs, ys) = remove\ zs$

$consQueue$ :: $Queue\ a \rightarrow [Queue\ a] \rightarrow [Queue\ a]$
$consQueue\ xs\ xss$ = **if** $isempty\ xs$ **then** xss **else** $xs : xss$

$wrapQueue$ :: $Queue\ a \rightarrow [Queue\ a]$
$wrapQueue\ xs$ = $consQueue\ xs\ [\,]$

Both definitions of *boxall* are loopless.

Final remarks

The term *loopless* was coined by Ehrlich (1973). A number of loopless algorithms for generating combinatorial patterns appear in Knuth's published drafts of three sections of Volume 4 of *The Art of Computer Programming* (Knuth, 2005). These fascicles contain references to much of the literature on looplessness. The quote from Knuth appears in Knuth (2001). Okasaki's implementation of queues can be found in Okasaki (1995).

References

Ehrlich, G. (1973). Loopless algorithms for generating permutations, combinations, and other combinatorial configurations. *Journal of the ACM* **20**, 500–13.

Knuth, D. E. (2001). SPIDERS: a program downloadable from www-cs-faculty.stanford.edu/~knuth/programs.html.

Knuth, D. E. (2005). *The Art of Computer Programming, Volume 4, Fascicles 2,3,4*. Reading, MA: Addison-Wesley.

Okasaki, C. (1995). Simple and efficient purely functional queues and deques. *Journal of Functional Programming* **5** (4), 583–92.

29

The Johnson–Trotter algorithm

Introduction

The Johnson–Trotter algorithm is a method for producing all the permutations of a given list in such a way that the transition from one permutation to the next is accomplished by a single transposition of adjacent elements. In this pearl we calculate a loopless version of the algorithm. The main idea is to make use of one of the loopless programs for the generalised boustrophedon product *boxall* developed in the previous pearl.

A recursive formulation

In the Johnson–Trotter permutation algorithm the transitions for a list of length n of length greater than one are defined recursively in terms of the transitions for a list of length $n-1$. Label the elements of the list with positions 0 through $n-1$ and let the list itself be denoted by $xs + [x]$. Begin with a downward run $[n-1, n-2, \ldots, 1]$, where transition i means "interchange the element at position i with the element at position $i-1$". The effect is to move x from the last position to the first, resulting in the final permutation $[x] + xs$. For example, the transitions $[3, 2, 1]$ applied to the string "abcd" result in the three permutations "abdc", "adbc" and "dabc". Next, suppose the transitions generating the permutations of xs are $[j_1, j_2, \ldots]$. Apply the transition j_1+1 to the current permutation $[x] + xs$. We have to increase j_1 by one because xs is now one position to the right of the "runner" x. Next, run x upwards again to the last position by applying the transition sequence $[1, 2, \ldots, n-1]$. This results in a final permutation $ys + [x]$, where ys is the result of applying transition j_1 to xs. For example, the transitions $[3, 1, 2, 3]$ applied to "dabc" result in four more permutations "dacb", "adcb", "acdb" and "acbd". For the next step, apply the second transition j_2 for xs and run x down again. We do not have to modify the transition j_2 after upward runs because the relevant permutation is to the left of x. Continue in the same fashion, interleaving runs of x downwards and upwards, with the transitions for $n-1$.

251

The above description codes quite easily using the boustrophedon product ($\square$) defined in the previous pearl:

$$
\begin{aligned}
jcode &\quad::\quad Int \rightarrow [Int] \\
jcode\ 1 &\quad=\quad [\,] \\
jcode\ n &\quad=\quad (bumpBy\ 1\ (jcode\ (n{-}1)))\ \square\ [n{-}1, n{-}2 \mathinner{\ldotp\ldotp} 1]
\end{aligned}
$$

The function $bumpBy\ k$ adds k to every item in even position:

$$
\begin{aligned}
bumpBy\ k\ [\,] &\quad=\quad [\,] \\
bumpBy\ k\ [a] &\quad=\quad [a + k] \\
bumpBy\ k\ (a : b : as) &\quad=\quad (a + k) : b : bumpBy\ k\ as
\end{aligned}
$$

Our task is to make *jcode* loopless.

The plan

The general plan is to express *jcode* in terms of *boxall*, the generalised boustrophedon product defined in the previous pearl, and then to appeal to the loopless algorithm for *boxall*. To do so we need to generalise *jcode*. Consider the function *code*, defined by

$$
code\ (k, n) \quad=\quad bumpBy\ k\ (jcode\ n)
$$

Clearly, $jcode\ n = code\ (0, n)$. We reason for an odd positive integer n that

$$
\begin{aligned}
&\quad code\ (k, n) \\
=&\quad \{\text{definition}\} \\
&\quad bumpBy\ k\ (jcode\ n) \\
=&\quad \{\text{definition of } jcode\} \\
&\quad bumpBy\ k\ (bumpBy\ 1\ (jcode\ (n{-}1))\ \square\ [n{-}1, n{-}2 \mathinner{\ldotp\ldotp} 1]) \\
=&\quad \{\text{claim, see below}\} \\
&\quad bumpBy\ (k{+}1)\ (jcode\ (n{-}1))\ \square\ bumpBy\ k\ [n{-}1, n{-}2 \mathinner{\ldotp\ldotp} 1] \\
=&\quad \{\text{definition of } code \text{ and } bumpDn \text{ (see below)}\} \\
&\quad code\ (k{+}1, n{-}1)\ \square\ bumpDn\ (k, n)
\end{aligned}
$$

where *bumpDn* (pronounced "bump down") is defined by

$$
bumpDn\ (k, n) = bumpBy\ k\ [n{-}1, n{-}2 \mathinner{\ldotp\ldotp} 1] \tag{29.1}
$$

The first claim is that

$$
\begin{aligned}
&bumpBy\ k\ (xs\ \square\ ys) \\
&\quad=\quad \textbf{if}\ even\ (length\ ys)\ \textbf{then}\ bumpBy\ k\ xs\ \square\ bumpBy\ k\ ys \\
&\qquad\quad \textbf{else}\ xs\ \square\ bumpBy\ k\ ys
\end{aligned}
$$

The claim can be proved from the definition of $\Box$ and the fact that

$$bumpBy\ k\ (xs \mathbin{+\!\!+} [y] \mathbin{+\!\!+} ys)$$
$$= \quad \textbf{if}\ even\ (length\ xs)\ \textbf{then}\ bumpBy\ k\ xs \mathbin{+\!\!+} bumpBy\ k\ ([y] \mathbin{+\!\!+} ys)$$
$$\textbf{else}\ bumpBy\ k\ xs \mathbin{+\!\!+} [y] \mathbin{+\!\!+} bumpBy\ k\ ys$$

The easy details are left as an exercise.

The case when n is even is treated similarly, and we arrive at the following definition of *code*:

$$code\ (k, 1) \quad = \quad [\,]$$
$$code\ (k, n) \quad = \quad code\ (k', n-1) \mathbin{\Box} bumpDn\ (k, n)$$
$$\textbf{where}\ k' = \textbf{if}\ odd\ n\ \textbf{then}\ k+1\ \textbf{else}\ 1$$

For example, bearing in mind that $\Box$ is associative, we have

$$code\ (0, 4) \quad = \quad bumpDn\ (2, 2) \mathbin{\Box} bumpDn\ (1, 3) \mathbin{\Box} bumpDn\ (0, 4)$$

Recalling that $boxall = foldr\ (\Box)\ [\,]$, we can now rewrite *code* in the form

$$code \quad = \quad boxall \cdot map\ bumpDn \cdot pairs$$

where

$$pairs \qquad\qquad :: \quad (Int, Int) \to [(Int, Int)]$$
$$pairs\ (k, 1) \quad = \quad [\,]$$
$$pairs\ (k, n) \quad = \quad pairs\ (k', n-1) \mathbin{+\!\!+} [(k, n)]$$
$$\textbf{where}\ k' = \textbf{if}\ odd\ n\ \textbf{then}\ k+1\ \textbf{else}\ 1$$

Again, the easy details are left as an exercise. Evaluating $pairs\ (k, n)$ takes $\Theta(n^2)$ steps, but this can be reduced to $\Theta(n)$ steps with the help of an accumulating parameter. Define *addpair* by

$$addpair\ (k, n)\ ps \quad = \quad pairs\ (k, n) \mathbin{+\!\!+} ps$$

Synthesizing a direct definition of *addpair* leads to

$$pairs\ (k, n) \qquad\quad = \quad addpair\ (k, n)\ [\,]$$
$$addpair\ (k, 1)\ ps \quad = \quad ps$$
$$addpair\ (k, n)\ ps \quad = \quad addpair\ (k', n-1)\ ((k, n) : ps)$$
$$\textbf{where}\ k' = \textbf{if}\ odd\ n\ \textbf{then}\ k+1\ \textbf{else}\ 1$$

Hence, since $jcode\ n = code\ (0, n)$, we obtain

$$jcode \quad = \quad boxall \cdot map\ bumpDn \cdot pairs$$
$$\textbf{where}\ pairs\ n = addpair\ (0, n)\ [\,]$$

Since we know how to make *boxall* loopless, this definition of *jcode* is a loopless algorithm. Or is it?

A loopless algorithm

No, it is not: part of the prologue is *map bumpDn* (*pairs n*), and this takes $\Theta(n^2)$ steps. The rules of the game only allow a prologue that takes $\Theta(n)$ steps.

What we really need to do is make *boxall* · *map bumpDn* loopless. It is easy to make *bumpDn* loopless, so let us first do that. Recall definition (29.1):

$$bumpDn\ (k, n) = bumpBy\ k\ [n-1, n-2\mathbin{..} 1]$$

To make *bumpDn* loopless we can set up a state consisting of a quadruple (j, k, m, n) in which the first component j begins with k and then flips alternately between 0 and k, the second and fourth components k and n do not change and the third component m counts down from $n-1$ to 1. Then we have

$$
\begin{aligned}
bumpDn &= unfoldr\ stepDn \cdot prologDn \\
prologDn\ (k, n) &= (k, k, n-1, 1) \\
stepDn\ (j, k, m, n) &= \textbf{if } m < n \textbf{ then } Nothing \\
&\quad\ \textbf{else } Just\ (m + j, (k-j, k, m-1, n))
\end{aligned}
$$

Similarly, we can make *reverse* · *bumpDn* loopless:

$$
\begin{aligned}
reverse \cdot bumpDn &= unfoldr\ stepUp \cdot prologUp \\
prologUp\ (k, n) &= (\textbf{if } even\ n \textbf{ then } k \textbf{ else } 0, k, 1, n-1) \\
stepUp\ (j, k, m, n) &= \textbf{if } m > n \textbf{ then } Nothing \\
&\quad\ \textbf{else } Just\ (m + j, (k-j, k, m+1, n))
\end{aligned}
$$

The functions *stepDn* and *stepUp* can be unified as one function, *bump* say (we need the name *step* for another purpose later on), by adding in a fifth component i, taking $i = -1$ for a down-step and $i = 1$ for an up-step. That gives

$$
\begin{aligned}
bumpDn &= unfoldr\ bump \cdot prologDn \\
reverse \cdot bumpDn &= unfoldr\ bump \cdot prologUp
\end{aligned}
$$

where

$$
\begin{aligned}
bump\ (i, j, k, m, n) &= \textbf{if } i * (n-m) < 0 \textbf{ then } Nothing \\
&\quad\ \textbf{else } Just\ (m + j, (i, k-j, k, m+i, n)) \\
prologDn\ (k, n) &= (-1, k, k, n-1, 1) \\
prologUp\ (k, n) &= (1, \textbf{if } even\ n \textbf{ then } k \textbf{ else } 0, k, 1, n-1)
\end{aligned}
$$

Next, recall from the previous pearl that one loopless definition of *boxall* takes the form *boxall* = *unfoldr step* · *prolog*, where

$$prolog = wrapQueue \cdot fst \cdot foldr\ op\ (empty, empty)$$

The function *op* was defined by

$$op\ xs\ (ys, sy) \quad = \quad \textbf{if}\ even\ (length\ xs)$$
$$\textbf{then}\ (mix\ xs\ (ys, sy), mix\ (reverse\ xs)\ (sy, ys))$$
$$\textbf{else}\ (mix\ xs\ (ys, sy), mix\ (reverse\ xs)\ (ys, sy))$$

$$mix\ [\,]\ (ys, sy) \qquad = \quad ys$$
$$mix\ (x : xs)\ (ys, sy) \quad = \quad insert\ ys\ (Node\ x\ (mix\ xs\ (sy, ys)))$$

The function *step* was defined by

$$step\ [\,] \qquad = \quad Nothing$$
$$step\ (zs : zss) \quad = \quad Just\ (x, consQueue\ xs\ (consQueue\ ys\ zss))$$
$$\textbf{where}\ (Node\ x\ xs, ys) = remove\ zs$$

$$consQueue \qquad :: \quad Queue\ a \to [Queue\ a] \to [Queue\ a]$$
$$consQueue\ xs\ xss \quad = \quad \textbf{if}\ isempty\ xs\ \textbf{then}\ xss\ \textbf{else}\ xs : xss$$

$$wrapQueue \qquad :: \quad Queue\ a \to [Queue\ a]$$
$$wrapQueue\ xs \quad = \quad consQueue\ xs\ [\,]$$

We reason:

$$jcode$$
$$= \quad \{\text{definition of } jcode \text{ in terms of } boxall\}$$
$$boxall \cdot map\ bumpDn \cdot pairs$$
$$= \quad \{\text{loopless definition of } boxall\}$$
$$unfoldr\ step \cdot wrapQueue \cdot fst \cdot foldr\ op\ (empty, empty) \cdot$$
$$map\ bumpDn \cdot pairs$$
$$= \quad \{\text{fold-map fusion}\}$$
$$unfoldr\ step \cdot wrapQueue \cdot fst \cdot foldr\ op'\ (empty, empty) \cdot pairs$$

where

$$op'\ (k, n)\ (ys, sy) \quad = \quad op\ (bumpDn\ (k, n))\ (ys, sy)$$

Unfolding this definition, and using the fact that $bumpDn\ (k, n)$ has even length if n is odd, together with the definitions of *prologDn* and *prologUp*, we find

$$op'\ (k, n)\ (ys, sy)$$
$$= \quad \textbf{if}\ odd\ n$$
$$\textbf{then}\ (mix\ (unfoldr\ bump\ (-1, k, k, n{-}1, 1))\ (ys, sy),$$
$$mix\ (unfoldr\ bump\ (1, 0, k, 1, n{-}1))\ (sy, ys))$$
$$\textbf{else}\ (mix\ (unfoldr\ bump\ (-1, k, k, n{-}1, 1))\ (ys, sy),$$
$$mix\ (unfoldr\ bump\ (1, k, k, 1, n{-}1))\ (ys, sy))$$

The function $op'\,(k, n)$ takes $\Theta(n)$ steps, so *foldr op'* (*empty, empty*) takes quadratic time. We can make op' less busy by taking *unfoldr bump* out of its definition and letting a modified version of *step* do all the work. In effect, we delay the evaluation of the first argument of *mix*. We will need a new data type to represent delayed evaluations, and we~take

> **type** *Forest a* $=$ *Queue* (*Rose a*)
> **data** *Rose a* $=$ *Node a* (*Forest a, Forest a*)

The new definition of a rose tree has a pair of forests as offspring rather than a single forest. Now consider a new version of *step*, defined by

> **type** *State* $=$ (*Int, Int, Int, Int, Int*)
> **type** *Pair a* $=$ (*a, a*)

> *step* :: [*Forest* (*Int, State*)] $\rightarrow$ *Maybe* (*Int*, [*Forest* (*Int, State*)])
> *step* [ ] $=$ *Nothing*
> *step*(*zs* : *zss*)
> $=$ *Just* (x, *consQueue* (*mix q* (*sy, ys*)) (*consQueue zs' zss*))
>   **where** (*Node* (x, q) (*ys, sy*), *zs'*) $=$ *remove zs*

where *mix* is modified to read

> *mix* :: *State* $\rightarrow$ *Pair* (*Forest* (*Int, State*)) $\rightarrow$ *Forest* (*Int, State*)
> *mix* (i, j, k, m, n) (*ys, sy*)
> $=$ **if** $i * (n-m) < 0$ **then** *ys*
>   **else** *insert ys* (*Node* ($m+j$, ($i, k-j, k, m+i, n$)) (*ys, sy*))

The function *step* generates the next transition x and passes the state q (a quintuple) to *mix*, which computes the next transition, if there is one, and a new state. We now claim that

> *jcode* $=$ *unfoldr step* · *wrapQueue* · *fst* · *foldr op'* (*empty, empty*) · *pairs*

where op' is redefined to read

> op' :: (*Int, Int*) $\rightarrow$ *Pair* (*Forest* (*Int, State*))
> $\rightarrow$ *Pair* (*Forest* (*Int, State*))
> op' (k, n) (*ys, sy*) $=$ **if** *odd n*
>   **then** (*mix* ($-1, k, k, n-1, 1$) (*ys, sy*),
>   *mix* ($1, 0, k, 1, n-1$) (*sy, ys*))
>   **else** (*mix* ($-1, k, k, n-1, 1$) (*ys, sy*),
>   *mix* ($1, k, k, 1, n-1$) (*ys, sy*))

Once again, details are left as an exercise. The rather long prologue

> *prolog* $=$ *wrapQueue* · *fst* · *foldr op'* (*empty, empty*) · *pairs*

takes $\Theta(n)$ steps when applied to n, and *step* takes constant time, so this finally is a genuine 24-carat loopless program for *jcode*.

Final remarks

If it were not for the very picky requirement that the prologue had to take linear time, we could have stopped calculating as soon as we had reached the definition

$$jcode \;=\; boxall \cdot map\; bumpDn \cdot pairs$$

What this definition really shows is the usefulness of the generalised boustrophedon product function *boxall* in the generation of many kinds of combinatorial patterns. We will see more uses in the final pearl.

The Johnson–Trotter algorithm was described independently in Johnson (1963) and Trotter (1962). As mentioned in the previous pearl, Ehrlich (1973), which introduced the concept of a loopless algorithm, was mainly devoted to describing a loopless program for the Johnson–Trotter algorithm.

References

Ehrlich, G. (1973). Loopless algorithms for generating permutations, combinations, and other combinatorial configurations. *Journal of the ACM* **20**, 500–13.

Johnson, S. M. (1963). Generation of permutations by adjacent transpositions. *Mathematics of Computation* **17**, 282–5.

Trotter, A. F. (1962). *Perm* (Algorithm 115). *Communications of the ACM* **5**, 434–5.

30

Spider spinning for dummies

> Oh what a tangled web we weave
> when first we practise to derive.
> *(With apologies to Sir Walter Scott)*

Introduction

Consider the problem of generating all bit strings $a_1 a_2 \ldots a_n$ of length n satisfying given constraints of the form $a_i \leq a_j$ for various i and j. The generation is to be in *Gray path order*, meaning that exactly one bit changes from one bit string to the next. The *transition code* is a list of integers naming the bit that is to be changed at each step. For example, with $n = 3$, consider the constraints $a_1 \leq a_2$ and $a_3 \leq a_2$. One possible Gray path is 000, 010, 011, 111, 110 with transition code $[2, 3, 1, 3]$ and starting string 000.

The snag is that the problem does not always have a solution. For example, with $n = 4$ and the constraints $a_1 \leq a_2 \leq a_4$ and $a_1 \leq a_3 \leq a_4$, the six possible bit strings, namely 0000, 0001, 0011, 0101, 0111 and 1111, cannot be permuted into a Gray path. There are four strings of even weight (the numbers of 1s) and two of odd weight, and in any Gray path the parity of the weights has to alternate.

Constraints of the form $a_i \leq a_j$ on bit strings of length n can be represented by a digraph with n nodes in which a directed edge $i \leftarrow j$ is associated with a constraint $a_i \leq a_j$. Knuth and Ruskey showed how to construct a Gray path provided the digraph was *totally acyclic*, meaning that the undirected graph obtained by dropping the directions on the edges is acyclic. They called a connected totally acyclic digraph a *spider*, because when an edge $i \leftarrow j$ is drawn with i below j the digraph can be made to look like an arachnid (see Figure 30.1 for a three-legged spider). They called a totally acyclic digraph a *tad*, but, since its connected components are spiders, we will continue the arachnid metaphor and call it a *nest* of spiders.

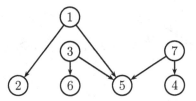

Fig. 30.1 A three-legged spider

Knuth named the problem of generating the associated bit strings in Gray path order *spider squishing*. The more formal rendering of the task is: "generating all ideals[1] of a totally acyclic poset in Gray path order". Since spiders are good for the environment and should never be squished, we will call it *spider spinning* instead.

A useful way to think of the problem of spider spinning is in terms of colourings. Think of the nodes of the spider of Figure 30.1 as being coloured black if the associated bit is 1 and coloured white if the bit is 0. Thus, every descendant of a white node has to be white. For example, if node 1 is white, then nodes 2 and 5 have to be white as well. The problem of spider spinning is then to enumerate all legal colourings by starting with one such colouring and changing the colour of exactly one node at each step. As we will see, the initial colouring cannot in general be chosen to be the all-white or all-black colouring.

Our aim in this pearl is to derive a loopless algorithm for spider spinning. Knuth and Ruskey gave an algorithm for spider spinning, but it was not loopless. There is a program, SPIDERS, on Knuth's website that does perform loopless spider spinning. It is quite complicated, as Knuth readily admits:

But I apologize at the outset that the algorithm seems to be rather subtle, and I have not been able to think of any way to explain it to dummies.

Hence our title. Our aim in this pearl is to calculate a loopless algorithm for spider spinning. I have no idea if my algorithm bears any relationship to Knuth's algorithm, since I can't explain his algorithm either.

Spider spinning with tree spiders

Let us first consider the simpler problem of spider spinning when each spider is just a tree, so all spiders' legs are directed downwards. This special case

[1] By an *ideal* of a poset S is meant a subset I of S such that if $x \in I$ and $x \leq y$, then $y \in I$.

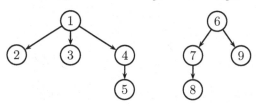

Fig. 30.2 A nest of two tree spiders

---

of spider spinning was considered by Koda and Ruskey. The relevant data
type declarations are

> **type** *Nest* = [*Spider*]
> **data** *Spider* = *Node Int Nest*

A nest of two tree spiders is pictured in Figure 30.2. We will suppose that
the labels of nodes in a nest of spiders of size n are the elements of $[1 .. n]$ in
some order. We can define *ncode* and *scode*, the transition codes for a nest of
spiders and a single spider respectively, using the generalised boustrophedon
product function *boxall*:

> *ncode*   :: *Nest* → [*Int*]
> *ncode*   = *boxall* · *map scode*
>
> *scode*   :: *Spider* → [*Int*]
> *scode* (*Node a xs*) = *a* : *ncode xs*

The transition code for a single spider consists of an initial transition to
change the colour of the root node (in fact, from white to black), followed by
a complete list of the transitions for the nest of its subspiders. The definition
of *ncode* is short and sweet, but not loopless.

A loopless program

The first step on the path to looplessness is dictated solely by the form of
the definition of *ncode*. Recalling that *boxall* = *foldr* ($\square$) [ ], an application
of the map-fusion law of *foldr* yields

> *ncode* = *foldr* (($\square$) · *scode*) [ ]

The focus now is on the function ($\square$) · *scode*. We calculate:

> $\quad$ *scode* (*Node a xs*) $\square$ *bs*
>
> = $\quad$ {definition of *scode*}
>
> $\quad$ (*a* : *ncode xs*) $\square$ *bs*

$=$ {definition of $\square$}

$\quad$ $bs \mathbin{+\!\!+} [a] \mathbin{+\!\!+} (ncode\ xs\ \square\ (reverse\ bs))$

$=$ {initial definition of $ncode$}

$\quad$ $bs \mathbin{+\!\!+} [a] \mathbin{+\!\!+} (boxall\ (map\ scode\ xs)\ \square\ (reverse\ bs))$

The third term of this expression takes the form

$$(foldr\ (\square)\ [\,]\ ass)\ \square\ cs$$

in which $ass = map\ scode\ xs$ and $cs = reverse\ bs$. This suggests the use of the fold-fusion law of $foldr$. Setting $f\ as = as\ \square\ cs$, we have that f is strict and $f\ [\,] = cs$, since $[\,]$ is the identity of $\square$. Hence, the fold-fusion law gives

$$(foldr\ (\square)\ [\,]\ ass)\ \square\ cs\ =\ foldr\ h\ cs\ ass$$

provided we can find an h such that $(as\ \square\ bs)\ \square\ cs = h\ as\ (bs\ \square\ cs)$. But $\square$ is associative, so we can take $h = (\square)$.

Putting these calculations together, we obtain:

$\quad$ $scode\ (Node\ a\ xs)\ \square\ bs$

$=$ {above}

$\quad$ $bs \mathbin{+\!\!+} [a] \mathbin{+\!\!+} (boxall\ (map\ scode\ xs)\ \square\ (reverse\ bs))$

$=$ {fold fusion}

$\quad$ $bs \mathbin{+\!\!+} [a] \mathbin{+\!\!+} foldr\ (\square)\ (reverse\ bs)\ (map\ scode\ xs)$

$=$ {map fusion}

$\quad$ $bs \mathbin{+\!\!+} [a] \mathbin{+\!\!+} foldr\ ((\square) \cdot scode)\ (reverse\ bs)\ xs$

Hence, setting $op = (\square) \cdot scode$, we have calculated that

$$
\begin{aligned}
ncode &= foldr\ op\ [\,]\\
op\ (Node\ a\ xs)\ bs &= bs \mathbin{+\!\!+} [a] \mathbin{+\!\!+} foldr\ op\ (reverse\ bs)\ xs
\end{aligned}
$$

The remaining steps are to eliminate *reverse* by computing both *ncode* and *reverse · ncode* at the same time, and to represent each of their results by a queue of rose trees under the abstraction function *preorder*. Rose trees are here declared by

$$
\begin{aligned}
\textbf{type}\ Forest\ a\ &=\ Queue\ (Rose\ a)\\
\textbf{data}\ Rose\ a\ &=\ Fork\ a\ (Forest\ a)
\end{aligned}
$$

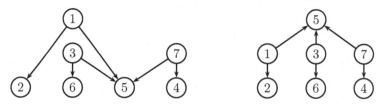

Fig. 30.3 A spider and an associated tree

We have performed these steps with the derivation of a loopless program for *boxall*, so we will just state the result:

$$ncode \;=\; unfoldr\ step \cdot wrapQueue \cdot fst \cdot foldr\ op\ (empty, empty)$$
$$op\ (Node\ a\ xs)\ (bs, sb)$$
$$\qquad =\; (insert\ bs\ (Fork\ a\ cs),\ insert\ sc\ (Fork\ a\ sb))$$
$$\qquad\quad \textbf{where}\ (cs, sc) = foldr\ op\ (sb, bs)\ xs$$

The remaining functions *step* and *wrapQueue* are exactly as they were defined in the loopless algorithm for *boxall*. Since *foldr op* (*empty*, *empty*) takes linear time in the size of the nest, this is a loopless program for *ncode*.

Spider spinning with general spiders

Now we are ready to tackle the general spider-spinning problem. First, observe that by picking a spider up by one of its nodes we get a tree with directed edges, such as that shown in Figure 30.3. Different trees arise depending on which node is picked up, but they all represent the same constraints. It follows that we can model general spiders with the type declarations

$$
\begin{array}{lll}
\textbf{type}\ Nest & = & [Spider] \\
\textbf{data}\ Spider & = & Node\ Int\ [Leg] \\
\textbf{data}\ Leg & = & Dn\ Spider \mid Up\ Spider
\end{array}
$$

A spider has legs, not edges. A spider's leg points upwards or downwards to another spider.

There is one complication when dealing with general spiders that does not arise with simpler species: the starting bit string is not necessarily a string consisting of all 0s. For example, with $n = 3$ and the constraints $a_1 \geq a_2 \leq a_3$, the five possible bit strings, namely 000, 001, 100, 101 and 111, can only be arranged in Gray path order by starting with one of the odd-weight strings: 001, 100, or 111. However, we postpone consideration of the function $seed :: Nest \rightarrow [Bit]$ for determining the starting string until later on.

As with tree spiders, we can define

$$ncode \quad :: \quad Nest \rightarrow [Int]$$
$$ncode \quad = \quad boxall \cdot map\ scode$$

We define $scode$ to be the concatenation of two lists, a white code and a black code:

$$scode \qquad\qquad :: \quad Spider \rightarrow [Int]$$
$$scode\ (Node\ a\ legs) \quad = \quad wcode\ legs \mathbin{+\!\!+} [a] \mathbin{+\!\!+} bcode\ legs$$

The white code, $wcode$, for a spider $Node\ a\ legs$ is a valid transition sequence when the head node a is coloured white (corresponding to a 0 bit) and the black code is a valid sequence when a is coloured black (corresponding to a 1 bit). Thus, $scode$ is defined as the sequence that goes through the white code, changes the colour of a from white to black and then goes through the black code. Note that when the spiders are tree spiders, so all legs point downwards, the white code is the empty sequence.

For $scode$ to be correct, the final spider colouring after executing $wcode\ legs$ has to be the initial colouring on which $bcode\ legs$ starts. In order for the colourings to match up we need to define $wcode$ in terms of a variant of $\square$, which we will denote by $\lozenge$ and pronounce "cox".[2] The operation $\lozenge$ is the *conjugate* of $\square$:

$$as \lozenge bs \quad = \quad reverse\ ((reverse\ as)\ \square\ (reverse\ bs))$$

Whereas $as \square bs$ begins with as and ends with either bs or $reverse\ bs$ depending on whether as has even length, $as \lozenge bs$ ends with bs and begins with either bs or $reverse\ bs$. For example:

$$[2,3,4] \square [0,1] \quad = \quad [0,1,2,1,0,3,0,1,4,1,0]$$
$$[2,3,4] \lozenge [0,1] \quad = \quad [1,0,2,0,1,3,1,0,4,0,1]$$

We can express $\square$ in terms of $\lozenge$ by conjugation, but there is another way:

$$as \square bs$$

$$= \quad \textbf{if}\ even\ (length\ as)\ \textbf{then}\ as \lozenge bs\ \textbf{else}\ as \lozenge (reverse\ bs) \qquad (30.1)$$

A similar equation defines $\lozenge$ in terms of $\square$. Equation (30.1) will be needed below.

---

[2] By the way, "to box and cox" means "to take turns", which is certainly what both operations do and is the real reason for their names. The term comes from the comic play *Box and Cox – A Romance of Real Life in One Act*, by John Maddison Morton. Box and Cox were two lodgers who shared their rooms – one occupying them by day and the other by night.

The operation $\Diamond$ is associative with the empty sequence as identity element. The proof is left as an exercise, but it depends on the fact that

$$(as +\!\!+ [b] +\!\!+ bs) \Diamond cs \;=\; (as \Diamond cs') +\!\!+ [b] +\!\!+ (bs \Diamond cs)$$

where $cs' = \textbf{if } even\,(length\;bs)\textbf{ then } reverse\;cs\textbf{ else } cs$. A similar property was needed to prove $\Box$ was associative.

Setting $coxall = foldr\,(\Diamond)\,[\,]$, we can now define

$$
\begin{array}{lll}
wcode, bcode & :: & [Leg] \rightarrow [Int] \\
wcode & = & coxall \cdot map\; wc \\
bcode & = & boxall \cdot map\; bc
\end{array}
$$

where $wc, bc :: Leg \rightarrow [Int]$ are yet to be defined. Use of $coxall$ in the definition of $wcode$ ensures that the final colouring after executing $wcode$ will be the union of the final colourings generated by the wc transitions, and use of $boxall$ in the definition of $bcode$ means that this colouring will also be the union of the colourings on which the bc transitions start.

It remains to define wc and bc. Given the choices above, the following definitions are forced:

$$
\begin{array}{lll}
wc\,(Up\,(Node\;a\;legs)) & = & wcode\;legs +\!\!+ [a] +\!\!+ bcode\;legs \\
wc\,(Dn\,(Node\;a\;legs)) & = & reverse\,(wcode\;legs) \\
bc\,(Up\,(Node\;a\;legs)) & = & reverse\,(bcode\;legs) \\
bc\,(Dn\,(Node\;a\;legs)) & = & wcode\;legs +\!\!+ [a] +\!\!+ bcode\;legs
\end{array}
$$

Look first at $wc\,(Up\,x)$. When the head of the mother spider of x is white and is connected to x by an upwards edge, there are no constraints on $wc\,(Up\;x)$, so we can define it to be either $scode\;x$ or its reverse. But the subsequent transitions affecting x are those in the list $bc\,(Up\;x)$, and the only way to match up the final colouring of the former with the initial colouring of the latter is with the definitions above. The reasoning is dual with $bc\,(Dn\;x)$ and $wc\,(Dn\;x)$.

Finally, we show that $ncode$ can be expressed in terms of $bcode$:

$$
\begin{array}{ll}
& ncode\;xs \\[4pt]
= & \{\text{definition of } ncode\} \\
& boxall\,(map\;scode\;xs) \\[4pt]
= & \{\text{definition of } scode \text{ and } bc\} \\
& boxall\,[bc\,(Dn\;x) \mid x \leftarrow xs] \\[4pt]
= & \{\text{definition of } bcode\} \\
& bcode\,[(Dn\;x) \mid x \leftarrow xs]
\end{array}
$$

ncode	::	$Nest \rightarrow [Int]$
ncode	=	$bcode \cdot map\ Dn$
bcode, wcode	::	$[Leg] \rightarrow [Int]$
bcode	=	$boxall \cdot map\ bc$
wcode	=	$coxall \cdot map\ wc$
bc, wc	::	$Leg \rightarrow [Int]$
bc (Up (Node a legs))	=	$reverse\ (bcode\ legs)$
bc (Dn (Node a legs))	=	$wcode\ legs + [a] + bcode\ legs$
wc (Up (Node a legs))	=	$wcode\ legs + [a] + bcode\ legs$
wc (Dn (Node a legs))	=	$reverse\ (wcode\ legs)$

Fig. 30.4 The starting program for *ncode*

The complete program for *ncode*, apart from *boxall* and *coxall*, is listed in Figure 30.4. Our task is to make *ncode* loopless.

A loopless algorithm

The transformation to loopless form follows the same path as the simpler problem of a nest of tree spiders. Specifically, we are going to:

(i) Eliminate *boxall* and *coxall* from the definition of *ncode* by appeal to map fusion and fold fusion.

(ii) Eliminate *reverse* by appeal to tupling.

(iii) Eliminate the remaining complexity by introducing queues.

It is the appeal to fold fusion in the first step that is the trickiest. As an easy first step we apply map fusion to the definitions of *wcode* and *bcode*, obtaining

$$bcode = foldr\ ((\square) \cdot bc)\ [\,]$$
$$wcode = foldr\ ((\lozenge) \cdot wc)\ [\,]$$

The focus of attention now is on the terms $(\square) \cdot bc$ and $(\lozenge) \cdot wc$. Everything we discover about the first will apply to the second with the obvious changes. We will follow the path of the tree-spider calculation as closely as possible.

There are two clauses in the definition of *bc* and we consider them in turn. First we have

$$bc\ (Up\ (Node\ a\ legs))\ \square\ cs$$

$=$ {definition of *bc*}

$$reverse\ (bcode\ legs)\ \square\ cs$$

$=$ {definition of *bcode*}

$$reverse\ (boxall\ (map\ bc\ legs))\ \square\ cs$$

As in the case of tree spiders, the next step is an appeal to the fold-fusion law: if a function h can be found so that

$$reverse\,(as \,\square\, bs)\,\square\, cs \;\; = \;\; h\; as\;((reverse\; bs)\,\square\, cs) \tag{30.2}$$

then

$$reverse\,(boxall\,(map\; bc\; legs))\,\square\, cs \;\; = \;\; foldr\; h\; cs\,(map\; bc\; legs)$$

The trouble is that there is no such h to satisfy (30.2). The reason is that $\square$ is not an injective function; for example

$$\text{``abab''} \,\square\, \text{``aaaba''} \;\; = \;\; \text{``ab''} \,\square\, \text{``aaabaaaba''}$$

If h existed to satisfy (30.2), then we would require

$$reverse\,(as \,\square\, \text{``baba''})\,\square\, \text{``aaaba''}$$
$$= \;\; reverse\,(as \,\square\, \text{``ba''})\,\square\, \text{``aaabaaaba''}$$

for all as. But the above equation is false: take for instance $as = \text{``c''}$. What we can do is find an h such that

$$reverse\,(as \,\square\, bs)\,\lozenge\, cs \;\; = \;\; h\; as\;((reverse\; bs)\,\lozenge\, cs) \tag{30.3}$$

Equation (30.3) has the same form as (30.2) except that the last $\square$ on either side has been changed into a $\lozenge$. To discover h we reason:

$$reverse\,(as \,\square\, bs)\,\lozenge\, cs$$
$$= \quad \{\text{definition of }\lozenge\}$$
$$(reverse\; as \,\lozenge\, reverse\; bs)\,\lozenge\, cs$$
$$= \quad \{\text{since }\lozenge\text{ is associative}\}$$
$$reverse\; as \,\lozenge\, (reverse\; bs \,\lozenge\, cs)$$

Hence, we can take $h\; as\; bs = reverse\; as \,\lozenge\, bs$. Appeal to fold fusion then gives

$$reverse\,(boxall\,(map\; bc\; legs))\,\lozenge\, cs \;\; = \;\; foldr\; h\; cs\,(map\; bc\; legs)$$

But all this helps only if we can change a $\square$ into a $\lozenge$. Fortunately, (30.1) comes to the rescue. Setting

$$cs' \;\; = \;\; \textbf{if}\; even\,(length\,(bcode\; legs))\; \textbf{then}\; cs\; \textbf{else}\; reverse\; cs$$

we can reason:

$$bc\,(Up\,(Node\; a\; legs))\,\square\, cs$$
$$= \quad \{\text{above}\}$$
$$reverse\,(boxall\,(map\; bc\; legs))\,\square\, cs$$
$$= \quad \{\text{using (30.1)}\}$$
$$reverse\,(boxall\,(map\; bc\; legs))\,\lozenge\, cs'$$

$=$ {fold fusion}

$$foldr\,((\lozenge) \cdot reverse)\;cs'\;(map\;bc\;legs)$$

Having transformed $\square$ into $\lozenge$ we now transform $\lozenge$ back into $\square$ with another application of fold fusion. The fusion condition

$$reverse\,((reverse\;as)\;\lozenge\;cs) \quad = \quad as\;\square\;(reverse\;cs)$$

is just the conjugate property of $\square$ and $\lozenge$ and it leads to

$$reverse \cdot foldr((\lozenge) \cdot reverse)\;cs' \quad = \quad foldr\,(\square)\,(reverse\;cs')$$

Thus:

$$bc\,(Up\,(Node\;a\;legs))\;\square\;cs$$

$=$ {above}

$$foldr\,((\lozenge) \cdot reverse)\;cs'\;(map\;bc\;legs)$$

$=$ {fold fusion}

$$reverse\,(foldr\,((\square) \cdot bc)\,(reverse\;cs')\;legs)$$

Introducing $bop = (\square) \cdot bc$, we have shown that $bcode = foldr\;bop\,[\,]$, where

$$bop\,(Up\,(Node\;a\;legs))\;cs \quad = \quad reverse\,(foldr\;bop\;cs'\;legs)$$
$$\textbf{where}\;cs' \quad = \quad \textbf{if}\;even\,(length\,(bcode\;legs))$$
$$\textbf{then}\;reverse\;cs\;\textbf{else}\;cs$$

Entirely dual reasoning with $wop = (\lozenge) \cdot wc$ establishes $wcode = foldr\;wop\,[\,]$, where

$$wop\,(Dn\,(Node\;a\;legs))\;cs \quad = \quad reverse\,(foldr\;wop\;cs'\;legs)$$
$$\textbf{where}\;cs' \quad = \quad \textbf{if}\;even\,(length\,(wcode\;legs))$$
$$\textbf{then}\;reverse\;cs\;\textbf{else}\;cs$$

That was quite a bit of effort, but it disposes of only two clauses, so more work remains. We now tackle the clause $bc\,(Dn\,(Node\;a\;legs))\;\square\;cs$ and start off by reasoning:

$$bc\,(Dn\,(Node\;a\;legs))\;\square\;cs$$

$=$ {definition of bc}

$$(wcode\;legs \mathbin{+\!\!+} [a] \mathbin{+\!\!+} bcode\;legs)\;\square\;cs$$

$=$ {distributing $\mathbin{+\!\!+}$ over $\square$}

$$(wcode\;legs\;\square\;cs) \mathbin{+\!\!+} [a] \mathbin{+\!\!+} (bcode\;legs\;\square\;cs')$$

where

$$cs' = \textbf{if}\;even\,(length\,(wcode\;legs))\;\textbf{then}\;reverse\;cs\;\textbf{else}\;cs$$

The rule for distributing $+\!\!+$ over $\Box$ was given in the first pearl on looplessness:

$$(xs +\!\!+ [y] +\!\!+ ys) \Box zs \;=\; (xs \Box zs) +\!\!+ [y] +\!\!+ (ys \Box zs')$$
where $zs' =$ **if** *even* $(length\ xs)$ **then** *reverse* zs **else** zs

We tackle each of the terms *bcode legs* $\Box\ cs'$ and *wcode legs* $\Box\ cs$ in turn. First:

$$
\begin{aligned}
&\quad bcode\ legs \Box\ cs' \\
=&\quad \{\text{definition of } bcode\} \\
&\quad foldr\ (\Box)\ [\,]\ (map\ bc\ legs) \Box\ cs' \\
=&\quad \{\text{fold fusion (exercise)}\} \\
&\quad foldr\ (\Box)\ cs'\ (map\ bc\ legs) \\
=&\quad \{\text{map fusion and definition of } bop\} \\
&\quad foldr\ bop\ cs'\ legs
\end{aligned}
$$

Second:

$$
\begin{aligned}
&\quad wcode\ legs \Box\ cs \\
=&\quad \{\text{using (30.1)}\} \\
&\quad wcode\ legs \Diamond\ reverse\ cs' \\
=&\quad \{\text{definition of } wcode\} \\
&\quad foldr\ (\Diamond)\ [\,](map\ wc\ legs) \Diamond\ reverse\ cs' \\
=&\quad \{\text{fold fusion (exercise)}\} \\
&\quad foldr\ (\Diamond)\ (reverse\ cs')\ (map\ bc\ legs) \\
=&\quad \{\text{map fusion and definition of } wop\} \\
&\quad foldr\ wop\ (reverse\ cs')\ legs
\end{aligned}
$$

Hence, we have derived

$$
\begin{aligned}
bop\ (Dn\ (Node\ a\ legs))\ cs \;=\;\; &foldr\ wop\ (reverse\ cs')\ legs +\!\!+ [a] +\!\!+ \\
&foldr\ bop\ cs'\ legs
\end{aligned}
$$
where $cs' =$ **if** *even* $(length\ (wcode\ legs))$ **then** *reverse* cs **else** cs

Dual reasoning establishes a similar result for *wop* (*Up* (*Node a legs*)) *cs* and leads to the program summarised in Figure 30.5. It is not very attractive and certainly not efficient, mostly on account of the repeated need to compute parity information.

$$\begin{array}{lll}
ncode & :: & Nest \rightarrow [Int] \\
ncode & = & foldr\ bop\ [\,]\cdot map\ Dn \\
bop, wop & :: & Leg \rightarrow [Int] \rightarrow [Int] \\
bop\ (Up\ (Node\ a\ legs))\ cs & = & reverse\ (foldr\ bop\ cs'\ legs)
\end{array}$$

$\quad$ **where** $cs' =$ **if** $even\ (length\ (foldr\ bop\ [\,]\ legs))$ **then** $reverse\ cs$ **else** cs

$$\begin{array}{lll}
bop\ (Dn\ (Node\ a\ legs))\ cs & = & foldr\ wop\ (reverse\ cs')\ legs +\!\!+ [a] +\!\!+ \\
& & foldr\ bop\ cs'\ legs
\end{array}$$

$\quad$ **where** $cs' =$ **if** $even\ (length\ (foldr\ wop\ [\,]\ legs))$ **then** $reverse\ cs$ **else** cs

$$\begin{array}{lll}
wop\ (Up\ (Node\ a\ legs))\ cs & = & foldr\ wop\ cs'\ legs +\!\!+ [a] +\!\!+ \\
& & foldr\ bop\ (reverse\ cs')\ legs
\end{array}$$

$\quad$ **where** $cs' =$ **if** $even\ (length\ (foldr\ bop\ [\,]\ legs))$ **then** $reverse\ cs$ **else** cs

$$\begin{array}{lll}
wop\ (Dn\ (Node\ a\ legs))\ cs & = & reverse\ (foldr\ wop\ cs'\ legs)
\end{array}$$

$\quad$ **where** $cs' =$ **if** $even\ (length\ (foldr\ wop\ [\,]\ legs))$ **then** $reverse\ cs$ **else** cs

Fig. 30.5 The code after eliminating $\square$ and $\lozenge$

Parity spiders

Instead of repeatedly computing parity information we will install this information in a *parity spider*, a spider in which each node is equipped with two Boolean values:

$$\begin{array}{lll}
\textbf{data}\ Spider' & = & Node'\ (Bool, Bool)\ Int\ [Leg'] \\
\textbf{data}\ Leg' & = & Dn'\ Spider'\ |\ Up'\ Spider'
\end{array}$$

The invariant on a parity spider $Node'\ (w, b)\ a\ legs$ is that

$$\begin{array}{lll}
w & = & even\ (length\ (wcode\ legs)) \\
b & = & even\ (length\ (bcode\ legs))
\end{array}$$

where *wcode* and *bcode* return the white code and black code on parity spiders.

Parity information can be installed in an ordinary spider by decorating it:

$$\begin{array}{lll}
decorate & :: & Spider \rightarrow Spider' \\
decorate\ (Node\ a\ legs) & = & node'\ a\ (map\ (mapLeg\ decorate)\ legs) \\
\\
mapLeg\ f\ (Up\ x) & = & Up'\ (f\ x) \\
mapLeg\ f\ (Dn\ x) & = & Dn'\ (f\ x)
\end{array}$$

The smart constructor $node'$ is defined by

$$node'\ a\ legs\ =\ Node'\ (foldr\ op\ (True, True)\ legs)\ a\ legs$$

where $op :: Leg' \rightarrow (Bool, Bool) \rightarrow (Bool, Bool)$ is defined by

$$\begin{array}{lll}
op\ (Up'\ (Node'\ (w, b)\ \_\_))\ (w', b') & = & ((w \neq b) \wedge w', b \wedge b') \\
op\ (Dn'\ (Node'\ (w, b)\ \_\_))\ (w', b') & = & (w \wedge w', (w \neq b) \wedge b')
\end{array}$$

$bop, wop :: Leg' \rightarrow [Int] \rightarrow Int$
$bop\ (Up'\ (Node'\ (w, b)\ a\ legs))\ cs$
$\quad =\quad reverse\ (foldr\ bop\ (revif\ b\ cs)\ legs)$
$bop\ (Dn'\ (Node'\ (w, b)\ a\ legs))\ cs$
$\quad =\quad foldr\ wop\ (revif\ (not\ w)\ cs)\ legs\ +\!\!\!+\ [a]\ +\!\!\!+\ foldr\ bop\ (revif\ w\ cs)\ legs$
$wop\ (Up'\ (Node'\ (w, b)\ a\ legs))\ cs$
$\quad =\quad foldr\ wop\ (revif\ b\ cs)\ legs\ +\!\!\!+\ [a]\ +\!\!\!+\ foldr\ bop\ (revif\ (not\ b)\ cs)\ legs$
$wop\ (Dn'\ (Node'\ (w, b)\ a\ legs))\ cs$
$\quad =\quad reverse\ (foldr\ wop\ (revif\ w\ cs)\ legs)$

$revif\ b\ cs\ =\ \textbf{if}\ b\ \textbf{then}\ reverse\ cs\ \textbf{else}\ cs$

Fig. 30.6 Spinning with parity spiders

To justify this definition of *op*, abbreviate *even · length* to *el*. We reason:

$\quad\quad el\ (wcode\ (leg : legs))$
$=\quad\quad \{\text{definition of } wcode \text{ (on parity spiders)}\}$
$\quad\quad el\ (wc\ leg\ \lozenge\ wcode\ legs)$
$=\quad\quad \{\text{since } el\ (as\ \lozenge\ bs) = el\ as\ \wedge\ el\ bs\}$
$\quad\quad el\ (wc\ leg)\ \wedge\ el\ (wcode\ legs)$
$=\quad\quad \{\text{assuming } leg = Up'\ (Node'\ a\ legs')\}$
$\quad\quad el\ (wcode\ legs'\ +\!\!\!+\ [a]\ +\!\!\!+\ bcode\ legs')\ \wedge\ el\ (wcode\ legs)$

But $as\ +\!\!\!+\ [a]\ +\!\!\!+\ bs$ has even parity if and only if *as* and *bs* have opposite parity. Similar reasoning justifies the other values of *op*.

Installing parity information takes linear time in the size of a spider and leads to the slightly simpler and much more efficient definitions of *bop* and *wop* given in Figure 30.6.

The remaining steps

The final steps are to eliminate *reverse* by tupling and to represent each component of the pair of results returned by *bop* and *wop* by the preorder traversal of a queue of rose trees, just as in the case of tree spiders. To eliminate *reverse* we represent a sequence *as* by a pair (as, sa), where $sa = reverse\ as$. Concatenation of pairs is implemented by

$$cat\ a\ (ws, sw)\ (bs, sb)\ =\ (ws\ +\!\!\!+\ [a]\ +\!\!\!+\ bs,\ sb\ +\!\!\!+\ [a]\ +\!\!\!+\ sw)$$

Reversal is then implemented by swapping the two lists. Next, each component is represented by a queue of rose trees in a way we have seen twice

$$ncode \quad = \quad unfoldr \, step \cdot prolog$$
$$prolog \quad = \quad wrapQueue \cdot fst \cdot foldr \, bop \, (empty, empty) \cdot map \, (Dn' \cdot decorate)$$

$$bop \, (Up' \, (Node' \, (w, b) \, a \, legs)) \, ps$$
$$= \quad swap \, (foldr \, bop \, (swapif \, b \, ps) \, legs)$$
$$bop \, (Dn' \, (Node' \, (w, b) \, a \, legs)) \, ps$$
$$= \quad cat \, a \, (foldr \, wop \, (swapif \, (not \, w) \, ps) \, legs) \, (foldr \, bop \, (swapif \, w \, ps) \, legs)$$
$$wop \, (Up' \, (Node' \, (w, b) \, a \, legs)) \, ps$$
$$= \quad cat \, a \, (foldr \, wop \, (swapif \, b \, ps) \, legs) \, (foldr \, bop \, (swapif \, (not \, b) \, ps) \, legs)$$
$$wop \, (Dn' \, (Node' \, (w, b) \, a \, legs)) \, ps$$
$$= \quad swap \, (foldr \, wop \, (swapif \, w \, ps) \, legs)$$

$$cat \, a \, (ws, sw) \, (bs, sb)$$
$$= \quad (insert \, ws \, (Fork \, a \, bs), insert \, sb \, (Fork \, a \, sw))$$

$$swap \, (xs, ys) \qquad = \quad (ys, xs)$$
$$swapif \, b \, (xs, ys) \quad = \quad \textbf{if } b \textbf{ then } (ys, xs) \textbf{ else } (xs, ys)$$

Fig. 30.7 The final loopless program

before. The result of these manoeuvres gives our final loopless program, summarised in Figure 30.7

Even though the prologue is now a four-act play, involving characters such as spiders, lists, queues and trees, and strange actions like swapping and folding, it nevertheless takes linear time in the size of the nest; so this finally is a loopless program for spider spinning.

The initial state

One task remains, namely to define *seed* :: *Nest* → [*Bit*], the function that returns the starting bit string $a_1 a_2 \ldots a_n$ for a nest of spiders whose labels are [1 .. n] in some order. We will just sketch the reasoning behind the definition of *seed*. We will need the Haskell library *Data.Map* of finite mappings for representing colourings. This library provides a type *Map k a* for representing finite mappings from keys (k) to values (a) and includes the following four functions:

$$empty \quad :: \quad Map \, k \, a$$
$$insert \quad :: \quad Ord \, k \Rightarrow k \to a \to Map \, k \, a \to Map \, k \, a$$
$$union \quad :: \quad Ord \, k \to Map \, k \, a \to Map \, k \, a \to Map \, k \, a$$
$$elems \quad :: \quad Map \, k \, a$$

The value *empty* denotes the empty mapping, *insert* inserts a new binding into a mapping, *union* unions two mappings and *elems* returns the range of values in a mapping in increasing key order. We define a spider's *state* to be a mapping from the integer node labels of the spider to bits, integers taking the values 0 and 1:

> **type** *State* = *Map.Map Int Bit*
> **type** *Bit* = *Int*

To avoid name clashes with similarly named functions in *Queue*, we define

> *install* :: *Int → Bit → State → State*
> *install* = *Map.insert*
>
> *union* :: *State → State → State*
> *union* = *Map.union*
>
> *start* :: *State*
> *start* = *Map.empty*

The function *seed* is defined in terms of two functions

> *wseed, bseed* :: [*Leg′*] → (*State, State*)

Both functions take a list of directed parity spiders and return a pair of states; *wseed* returns the initial state on which *wcode* operates and the final state that results. Similarly for *bseed*. We need both initial and final states and we need parity spiders because parity information plays a part in determining the correct initial state. We define *seed* by

$$seed = elems \cdot fst \cdot bseed \cdot map\,(Dn' \cdot decorate)$$

This function takes a nest of spiders, converts it into a list of downwards-directed parity spiders, computes the initial and final states associated with *bcode*, extracts the first component and returns a list of bits, the starting string for $a_1\,a_2 \ldots a_n$.

We define *bseed* and *wseed* by following the code of Figure 30.4, except that we compute states rather than transitions. First:

> *bseed* = *foldr bsp* (*start, start*) · *map bs*
> *wseed* = *foldr wsp* (*start, start*) · *map ws*

The function *bs* returns the initial and final states for the transitions *bc*; similarly for *ws*. In fact, *bs* returns a triple, the first component of which is parity information needed for the computation of *bsp*. The function

> *foldr bsp* (*start, start*)

returns the initial and final states for *boxall*, and *foldr wsp* (*start, start*) is a similar function for *coxall*.

Here is the program for *bs*:

$$bs \, (Up' \, (Node' \, (w, b) \, a \, legs)) \;=\; (b, install \, a \, 1 \, fs, install \, a \, 1 \, is)$$
$$\textbf{where} \; (is, fs) = bseed \, legs$$
$$bs \, (Dn' \, (Node' \, (w, b) \, a \, legs)) \;=\; (b, install \, a \, 0 \, is, install \, a \, 1 \, fs)$$
$$\textbf{where} \; is \;=\; fst \, (wseed \, legs)$$
$$fs \;=\; snd \, (bseed \, legs)$$

Recalling that $bc \, (Up \, (Node \, a \, legs)) = reverse \, (bcode \, legs)$, we see that the initial and final states of *bseed legs* have to be reversed in computing *bs*. Moreover, since we are considering the black code, the value associated with label *a* is 1, so this information is installed in the state. The parity information provided by *b* is also returned.

For the second clause, recall that

$$bc \, (Dn \, (Node \, a \, legs)) \;=\; wcode \, legs \mathbin{+\mkern-8mu+} [a] \mathbin{+\mkern-8mu+} bcode \, legs$$

Here, the initial state corresponding to *wcode legs* and the final state corresponding to *bcode legs* are the correct initial and final states to choose. Moreover, the label *a* starts off being associated with a 0 bit and ends up being associated with a 1 bit.

The definition of *ws* is similar. It remains to consider *bsp* and *wsp*, whose definitions are

$$bsp \, (b, ia, fa) \, (ib, fb) \;=\; (union \, ia \, ib, union \, fa \, (\textbf{if} \; b \; \textbf{then} \; fb \; \textbf{else} \; ib))$$
$$wsp \, (w, ia, fa) \, (ib, fb) \;=\; (union \, ia \, (\textbf{if} \; w \; \textbf{then} \; ib \; \textbf{else} \; fb), union \, fa \, fb)$$

Recall that $as \,\square\, bs$ begins with *bs* and ends with *bs* if *as* has even length, or ends with *reverse bs* if *as* has odd length. Hence, the initial state is the union of the two initial states associated with *as* and *bs*, but the final state is the union of the initial state associated with *as* and either the final or initial state associated with *bs*, depending on the parity of *as*. In the definition of *bsp* the Boolean *b* determines the parity. The complete code for *seed* is summarised in Figure 30.8.

Final remarks

The Knuth and Ruskey (2003) non-loopless algorithm for spider spinning made heavy use of coroutines. Knuth's (2001) loopless version is on his website. The simpler problem of spinning with tree spiders was first considered in Koda and Ruskey (1993). A non-loopless algorithm based on continuations appeared as a Functional Pearl in Filliâtre and Pottier (2003).

$$
\begin{aligned}
seed &= elems \cdot fst \cdot bseed \cdot map\,(Dn' \cdot decorate) \\
bseed &= foldr\ bsp\ (start, start) \cdot map\ bs \\
wseed &= foldr\ wsp\ (start, start) \cdot map\ ws \\
bs\,(Up'\,(Node'\,(w, b)\ a\ legs)) &= (b, install\ a\ 1\ fs, install\ a\ 1\ is) \\
&\quad \textbf{where}\ (is, fs) = bseed\ legs \\
bs\,(Dn'\,(Node'\,(w, b)\ a\ legs)) &= (b, install\ a\ 0\ is, install\ a\ 1\ fs) \\
&\quad \textbf{where}\ is = fst\,(wseed\ legs) \\
&\qquad\quad\ \, fs = snd\,(bseed\ legs) \\
ws\,(Up'\,(Node'\,(w, b)\ a\ legs)) &= (w, install\ a\ 0\ is, install\ a\ 1\ fs) \\
&\quad \textbf{where}\ is = fst\,(wseed\ legs) \\
&\qquad\quad\ \, fs = snd\,(bseed\ legs) \\
ws\,(Dn'\,(Node'\,(w, b)\ a\ legs)) &= (w, install\ a\ 0\ fs, install\ a\ 0\ is) \\
&\quad \textbf{where}\ (is, fs) = wseed\ legs
\end{aligned}
$$

$$
\begin{aligned}
bsp\,(b, ia, fa)\,(ib, fb) &= (union\ ia\ ib, union\ fa\ (\textbf{if}\ b\ \textbf{then}\ fb\ \textbf{else}\ ib)) \\
wsp\,(w, ia, fa)\,(ib, fb) &= (union\ ia\ (\textbf{if}\ w\ \textbf{then}\ ib\ \textbf{else}\ fb), union\ fa\ fb)
\end{aligned}
$$

Fig. 30.8 The function *seed*

References

Filliâtre, J.-C., and Pottier, F. (2003). Producing all ideals of a forest, functionally. *Journal of Functional Programming* **13** (5), 945–56.

Knuth, D. E. (2001). SPIDERS: a program downloadable from www-cs-faculty.stanford.edu/~knuth/programs.html.

Knuth, D. E. and Ruskey, F. (2003). Efficient coroutine generation of constrained Gray sequences (aka deconstructing coroutines). *Object-Orientation to Formal Methods: Dedicated to The Memory of Ole-Johan Dahl.* LNCS 2635. Springer-Verlag.

Koda, Y. and Ruskey, R. (1993). A Gray code for the ideals of a forest poset. *Journal of Algorithms* **15**, 324–40.

Index